**DISCARDED**

# THREE EPISODES OF
MASSACHUSETTS HISTORY

# THREE EPISODES OF
# MASSACHUSETTS HISTORY

THE SETTLEMENT OF BOSTON BAY
THE ANTINOMIAN CONTROVERSY
A STUDY OF CHURCH AND TOWN GOVERNMENT

BY

CHARLES FRANCIS ADAMS

VOLUME II
*REVISED*

*New York*
RUSSELL & RUSSELL
1965

Copyright, 1892,
By CHARLES FRANCIS ADAMS.
REISSUED, 1965, BY RUSSELL & RUSSELL, INC.
L.C. CATALOG CARD NO: 65—18782
PRINTED IN THE UNITED STATES OF AMERICA

## CONTENTS OF VOL. II.

### THE ANTINOMIAN CONTROVERSY.
*Continued.*

| CHAPTER | | PAGE |
|---|---|---|
| X. | The Fate of the Outcasts | 533 |
| XI. | "And Shem and Japheth took a Garment and covered the Nakedness of their Father" | 559 |

### A STUDY OF CHURCH AND TOWN GOVERNMENT.

| | | |
|---|---|---|
| I. | Old Braintree | 581 |
| II. | The Braintree North Precinct Church | 590 |
| III. | Land Titles and the Town Commons | 646 |
| IV. | The Highways | 666 |
| V. | Dwellings and Modes of Life | 680 |
| VI. | Population and Wealth | 689 |
| VII. | Social Life | 699 |
| VIII. | The Vicious, the Poor and the Insane | 722 |
| IX. | The Meeting-house | 732 |
| X. | The Church, and Church Discipline | 747 |
| XI. | The Training-field and the School-house | 764 |
| XII. | Intemperance and Immorality | 783 |
| XIII. | Health, Reading, Diversions | 800 |
| XIV. | Town-meetings | 810 |
| XV. | Colonial Wars and Town Contentions | 827 |
| XVI. | The Revolutionary Epoch | 838 |
| XVII. | Exhaustion | 889 |
| XVIII. | Recuperation | 899 |
| XIX. | The Era of Change | 922 |
| XX. | The Quincy School System | 933 |

## CONTENTS OF VOL. II.

| | | |
|---|---|---|
| XXI. | The Alien Infusion . . . . . . | 944 |
| XXII. | The Rebellion . . . . . . . | 961 |
| XXIII. | Town-meetings again . . . . . | 965 |
| XXIV. | A Long Battle won . . . . . | 975 |
| XXV. | "The King is dead! Long live the King!" | 980 |
| INDEX | . . . . . . . . . . | 1011 |

## CHAPTER X.

### THE FATE OF THE OUTCASTS.

OF the subsequent fate of Anne Hutchinson and John Wheelwright, little need here be said; their stories, — and that of Mrs. Hutchinson is a sufficiently tragic one, — are told in the biographies which have been written of them. Before her excommunication was an accomplished fact, Winthrop says that Mrs. Hutchinson "seemed to be somewhat dejected." She could hardly have been otherwise; for to her the action of the Boston church, when at the meeting of March 15th Cotton solemnly admonished her, must have been a complete surprise, — a revelation of changed public feeling. During the whole four months which preceded it she had been under restraint at Roxbury, and practically shut off from direct intercourse with the body of her fellow-communicants. When her trial before the Court closed in November she was still the central figure and the animating spirit of a formidable party, which in the town and church of Boston, at least, was wholly and even aggressively predominant. The Boston deputies to the legislature had been elected without opposition to sustain her; and they had sustained her to the extent of their power and to the very end. So strong indeed was the feeling locally that it has been seen how even Winthrop, the governor of the colony, had been in imminent danger of being called to account before the church after the trial, for his course in connection with it; and had felt it necessary to forestall action by publicly telling the congregation, that as a magistrate he could not hold himself answerable to a congregation. The elders were on his side, and the malcontents abandoned their project; but that they entertained it, and that Winthrop should have taken such public action to anticipate them, is complete evidence of how strong and general the feeling was. During the winter which followed, a great change had occurred. In the first place the minority was completely vanquished; in the second place, a system of terrorism was established. People no more wanted to be sent into banishment to Rhode Island or New Hampshire then, than now they would want to be banished to New Mexico or to Wyoming. Yet banishment, prompt and perpetual, was the alternative to complete submission. The leaders, it was understood, were to go. So much was settled. Indeed, some of them had already gone, and others were soon to follow. Public meetings of the dissatisfied were not tolerated, and their most private utterances were laid hold of and repeated, in order to be heralded in public, and stamped out as heresies.[1] Moreover, the influence and example of Cotton were potent. After Vane left the colony, Cotton was the virtual leader of the minority, and those composing it had sought to shelter themselves under the authority of his name. But Cotton had now wholly accepted the situation. He had done even more than this, — he had, heart and soul, gone over to the other side. He was, indeed, inquisitor-in-chief, and, "finding how he had been abused, and made (as himself said) their stalking horse," he spent most of his time discovering

[1] Cotton, *Way Cleared*, 58, 85.

errors and leading back such as were gone astray.[1]
The clergy, therefore, were united as one man. So
was the magistracy. To stand up in that community,
against church and state combined, called for great
moral courage. Not one in a hundred would dare do
it. Under these circumstances, the fact that all opposition ceased calls for no explanation. The silence
which prevailed may have been sullen, but it was complete. The minority surrendered their arms and held
their tongues. Order reigned in Boston.

While Mrs. Hutchinson could have had little idea
of all this when she was brought in from Roxbury to
confront the church, a realizing sense of it must have
come to her when she, whose utterances a few short
months before had been received by all as those of a
prophetess, found not one to oppose her public censure. The utter downfall of her faction and the
collapse of her ambitious projects were apparent. For
the moment her mind must have been crowded with
very mundane misgivings. A wife and the mother of
many children, she was under sentence of banishment;
and even then her husband and brethren were seeking
out a home in some uninhabited place. The marvel
is how a woman in delicate health and of sensitive
organization, burning with religious fervor and soon
once more to become a mother,[2] bore up against such
a sea of troubles.

[1] Winthrop, i. *253.

[2] The miscarriage of Mrs. Hutchinson, over the details of which
Governor Winthrop and Messrs. Weld and Cotton all gloated with
singular pleasure, seems to have occurred in Rhode Island in July
or August, 1638, some four months after her excommunication. Six
weeks before it occurred — that is, in June — she had been forced to
consult a physician, perceiving "her body to be greatly distempered
and her spirits failing, and in that regard doubtful of life." Winthrop, i. *271; *Short Story*, Preface, 12.

The ordeal fairly passed and the worst befallen, her spirits rose once more. Indeed she seems to have now worked herself into a state of exaltation, glorying in her trials and declaring that, next to Christ, they were the greatest happiness that ever befell her. At the time of her excommunication the snow still lay deep upon the ground, though it was our first of April, nor did the winter break up until some days later.[1] The exile could not, therefore, at once be driven forth; but until she could be, she was freed from her semi-imprisonment at Roxbury, and allowed to remain, though closely within doors, at her own house in Boston. At length, some days later, Governor Winthrop sent her a warrant to depart the jurisdiction, and in obedience thereto, on the $\frac{28\text{th}}{7\text{th}}$ of $\frac{\text{March}}{\text{April}}$, she left her home, and, going down to the shore, was conveyed in a boat across the bay to a landing near her husband's farm at the Mount.[2] It was the first stage of her journey. She was under injunction to leave the province before the close of the month. Her original plan was to join Wheelwright's family at Mt. Wollaston, and go with them by water to Portsmouth. Meanwhile her husband and his companions, after being refused an abiding-place within their limits by the Plymouth authorities, found a site for a plantation to their liking in the island of Aquidneck, near where Newport now is. Receiving tidings of this before she had started for New Hampshire, Mrs.

[1] Winthrop, *264.
[2] The precise site of William Hutchinson's house in what is now Quincy is not known, but his allotment (*supra*, 366, n.) covered the territory in the immediate neighborhood of the Wollaston Heights station on the Old Colony railroad, including what is known as Taylor's hill and a part of the large plain north thereof. Lechford's *Note-Book*, [177], [214].

Hutchinson changed her plans, and, in the early days of April, journeyed by land to Providence, and to the island of Aquidneck in Narragansett Bay.

There she lived for a few troubled years, and there in March, 1640, she was visited by a formal delegation of the Boston church, whose mission was to require her companions in exile to explain " their unwarrantable practice in communicating with excommunicated persons." There are two accounts of what took place between those composing this delegation — one of whom was Major Gibbons — and Mistress Hutchinson. According to the more reliable of these accounts, the brief conference was brought to a close by her remarking that she would not acknowledge the Boston church to be any church of Christ; according to the other and less reliable account, the mere mention of " the church of Christ at Boston" brought on an expression of temper on her part, in which she coupled the name of that body with epithets common enough in Shakespeare's day, but which are now classed as archaic. That the mission was fruitless hardly needs to be said.[1]

In 1642 William Hutchinson died; and, shortly after, his wife removed to a point on Manhattan Island, it would seem, " neare a place," as Mr. Weld took care to note down, " called by Seamen, and in the Map, Hell-gate." While the reason of this removal is not certainly known, a plan for bringing Rhode Island within the jurisdiction of the Massachusetts colony was under consideration at the time; and it has been surmised that the mere apprehension of such a thing led to her again going into exile. On the other hand,

[1] Arthur Ellis, *First Church of Boston*, 65; G. E. Ellis, *Puritan Age*, 351.

her old enemies in Massachusetts very pointedly insinuated that she found herself after a while no longer appreciated in her place of exile, and so moved away, "being weary of the Island, or rather the Island being weary of her." If the least charitable, the last explanation is, on its face, the more likely of the two. It was the woman's nature to crave excitement and notoriety. She could not be happy without it. As soon, therefore, as she found herself a sensation of yesterday, she grew restless and felt a call to go elsewhere. If such was, indeed, the true explanation of her removal to the Dutch settlement at the mouth of the Hudson, time was not given her to weary of her new and final place of abode, for she could have been there but a few months when, in August, 1642, "the Indians set upon them, and slew her and all her family, her daughter and her daughter's husband, and all their children" save one daughter that was carried into captivity. This child was then eight years old; in 1647 she was recovered by the General Court and brought back to Massachusetts. When the news of this terrible ending reached Boston, the people there were deeply moved. They called to mind the defiant words in which the would-be prophetess had told the Court that the Lord would surely deliver her from impending calamity, and would ruin them and their posterity and their whole State; and so bade them take heed how they proceeded against her. And now the clergy of Massachusetts Bay grimly pointed out to all their congregations that the Lord God of Israel — the God of Abraham and Isaac — had indeed and in his own good way shown himself to his chosen people. He had smote the American Jezebel a dreadful blow. Thus the Lord heard his servants' groans to heaven, and freed them from this great and sore affliction; neither had he shown himself through the devilish delusion of miracles, but in the way of his wonderful providence he had picked out this woful woman, to make her and those belonging to her an unheard-of heavy example.

The subsequent fate of John Wheelwright, if less dramatic than that of Anne Hutchinson, was sufficiently checkered. He had, it will be remembered, made his way to Exeter during the severe winter of 1637–8. Joined there by his family the following spring, he once more settled down in the practice of his ministry. As would naturally have been expected, he was now pressed by his brother exiles to join them in Rhode Island. " They sent to him," Cotton says, " and urged him much to come to them, to a far richer soil, and richer company than where he lived : yet he constantly refused " upon the " ground of the corruption of their judgments: ' Professing often, whilst they pleaded for the Covenant of Grace, they took away the Grace of the Covenant.'" But Exeter was not destined to remain his home. Three years later only, in 1641, the New Hampshire towns voluntarily put themselves within the jurisdiction of Massachusetts Bay; and then Wheelwright, being brought again under the ban of the law, betook himself further east to Sir Ferdinando Gorges' province of Maine, where he sat down not far from Cape Porpoise, founding what is now the town of Wells. He was accompanied by his mother-in-law, the mother of the Hutchinsons, who, as she sat in the twilight of those later days, must often have thought regretfully of her early home at Alford in the fens of Lincolnshire, — and here, in dreariest exile, the poor, buffeted old Englishwoman died. But as Wheelwright calmly meditated in this last place of refuge over his stormy career, its events gradually assumed a new character in his eyes, and he bethought to make his peace with his brethren. Not improbably he felt the more moved to this course when tidings of his sister Hutchinson's fate reached him, leading him to reflect on the real character of the issues upon which her life had been wrecked. In any event, a letter of reconciliation from Wheelwright to Winthrop followed hard upon the destruction of the Hutchinson family. It was a thoroughly manly effort, and its terse, pointed admissions gave evidence that it was the fruit of "an overruling conscience." He expressed his deep contrition for the part he had taken in "those sharp and vehement contentions," and intimated his more mature sense of the inanity of the points at issue. He confessed that, as he now saw it, he had then acted sinfully, and he humbly craved forgiveness. In reply a safe-conduct to Boston was sent him, and he was practically invited to go there and abase himself before the General Court. This he declined to do, taking the ground that, however willing he might be to confess himself wrong in respect to "justification and the evidencing thereof," yet he could not with a good conscience condemn himself for such "capital crimes, dangerous revelations and gross errors" as were charged upon him and had caused his sufferings. Some further correspondence followed, as the result of which the General Court in May, 1644, placed upon its records a vote remitting Wheelwright's sentence of banishment "upon particular, solemn and serious acknowledgment, and confession by letter, of his evil carriages and of the Courts justice upon him for them." It is to be hoped that Winthrop did not draw up this entry as it stands recorded, for it was couched in a very different spirit from the letter which invited it. Wheelwright had made no such confession of guilt and of the justice of his civil sentence. He could not, nor would he, avail himself of a pardon, the acceptance of which bound him to so humiliating a confession.[1]

Accordingly, for three years more, the former student at Cambridge and incumbent of Bilsby, now a man of over fifty, remained buried in the frontier wilderness of Maine. In 1647 he received a call from Hampton, near Exeter, and, removing thither, he there ministered for nearly eight years. At last, in May, 1654, in answer to some echo of the old Antinomian controversy, — for such echoes still from time to time came back to New England from the English press, — the people of Hampton drew up a petition to the General Court, intended to bring out from that body some kindly testimonial in Wheelwright's behalf. It was to be a sort of certificate of restored fellowship and regular standing. Winthrop had now been dead four years, and Endicott had succeeded him as governor. Cotton, too, was dead. Weld and

---

[1] It was at the time this correspondence between Winthrop and Wheelwright was going on, and the rescinding of the sentence of exile was under advisement, that Weld's *Short Story*, etc., was printed in London. As Winthrop was the author of that pamphlet, and knew better than any one else that the statements contained in it must occasion controversy, he could not but have seen how very desirable it was to secure the complete confession of Wheelwright in advance. The pamphlet could hardly have reached America when the vote of May 29th was recorded. This fact may account for the peculiar wording of that vote. A confession was manufactured in advance by the other party to the controversy, and put on record. None of the public men of that time were above such tricks. The best of them seem to have looked upon low cunning as an admitted feature in statecraft.

Peters, having gone to England years before, were not destined to return. The old controversial fire, in that particular form with which Wheelwright had been concerned, was wholly burned out, and it was also a period during which the local persecuting spirit was comparatively quiet, — resting, indeed, preparatory to its next fierce outburst against the Ranters and Quakers, two years further on. Accordingly, when the petition of the people of Hampton reached the General Court, it presently, in answer thereto, judged "meete to certifie that Mr. Wheelwright hath long since given such satisfaction both to the Court and elders generally as that he is now, and so for many years hath been, an officer in the church at Hampton within our jurisdiction, and that without any offence to any, so far as we know." The words were somewhat negative in their character, but they were the last in the, so called, Antinomian controversy.

Some two years later than this, towards the close probably of 1656, Wheelwright left Hampton and sailed for England. It then lacked a few months only of being twenty full years since he had first landed in Boston, a man of forty-four, and there rejoined his sister Hutchinson. The retrospect could not have been a pleasant one. He was now sixty-four; the end of all his ambitious dreams had been a banishment, and more than ten years had elapsed since the blood of Anne Hutchinson was poured upon the ground. While he had been languishing under the provincial ban of Massachusetts Bay, his old schoolfellow and familiar friend had become the Lord Protector of England. Nevertheless, the six years he now passed in England — those which saw the end of the Commonwealth and the beginning of the Restoration —

could hardly have been other than the halcyon years of his life. During them he was treated with consideration by eminent men; for not only, it would seem, did he live at Belleau, — the home of Sir Harry Vane, his old friend and protector, who now " greatly noticed him," — but he was singled out by Cromwell for marks of especial regard; and when he went up to London for a visit " my Lord Protector was pleased to send one of his guard " for him, and gave him an hour's interview.

Pleasure-trips across the Atlantic were not taken in those days, and the probabilities are that when Wheelwright returned to England in 1656, he proposed to finish his days there. If such was his intention, the course of political events may well have induced him to change it. Cromwell died; and even before the Restoration, Vane had been committed a prisoner to his own house. The old Puritan divine had fallen again upon evil days. On the 4th of June, 1662, Vane was arraigned in the court of King's Bench, and ten days later he laid his neck on the block upon Tower Hill. Then Wheelwright seems to have shaken from his feet the dust of his native land, though he had passed his seventieth year when, later in the same summer, he next landed in Boston. His pulpit at Hampton had long since been filled, but he now received a call from the neighboring church at Salisbury, where he was formally installed on the 9th of December following his return. This was his last and also his longest settlement, for it continued seventeen years, until his death in 1679. He was then the oldest minister in New England. He had outlived all the contentions of his middle life, and every one of his contemporaries who had taken part in them. He belonged to a past generation. But priesthoods have long memories. At the time his brethren took no special notice of the patriarch's death, nor does any stone now mark his grave. A portrait, believed on such evidence as is now attainable to be of him,[1] for years hung in the Senate Chamber of Massachusetts, and is now preserved in one of the rooms occupied by the Secretary of State. Painted by an unknown hand in 1677, it represents an aged minister in the sombre Calvinistic garb of the time, — the broad white Geneva bands and black coif, while from under the last straggle thin gray locks. The features, neither large nor harsh, are suggestive of the Shakespeare type of face so common among the English of that time, and in them, though drawn by an unskilled hand and faded now, it yet seems possible to read an expression of sadness and disappointment such as would be not unnatural to a man of eighty-four, so much of whose life had been passed in losing strife and weary exile.

Finally, like most of the Puritan breed, John Wheelwright was far from being a lovable character. His proper place was not the pulpit. He should have been a man of affairs, — a lawyer, a magistrate, possibly a soldier; for he was strong, self-willed, enterprising and courageous. He was ambitious also, naturally craving prominence and taking a grim delight in controversy. Nor did he shrink from conflict with nature, any more than he shrank from it with man. He was not afraid to be alone in a minority, or alone in the woods. A clergyman, he was often engaged in lawsuits; for in matters temporal, as well as in those spiritual, he had the full courage of his convictions and entire faith in himself. That he was an attractive

[1] 250th *Anniversary, First Church, Quincy,* 12, 151-2.

man in domestic life does not seem probable; he leaves the impression of one deeply conscientious, but still rigid, overbearing, and hard to please at home, as everywhere else.

None the less, Wheelwright was essentially a man of mark; and a man who, wherever he might have gone, would have left his mark. It may be mere accident, but those familiar with the subsequent history of the Mount have thought they could detect in it indications of the man's power of thus impressing himself on those about him. As will presently be seen, in 1640 that region was incorporated as a town, under the name of Braintree. Again, in 1792, the north precinct of Braintree, which included Mt. Wollaston, was set off as the town of Quincy. It was in what is now the city of Quincy that Wheelwright ministered, and there is no doubt that his parishioners sympathized fully in his views. The first teacher of the church regularly gathered there, two years later, was one of his disciples, whose name was blotted from the famous Boston remonstrance only so late as May, 1640.[1] In subsequent years the north precinct of Braintree, — both as such, and as the town of Quincy, — always showed a marked leaning towards a liberal theology, the more noticeable from the contrast in this respect offered to the rigid orthodoxy which ever characterized the south precinct, still retaining the original name. During the eighteenth century the two precincts more than once, through their pastors, engaged in sharp controversy, never changing their sides,[2] — the original leaven apparently continuing to work, as the pastor influenced the people, and the tendency of the people operated back in the selection of pastors,

[1] *Infra*, 603.   [2] *Infra*, 638, 944.

— until the old order of things passed wholly away. As the twig is bent, the tree inclines; and so it may even be surmised that the seed sown by Wheelwright, in 1637, bore active fruit in the great New England protest, under the lead of Channing, two centuries later, deciding the course then pursued by the descendants in the seventh generation of those who at the Mount had listened to him.

Of the others who shared Mrs. Hutchinson's exile, William Coddington was the most prominent. He seems to have been the immediate successor of Thomas Morton in the ownership of Mt. Wollaston; and, singularly enough, the record of every annual town-meeting of Quincy, so long as Quincy continued to be a town, bore recurring evidence to the fact that he once lived there, and thence went into exile. Since the year 1640, a portion of the extensive grant made to him and to Edmund Quincy, jointly, in December, 1635, has been public property, and is spoken of on the first page of the Braintree records as "The Schoole Lands." Each year, by a formal vote, — the reason of which long since passed into a meaningless tradition, — the town of Quincy, as tenant of the land thus held, appropriated to school purposes a sum of money as a nominal rent.[1] The name of the school in which the children of the district including Mt. Wollaston are taught, and the street upon which its building stands, still perpetuate the name of Coddington.

[1] The record of the process through which this land came into the possession of the original town of Braintree is inexplicably defective; but some facts connected with it lead to a suspicion that Coddington, after going into exile, instead of freely giving the land, was judicially despoiled of it. See communication referred to in the *Proc. Mass. Hist. Soc.* Series II. vii. 23.

The dominant faction dealt with Coddington in much the same arbitrary spirit with which it had dealt with Wheelwright and Anne Hutchinson. He was neither " convented " nor formally banished; but, though a firm, self-asserting man of a business turn of mind and somewhat grasping disposition, the action of those with whom he had been seven years associated offended him, and, as intense religious bigotry has at no time been conducive to social amenities, the private bearing towards him of many of his old friends doubtless aggravated the difficulties of the situation. Even as early as the autumn of 1637, therefore, Coddington thought of removing with a number of others from the Massachusetts jurisdiction, and obtained leave so to do, a year's time being allowed them for the purpose : but, before their plans were matured, the General Court, at its March session of 1638, — at the very time of the excommunication of Mrs. Hutchinson, — took cognizance of the matter on the strength of a rumor that the emigrants proposed only to withdraw themselves " for a season." Their movements were accordingly expedited by a summons commanding them to appear before the next Court, unless, accompanied by their families, they had previously taken themselves off. The next Court was fixed to be held two weeks later. Deeply indignant, but being, as he himself subsequently expressed it, " not willing to live in the fire of contention," Coddington, together with the others designated in the summons, six in number, made their way to Providence within the designated time. It was in the early days of our April that he left his brick house, on the north side of what is now Liberty Square, said to have been the first brick house ever built in Boston, and he afterwards wrote to Winthrop "what myself and wife and family did endure in that removal, I wish neither you nor yours may ever be put unto." But when, in 1640, — two years later, — he thus expressed himself, his animosities had already passed away; for in yet another letter, written shortly after and likewise to Winthrop, he took occasion to say that he well approved " of a speech of one of note amongst you, that we were in a heate and chafed, and were all of us to blame; in our strife we had forgotten that we were brethren."[1] Though Wheelwright was eight years his senior, Coddington died first, in 1678. His name is still venerated in Rhode Island, as that of Winthrop is in Massachusetts; and, while the portrait of the latter looks down from the walls of the Senate chamber of the State-House in Boston, that of the former hangs in the Council-room at Newport. Through several generations his descendants dwelt in the home he had helped to build up and rule over; but in time they also experienced the decay common to families, and the last of them is reported to have died in the almshouse of the place her ancestor founded, lying on a bed which still showed the armorial bearings of her family.

It will be remembered that when Mrs. Hutchinson left the Boston church, after excommunication, Mary Dyer walked at her side. She was a very proper and comely young woman, the wife of one William Dyer, sometime a citizen of London, and a milliner in the New Exchange; though as Winthrop, to whom we owe these particulars, goes on to say, she and her husband were in Boston "notoriously infected with Mrs. Hutchinson's errors, and very censorious and

[1] IV. *Mass. Hist. Soc. Coll.* vi. 314, 317.

troublesome, she being of a very proud spirit, and much addicted to revelations." They both went with the Hutchinsons to Rhode Island. Mary Dyer would seem to have been one of that class, numerous in those days, whose brains were wholly unsettled by their religion. She remained in Rhode Island, in apparently undisturbed enjoyment of her revelations, for many years, becoming a Quaker in the mean while; but at last, in 1659, hearing of the persecution of that sect in Massachusetts, and loathing her place of refuge "for that there they were not opposed by the civil authority, but with all patience and meekness were suffered to say over their pretended revelations and admonitions," — feeling this call to persecution she came to Boston. What she there did does not appear, but she was speedily arrested and brought before the Court in company with three others. She simply said in her own defence that she came from Rhode Island to visit the Quakers, that she was of their religion, and that the light within her was the rule. They were banished, under pain of death if they returned. Mary Dyer and one other "found freedom to depart;" but within a month they were back again, in company with another woman, who brought some linen for the examination of Governor Endicott, intended to be used as the grave-clothes of that magistrate's victims. They were at once all thrown into prison, and then brought again before the Court, which now sentenced them to death. Mary Dyer's son at this time filled the important office of secretary of the province of Rhode Island, and at his earnest solicitation the death-penalty was remitted in the case of his mother, on condition that she should leave Massachusetts within forty-eight hours. Her companions, William

Robinson and Marmaduke Stephenson, were left for execution. When the day fixed for their hanging came, the town had to be put under guard, so great was the sympathy felt for the condemned. Surrounded by a heavy escort, the three prisoners walked together from the jail in Cornhill to the gallows, which had been erected on the Common, Mary Dyer going between the two others and holding a hand of each. She must then have been a woman of middle life, but Edward Nicholson, the marshal, asked her if she was not "ashamed to walk hand in hand, between two young men?" "It is," she answered, "an hour of the greatest joy I can enjoy in this world. No eye can see, no ear can hear, no tongue can speak, no heart can understand, the sweet incomes and refreshings of the Spirit of the Lord which now I enjoy."[1]

When her companions were hanged, she sat beneath the gallows with the halter about her neck, calmly looking at the multitude of horrified spectators, whom a hundred armed men of the train-band kept back from the scaffolding; for so great was the throng upon the Common that day, that the draw-bridge over the canal, which then separated the North End from the town, broke down under the weight of those returning home. When her companions were dead Mary Dyer was taken back to prison, and there she first learned of the circumstances of her reprieve. She at once wrote to the governor, repudiating her son's action, and offering her life as a sacrifice. It was necessary to use force to get her out of the jurisdiction. She was at last taken back to Newport, where for a time she seems to have been kept under

---

[1] *Supra*, 408.

restraint; but in the following spring she succeeded in eluding those having her in charge, and, journeying "secretly and speedily," found her way back to Boston. She was again thrown into prison; and again her family piteously interceded for her. She was sentenced once more to be hanged, but at the gallows her life was offered her if she would keep away from Massachusetts. Her reply was: — "In obedience to the will of the Lord I came; and in his will I abide faithful to the death." She now lies buried in some undistinguished part of Boston Common. Assuredly the fate of those two women, who, side by side, walked forth out of the church on that 22d of March, 1638, was sufficiently tragic, — one murdered by savages, the other put to death by her brethren!

To turn from Mary Dyer to John Underhill is like suddenly passing from the solemnity of a funeral to the buffoonery of a pantomime. Captain John Underhill was a Puritan of that Trusty Tompkins type common enough a few years later on in the armies of the Commonwealth, — a curious mixture of fervor, which was apparently genuine, and of licentiousness which was unquestionably so. He seems to have taken religion, as he would have taken any other epidemic which might have chanced to prevail, — and to have felt it sufficiently, not to prevent his scoffing or indulging the flesh, but to make him extremely uncomfortable after he had done so. As a soldier he had seen some service under Prince Maurice of Nassau in the Low Countries; and he came out with Winthrop in a semi-military capacity in 1630. More recently he had served under Endicott in the latter's inglorious Pequot campaign.

Though Underhill belonged to Mrs. Hutchinson's faction, his more earnest efforts seem to have been put forth in Wheelwright's behalf. After the sentence of the latter he sent a strong appeal to Winthrop not to enforce it,[1] and later on he followed Wheelwright to New Hampshire. When called to account for putting his name to the remonstrance he at first retracted in writing, and put the paper in the Governor's hands; but presently he made up his mind to follow the exiled minister, and petitioned the Court for a grant of land which had been promised him. Hereupon he was questioned as to certain heretical opinions alleged to have been uttered by him some time before to the effect, —

"That we were zealous here, as the Scribes and Pharisees were, and as Paul was before his conversion, &c. Which he denying, they were proved to his face by a sober, godly woman, whom he had seduced in the ship, and drawn to his opinions (but she was afterwards freed again). Among other passages he told her how he came to his assurance, and that was thus : — He had lain under a spirit of bondage and a legal way five years, and could get no assurance ; till at length, as he was taking a pipe of tobacco, the Spirit set home an absolute promise of free grace with such assurance and joy, as he never since doubted of his good estate, neither should he though he should fall into sin."

His answers and explanations were not edifying on doctrinal grounds, and so the matter of his signing the remonstrance was brought in question. His retraction was produced by the Governor and read to the Court, but he now said it applied only to the manner, not to the matter of the paper ; in regard to the

[1] iv. *Mass. Hist. Soc. Coll.* vii. 171.

latter he was of the same mind still as he was when he affixed his name. When asked for a Scripture "rule by which he might take so much upon him, as publickly to contradict the sentence of the Court, &c., hee alleged the example of Joab his rough speech to David." The precedent thus adduced having been disallowed for causes elaborately specified, he then insisted much "upon the liberty which all States do allow to Military officers, for free speech, &c., and that himself had spoken sometimes as freely to Count Nassau." This argument weighed no more with the Court than the other; so the captain was committed, and the next day he was again sent for and banished.

"The Lord's day following he made a speech in the assembly, shewing that, as the Lord was pleased to convert Paul as he was in persecuting, etc., so he might manifest himself to him as he was taking the moderate use of the creature called tobacco. He professed withal, that he knew not wherein he had deserved the sentence of the Court, and that he was sure that Christ was his, etc. . . .

"The next Lord's day the same Capt. Underhill, having been privately dealt with upon suspicion of incontinency with a neighbor's wife, and not hearkening to it, was publicly questioned, and put under admonition. The matter was, for that the woman being young, and beautiful, and withal of a jovial spirit and behaviour, he did daily frequent her house, and was divers times found there alone with her, the doors being locked on the inside. He confessed it was ill, because it had an appearance of evil in it; but his excuse was, that the woman was in great trouble of mind, and sore temptations, and that he resorted to her to comfort her; and that when the door was found locked upon them, they were in private prayer together. But this practice was clearly condemned also by the elders, affirming, that it had not been of good report for any of them to have done the like, and that they ought in such case, to have called in some brother or sister, and not to have locked the door, etc."

In September, 1638, after leaving Boston, Underhill went to New Hampshire. The rest of his ludicrous story loses point when told in other than the unconsciously solemn words in which Winthrop first recorded it: —

"The General Court in September gave order to the Governor to write to them of Pascataquack, to signify to them, that we looked at it as an unneighborly part, that they should encourage and advance such as we had cast out from us for their offences, before they had inquired of us the cause, &c. (The occasion of this letter was, that they had aided Mr. Wheelwright to begin a plantation there, and intended to make Capt. Underhill their governor.) Upon this Mr. Burdet returned a scornful answer, and would not give the governor his title &c. and Capt. Underhill wrote a letter to a young gentleman, who sojourned in the house of our governor, wherein he reviled the governor with reproachful terms and imprecations of vengeance upon us all. This letter being shown to the governor and council, the governor by advice wrote to Edward Hilton. He intimated withal how ill it would relish, if they should advance Capt. Underhill, whom we had thrust out for abusing the Court with feigning a retraction both of his seditious practice and also of his corrupt opinions, and after, denying it again; and for casting reproach upon our churches, &c. : signifying withal, that he was now found to be an unclean person, for he was charged by a godly young woman to have solicited her chastity under pretence of Christian love, and to have confessed to her that he had his will oftentimes of the cooper's wife, and all out of strength of love; and the church had sent for him, and sent him a license to come and go under the hands of the governor and deputy ; but he refused to come, excusing himself, by letters to the elders, that the license was not sufficient, &c., and, by letters to the Governor, that he had no rule to come and answer to any offence, except his banishment were released. But, to the matter he was charged with he gave no answer, but sought an evasion.

"The Pascataquack men had chosen Captain Underhill their governor before the letter came to them, and it was intercepted and opened by Mr. Burdet and him. The captain was much nettled with this letter, and especially because his adulterous life with the cooper's wife at Boston was now discovered, and the church had called him to come and make answer to it. And upon this he wrote a letter to Mr. Cotton, full of high and threatening words against us; but he wrote another, at the same time, to the governor in very fair terms, entreating an obliterating of all that was past, and a bearing with human infirmities, &c., disavowing all purpose of revenge.

"But, instead of coming to Boston to make answer to the church, he procured a new church at Pascataquack of some few loose men to write to our church in his commendation, wherein they style him the right worshipful, their honored governor. All which notwithstanding the church of Boston proceeded with him. After this, Capt. Underhill's courage was abated, for the chiefest in the river fell from him, and the rest little regarded him, so as he wrote letters of retraction to divers. And presently [about a year later] being struck with horror and remorse for his offences, both against the church and civil state, he could have no rest till he had obtained a safe conduct to come and give satisfaction; and accordingly, at a lecture at Boston, (it being the court time,) he made a public confession both of his living in adultery with Faber's wife, and attempting the like with another woman; and also the injury he had done to our state, &c.; and acknowledged the justice of the court in their proceedings against him. Yet all his confessions were mixed with such excuses and extenuations, as did not give satisfaction of the truth of his repentance, so as it seemed to be done rather out of policy, and to pacify the sting of his conscience, than in sincerity. But, however, his offences being so foul and scandalous, the church presently cast him out; which censure he seemed to submit unto, and, for the time he staid in Boston, (being four or five days) he was very much dejected, &c.; but, being gone back, he soon recovered his spirits again, or, at least, gave not that proof of a broken heart, as he gave hope of at Boston."

At Dover — as the New Hampshire settlement presided over by Underhill and Burdet was now called — the captain had other troubles to encounter besides those which his conscience caused him. In fact a species of civil war, of the smallest conceivable proportions, broke out between that town and the adjoining town of Exeter, as a result of which Underhill was deposed and one Roberts chosen president in his place.

Soon after this downfall the ex-governor again went to Boston, trying once more to make his peace with the church. Not being satisfied of his repentance, the church declined to listen to him; and so, after a week's waiting, he went back to New Hampshire, where he seems to have now been in open disgrace. At last, in the course of the spring and summer of 1640, he came to the last act in this drama of colonial life and manners, — the closing, ludicrous scene being again in that meeting-house which a little more than two years before had witnessed the solemn excommunication of Mistress Hutchinson. There is nothing better recorded by Winthrop.

"Captain Underhill being brought, by the blessing of God on this church's censure of excommunication, to re-

morse for his foul sins, obtained, by means of the elders
and others of the church of Boston, a safe conduct under
the hand of the governor and one of the council to repair
to the church. He came at the time of the court of assistants, and upon the lecture day, after sermon, the pastor
called him forth and declared the occasion, and then gave
him leave to speak. Indeed it was a spectacle which caused
many weeping eyes, though it afforded matter for much
rejoicing to behold the power of the Lord Jesus in his own
ordinances, when they are dispensed in his own way, holding forth the authority of his regal sceptre in the simplicity
of the gospel. He came in his worst clothes (being accustomed to take great pride in his bravery and neatness)
without a band, in a foul linen cap pulled close to his eyes;
and standing upon a form, he did, with many deep sighs
and abundance of tears, lay open his wicked course, his
adultery, his hypocrisy, his persecution of Gods people
here, and especially his pride (as the root of all, which
caused God to give him over to his other sinful courses)
and contempt of the magistrates. He justified God and
the church and the court in all that had been inflicted on
him. Indeed he appeared as a man worn out with sorrow,
and yet he could find no peace. Therefore he was now
come to seek it in this ordinance of God. He spake well,
save that his blubbering &c. interrupted him, and all along
he discovered a broken and melting heart, and gave good
exhortations to take heed of such vanities and beginnings of
evil as had occasioned his fall; and in the end he earnestly
and humbly besought the church to have compassion on
him, and to deliver him out of the hands of Satan.

"So accordingly he was received into the church again;
and after, he came into the court (for the General Court
began soon after) and made confession of his sin against
them, &c. and desired pardon, which the court freely
granted him, so far as concerned their private judgment.
But for his adultery they would not pardon that for ex-

amples sake; nor would restore him to freedom, though they released his banishment, and declared the former law against adultery to be of no force; so as there was no law now to touch his life, for the new law against adultery was made since his fact committed.

"He confessed also in the congregation, that though he was very familiar with that woman, and had gained her affection, &c., yet she withstood him six months against all his solicitations (which he thought no woman could have resisted) before he could overcome her chastity, but being once overcome she was wholly at his will. And to make his peace the more sound he went to her husband (being a cooper) and fell upon his knees before him in the presence of some of the elders and others, and confessed the wrong he had done him, and besought him to forgive him; which he did very freely, and in testimony thereof he sent the captain's wife a token." [1]

[1] It is unnecessary in the present work to follow the Captain's career after he thus made his peace with the church of Boston, the magistrates of Massachusetts Bay and Joseph Faber, cooper. He removed to Stamford in Connecticut, and afterward to Flushing, on Long Island. He performed other military duties; he was a delegate to the Assembly and an under-sheriff, — an altogether respectable and useful man. He was far from being a man of education, and in IV. Mass. Hist. Soc. Coll. vii. are a number of letters from him, the spelling of which is remarkable. The following is a specimen taken from a letter to "John Wenthrop esquier, Goferner of the Macetuchets baye," and written from the house of Captain Gibbons, where he apparently tarried during his brief and fruitless visit to Boston in April, 1640: —

"A mong the rest of my aflickchons, jusli imposed by my sinnfull lif and backsliding prodigalliti in my whole corce, this is on that doth and will agrefate my grefe, thut I am deprife of that chrischan liberti I once had, boght by the preschous blud of the Lord Jesous; but I hafe made the blod and deth of Christ of non efeckt, therfor I am justli depriued of liberti to visset you, nor dare I aproch youer presenc, tel the Lord mofe you there unto." This queer specimen of one type of Puritan life is supposed to have died at Oyster Bay, L. I., in 1672.

## CHAPTER XI.

### "AND SHEM AND JAPHETH TOOK A GARMENT AND COVERED THE NAKEDNESS OF THEIR FATHER."

THE course pursued by those in authority in Massachusetts Bay towards Mrs. Hutchinson and her adherents has ever been, and will probably long remain, one of the hotly contested issues in early New England history. So far as external authority is concerned the verdict has been distinct. The action of the General Court of 1637 has been treated as an unjustifiable persecution, which has left a dark stain on the earliest pages of the history of the Puritan Commonwealth.[1] But, on the other hand, the founders have not lacked champions to extenuate, and even to justify their proceedings.[2] By these it has been argued that the colonists came to New England with certain great and laudable objects in view; that to the attainment of these objects unity of opinion and effort was clearly desirable, if, indeed, not absolutely essential. Beset as it was with enemies, and regarded with, at best, unfriendly eyes by those in authority at Whitehall, the continued existence of the enterprise often in those early days hung upon a thread. A mere scandal, a rumor even of internal dissensions, might afford the pretext for a fatal exercise of royal authority. This peril, it cannot be denied, was never absent

[1] Doyle, *The English in America; the Puritan Colonies*, i. 186–8.
[2] Palfrey, i. 488–511.

from the minds of Winthrop and his associates. The whole enterprise, moreover, was a business undertaking, those engaged in which formed a society or partnership by themselves, in which no provision had been made, or was intended to be made, for hostile or antagonistic elements. Massachusetts, within the chartered limits, was to the members of this partnership what his farm or his dwelling is to a freeholder; and they had the same right as the freeholder to expel intruders or dissentients, or persons distasteful to them. Those responsible for the success of the undertaking finally, after careful consideration, were persuaded and fully believed that the expulsion of the more prominent of the so-called Antinomian faction was necessary to peace and prosperity, temporal and spiritual; and, if the whole thing is viewed from the standpoint of the seventeenth century instead of the nineteenth, it will probably be conceded that they were correct in their conclusion.[1] The event certainly vindicated the substantial justice of their course, as a long period of internal tranquillity followed the proceedings of 1638.

This line of argument is plausible, but there are difficulties connected with its acceptance. The analogy of the freeholder may, from a legal point of view, be correct; and yet a freeholder who invited his brethren to come and abide with him and labor on his farm, and who then sternly visited each expression of opinion different from his own with stripes and banishment, would not be regarded as a desirable neighbor or as a judicious man. In its wider scope, also, the same line of argument might equally well be used to palliate the course of those whose persecutions

[1] Lodge, *Short History*, 351.

forced the colonists into exile. In their desire to defend Winthrop, those who reason thus also defend Laud. He, too, as well as his master and Philip II. and Louis XIV., had great public ends in view, the attainment of which was not in his belief consistent with toleration. Even more than Winthrop, Laud might a little later have pointed to terrible civil calamities which had resulted from his inability to carry out a policy of wholesome repression. If, indeed, he had lived only ten years longer he might have cited exultingly the conformity enforced in Massachusetts and the tranquillity resulting therefrom; and then turned to the dissensions which tore England, and have asserted, truly enough, that he only tried to do in his own country, and failed, what Winthrop had tried to do in Massachusetts, and succeeded. He had striven for the peace of absolute conformity. It is well to consider in the discussion the seventeenth century standpoint; but, in the seventeenth century, good public intentions were not confined to the founders of New England. Others, as well as they, had high considerations of state always in view; and a concurrence of opinion to a given end was in the seventeenth century eagerly desired by those who ruled elsewhere as well as by those who ruled in Massachusetts.

In the treatment of doubtful historical points, there are few things which need to be more carefully guarded against than patriotism or filial piety. Admirable in their place, these sentiments have less than nothing to do with that impartiality which should be the historian's aim; and the appeal to them is generally accompanied by some suggestion that the matter in dispute should be viewed, not according to immutable principles, but from the standpoint of the period or the individual. When viewed in this way, there are few historical events which do not admit of some defence. The door is open wide for sophistry as well as charity. True, it is neither safe nor just to apply the standard of one century to the acts of individuals of another century; but, none the less, the fact of being in advance of one's century constitutes greatness, both in the individual and in the people. If, also, the standards of the period are to be exhumed and adopted, they should be applied with rigorous impartiality. Love of country and piety, whether filial or religious, should not be permitted to intervene in one case, and be excluded in another. Judged in the full light of subsequent events, the protestant, civil or religious, of the seventeenth century was better than the seventeenth century inquisitor and persecutor; but when, circumstances being altered, the protestant himself turned inquisitor and persecutor, it is not easy to see on what judicial principle the historian, who has been exciting sympathy by the ancient tale of wrong, can suddenly put in that plea of altered times for the one, which he has systematically disallowed for the others. To do so may be filial, but it is not rational and it is not fair.

In the controversy of 1637-8 Winthrop and his associates seem to have felt the weakness of their position far more than their modern defenders; and they labored hard to hide it. In England the so-called Antinomian persecution was generally and correctly regarded as a religious one. To deny that it was such is impossible now, and was not easy then. In the face of the record of the Synod at Cambridge, with its endless list of erroneous opinions and "unsavory speeches," — in the face of the church indictment of Mrs. Hutchinson with its twenty-nine several counts, — it might almost as well have been contended that the issue between Luther and Leo X. was not a religious issue, and that the German reformer was proceeded against simply because his course led directly to sedition and civil strife, — which it unquestionably did. But, for obvious reasons, the fathers of the colony were sensitive on this point. The principles of religious toleration were much better understood at that time, by minorities at least, than modern investigators seem disposed to admit. The Long Parliament had not then met, and Laud was in the full enjoyment of power. The friends of Winthrop and Weld in England were accordingly, in 1636–8, themselves undergoing persecutions, and those in New England were loath to supply the prelates with new examples as well as fresh arguments. Their casuistry was equal to this, as it was equal to all other occasions. They flatly denied that religious considerations had anything to do with their proceedings. Whatever they had done, had been done on civil grounds. They had, it was true, labored and wrestled with their brethren over matters spiritual, but the punishments inflicted had been for temporal miscarriages.

Thomas Weld, for instance, in a narrative prepared especially for use in England, after referring to the recantation of Cotton, thus stated the case as respected the others: —

"But for the rest, which (notwithstanding all these meanes of conviction from heaven and earth, and the example of their seduced brethrens returne) yet stood obdurate, yea more hardened (as we had cause to feare) than before; we convented those of them that were members before the churches, and yet laboured once and againe to convince them, not onely of their errors, but also of sundry exorbitant practices, neglecting to feare the Church, and lying, &c., but after no meanes prevailed, we were driven with sad hearts to give them up to Satan: Yet not simply for their opinions (for which I find we have beene slanderously traduced) but the chiefest cause of their censure was their miscarriages (as have beene said) persisted in with great obstinacy." [1]

So when Coggeshall was arraigned before the Court, he had met the charges preferred against him by saying that they amounted to nothing "but matter of different opinion, and that he knew not one example in Scripture that a man was banished for his judgment." To this Winthrop, in the account of the proceedings he prepared for publication in England, says he replied that if the prisoner "had kept his judgment to himself, so as the public peace had not been troubled or endangered by it, we should have left him to himself, for we do not challenge power over mens consciences, but when seditious speeches and practices discover such a corrupt conscience, it is our duty to use authority to reform both." [2] Cogges-

[1] *Short Story*, xii., xv.
[2] In the letter of the Rev. Thomas Shepard, entitled *New England's Lamentations for Old England's Errors*, the distinction suggested here is very clearly drawn: — "We never banished any for their consciences, but for sinning against conscience, after due means of conviction." This is very like Cotton's argument in his reply to Saltonstall, that a magistrate in compelling a man to religious observances does not compel him to sin, "but the sin is in his will that needs to be compelled." (Hutchinson's *State Papers*, 404.) But the statements made for English effect are ludicrously at variance with Winthrop's emphatic laying down of the law at the Hutchinson trial: — "We see not that any should have authority to set up any other exercises besides what authority hath already set up." (Hutchinson, ii. 486.)

hall's offence, it will be remembered, consisted in his saying, from his place in the Legislature, that he approved of a paper presented to a previous Legislature, though his name was not signed to it. It was a case of constructive sedition; but constructive sedition resulting in banishment is only in degree a lesser outrage than constructive treason resulting in death. Whatever their party or country, zealots are all formed of one material, and Hugh Peters was but Ignatius Loyola under other conditions; nor can the fact that the founders of Massachusetts did the deed influence the verdict of history. The "conscientiously contentious" John Wheelwright, silenced for opinion's sake, and expelled from his pulpit at Mount Wollaston, was a persecuted man no less than the "conscientiously contentious" John Wheelwright silenced and expelled for the same cause from his vicarage at Bilsby.

By investigators of another class it is argued that these proceedings were reasonable measures of self-preservation. Those holding this view insist that it is impossible to arrive at any correct understanding of the motives which impelled the dominant party in Massachusetts to their rigorous measures without extending the range of vision so as to take into view the general condition of European thought and political and religious movement at that time. They say, and with truth, that the human mind in many countries was then in a condition of violent seething; the old ligaments which had bound men together were loosened, and the new had not begun to knit. The world was full of crude abominations. The Anabaptists of Munster were but a century gone, and the saints of the Fifth Monarchy were yet to come. The human mind was sick with *isms* — sick in England and Scotland, sick in France, sick in Germany. For the time all things seemed to tend towards subversion. The startling success of Mrs. Hutchinson in her rôle of a prophetess in Boston, "raised up of God for some great work now at hand," was significant. It demonstrates at least how thoroughly the Massachusetts community was impregnated with this uneasy spirit, how strongly it sympathized with the morbid tendencies of the age. In and of herself, Mistress Anne Hutchinson was nothing. At any other time she might have come to Boston and criticised each Sunday's sermons to her heart's content, — talking her mystical nonsense until she stopped from sheer weariness, — and, while few would have hearkened to her, nobody would have molested her. She would have passed away as thousands like her have before and since, and the most diligent search of the antiquarian would fail to detect any ripple made by her in the great current of events. But Mrs. Hutchinson chanced happily. She thirsted for notoriety, and she struck just the combination of circumstances which secured it to her. The historian of to-day, therefore, sees that her success was a symptom, not a cause. It denoted a condition of the body politic. The clergy were supreme; the people were restless, and she gave voice to their restlessness. Thus the great struggle for New England, between the vague unrest of the time and its conservative forces, chanced to happen over her body. Had the conflict resulted otherwise than it did, — had Mrs. Hutchinson sustained herself and had the clergy been vanquished, — she and Wheelwright and the rest would have been like many others, before and since, who have inaugurated revolution when they fondly supposed they were guiding reform. She would soon have been made to realize that the spirit she had invoked far exceeded her powers of control. She would have disappeared aghast at the excesses and absurdities of those who had once been her followers. Theoretical toleration then meant in practice, what theoretical liberty meant in practice a century and a half later in France, — anarchy, pure and simple. The fault was not in the food: that was as good and strong and nourishing in 1637 and in 1793 as it is now; but the stomach of the body politic was not yet educated up to the point of assimilating it. Thus the battle over Mrs. Hutchinson involved the question whether Massachusetts was to be radical and doctrinaire, or conservative and practical, — a man's home or a fool's paradise. The doctrinaire Vane was wise in principle and wrong in practice; Winthrop, cool and prudent, was wrong in principle but right in practice. Even in his bigotry, he saved Massachusetts.

To this somewhat fanciful and overwrought line of argument, it may be replied, that it is a doubtful expedient to justify persecution on the ground that, but for it, a long train of calamities, which never did happen, might have happened. In the early days of New England the clergy never wearied of reminding their flocks of the evil deeds of the Anabaptists; and they were always predicting a renewal of the horrors of Munster as a certain result of toleration. That picture produced much the same effect on the minds of the timid of those days, as the thought of another Reign of Terror has produced on the well-to-do of Europe throughout the present century. There were alarmists in the seventeenth century just as there are in the nineteenth; but the realities of history and the imaginings of excited men are two very different things. In 1629 the charge made against the first body of emigrants to Salem in Endicott's company was that " they were Separatists, and would be shortly Anabaptists." In 1637 Winthrop doubtless believed in his heart — what he stated at the trial and spread on the Records of the Province and reiterated in his narrative of the proceedings — that the Covenant of Grace, as taught by Mrs. Hutchinson, and social anarchy, or worse, were convertible terms.[1] It is barely possible that at one stage of the controversy there might have been danger of actual strife; though the presumption — as gathered from the calm, law-abiding tone of the papers which emanated from the minority, and from the submissive way in which they allowed themselves at the close to be disarmed, fined, whipped, disfranchised and banished — is decidedly the other way. There is no evidence of any material in that little community out of which to manufacture revolutions. Certainly Coddington, Coggeshall, Hough, Balston, Hutchinson, Dummer, and even blubbering Captain John Underhill, are strange subjects out of which to conjure up hosts of prophets of Munster, Latter-day Saints, or Fifth Monarchy Men.

But the common-sense view of the controversy of 1637, and its unhappy outcome, would seem to lead the modern investigator to wholly different and more sober-colored conclusions. It was a struggle for civil power and ecclesiastical supremacy in a small village community. As such it naturally — it almost necessarily — resulted in a display of the worst qualities of those engaged in it. It illustrated also with singular force the malign influence apt to be exercised by the

[1] Hutchinson, ii. 514; *Records*, i. 211; *Short Story*, 40.

priest and the woman as active elements in political life. Stirred by an access of ill-considered popular enthusiasm, the body of the freemen had, at the election of 1636, put a slight upon the time-honored magistrates of the colony, by placing the boyish Vane over their heads, in the office of governor. An ambitious woman, with her head full of Deborahs and the like, and with a genius for making trouble, had then sought to drive from his pulpit, in the chief town, its long-settled pastor, in order to install her own favorite preacher in his place, with her kinsman as that preacher's associate and successor. In her day-dreams she herself probably occupied, in the new order of things she proposed to bring about, the position of a prophetess, — the real guiding-spirit of the whole, — with her husband possibly in the judge's seat. Altogether it was an exhilarating vision, — such a vision as self-conscious and usually unappreciated natures have in every time and most places been wont to revel in. But it did so chance that Mrs. Hutchinson fell into just that combination of circumstances which enabled her to succeed up to a certain point. Her success was indeed marvellous; and it turned her head. Presently she became reckless. She put wanton affronts on the pastor; and when his brethren rallied to his support, she did not hesitate to assail them also. She made enemies of the whole body of the clergy. Vane sympathized with her; Winthrop with them. The contest over the possession of the civil offices came first, and resulted in an easy conservative triumph. Vane made the best fight he could; but the odds were too heavy, and he went helplessly down. Winthrop was reinstated in his old place; and, practically, the struggle was then over.

This fact both Vane and Winthrop recognized. They were men trained in public affairs and accustomed to their ways. When beaten, the latter, with a sense and dignity which did him infinite credit, accepted the situation as a man should, and patiently bided his time; the former, when his turn to be defeated came, left the country. The real issue was then decided, and there was no longer anything to quarrel over. Unfortunately there was a woman in the case, and the implacable spirit of theological hate had been aroused. The priesthood demanded a victim; and the victim met the priesthood at least half-way. It now became a struggle, which would have been ludicrous had it not been so earnest and so painful, between the whole body of the clergy and a female enthusiast, politician and tease. Had Winthrop then been in real control and able to assert a policy, the excitement would speedily have worn itself out, as purely factitious excitements always have worn themselves out when left alone, and always will. In six months from his return to office Mrs. Hutchinson would have been a sensation of yesterday; while John Wheelwright for the rest of his life would have quietly ministered to his people at the First Church in Braintree. As for real danger to the existence of the colony, there was none. The strength and permanence of the English settlement of Massachusetts rested on too strong a basis to be jeopardized by a change of magistrates, or a noisy quarrel in a vestry. The success of Charles I. and Strafford and Laud in their schemes in England would have placed the colony in much peril; but in New England its safety lay, not in the fact that Winthrop, or any other man or set of men, held office, but in the oneness, the hard practical sense, and power of political afterthought and self-restraint, of the twelve or fifteen thousand Englishmen who composed it. They were no sheep, to whom Anne Hutchinson was a ravening wolf and for whom John Winthrop was the only shepherd.

The issue was then finally and completely settled at Cambridge on the $\frac{17\text{th}}{27\text{th}}$ of May, 1637. The whole theory of a continuing danger, to the time when six months later the persecution took place, is without any evidence in its support. The procession of his friends which escorted Vane to the shore, when on the 13th of August he embarked for England, was a final demonstration, — the salvo of musketry which saluted his departing vessel was the volley fired over the grave of a lost cause. The demonstration may under the circumstances have been indiscreet, but it could hardly have excited alarm. The Pequot war had then been brought to a triumphant close; the conservative party was in undisputed control of every branch of the government; the immigration was large; the alien law was in operation. The adherents of Mrs. Hutchinson, the so-called Antinomians, were in a majority in a single town only of the whole province, and their party was so completely broken that its leaders were already seeking a place of refuge outside the jurisdiction of Massachusetts. The struggle with them was no longer for power, but for self-preservation. So far from threatening the safety of the community, they were notoriously unable to protect themselves.

Unfortunately Winthrop's course was not now a free one. It was hampered by the presence of those ecclesiastical allies who had borne him back into power. The clergy verifying in their conduct Milton's assertion that "Presbyter was but Priest writ large,"—the clergy insisted on the extirpation of an indefinable heresy. They pointed to the compact of January, two years before, wherein "Mr. Winthrop acknowledged that he was convinced that he had failed in overmuch lenity and remissness, and would endeavor to make a more strict course hereafter." They demanded the letter of the bond. Dudley and Endicott also were there, sitting on his either hand at the council-table: Dudley, to whom a faction among the people had adhered because he carried matters with "more severity;" and Endicott, afterwards the persecutor of the Quakers, and now the mouthpiece of Hugh Peters.[1] The mild-tempered but prudent Win-

[1] That this is the correct explanation of Winthrop's course is, I think, plainly to be inferred from his own language. In May, 1635, he had failed of a reëlection as governor, and subsequently, in January, 1636, had been informally arraigned before the clergy on the charge of dealing "too remissly in point of justice." He had made the issue that "justice should be administered with more lenity in the infancy of a plantation than in a settled state." The next morning the ministers had "set down a rule in the case" in favor of "strict discipline." Then Winthrop confessed himself, in the language cited in the text, and promised to err no more on the side of lenity. (Winthrop, i. *178.) Sixteen months later, through the direct interposition of the clergy, he had been again chosen governor, and now as the exponent of their policy. Immediately on his return to office he wrote as follows of the Antinomian controversy:—"Few could see where the difference was; and indeed it seemed so small, as (if men's affections had not been formerly alienated, when the differences were formerly stated as fundamental) they might easily have come to reconciliation." (Ib. *221.) Six months later he records the meeting of the General Court, when its members, "finding upon consultation that two so opposite parties could not contain in the same body, without apparent hazard to the whole, agreed to send away some of the principal." (Ib. *245.) These extracts, with Dudley's and Endicott's interpolations at Mrs. Hutchinson's trial, apparently tell the whole story. Hugh Peters' influence on Endicott, who "as a magistrate did not bear his sword in vain," is set forth in I. *Mass. Hist. Soc. Coll.* vi. 253-5.

throp remembered his promise, and bent to the storm he could not withstand. What followed was a simple ecclesiastical persecution, of the more moderate kind. "Jezebel" was hunted out. With Winthrop, therefore, all the proceedings subsequent to the May election of 1637 were a political necessity. Like many another public man, he found himself driven by the clamor of those behind him further than he wished, or thought it wise to go. There is reason, also, to believe that his own conscience was thereafter ill at ease in regard to the course he then pursued, and that he feared, because of the sufferings and banishments inflicted, God would visit his wrath and sore displeasure upon the land.[1] The recollection of these things even cast a shadow of remorse over the closing hours of his well-spent life; for when, twelve years later, the Father of Massachusetts lay dying in his house in Boston, an order for the expulsion of some religious dissentient was brought to him. Turning from Dudley, ever prone to severity, who pressed him to sign it, the dying magistrate refused, saying, — "Of that work I have done too much already."[2] As he uttered those words the memory of murdered Anne Hutchinson, upon whose former home, standing opposite his own, his fading vision may at the moment well have rested, must needs have been uppermost in his thoughts.[3]

The business of the historian is to state facts and conclusions exactly as he sees them. On the one hand it would appear that the Boston movement of 1636-8 — the miscalled Antinomian movement —

---

[1] IV. *Mass. Hist. Soc. Coll.* vii. 187.
[2] Hutchinson, i. 151.
[3] Ellis, *Puritan Age*, 25.

was a premature agitation, based on a false issue. The power of the clergy could not then have been successfully assailed in Massachusetts; nor was it desirable that it should be. There was need enough for reform; but, to be useful and healthy, reform had to come more slowly and from another direction. Neither did Anne Hutchinson or her following hold forth any promise of better things. Theirs was no protest against existing abuses. On the contrary, in their religious excesses they outdid even the clergy, — they out-heroded Herod. Their overthrow, accordingly, so far as it was peculiar to themselves and did not involve the overthrow of great principles of religious toleration and political reform, was no matter for regret. Knowingly and intelligently they represented nothing that was religiously good or politically sound. But, unfortunately, their action — as false, premature action is wont to do — brought wiser action and sound principles into disrepute, and seriously retarded progress in Massachusetts. This was conspicuously apparent in the ruthless treatment a subsequent and more deserving reform movement shortly after received at the hands of the party in power; for the fate of Robert Child and his associates in 1646 was a mere political corollary of that of Anne Hutchinson in 1637. At the hands, therefore, of an historian whose intelligence is not mastered by his sympathies, she and her friends, including Governor Vane, are entitled to no consideration. They went on a fool's errand, and they brought great principles into lasting odium.

On the other hand, the way in which the adherents of Vane and Mrs. Hutchinson were suppressed cannot be defended, without including in the defence the whole system of religious and political intolerance of that time. But why should it be defended? It is impossible to ignore the fact, and worse than useless to deny it, that the New England Puritans were essentially a persecuting race. They could not be otherwise. They believed that they were God's chosen people. As such, they were right; all others were wrong. If, therefore, they failed to bring up their children in the strait and narrow way, and to protect them and all the people from the wiles of the Evil One, God would not hold them guiltless. The Israelites were their models in all things, and the precedents which guided their action were precedents drawn from the books of the Old Testament. "So, by the example of Lot in Abraham's family, and after Hagar and Ishmael, he saw they must be sent away." The Israelites were not an attractive or an amiable or a philosophical race; they were narrow, devout and clannish. No one ever presumed to sophisticate away their cruelties or their persecutions. Yet withal they were a strong and an aggressive people, believing certain things implicitly; and, accordingly, they impressed themselves and their beliefs on the human mind. Their very imperfections were essential elements of their strength. They believed to fanaticism; and it was the strength of their fanaticism which caused their belief to dominate. It was the same with the Puritans of New England. They persecuted as a part of their faith.

It is true that in so doing the Puritan exiles to New England showed that they were not in advance of their times. That they were not, was again an element of their strength; for they were essentially practical men, and not idealists. As such, being of the seventeenth century, they objected to persecution chiefly as applied to themselves. It was enough for them that their charter and the fundamental principles of their community gave them the right to prescribe who might settle among them, and to expel dissentients and intruders. They exercised that right.

But is there any good reason to suppose that the crushing-out process of 1637 resulted more favorably in Massachusetts than elsewhere? The historians of the New England school have insisted that it did,—that in this case at least, whether harshly and oppressively used or not, persecution was justified by the result.[1] They point to the fact that peace, quiet and safety were by means of it restored, and that a long period of internal tranquillity followed the year 1637. The exiles even, in many cases, made their submission and returned. All this is true. Exiles have usually, in all ages and in all countries, looked fondly back on their old homes, and returned to them as soon as they were permitted so to do. As respects the long period of peace and tranquillity, there can be no question that such a period followed the violent measures of 1637-8. This was well expressed in a tract published in London in 1643, in which the boast was made that, since the banishment of the friends of Mrs. Hutchinson, "not any unsound, unsavourie and giddie fancie have dared to lift up his head, or abide the light amongst us." [2] But, though there can be no question that a period of peace and tranquillity did then settle down on Massachusetts, or that it lasted through the lives of six generations of those born on the soil, there may well be great question whether this peace and tran-

---

[1] Palfrey, i. 509; Lodge, 351.
[2] 1. *Mass. Hist. Soc. Coll.* i. 247.

quillity were good things, — whether, indeed, those blessings were not purchased for Massachusetts, as they have been for other countries, at a heavy price. When Vane, in the December council of 1636, was cowering under the fierce diatribe of Hugh Peters, he showed true insight in exclaiming, "the light of the Gospel brings a sword."[1] These few words, like a sudden electric flash, revealed the whole situation, laying bare the errors of those with whom he was contending. Then and afterwards, it was in New England as it has been and still is elsewhere: "the spiritual growth of Massachusetts withered under the shadow of dominant orthodoxy; the colony was only saved from atrophy by its vigorous political life," and the rule of its established church, "so long as it endured, was a rule of terror, not of love; her ways were never ways of pleasantness, her paths were never peace."[2]

Yet it has more than once been assumed by the Massachusetts historians, in a sort of matter-of-course way, that the sterile conformity, which for more than a century after the suppressions of 1637–8 prevailed in the Puritan Commonwealth, was desirable, — that magistrates like Stoughton and divines like Mather, and a literature of forgotten theology and unreadable homilies, were fruits indicating a good tree. That what happened then did happen is true; that it naturally resulted from what went before is equally true; but that better things could not have happened is taken for granted. That in time the intellect of Massachusetts — schooled by self-government through a long struggle with nature and against foreign en-

[1] *Supra*, 424.
[2] Doyle, *Eng. in Am.; the Puritan Colonies*, i. 187–8.

croachments — did work itself out from under the incubus of superstition, prejudice and narrow conformity imposed upon it by the first generation of magistrates and ministers, cannot be denied; but it is certainly going far to infer therefrom that, in this especial case, superstition, prejudice and narrow conformity were helps instead of obstacles. It is not easy indeed to see how the *post ergo propter* fallacy could be carried further. It is much like arguing, because a child of robust frame and active mind survives stripes and starvation in infancy, and bad instruction and worse discipline in youth, — struggling through to better things in manhood, — that therefore the stripes and starvation, and bad instruction and worse discipline, in his case at least worked well, and were the cause of his subsequent excellence. It is barely possible that New England, contrary to all principle and precedent, may have profited by the harshness and bigotry which for a time suppressed all freedom of thought in Massachusetts; but it is far more likely that the slow results afterwards there achieved came notwithstanding that drawback, rather than in consequence of the discipline it afforded. Certainly the historians who with such confidence set aside all the lessons of human experience — in order to assert that, in the case of their ancestors, whatever was, was right, as well as best — would be slow to apply the same rules or draw similar conclusions in the case of such as persecuted, banished or suppressed those who thought like their ancestors.

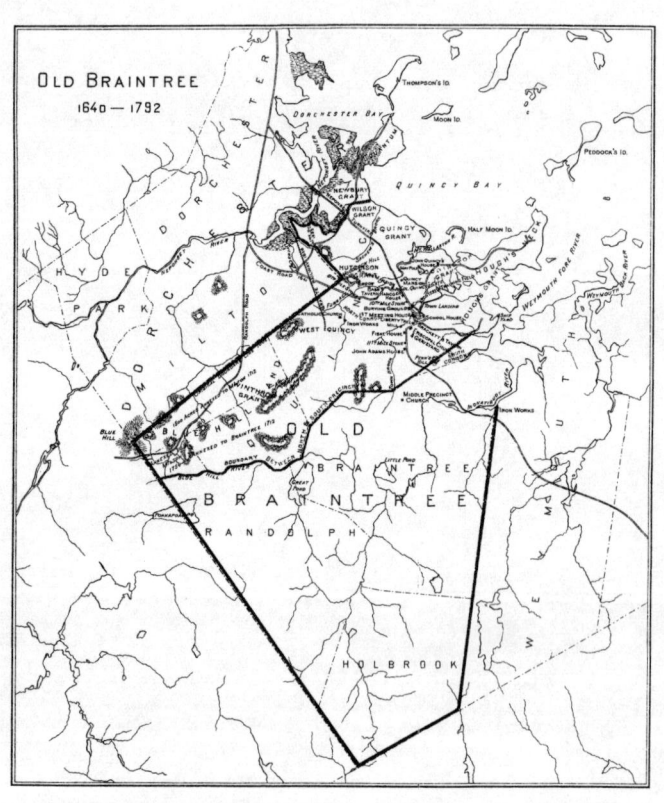

# III.

# A STUDY OF CHURCH AND TOWN GOVERNMENT.

# A STUDY OF CHURCH AND TOWN GOVERNMENT.

## CHAPTER I.

### OLD BRAINTREE.

ON the 18th of November, 1637, according to the calendar now in use, sentence of banishment was passed on John Wheelwright; and, before the 1st of December, the preacher at "the Mount" had forever left his people there, and was on his way to New Hampshire. The character and extent of the settlements on the shores of Boston Bay south of the Neponset, at that time, have already been referred to. Practically, the region was still a forest wilderness of swamp, salt marsh and upland. There was as yet no road from Boston to Plymouth, for the path to the latter place — in trying to follow which Phinehas Pratt had lost his way thirteen years before [1] — began at Wessagusset, and such little intercourse as there was between those dwelling at Wessagusset and at Boston was by boat across the bay. The Indian trail did not follow the shore, nor could it be called a path, for the eye of the trained woodsman was needed to detect its devious way as it wound about the head-waters of tidal inlets and circled the uplands in search of fords, or

[1] *Supra*, 86–8.

those points where alone it was possible to cross the swamps. While a forlorn remnant of the Massachusetts, the stricken survivors of plague and small-pox, haunted the forest, between the Neponset and the Monatoquit there were absolutely no white inhabitants. First Morton and the Merry-Mount company had been rooted out by the magistrates, who afterwards hunted Gardiner into the wilderness; and, so far as those two earliest attempts at settlement were concerned, axe and fire had done the work of obliteration with all possible thoroughness, as Alderman, the pioneer settler at Hingham, found when, in 1634, having had occasion to be in Boston, he undertook to return home by trail instead of by boat. His experience has already been referred to,[1] and it was even more severe than that of Phinehas Pratt eleven years earlier; for, losing his way, Alderman, during three days and nights, wandered through woods and swamps without falling in with a habitation, either house or wigwam, or a human being, white or red. Then, at last, exhausted and starved, with torn clothing and bruised body, he struggled out of the wilderness to find himself in Scituate. The Neponset was the southern limit of the Massachusetts settlement, and the region beyond it remained a wilderness, through which, and beneath the dense tangle of the primeval forest, the sluggish streams that had their sources among the Blue Hills worked their slow way by clogged and crooked channels into the coast-indenting tidal creeks, whose wide margins of spongy salt-marsh were submerged at times of flood.

Of the original settlers thereabouts, — the "old planters," as they were called, — the widow of David

[1] *Supra*, 337, 364.

Thomson only had been left, dwelling with her infant son and a few servants on the farm cleared and cultivated by her husband at the very point where Miles Standish and his party landed, when, thirteen years before, they first visited Boston Bay. Reference has also been made to the order of the General Court of May, 1634, that Boston, being "too small to contain many," should have a convenient enlargement at Mount Wollaston.[1] In the following September the "enlargement" was formally approved, and on the 8th of December a grant of land was made to "Mr. Willson the Pastor." The Rev. John Wilson of the first church of Boston was therefore the earliest landowner under the Massachusetts charter in what subsequently became, and for a century and a half remained, the township of Braintree. Two years later still further large assignments were made, and the entire bay-front from the Squantum headland to the mouth of the Monatoquit opposite Wessagusset passed into the hands of three men, Atherton Hough, William Coddington and Edmund Quincy.

Thus the region immediately south of the Neponset constituted an exception to the well-defined general policy under which the earlier land allotments were made in Massachusetts. That policy, — a distinct negation of the feudalism which Gorges had sought to transplant,[2] — unquestionably looked as a whole to a careful husbanding of resources in the interest of all; to a methodical occupation of territory; to an avoidance of even the beginnings of great accumulations of landed property: so that, during the twenty-five years

[1] *Supra*, 365.
[2] Egleston, *The Land System of the New England Colonies*, 26–7. *Johns Hopkins University Studies*, IV.

which immediately followed the settlement, but little more than a hundred special grants were made, the largest of which was 3,200 acres, while most of them did not exceed 250 acres.

Yet while this wise and far-sighted policy was followed in the colony as a whole, in the case of "the Mount," nearly the whole of the bay-front, as has been seen, was allotted to three men, while three others secured a large portion of the adjacent upland; and great tracts, one of them of 3,000 acres and another of 2,000, were set aside and devoted to special purposes: and this deviation from the general scheme became, as will presently be seen, the cause of subsequent grave complications.

Although in December, 1636, a committee, at the head of which was Winthrop, was appointed "to Consider of the Mount Woolistone businesse, and for the ripening thereof how there may be a Town there" with the consent of Boston, "the Mount" still seems at that time to have been looked upon as a remote, outlying dependency, to be reached conveniently enough by boat in summer, but in winter practically inaccessible. A little over one month before the Winthrop committee was appointed, on the $\frac{30\text{th}}{9\text{th}}$ of $\frac{\text{October}}{\text{November}}$, it will be remembered John Wheelwright had been "granted unto for the preparing for a church gathering" there. It was evidently intended to incorporate a town at once; and little doubt exists that the body of immigrants who during the summer of 1637 came, as Winthrop says, "out of England from Mr. Brierly his church," would have joined the flock to which Wheelwright ministered, and consequently become freeholders of the proposed new town, had they not been confronted at landing with that alien law, the purpose and operation of which has already been described.[1] They were consequently obliged to find a place for settlement elsewhere, and outside the Massachusetts jurisdiction.

Naturally, amid the complications and fierce quarrels of 1637, nothing was done by the committee of December 10th in the " ripening " way; nor, for the next three years, was anything more heard of the project of a new church and another town south of the Neponset. It lay in abeyance, awaiting the advent of quieter times. During the interval the dwellers at and about Mount Wollaston would seem to have been poor people, the " servants " as they were described of the large landholders; for there is no reason to suppose that any person of note or substance had yet actually made his home there, though several such unquestionably cultivated farms upon which they erected dwellings for their servants, and barns and outbuildings to shelter their stock. During the subsequent years to 1640 other large allotments, of from 100 to 400 acres, were made to non-residents, exceptional grants well calculated to foster a race of landed gentry, but adding little either to the population or the prosperity of the region. But large grants were no longer the rule. Another system was all this time being pursued towards " the common people," as they were called, who were coming over to New England in crowds. The custom was to allot such, irrespective of sex or age, but grouping them in families, four acres a head; and in the case of Boston the smaller allotments were made largely at the Mount, twenty-six such being recorded in 1638, and fifteen more in 1639. Prior to the incorporation of Braintree in

[1] *Supra*, 458–60.

May, 1640, one hundred and five such allotments in all had been parcelled out to families, numbering 565 persons, showing that the average family, including probably servants as well as children, was between five and six persons. But though these allotments are recorded, it cannot be inferred that all those to whom they were made actually settled at the Mount. On the contrary, the names of only a small portion of them are at a somewhat later period to be found in the town and parish records, and the natural inference is that many received their allotments in one place, and, in those days of abundant land, preferred to settle elsewhere.

Nevertheless, a certain portion of these poorer people did go out and build dwellings south of the Neponset; and at last a decisive movement was made towards the establishment of an independent church there. The "Chapel of Ease" arrangement, as it of necessity involved dependence on a mother church, no longer sufficed for the spiritual needs of a growing population. The region had also stood an unoccupied gap of heathendom long enough; for the Dorchester church, on the north, went back to June, 1630, while the societies of Weymouth and Hingham, on the south, dated respectively from July and September, 1635. Without, therefore, waiting for a formal adjustment of all questions with Boston, on the 16th of September, 1639, those dwelling at the Mount, in the words of Governor Winthrop, " gathered a church after the usual manner, and chose one Mr. Tomson, a very gracious, sincere man, and Mr. Flynt, a godly man also, their ministers." In the case of the church at Braintree, the signatures of six persons, besides those of the pastor and teacher, were affixed to the covenant. Drawn up in the simple but not unimpressive form then in common use, by virtue of it those entering into the compact — " poor unworthy creatures, who have sometime lived without Christ and without God in the world " — promised thereafter " to worship the Lord in spirit and truth, and to walk in brotherly love and the duties thereof according to the will of the gospel." In witness of which, they made public profession of faith in presence of those assembled, and gave to one another the right hand of fellowship. The church at Braintree was the fifteenth which had been gathered in the province of Massachusetts Bay during the ten years of its settlement.

The incorporation of the town followed hard upon the gathering of the church, for, at the following session of the General Court, that of May, 1640, the " petition of the inhabitants of Mount Wollaston was acceded to, and it was granted them to be a town, to be called Braintree;" though no well-authenticated or wholly satisfactory reason for the choice of this name has ever been given, nor is there any bond of connection apparent between the Suffolk Braintree, of New England, and the Essex Braintree, of Old England. The vote incorporating Braintree contained detailed reference to an agreement which had been effected between certain representatives of those dwelling at the Mount and the authorities of Boston. The vested interests of the latter place in the former had again been asserted, and the question thus raised proved one not easy to settle. There had evidently been much bickering. Appealing to the " enlargement " vote of 1634, it was contended on the one side that Boston and the Boston church would, through the incorporation of the new town, be shorn of their proportions; while on the other side a growing population asserted their natural rights. The result was a compromise, the terms of which are by no means free from ambiguity. Under it all the lands in the new township seem to have been released from a liability to taxation as a part of Boston, and also from future county taxes, upon the payment to Boston of a trifle over a shilling an acre on the land "formerly granted to divers men of Boston upon expectation they should have continued still with us," and three shillings an acre for every acre that had been, or thereafter should be, granted to any others not inhabitants of Boston. In other words, the actual settlers in Braintree were to pay into the Boston treasury a sum of money on their holdings in commutation. At the same time further large allotments at the Mount were made, including five hundred acres "for the use of the Canoneere of Boston Wheresoever he is, or shall be, in the service thereof, from time to time," and "two thousand acres to be sett apart for the use of (Boston) in the most Convenient place unallotted."

This agreement was made on the 11th of January, 1639, some five months before the General Court acted on the petition to incorporate; and when the court did act, it made a further proviso that, if the inhabitants of the newly-created town failed to fulfil the covenant they had entered into, it should be in the power of Boston to recover its dues by action against the Braintree people, collectively or individually. That the burden thus imposed on Braintree was an unusual and most oppressive one does not need to be said. It was the case of a poor, struggling community being compelled to buy out alien vested interests in the soil, which ought never to have existed. Accordingly, at a later time it proved a fruitful source of heart-burnings and litigation. Nevertheless the arrangement, favorable or otherwise, seems to have been the best it was possible to effect at the time, and under it Braintree came into existence as an independent political community on what is now the 23d of May, 1640. Those dwelling in the new town were also made to realize at once that political privileges carried with them corresponding obligations, for by the same court they were assessed twenty-five pounds in a total levy of twelve hundred pounds. In payment of this levy old silver plate was to be received at five shillings the ounce, " good old Indian corn, being clean and merchantable," at five shillings the bushel, summer wheat at seven shillings, and rye at six shillings. In which of these several staples the whole or any portion of this earliest tax levy was paid, nowhere appears; but that it was paid admits of no doubt, and at the next session of the General Court, held in Boston on the 7th day of the following October, William Cheeseborough and Stephen Kinsley appeared, and took their seats as the first representatives of Braintree.

## CHAPTER II.

### THE BRAINTREE NORTH PRECINCT CHURCH.

THE original Braintree settlement was along the shore of the bay, and on the upland and in the valleys adjacent thereto. Only by slow degrees did population work its way back among the hills and interior valleys. In 1708 the church of Braintree was divided, and the original settlement became the North Precinct. In 1792 this North Precinct was set off from the rest of the town, and became Quincy.

Until 1708, therefore, the original Braintree church was the one church of the town; from 1708 to 1792 it was the North Precinct church; from 1792 to 1820 it was the Quincy church. The revised constitution of Massachusetts went into effect in 1820, and under its provisions a complete separation of church from state took place: but the habits of the people were fixed, and several years elapsed before this change in the organic law began to produce its full results;[1] for people went on attending divine worship in the meeting-house of their fathers, and in Quincy it was ten years yet before another meeting-house was built. Accordingly,

[1] So fixed was the belief that obligatory support of a church was essential to its continued existence that the late Judge Story voiced a very common sentiment when, at the time the amended constitution took effect, he expressed the opinion that in twenty-five years there would not be a church open in Massachusetts in which the old religious services would be held.

the sole church of the Braintree of 1639 was still, until 1830, the sole church of Quincy.

The society had then worshipped in four successive buildings, the last of which was in 1830 almost new, having been finished only two years before. Built of stone, it was called a "temple," and it replaced an old New England meeting-house which for ninety-six years had stood on the training-field in the centre of the town. Thus, when this meeting-house of 1732 was removed in 1828, the visible emblem which connected the modern with the colonial town may be said to have disappeared. The connecting link between two chains was broken. The period, therefore, of one hundred and eighty-nine years which elapsed after the gathering of the First Church of Braintree, and before the pulling down and moving away of the third meeting-house in Quincy, must historically be considered by itself. It was not the less one and the same period because during it the colonies were severed from Great Britain, and Quincy was severed from Braintree. These were both mere political changes, scarcely affecting to a degree outwardly perceptible the occupations of the people who lived at what in 1635 was known as the Mount, or their modes of life and thought, or their social and material condition. The real elements of change in all these respects were not political; nor had they begun to make their presence felt when the eighteenth century came to its close. Thirty years later it was no longer so. The original Granite railway was built in Quincy in 1826; the first Massachusetts railroad company was incorporated in 1830. These events marked epochs. They from top to bottom altered in America, as in Europe, — and at "the Mount" as in Massachusetts,

— that which French and Indian wars, and wars of independence, and church and municipal divisions, had affected scarcely at all.

The long period from 1640 to 1830 was therefore with the Massachusetts towns the primitive period, — that of formation. Though it led directly to the present, it had little in common with the present. Nevertheless, during that period five generations lived on the soil, and were buried in it; and concerning these there was, as a rule, little more to record. A simple, laborious, unaggressive race, they were born and died, — each following generation much the same as the generation which preceded it. Wealth and population increased slowly. With vessels of the same build, they fished familiar seas; with similar utensils, they cultivated the same fields. Dwelling in houses built on an identical plan, they preserved the old domestic and social customs. The outer world made itself little felt in the remote village community; and the village community in no way influenced the outer world. Few elements of change existed, and accordingly little change took place. The Quincy of 1830 was only the Braintree of 1640, a little more thickly peopled and a little more prosperous.

The social and material conditions of the town during this period of one hundred and ninety years will be treated in another chapter. Meanwhile the year 1830 brought the early theological period to a close. Up to that time the life of the church and the life of the town were interwoven, and until 1824 parish and town were legally one; so the history of the church, as being the more ancient of the two, precedes that of the town.

In September, 1739, the Rev. John Hancock, father

## 1637. THE FIRST MEETING-HOUSE. 593

of the patriot and then the North Precinct minister, preached two centennial sermons in the new meeting-house removed in 1828, but which then was new. In one of these sermons he said, — " This is the third house, in which we are now worshipping, that we and our fathers have built for the public worship of God." There is reason to suppose that the second of these three houses was built in the year 1666, as the quaint old weather-vane which surmounted it, still in existence, bears that date. Of the first Braintree meeting-house, there remains no detailed account or description. Completed, and in use, before the month of May, 1641, a familiar, recognized landmark, standing near the end of a short bridge even then referred to as "old," this house " for the public worship of God" was probably built during the summer of the year 1637 for the use and under the supervision of John Wheelwright. Possibly it may have been even older, and already serving as the "Chapel of Ease" at Mount Wollaston on that day of fast at the end of May, 1637, when Vane and Coddington, to emphasize their dissent from the methods of their opponents, ignored the Boston assembly, and went " to keep the day at the Mount with Mr. Wheelwright." It may well, therefore, have been that the Fast-day services of 1637, on what now is reckoned as the 3d of June, were the first ever solemnized within those newly-erected walls, standing that day fresh from the hands of the builders; while Vane was there to lend dignity and interest to the event, as well as give public evidence of his sympathy with the preacher. If such perchance was the case, a new interest attaches to those walls, and to the church which within them, a little later on, began its organized life. John Wheelwright, the schoolmate and friend of Cromwell, the proscribed in two continents, there preached that day in presence of young Harry Vane, moving steadily and fatefully forward from the chair of state in Boston to the block on Tower-hill.

Whether this was so or not, that first church edifice stood in 1640 on rising ground just south of the place where the principal travelled way of the little settlement — the way which a few years later became a part of the colonial coast-road connecting Boston and Plymouth — crossed a brook, then and subsequently known as the Town River. At the time the first meeting-house was built, the road could have been hardly more than a well-beaten trail, for it was not formally laid out until at least seven years later, in 1648. The brook, which for some distance higher up had forced its way through a well-nigh impenetrable tangle from which the larger forest animals had hardly vanished and which yet swarmed with reptile life, here flowed over a hard gravel bottom between two converging bits of upland. It was a fording-place, — a natural point of crossing. For that reason the meeting-house was put there. It was a point convenient for those living on both sides of the watercourse.

The meeting-house stood in the open, and when the " country highway " from Weymouth to Dorchester was formally laid out, in 1648, it here diverged, passing the building at both its ends, for it faced east and west. The diverging ways then shortly turned and joined again. At no great distance from the front of the meeting-house, looking westward, lay the tangled bottom through which the Town River sluggishly crept. Beyond this, and half a mile or so away, rose the rough, heavily-wooded granite hills, while to the east there stretched a broad, and comparatively level, upland plain. Such in 1640 was the centre of the town.

In the humble church edifice, which, nevertheless, was "as fair a meeting-house" as that people could provide, William Tompson, "a very holy man, who had been an instrument of much good at Accomenticus," was formally ordained as first regular minister. At that time the gathering of a new church was a great event in Massachusetts, — another candle was lighted in the tabernacle. The gathering at the Mount also was a special occasion. A true church — one to which none but orthodox doctrines were to be preached — was to be established in the Antinomian hot-bed. The last vestiges of the banished Wheelwright's teachings were to be eradicated, and his flock, renouncing "the devil, the wicked world, a sinful flesh, with all the remnants of Anti-Christian pollution wherein sometimes we have walked, and all our former evil ways," were to become members of the common fold.

Of those who were present, or of those who took part in the services, no record has come down. Winthrop noted the event in his journal, but there is nothing to indicate that either he or Dudley, during that year Governor and Deputy-Governor, were there. Probably Peter Hobart, that "bold man who would speak his mind," came over from Hingham; while from Dorchester came Richard Mather, together with his young associate, John Wilson, son of the pastor of Boston, and himself just graduated from Cambridge. The Rev. John Allen may have found his way through the forest paths from Dedham, as Wilson and Cotton sailed across the bay from Boston. Earnest, devout men, they gathered from far and near in the primitive wilderness meeting-house on that September day, and there extended the right hand of fellowship to the little congregation who now covenanted one with another " to worship the Lord in Spirit and in Truth, and to walk in brotherly love." The church then founded was destined to centuries of unbroken existence.

The pastorate of William Tompson extended through a period of nineteen years. Represented by the writers of his own time as having been " a very powerful and successful preacher," and one " abounding in zeal for the propagation of the gospel," Tompson was likewise of a " very melancholic mien and of a crazy body," and his ministry at Braintree can be accounted successful neither for himself nor his people. A graduate of Oxford, and belonging to that earliest generation of New England clergymen who had been settled over English churches, the new Braintree pastor resigned a living in Lancashire in order to come to New England, and landed in Boston at about the time the Antinomian Synod of 1637 was sitting. Settled at Braintree in September, 1639, in the following March Henry Flynt was ordained as teacher of the church, which would seem to indicate that the pastor from the very beginning proved unequal to the performance of all his duties ; for the teacher in the early New England churches was practically an associate pastor,[1] and it is not likely that a small and poor community, such as Braintree, assumed with-

---

[1] As to the distinctive functions of Pastor and Teacher in the early New England church organization, see Walker's *Thomas Hooker*, 69-70.

out reason the support of two ministers. In any event
the society seemed not unwilling to allow Mr. Tompson to seek other fields of usefulness, and in 1642 his
brother ministers selected him with two others to go
forth on a strange sort of missionary service among
the Church of England heathen of Virginia; for a
cry had come up from "many well-disposed people,
. . . to the elders here, bewailing their sad condition
for want of the means of salvation, and earnestly entreating a supply of faithful ministers, whom, upon
experience of their gifts and godliness, they might
call to office." So far from turning a deaf ear to
this call, the Massachusetts elders "accounted it no
small honor that God had put upon his poor churches
here, that other parts of the world should seek to us
for help in this kind;" and so, the letters from Virginia having been "openly read in Boston upon a
lecture-day, the elders met, and set a day apart to
seek God in it." This done, they made choice for
the work in hand of three of their number "who
might most likely be spared;" and among the three
was Mr. Tompson, his church having two ministers.
Accordingly, on the $\frac{7th}{17th}$ of October, 1642, Mr. Tompson set out for Taunton, the first stage on the way
to Virginia, in company with the Rev. John Knowles
of Watertown, "a godly man and a prime scholar,"
who only, besides himself, accepted the call.

Their journey was over what now is a familiar
route, for they were "to meet the bark at Narragansett;" in other words, they were to go to Norfolk,
in Virginia, by way of Newport and New York, or
Aquidneck and New Amsterdam, as those places were
then called. The "bark" referred to was probably
one of the sloops or ketches of those days, — little one

and two masted crafts used in the coasting trade, — and George Fox has described how, thirty years later, he made the same voyage from Newport to New York, coming to anchor one night before Fisher's Island, where "there fell abundance of rain, and our sloop being open, we were exceeding wet." It was nearly three months before the missionaries reached their destination; for at first they were wind-bound in Narragansett Bay, and then, in passing through Hell-Gate, their boat was swept upon the rocks and so damaged that they barely succeeded in reaching the shore. Cotton Mather says of Tompson in this emergency, —

"Upon a ledge of craggy rocks near stav'd,
His Bible in his bosom thrusting, sav'd;
The Bible, the best of cordial of his heart,
'Come floods, come flames,' cry'd he, 'we'll never part.'"

The shipwrecked missionaries received "slender entertainment" at the hands of Governor William Kieft, the Dutch commandant at New Amsterdam, who had no fondness for New Englanders; but Isaac Allerton, formerly of Plymouth though then of New Haven, chanced to be there, and exerted himself greatly on behalf of his countrymen. Through his assistance another pinnace was procured, and in the dead of winter the three ministers set sail for Virginia. They encountered much foul weather, and the difficulty and danger through which they reached their destination caused them to entertain grave "question whether their call were of God or not." Once in Virginia, they were "bestowed in several places" where they "found loving and liberal entertainment;" and the change to another and less rigorous climate seems to have proved most beneficial to Mr. Tompson, who wrote back to his friends that he was better in health and spirits than at any time since he came over from England.

But Virginia has never proved a fruitful field for New England 'workers, whether religious or political, and the civil authorities there now looked askance at this earnest attempt at propagandism. Accordingly they soon put a stop to the public preaching of the newcomers, on the ground that they did not conform to the orders of the Church of England. Yet, if we can believe the report made on their return by the missionaries, the people, " their hearts being much influenced with an earnest desire after the gospel," continued to resort to them in private houses; seeing which, the rulers "did in a sense drive them out, having made an order that all such as would not conform to the discipline of the English Church should depart the country by such a day."

The summer of 1643 accordingly found Mr. Tompson and his associates back with their New England flocks; nor can their Virginia labors have been accounted fruitful, inasmuch as they seem to have made but a single convert. He, Daniel Gookins by name, followed his teachers back to Massachusetts, where at a later day he became a man of note; so that as Cotton Mather tunefully expressed it,

"by Tompson's pains,
Christ and New England a dear Gookins gains."

During his absence a severe bereavement had fallen on the unhappy Braintree clergyman. He had left his wife, who is described as "a godly young woman and a comfortable help to him," in charge of a family of small children, with scanty means of support. She died; and he returned to find his home broken up and his offspring scattered, though it is said they were "well disposed of among his godly friends." Marrying again some years later, the next glimpse which is obtained of Tompson, through Governor Winthrop's diary, is singularly illustrative of the time. In 1648 a synod met at Cambridge for the purpose of framing a code of church discipline. Before this representative gathering the Rev. John Allen, of Dedham, delivered a discourse which proved "a very godly, learned, and particular handling of near all the doctrines and applications" touching the matter in hand.

"It fell out about the midst of his sermon, there came a snake into the seat, where many of the elders sate behind the preacher. It came in at the door where people stood thick upon the stairs. Divers of the elders shifted from it, but Mr. Thomson, one of the elders of Braintree (a man of much faith), trod upon the head of it, and so held it with his foot and staff with a small pair of grains,[1] until it was killed. This being so remarkable, and nothing falling out but by divine providence, it is out of doubt the Lord discovered somewhat of his mind in it. The serpent is the devil; the synod, the representative of the churches of Christ in New England. The devil had formerly and lately attempted their disturbance and dissolution; but their faith in the seed of woman overcame him and crushed his head."

The mental and physical benefit which Tompson derived from his sojourn in Virginia was but temporary, and as he advanced in years his infirmities grew upon him. He seems to have had a morbid tendency, which at times verged on insanity. Cotton Mather's explanation of this, and of the course of treatment adopted for its cure, is curiously suggestive. There were then no insane asylums.

[1] A prong, or fork; obsolete.

"Satan, who had been after an extraordinary manner irritated by the evangelic labors of this holy man, obtained the liberty to sift him; and hence, after this worthy man had served the Lord Jesus Christ in the church of our New English Braintree, he fell into that *Balneum diaboli*, 'a black melancholy,' which for divers years almost wholly disabled him for the exercise of his ministry; but the end of this melancholy was not so tragical as it sometimes is with some, whom yet, because of their exemplary lives, we dare not censure for their prodigious deaths. . . . Accordingly, the pastors and the faithful of the churches in the neighborhood 'kept resisting of the devil' in his cruel assaults upon Mr. Tompson, by continually 'drawing near to God,' with ardent supplications on his behalf: and by praying always, without fainting, without ceasing, they saw the devil at length flee from him, and God himself draw near unto him, with unutterable joy. The end of that man is peace."

This means that Mr. Tompson did not commit suicide, and towards the close of his life the cloud lifted from him. He died on the 10th of December, 1666, having, it is said, resigned his pulpit some seven years before; but at the time of his death he was still an inhabitant of Braintree, and would seem, from the following quaint entry made by the Rev. Samuel Danforth in the records of the neighboring church of Roxbury, to have yet retained some pastoral relations with his former flock: —

"12. 10$^m$ 66. mr. William Tompson Pastor to the church at Braintree departed this life in the 69 year of his age. He had been held under the power of melancholy for the space of eight yeares. During which time He had diverse lucid intervales, and sweet revivings, especially the week before he dyed, in so much that he assayed to go to the church and administer the Lord's supper to them, but his body was so weak that he could neither go nor ride."

In the copy of verses bestowed on Tompson in the Magnalia by Cotton Mather, after his usual wont in such cases, there is one line of unusual strength, in which, referring to the departed "light," whom Oxford "with Tongues and Arts doth trim," the writer speaks of his

> "Tall, comely presence, life unsoil'd with stains,"

though further on a grim and pitiful gleam is thrown on the treatment for insanity in vogue during the seventeenth century in lines which tell us that

> "By his bed-side an Hebrew sword there lay,
> With which at last he drove the devil away."

Both Tompson and his second wife would seem to have been lacking in the quality of thrift, and during the closing years of his life the former minister of Braintree was wretchedly poor, — so poor, indeed, that in March, 1665, a public collection was taken up for him in the Dorchester church, which amounted to £6 9s., "besides notes for corn, and other things, above 30s."[1] Not without reason, therefore, Mather wrote of the dead clergyman, when at last he had "labored into rest,"

> "His inventory then, with John's, was took;
> A rough coat, girdle, with the sacred book."

The body of William Tompson lies in the old burying ground of Quincy, and the original stone, bearing quaint witness to his learning, piety and force as a divine, still marks the spot. He left by his two marriages numerous descendants, both sons and daughters; but no trace of his lineage is now found in the town over which first he ministered.

Teacher Henry Flynt, who became pastor on the

[1] See *Dorchester Town Records* [181].

resignation of Mr. Tompson in 1659, survived the latter only one year and four months, dying on the 27th of April, 1668. Born, it is supposed, in Derbyshire, England, he landed in New England in October, 1635, being then about twenty-nine years old. Coming over at the same time, if not in the same vessel, with young Sir Harry Vane, Henry Flynt seems to have been in political sympathy with him, while theologically he was an ardent admirer of Cotton. Indeed, almost the only fact recorded of Flynt by Mather in the Magnalia is that, having twin sons born to him in 1656, he named one John and the other Cotton, in memory of his revered mentor, then four years dead; but Mather does not add that the children in question lived but a few weeks, for, born on the 16th of September, their deaths were registered on the 20th of the following November. It has already been mentioned that Mr. Flynt, during the Antinomian controversy, adhered stanchly to Wheelwright.[1] Accordingly, though his name is appended as teacher to the Braintree church covenant of September 16, 1639, and Winthrop speaks of him as "a godly man" then ordained, it was not until the succeeding May that he made his submission to the General Court, acknowledging his sin in subscribing his name to the church of Boston memorial of March, 1637. As his formal ordination did not take place until March 17, 1640, it has been confidently surmised[2] that the postponement was in order to afford the distinguished young divine ample opportunity for recantation. If so, he at last availed himself of it; but there is no reason to suppose that in doing so he imitated the discreditable zeal which Cotton had

[1] *Supra*, 545.    [2] Savage, *note in Winthrop*, i. *247.

already shown in the work of hunting down his former associates; though it was asserted that through the exertions of its new teacher Braintree was " purged from the sour leaven of those sinful opinions that began to spread," and if any such remained there they were very covert. Of Mr. Flynt's later doctrinal views nothing is known; it is simply recorded of him that in his day he bore "the character of a gentleman remarkable for his piety, learning, wisdom and fidelity in his office." Unlike Mr. Tompson, the Flynts, husband and wife, appear to have been thrifty people, and the teacher died in comfortable circumstances. By his will he left the " great lot " of eighty acres granted to him by the town of Boston in 1640 to one son, and his dwelling-house, with the two lots it stood upon, to another son, both bequests subject to a life-estate in their mother, provided she remained unmarried. Then his will closed with this quaint provision: — " For the present, I know not what portion of my estate to assign to my wife, in case God call her to marriage, otherwise than as the law of the country does provide in that case, accounting all that I have too little for her, if I had something else to bestow on my children." Teacher Flynt's wife, whose maiden name was Margery Hoar, had evidently been a good and useful helpmeet to him; and indeed it is recorded, on the stone which marks the spot in the old graveyard where side by side they are buried, that, like her husband, descended from an "ancient and good" English family, she was also " a gentle-woman of piety, prudence, and peculiarly accomplished for instructing young gentlewomen, many being sent to her from other towns, especially from Boston." Mrs. Margery Flynt died in March, 1687, having survived her husband nearly twenty years. During that period " God [did not again] call her to marriage."

Henry Flynt left a numerous family, though no descendants of his name now live in Quincy. It was a granddaughter of his, Dorothy, child of the Rev. Josiah Flynt, of Dorchester, who married Judge Edmund Quincy, of Braintree, and from them a progeny than which none in Massachusetts has been more distinguished, traces descent. A daughter of hers was that " Dorothy Q." whose name has been embalmed in the familiar verses written upon her portrait by the most famous of her offspring in the Holmes family. From her, also, are descended the Wendells, the Jacksons, the Lowells and the Quincys; and indeed it is from Josiah Flynt the last family derives that given name which, handed down from generation to generation, is in Massachusetts almost conceded to it as a peculiar patronymic.[1] It was another Dorothy Quincy who in 1775 became the wife of John Hancock. The original Dorothy Flynt Quincy (1678–1737) dwelt in the house which Colonel Edmund Quincy built in Braintree in 1685, and which still remains one of the most interesting of all our colonial structures, quaintly typical of bygone times. In this house, still looking towards the brook, is the room in which Judge Sewall slept one rainy night in March, 1712. Next to it is the room still known as Tutor Flynt's chamber, for it was long occupied by Dorothy's brother Henry, for more than half a century a tutor at Harvard College and a fellow of the corporation through sixty-five years. To this day, indeed, the grandson of the old

---

[1] It was on some festive occasion wittily said of the Quincys that, while with other families the descent was from sire to son, in their case it was from 'Siah to 'Siah.

Braintree teacher is a tradition of the university. A genuine product of New England soil, his curt, dry sayings are still repeated. He lived until 1760, and left behind him the reputation of "a man of sound learning, of acute and discriminating intellect; firm but moderate; steadfast in opinion but without obstinacy; zealous and faithful in the discharge of his various duties." He lies buried in the ancient graveyard close to the buildings of the college which he served so long.

After the death of Teacher Flynt the church of Braintree, to use the language of a subsequent pastor, "fell into unhappy divisions, one being for Paul, and another for Apollos (as is too often the case in destitute churches), and were without a settled ministry above four years." No definite account of the cause of strife in this case has come down, but the contest was a heated one, in which "many uncomfortable expressions passed about." In the course of it things occurred which led some to suspect that the "sinful opinions" of John Wheelwright were perhaps not so covert in Braintree as had been asserted. That "sour leaven" may still have worked; for Mr. Josiah Flynt, the recently graduated son of the previous minister and one of the candidates for settlement, was openly charged with uttering "divers dangerous heterodoxies, delivered, and that without caution, in his public preaching." In view of this dissension, more than one day was set apart by the church "to seek the Lord by fasting and prayer," and at the frequent meetings there was much "uncomfortable debate," and at one of them at least "an awful division." A widespread scandal went abroad over these proceedings, and on the 25th of July, 1669, "God sent a very solemn,

awakening message to the church" by the mouth of
Mr. Eliot, it would seem the Indian apostle. But that
did not prevent the church from meeting on the 21st
of the following January, and acknowledging " several things scandalous and offensive, one to another."
Finally it was determined to call a counsel of sister
churches, and even then a debate took place, " wherein
much provocation to God and each other did appear."

Wearied as well as distressed by the angry turmoil,
Josiah Flynt at about this time received a call from
the church at Dorchester, which he accepted; and
there he remained until his premature death, in 1680.
Meanwhile Braintree continued for nearly two years
longer in a " destitute, divided state." At last things
came to such a pass that in May, 1671, the County
Court interfered, and sent out letters "in which they
did sterr up [the Dorchester] church together with
the Church at the North end of Boston and Deadham
and Weymouth; for to send by ther messengers for
to enquier into the reason of ther great difference and
slownes in providing a minester of the word"[1] in
Braintree; then, as this mission resulted in nothing,
the court again took the matter in hand, and in November, after due consideration of " the many means
that have been used with the church of Braintree, and
hitherto nothing done to effect, as to the obtaining
the ordinances of Christ among them," — taking this
into consideration, the court ordered and desired Mr.
Moses Fiske " to improve his labors in preaching the
word at Braintree until the church there agree, and
obtain supply for the work of the ministry." Mr.
Fiske seems to have obeyed this command in the true
church militant spirit; for, he says, " being ordered by

[1] *Dorchester Church Records*, 64.

the court, and advised by the reverend Elders and other friends, I went up from the honored Mr. Edward Tyng's, with two of the brethren of this church sent to accompany me, being the Saturday, to preach God's word unto them." The next day, December 3, 1671, he took his place in the Braintree pulpit, and delivered his first discourse, not failing at the close of the afternoon service to apologize as to his coming. But so well did he "improve his labors" on this occasion that the next day "about twenty of the brethren came to visit him, manifesting (in the name of the church) their ready acceptance of what the learned Court had done, and thanking him for his compliance therewith." On the 24th of February, 1672, Mr. Fiske received a unanimous call from the weary church, and on the 11th of the following September he was formally ordained; or, as he himself phrased it, that was "the day of my solemn espousals to this church and congregation."

At the time of his ordination Mr. Fiske was thirty years old; and his pastorate lasted thirty-six years, until his death, in 1708, an important period in the history of the town and church; for during it not only was the second parish organized, but a small Episcopal society, one of the earliest in New England, was formed. Of the Rev. Moses Fiske himself, his religious tenets or intellectual force, not much has been handed down, though it is recorded of him that, through a long pastorate he "was zealously diligent for God and the good of men, — one who thought no labor, cost or suffering too dear a price for the good of his people."

The manner in which the New England clergy intermarried, continually, so to speak, breeding-in, has often been remarked upon, and was suggestive; for, according to all known laws of generation and heredity, the result should have been of exceptional interest. That it was not, is probably due to the necessary limitations of theological development, of which, in New England, the Rev. Cotton Mather, perhaps, indicated the climax. Mr. Fiske was a case in point. Himself the son of a clergyman, he married successively two daughters of clergymen; three of his own daughters — Mary, Anne and Margaret — married clergymen; and two of his sons were clergymen. By his first wife, a daughter of Mr. Symmes, of Charlestown, Mr. Fiske had fourteen children. Through a period of nineteen years the unfortunate woman gave birth to infants on an average of one to each seventeen months, and two were born at separate births within a twelvemonth. Naturally several of them died in early infancy; and at last the mother was herself released by death from incessant child-bearing. Such cases were not unusual in early New England, and of Mrs. Sarah Symmes, the grandmother of Mrs. Fiske, it is recorded that "her courage exceeded her stature and she raised up ten children to people this American wilderness." She was the mother of thirteen. By his two marriages, Mr. Fiske had sixteen children; yet his family was small compared with that of Samuel Bass, the senior elder of his church, who died in 1694, after having sat in the deacon's seat for more than fifty years, and since the first organization of the church. At his death Deacon Bass numbered an offspring of one hundred and sixty-two souls; while among his contemporaries and the parishioners of Mr. Fiske, Henry Neal was the father of twenty-one children, and William Rawson had at one time twenty living sons and daughters the fruit of his loins by a single wife. Of Mrs. Sarah Thayer, wife of Ephraim Thayer, who died in 1751, a local bard recorded at the time, —

> "Also she was a fruitful vine,
> The truth I may relate, —
> Fourteen was of her body born,
> And lived to man's estate.
>
> "From these did spring a numerous race,
> One hundred thirty-two;
> Sixty and six each sex alike,
> As I declare to you.
>
> "And one thing more remarkable,
> Which here I shall record:
> She'd fourteen children with her,
> At the table of her Lord."

The simplicity of life and the severe economy habitual in those days is shown in the fact that Mr. Fiske brought up his family of sixteen children, sending three sons to college and marrying off his daughters, on a stipend which never exceeded ninety pounds a year, and which was usually sixty or eighty pounds, payable in part in corn and wood at stated valuations, or, as was expressed in the vote of the year 1704, "in money or in Indian corn at Two shillings and six pence per bushel, and barley molt at Two shillings and six pence per bushel or in other good merchantable pay at money price."

When in 1700 the new century began, the parish numbered about one hundred and forty families, representing an entire population of not far from eight hundred souls; but those composing this population no longer dwelt together in the neighborhood of Mount Wollaston and about the stone meeting-house. They were scattered over a wide extent of territory;

and this fact led to bitter contentions in the original church, which, recalling the evil days preceding Mr. Fiske's pastorate, saddened its closing years. In point of fact, town and church were passing through a natural stage of growth. That was being enacted on a small stage in Braintree which, when enacted on the larger stage of nationality, forms the most interesting part of history. A process of differentiation was going on, and that process, before it completes itself, is apt, on the smaller as on the larger stage, to call forth a great deal of human nature. It certainly did so in the case of Braintree.

The struggle seems first to have assumed definite shape about the year 1695. The old meeting-house was then pronounced inadequate to the growing needs of Braintree. It was small, inconveniently situated and out of repair. Those dwelling in the south part of the town complained that it was "very irksome, especially in winter, to come so far as most of them came to meeting, and through such bad ways, whereby the Lord's day, which is a day of rest, was to them a day of labor rather." Accordingly, the first proposition was that a new and larger church edifice, sufficient for the whole town, should be built at a more central point. This did not meet the views of old Colonel Edmund Quincy and others, who lived in the northern limits; consequently they set to work to prevent anything being done at all, and at a private meeting held at Colonel Quincy's they "did agree among themselves to shingle the old house, pretending to be at the whole charge themselves." But, none the less, "several pounds were afterwards gathered by a rate upon the whole town."

The project of a new and common meeting-house at

a more generally convenient site having been defeated by means such as this, the organization of a separate church was next agitated. This was opposed, for the reason that such a secession would throw the burden of the minister's salary on a smaller number. Accordingly in 1704–5 party feeling ran high. Two church meetings were held in January, whereat there was "much debate and some misapprehension about church discipline," by reason whereof there was "much sinful discourse" in the town. "Nine of the church withdrew from the Lord's table," and one of Parson Fiske's adherents pathetically remarked, as he noted these events, "the disorders among us call for tears and lamentations rather than to be remembered."

Getting no satisfaction, but, on the contrary, being "squib'd and floured by several of the other end of the town," those of the south part in the winter of 1705 began to talk "very hotly of building a meeting-house by themselves;" and on the 2d of May, 1706, the frame of the new edifice was raised. In the autumn of that year it was so far finished that they might comfortably meet therein. The matter had been "hitherto carried on in a way of great contention and disorder;" but a final difficulty, and the most serious of all, now presented itself. The people of the south had organized themselves into a new church, but the people of the north wholly declined to release them from their share of the burden of supporting the minister of the old church. An angry town-meeting was held to consider this matter on November 25, 1706, and the seceders certainly made what seems now a fair and even a liberal proposition. They offered to maintain their own church, and also to pay £20 of Mr. Fiske's salary. Even this was not satisfactory, and the town insisted that their "south end neighbors and brethren should not be released from bearing their usual part of the charge for the support of the Rev. Moses Fiske, which they were forward in the day of it to vote for and agree to."

The matter was then carried before the General Court; but there no immediate action was taken, and in the spring of 1707 the contention and disorder were greater than ever. A council of churches was suggested, and agreed to on the 27th of April. Accordingly, on the 7th of May delegates from nine neighboring societies met within the stone walls of the old Braintree meeting-house and listened to the aggrieved brethren. Those composing this council do not seem to have succeeded in pouring oil on the troubled waters; and, on the 10th of the following September, the Rev. Hugh Adams was formally ordained as first pastor of the South Church, which forthwith petitioned the General Court to be regularly set off as a distinct precinct. This prayer was dated in the true theological spirit of the time, — "From (Naphtali, if your honors please so to name our neighborhood, or) South Braintree;" the significance of which grim Puritan jest is found in Genesis (xxx. 8): — "And Rachael said, With great wrestlings have I wrestled with my sister, and I have prevailed : and she called his name Naphtali." Nevertheless, the dwellers in the south did not prevail on this occasion, for five days later, after an oral hearing, the General Court voted that, during the exercise of his ministry by Mr. Fiske, "the whole town" was obliged, in conformity with the provincial law then in force, to raise annually whatever sum was voted for his support. Meanwhile steps were to be taken towards forming a second precinct, the inhabitants of which, during Mr. Fiske's ministry, were " to take care by subscription to raise a maintenance for the minister there."

It is, of course, obvious now that the separation proposed was a mere question of time. Considering how universal and even obligatory church attendance then was, the cause for present wonder is that through more than sixty years the people of so large a territory were content to travel, summer and winter, such distances over their primitive roads to reach the common meeting-house. It is doubtful whether even the intense religious sense of the period, backed though it was by both spirit and letter of law, would have induced them to do so, had they not been impelled by the desire to gratify a social, as well as a spiritual, craving. The Sabbath and the meeting-house were all they had to relieve the monotony of week-day existence. In their widely-separated houses were no newspapers, fewer books, and fewer still strange faces; and so they eagerly went to meeting unmindful of weather or of distance, because there they met friends and relatives, while between the services they gossiped over the news. Whispers might then reach them, also, of events in that great outside world from which in their homes they were as much excluded as though encircled by a Chinese wall.

The separation of old Braintree into several church precincts also foreshadowed a further political separation not less desirable. But the slow course of growth and sequence of events during the colonial period of New England life is a characteristic of that time and people to which attention will frequently be called in the course of this narrative, for it contrasts strangely with what this generation has been accustomed to in

more recent times and in other parts of the country.
Nowhere is the slowness of the pace at which that
people were content to move more strikingly illustrated
in the case of Braintree than by the fact that, while
the development of two thirds of a century preceded a
separation into precincts, nearly ninety years more had
to pass away before the original town was divided.

Though foiled in its efforts for complete independence before the General Court of 1707, the South Precinct had not long to wait. The court had held it liable for its share of the support of the pastor of the old church during the ministry of Mr. Fiske only. Mr. Fiske's second wife, Anna, died on the 24th of July, following this decision. The widow of Daniel Quincy, a peculiar interest attaches to Mrs. Fiske as the mother of that John Quincy, of Mount Wollaston, from whom the North Precinct subsequently took its name as a town; and who, a youth of eighteen, graduated at Harvard College during the summer in which his mother's death took place. Parson Fiske did not long survive his wife. At the time of her death he seems to have been in feeble health, and a few days later he was stricken with "a sore malignant fever, and on the 10th day [of August], being Tuesday, about one of the clock, P. M., he died, willingly, patiently, blessed God, and forgave all his enemies. . . . He was, with suitable solemnity and great lamentations, interred at Braintree in his own tomb the 12th day." Of him an humble but devout parishioner wrote that he was "a dilligent, faithful laborer in the harvest of Jesus Christ; studious in the Holy Scriptures, having an extraordinary gift in prayer above many good men, and in preaching equal to the most, inferior to few."

Mr. Fiske's death was in one respect timely. It settled once for all the vexed question of parish division. On the 3d of November following, a town and parish meeting was held, at which it was voted that thenceforth "there should be two distinct precincts or societies in this town, for the more regular and convenient upholding of the worship of God." The ill-feeling which had existed between the sections then gradually passed away ; though, as late as 1710, the good offices of neighboring ministers seem to have been called for, and on the 19th of February their " advice for reconciliation " was read from the pulpit. As usual in the Massachusetts of that time, a special fast was thereupon ordered " on account of the late disturbances ; " and then at last, on March 19th, the Sabbath, the reconciliation was made complete by the clergymen of the two precincts exchanging pulpits, and preaching each to the other's congregation.

The pulpit of the First Precinct was then filled by Mr. Fiske's successor, the Rev. Joseph Marsh. His pastorate and that of the Rev. John Hancock covered, respectively, sixteen and eighteen years, and the two carried the history of the church into its second century. It was an uneventful time the world over, that of the first two Georges and Louis XV. The Massachusetts colony had now struggled through the more interesting early period, and, slowly as unconsciously, was preparing itself for the career which a century later was to open before it. Meanwhile the royal governors — Shute and Dummer, Burnet and Belcher — ruled a community numbering about a hundred thousand souls, and squabbled incessantly over petty questions with intractable 'General Courts. Locally, it was the period in which Judge Edmund Quincy and Colonel John Quincy flourished in Braintree, and largely directed the course of the town's affairs; while of men destined to a later prominence, John Adams and John Hancock were born, the former at the foot of Penn's Hill, October 19, 1735, and the latter the 12th of January, 1737, in a house then standing on the lot which, now the site of an academy, still bears the Hancock name.

The Rev. Joseph Marsh himself was ordained as pastor of the First Precinct on May 18, 1709. A graduate of the college in the class of 1705, during the winter of 1708–9 he was preaching, by request of the General Court, at Tiverton, the inhabitants of which place had failed to " comply with the law and provide themselves with a minister." He first " exercised " in Braintree on Sunday, October 31, 1708, less than three months after Mr. Fiske's death, and seems at once to have impressed himself on the people there as " a person of singular accomplishments, both natural and acquired." Accordingly, in November they gave him a call, and on the 16th of December, after extensive preparations had been made properly to receive him at his predecessor's house, " he came at night attended with the most of the inhabitants of this precinct." His salary was fixed at seventy pounds a year, and one hundred pounds additional was voted to him on his settlement, " and that to be paid for said settlement." Then on the 4th of May a special fast was kept " in order to ordination," which took place two weeks later. On the 30th of the following June the young pastor married the daughter of his predecessor, and in April, 1710, he bought the Fiske homestead, where he lived until his death, in March, 1726. He was then in his forty-first year.

Again the pulpit was but a short time vacant, for, on June 29th, John Hancock, the son of a father of the same name, was called to fill it. John Hancock, the father, was minister at Lexington, and so high was his professional standing and so great his influence that he was commonly known as "Bishop" Hancock. The son may have enjoyed a certain clerical prestige from the father's fame, for when called to Braintree in 1726 he was but twenty-four, though he had graduated in 1719. The salary voted to him (£110) was larger than had been given to any of his predecessors, and he received a further sum of £200 upon his settlement. But the vote giving these larger sums was expressed in ominous words, for it ran that the obligations were payable " in good and lawful bills of public credit on this Province." The colony was embarked on that troubled sea of depreciated paper money which was destined long to outlast the Hancock pastorate. In Mr. Hancock's letter accepting the call there is, also, one singular passage. The young candidate had expressed in the usual language of the day his sense of the "seriousness, solemnity and affection" of the occasion, and his belief that " Divine Providence calls and obliges me to an acceptance; " he then suddenly adds, immediately before closing his letter, " I would just take leave to recommend to your consideration the article of wood, which I understand is, or is likely to be pretty dear and scarce in this place." The result showed that this innocent-looking proviso was not devoid of either significance or worldly wisdom, for, some six or seven years later, in March, 1733, the precinct was called upon to vote that " twenty Pounds be raised . . . and added yearly to the Rev[nd] John Hancocks Sallery to supply him with fire-wood yearly During his Ministre;" and "against this vote Mr. Benjamin Neal entered his dissent."

The ordination of Mr. Hancock on the 2d of November, 1726, was a great occasion, for the pastors of seven sister churches took part in it, while the elder Hancock preached the sermon. The ceremonies were held in the old stone meeting-house of 1666. It must even then have been in poor repair, for during the winter of 1730 "cartloads of snow" were blown into it, and had to be shovelled out. As usual, it was not difficult to get the parish to vote the building of a new meeting-house; the trouble came in its location. Two meetings barely sufficed for the discussion of the question. The site first proposed was "at Col. Quincy's gate."[1] This was rejected. The site of the old stone church was next proposed, and rejected. Finally it was decided by a majority vote that the new edifice should be "at the ten milestone, or near unto it;" and at the next meeting an exact site was fixed "on the training-field," a few hundred yards south of the tenth milestone from Boston. The new house, large and commodious for the time, was in point of fact a bald, oblong, wooden structure, of the kind common to all New England towns. It was entered by doors at the two sides, and in front of it stood a tower, surmounted by an open cupola in which hung the bell, now increased in weight to two hundred and ninety pounds.

This edifice was dedicated on the 8th of October, 1732, "in peaceable times;" and it was voted "that Jonathan Webb keep the key of the old Meeting

[1] The point where the Old Colony railroad now passes under Adams Street, in Quincy. The present Bridge Street was the private avenue from the "coast road" (*Infra*, 672) to the old Quincy mansion.

house have the Caire of said house take down the glass and led of the windows of said house for the service of the Precinct and Naile Bords up at the Windows." Yet, though thus stripped and abandoned, the ancient edifice in which two generations of the inhabitants of Braintree had Sabbath by Sabbath assembled still had its uses, for in it both town and precinct meetings were held, summer and winter, for fourteen years to come, and it was not until 1748 that the structure was finally sold at auction and removed; and that it should have thus stood there, an unsightly ruin, serving, through sixteen years, almost no useful purpose, is significant of the slow growth and inanimate condition of the Massachusetts town during the first half of the seventeenth century. When sold at last, the material of the building brought £100 in currency of the old tenor, or, on the basis of conversion fixed by law two years later, about $55 of modern money. Nine years before, on September 16, 1739, "being Lord's day, the First Church of Braintree, both males and females, solemnly renewed the covenant of their fathers, immediately before the participation of the Lord's supper." A century of church life was complete.

On this occasion, in his discourse which is still extant, the pastor described himself as having been with his people almost thirteen years "in weakness, and in fear, and in much trembling." He continued with them five years more. These were the years of "the great awakening," during which Whitefield, Tennent and Davenport held forth continually to excited audiences, and New England was lashed into such a state of religious frenzy as was never known on the continent before or since. It is scarcely probable that Braintree wholly escaped the contagion of the craze; but when, shortly after reason had resumed its sway, Hancock died, the brother clergyman who preached his funeral discourse spoke of him "as a wise and skilful pilot," who had steered " a right and safe course in the late troubled sea of ecclesiastical affairs;" so that his people had " escaped the errors and enthusiasm which some, and the infidelity and indifferency in matters of religion which others had fallen into." These words were in themselves no poor tribute to the preacher cut off " in the midst of his days and growing serviceableness."

It was in 1728, the third year of the Hancock pastorate, that the first Episcopal church edifice in Braintree was finished, and on Easter Monday of that year services were performed in it. Dr. Ebenezer Miller, a Harvard graduate of 1722, was its rector, and for a century and a half thereafter descendants of his name continued to live in the town. Though it had no church of its own until 1728, this society had long been forming, and, as the result of careful investigation, one of its recent rectors has expressed a confident belief that Christ Church in Quincy, now that King's Chapel has changed hands, is, with the " exception, possibly, of Trinity Church, Newport, the oldest Episcopal parish in New England."[1] There is, indeed, evidence that, as early even as 1689, there was in Braintree a little body of Church of England communicants, and that, in one house at least, prayers from the liturgy were daily read. It was the head of this house, probably, who, as " L$^t$. Veazey," stands recorded in the 1689 list of those " sure, honest and well-disposed persons that Contributed their assistance

[1] Pattee, *Old Braintree and Quincy*, 245–8.

for and towards erecting a Church for God's worship in Boston, according to the Constitution of the Church of England as by law Established."[1] "L$^t$. Veazey" put his name down for one pound. In 1701 the Society for the Propagation of the Gospel in Foreign Parts was formed in London, and, for some reason now unknown, Braintree was early selected by it as a promising field in which to labor. In 1702 one zealous in the cause wrote to a leading church dignitary: — " Braintrey should be included; it is in the heart of New England, and a learned and sober man would do great good and encourage the other towns to desire the like. If the church can be settled in New England, it pulls up schisms in America by the roots that being the fountain that supplies with infectious streams the rest of America." Accordingly, " an annual encouragement of fifty pounds and a gratuity of twenty-five pounds for present occasions " was granted by the society to Mr. William Barclay, " the minister of the Church of England at Braintree in New England." At the same time a collection of books to form the basis of a church library was sent out, the twenty volumes or so of which, bearing the quaint seal of [2] the mother society, — massive seventeenth century accumulations of forgotten theological lore, — are still on the shelves of the Quincy rectory. Thus, in 1704, Christ Church in Braintree was fully organized, several of the names found earliest in the town records, such as Veazie, Saunders and Bass, being those of its wardens and vestrymen.

The movement did not pass unnoticed. The time was gone by when it could be suppressed with a high hand, for not only had the rigor of the primitive

[1] Foote, *Annals of King's Chapel*, 89.  [2] Ib. 147.

church discipline relaxed, but under the royal governors the Episcopalian ritual had for years been familiar in Boston; though still on the 25th of December those of the antique faith took occasion to " dehort their families from Christmas keeping and charge them to forbear." Accordingly when in August, 1704, the increase of the Rev. Mr. Fiske's salary from £80 to £90 was the burning question in Braintree, Judge Edmund Quincy urged as an argument in favor of the increase that the Church of England people would have to pay their proportion, calling Samuel French out of Captain John Mill's house, and saying to him, — "You know what has fell out in the town, the churchmen are now scheming to get a foot in the town; if you will join with us in a vote, we'll suppress the churchmen; I have got sixteen already."

By 1704 Mr. Barclay had returned to England, and for several years thereafter only a skeleton organization of the church was maintained. In 1713 the case was pronounced desperate by the Rev. Thomas Eager, who had apparently been sent out to look the field over, and who mentioned, as obstacles in the way of any growth of the church, that its members were taxed for the support of the regular precinct minister, and that they had no place of worship of their own. They feared censure as conventiclers if they assembled for worship in a private house. Yet he claimed to have at times as many as thirty attendants at service, with twelve regular communicants. Mr. Eager seems to have remained in Braintree nearly two years, and the account he gave of the dwellers there was not a flattering one.

"I have had a very hard way of living since my abode in this place, provisions being very scarce, and people generally very poor. The whole province has been very much disturbed on the account of my coming to this place, and accordingly have not failed to affront and abuse me wherever they meet me, — 'atheist and papist,' the best language I can get from them. The people are Independents, and have a perfect odium to those of our Communion. These few which adhere to our church are taxed and rated most extravagantly to support the dissenting clergy. Had this province been called New Creet instead of New England it had better suited, for the people are very great strangers to truth, and I do really believe that I have not passed one day since my arrival without one false report or other raised upon me. Thus you see my case is very pitiful; yet by the assistance of God's grace I shall have constancy and resolution enough to put forward the good work that I was sent about." [1]

On the other hand, judging by the statements contained in the following passage of a letter of Governor Dudley to the secretary of the Society for Propagating the Gospel, the Rev. Thomas Eager was by no means one of those "able and sober ministers" and "discreet" gentlemen, such as Edward Randolph had in 1682 entreated the Bishop of London to appoint "to performe the officies of the church with us." Far otherwise, he would seem to have been a parson of a type not unfamiliar to the readers of Fielding and Smollett, — a man carnally inclined, and of a temper the reverse of meek. The letter of Governor Dudley was dated May 1, 1714, and in it he wrote: —

"There has been some trouble at Braintree about the arrear, which I hope is over also; but I have heard a sorrowful account from everybody referring to Mr Eager. I had heard of his rude life in his passage hither, being frequently disguised in drink and fighting with the saylors,

[1] Foote, *Annals of King's Chapel*, 257–8.

even to wounds and taring his cloaths ; and during the few months of his stay here he was frequently in quarrels and fighting, and sending challenges for duells, that at length the auditory at Brantry were quite ashamed and discouraged; and he is gone to Barbadoes without any direction or order, and the Congregation without any Minister."

But there was ground for the complaint of Mr. Eager as to the taxing of his people for the support of the precinct ministers. The matter had already been before the Governor and Council on the complaint of William Veazie, the churchwarden, who, in 1696, had been fined "for ploughing on the day of Thanksgiving;" and this Veazie incident of 1696 is not without its significance, as throwing a curious gleam of light on the extreme Jacobite tendencies of a portion, at least, of the adherents of the Church of England who had in some way drifted to Massachusetts. In early June, news of the Barclay and Charnock plot to assassinate King William, the details and consequences of which Macaulay has described,[1] reached Boston, and the 18th of the month was fixed as a day of public thanksgiving over the failure of the popish plot and the preservation of the protestant monarch. When the day came William Veazie, instead of observing it like his fellow-townsmen, was, about eleven o'clock in the forenoon, seen to be ploughing the corn on his farm at Hough's Neck[2]

[1] *History of England*, chap. xxi.
[2] A portion of the grant to Atherton Hough, or Howgh (*Boston Town Records* [54], 1641) of 1634, and still known as Hough's (pronounced How's, corrupted to Hoar's) Neck. A somewhat singular instance of the permanence of local traditional nomenclature, as the grant was made over two centuries and a half ago; no one of the name of Hough, or How, or Hoar, so far as is known, ever lived on it; and the popular idea is, that the name is derived from some supposed resemblance of the locality to a horse's neck.

"with an Indian Boy and Two Horses." When remonstrated with for such conduct by certain of his scandalized neighbors, Veazie replied "that he did not know but that there was a great deal of Sin committed in setting apart dayes of Thanksgiving and Humiliation;" and further that "the King had granted Liberty of Conscience; and that King James was his Royal Prince; and that he did not know how this King came to the Crowne; and that the Crowne belonged to heires by Succession." To all of which utterances William Veazie, when subsequently arraigned, pleaded guilty; and thereupon he was promptly fined ten pounds and ordered "to be set in the pillory in the market place in Boston to morrow about noon, there to stand by the Space of An Hour." [1]

This was in 1696; and in 1713, seventeen years later, the obdurate Veazie was again in trouble, the town constable having seized and sold a cow of his because her owner refused to pay his portion of the tax levied on account of the Rev. Mr. Marsh's salary. Joseph Dudley, it has been seen, was then governor of the province, and it appeared that an order of the governor and council had been made directing the town officials to forbear the levying of the tax until after the next General Court. This order had been sent to Veazie, who not only refused to allow the constable to take a copy of it, but otherwise "provoked him." So the constable, one Owens by name, seized and sold the cow in contempt of the order. For this reason, when in due course the matter came before the Council, Governor Dudley evinced a decided bias in favor of Veazie, much to the displeasure of Judge Sewall, a member of Council, to whom anything which

---

[1] *Records of Supreme Court of Judicature*, v. 1686–1700, p. 117.

savored of the liturgy was a thing abhorred, — the Common-Prayer was an "invention of man," the use of which in his presence he reckoned "an Indignity and affront," while the "Office for burial [was] a Lying, very bad office; [making] no difference between the precious and the vile." So in his journal for June 2, 1713, Sewall gave a characteristic account of what took place in the Council Chamber on the complaint of the Braintree church-warden, in the course of which, the governor having put the question whether the cow should be returned to her owner, the judge bluntly expressed his opinion that "the Governor and Council had not Authority to rescind the Laws by nulling an execution." But on this occasion "Constable Owen" escaped on easier terms than Veazie seventeen years before, for, after being bound over to the next sessions of the court, it was subsequently thought advisable to "Chide him, and let him go."

Returning to the record of the Braintree church, the drinking and fighting parson Eager was succeeded by the Rev. Henry Lucas, who, after a short rectorship, removed to Newbury, and for several years thereafter the Braintree organization lay dormant; nor, indeed, was it until 1726 that any steps were taken toward building a church edifice. Ebenezer Miller, son of Samuel Miller, of Milton, was then a recent graduate of the college, and student of divinity. As such he early manifested a strong leaning towards Episcopacy, being, it has been said, the first native descendant of the colony ordained to the ministry of that church.[1] To him the members of the Braintree society went, and two agreements were entered into,

[1] *History of Milton, Mass.*, 130.

— one for the building a church edifice, the other for sending young Miller to England, there to receive orders. Both agreements were carried out. A site for the proposed edifice was conveyed by deed, bearing date of August 25, 1727, as the free gift to the society, of William and Benjamin Veazey, "for the building of a Church of England on, and no other purpose;" and, two years later, in the autumn of 1727, an unpretentious wooden structure had been erected, and was ready for occupancy. It stood near the main street of the town, and parallel with it, only a few hundred yards south of that crossing of the town river near which was the old stone meeting-house. For over a century, this building, from time to time enlarged, sufficed for the religious needs and shared in the fluctuating fortunes of those in Braintree and its vicinity who adhered to the Church of England faith and forms; and, in course of years, the ground about it grew thick with stones marking the last resting places of some who had worshipped within those walls. These stones still remain the sole memorial of a site upon which for over a hundred years stood one of the earliest offshoots in Puritan Massachusetts of that Established Church which John Winthrop, when turning his back forever on his native land, referred to as " our dear mother, . . . acknowledging that such hope and part as we have obtained in the common salvation we have received in her bosom, and sucked it from her breasts."

Receiving his degree of Master of Arts at Oxford in July, 1727, Mr. Miller was at the same time licensed to preach the gospel. The next month he was appointed to the living at Braintree, in New England, and, in September following, chaplain to the

Duke of Bolton. He came home to his own people
in the autumn of 1727, arriving in season to begin
his pastorate on Christmas-day. Accordingly, Judge
Sewall, in Boston, made the following entry in his
journal : — " Monday, Dec. 25, 1727. Shops open,
and people come to Town with Hoop-poles, Hay,
Wood, &c. Mr. Miller keeps the day in his New
church at Braintey: people flock thither."

Through the active intervention of Lieutenant-
Governor Dummer the vexed question of taxation
was now at last settled, and at a meeting of the North
Precinct held on the 29th of the next month (May,
1727), the Episcopalians appeared and presented their
case. There is no record of what was said in debate,
but the meeting finally voted to remit future taxes,
and also " to reimburse the petitioners whatever sums
they might have been assessed for Mr. Hancock's
ordination charge and settlement." This was also
done, as Mr. Hancock did not fail to record with
pride, " before ever any act of this nature passed in
the government." That it was settled in a way so
creditable seems to have been largely due to Mr. Hancock's influence, who then gave evidence that he was
possessor not only of some Christian spirit, but of
much good judgment. He always cultivated friendly
relations between the two societies, as well as personally between himself and Mr. Miller; and, before Mr.
Miller came, the precinct church " admitted to their
communion all such members of the Church of England as desired to have occasional communion with
them, and allowed them what posture of devotion they
pleased ; and they received the sacrament standing." [1]

[1] That this liberality in regard to partaking of the communion was
not confined to Mr. Hancock and the Braintree church, among New

But, though what had been a burning question through twenty-five years was thus properly disposed of, the disposition did not prove altogether final; for nearly twenty years later the old question presented itself in a new form, the almost necessary outcome of the law of compulsory contribution to religious worship as it then stood. The issue was now formally tried in court, and the precinct church not only won its case, but the result showed that litigation was far less costly in 1750 than it has subsequently become, inasmuch as the expense the committee appointed to take charge of the matter was at in " Attendance and Lawyers Fees" amounted "in the whole to the sum of £5/16."

Through thirty-six years Dr. Miller remained the rector of Christ Church, devoted to his parish, and accounted one of the ablest defenders of Episcopacy in New England; and as such he received the highest recognition then possible, for when, in 1747 he again visited England, the university of Oxford conferred on him the degree of Doctor of Divinity. At that time such degrees were not conferred by any institution in America, and some thirty-seven years before the university of Glasgow had to his intense gratification honored Cotton Mather [1] in the way in which the far greater Oxford now honored the incumbent of

England congregations, is proved by the following from one of Cotton Mather's publications. In his Manuductio ad Ministeriun; or, *Angels preparing to Sound the Trumpets*, published in 1727, he said (p. 127),—"And let the *Table* of the Lord have no *Rails* about it, that shall hinder a Godly *Independent*, and *Presbyterian*, and *Episcopalian*, and *Antipedobaptist*, and *Lutheran*, from sitting down together there. *Corinthian Brass* would not be so bright a *Composition*, as the people of GOD in such a *Coalition*, feasting together on His *Holy Mountain*. . . . Tho' in the church that I serve, I have seen the grateful Spectacle!"

[1] Wendell, *Cotton Mather*, 231.

Christ Church. At the close of Dr. Miller's ministry his society numbered fifty families and as many communicants. Indeed, he and his immediate successor so raised the Braintree church that for a time it seems "to have exercised a maternal care over those of the same communion in this vicinity;"[1] and not impossibly the pre-revolutionary rectors of Christ Church in Braintree might have been ordained as Bishops, had a diocese of Massachusetts, or even of New England then existed; but not until 1784 was such a diocese formed, and on the 11th of February, 1763, "to the very great loss of this church, his family and friends, [Dr. Miller] departed this life."

Not much more remains to be said of Christ Church prior to 1830, the period now under consideration. It had already seen its best days, for the Revolutionary troubles were at the time of its first rector's death already impending. Indeed, a posthumous attack made on him just after his death, because of his connection with a project for establishing an American bishopric, led to one of the angry paper controversies which paved the way to war.[2] The Rev. Edward Winslow, a Bostonian by birth and a graduate of Harvard college in the class of 1741, succeeded Dr. Miller. He was inducted into the living in July, 1764, and his connection with the society lasted through thirteen troubled years, until 1777.

Until after the middle of the nineteenth century, Episcopacy was an exotic in Massachusetts; and the cultivation of exotics is always expensive. The mother English society was most liberal in dealing with its sickly Braintree offshoot, and, until the Revo-

---
[1] Cutler, *Century Sermon* (1827), 7.
[2] John Adams, *Works*, x. 187.

lutionary troubles took the shape of actual war, it annually sent over sixty pounds sterling for the support of the minister. Naturally the society was inclined to a friendly feeling toward the hand which fed it. To it the Apthorps, the Vassalls, the Borlands, the Cleverlys and the Millers — indeed, all the gentry of the neighborhood, with the exception of the Quincys — belonged. The gentry were apt to be Tories; and, as early as 1765, John Adams noted in his diary that most of the churchmen in Braintree were favorers of the Stamp Act. Ten years later they had not changed their views, and when the news arrived of the passage of the Quebec Bill by Parliament in April, 1774, Mrs. Adams wrote, " all the Church people here have hung their heads," and, " no matter how much provoked by those of the other side, they would not discuss politics." Before that, " parties ran very high, and very hard words and threats of blows upon both sides were given out." A few months later there was something closely resembling an actual outbreak in the town, the North Precinct of which had the reputation of being a nest of Tories. The stock of public powder was removed from it by an organized mob, and Mrs. Adams again wrote, — " The church parson thought they were coming after him, and ran up garret "; and the story was that another member of the church " jumped out of his window and hid among the corn, whilst a third crept under a board fence and told his beads." As it was in Braintree, so was it elsewhere; for this was the time when, throughout the colonies, the ministers of the Established Church of England stood condemned in the eyes of all patriots, — the time when a Pennsylvania rector wrote to England that a militia captain " had lugged his company to church on a fast day, to hear that old wretch (*meaning me!*) preach," — the time when "neither seclusion, insignificance, nor high character was able to save the clergy from the fury of the populace."[1] Braintree did but share in the common feeling, and though, as will presently be seen, no record exists of any act of overt violence committed, there can be no doubt Mr. Winslow found his situation uncomfortable in the extreme, nor was it any longer safe for him to read the prayer for the King. Yet he seems to have struggled on, vainly hoping for better days, until his salary was stopped and many of his people had moved away. Then, in 1777, taking very properly the ground that his ordination oath compelled him to conform literally to the Prayer-Book, he, "with sad and silent musings," resigned his charge; while Mrs. Adams, actuated by the patriotic fervor of the day, wrote of him in a spirit marked with no excess of charity, — "The conscientious parson had taken an oath upon the Holy Evangelists to pray for his most gracious Majesty as his sovereign lord, and having no father confessor to absolve him, he could not omit it without breaking his oath." Going to New York, which was in British occupation, Mr. Winslow died there in 1780, before the close of the war. He lies buried under the altar of St. George's Church, in that city.

The English society had spent, it is said, over thirteen thousand dollars in the attempt to build up the Braintree church, and it was now less than ever able to stand alone. Though the ritual was again in as great public odium as it had been a whole century before, and the mutilated pages of the great book of services

[1] McConnell, *American Episcopal Church*, 208-10.

still in the possession of Christ Church bears curious evidence to the fact that the prayers for the King were no longer read in Braintree, Mr. Joseph Cleverly to a certain extent faced the storm, and filled, as best he could, the place Mr. Winslow had left vacant. A native of the town, and coming of a family long resident there, he was graduated at Harvard College in 1733, and, though never in orders, an earnest Episcopalian, he now for several years read prayers and services, and is referred to in the church's records as its teacher. He lived to extreme old age, dying in 1802.

After Mr. Cleverly's death the society for many years continued in what might fairly be called a state of suspended animation. It did not wholly die, for the church edifice was there, and the society owned also a piece of land on which stood a rectory, the whole having cost it £300 in 1765; and now the rent collected from the rectory sufficed to keep the church from tumbling down. The parish committee secured the assistance of clergymen and readers, so that from time to time church services were performed; but, as a religious force affecting town life, Christ Church hardly made itself felt between the close of the Revolution and the year 1825: and, indeed, with one period of faint revival, it continued to languish until long after 1830; when at last the increase of wealth and the change in modes of life of the whole outside community brought in new and influential families, largely summer residents, introducing elements in which the Episcopal form of worship found natural support. But the town had then lost its individuality. During the first hundred years of its existence the history of Christ Church in Braintree and Quincy is most interesting as showing how foreign Episcopacy was to the original Massachusetts civilization; how practically impossible it was for it there to take root and to flourish; and how, supported for a time at great effort and cost from without, when that support was withdrawn it languished and died away, having, so far as could be seen, in no way influenced the growth of the native community. The Established Church of England, like that of Rome, was a wholly alien institution; and Episcopacy, like Roman Catholicism, secured a firm hold on the soil only when a new and an alien element was infused into the population of the Massachusetts town.

Returning to the history of the original precinct church, about which the whole religious life and mental activity of Braintree still centred, the Hancock pastorate, ending in May, 1744, was followed by an interim of a year and a half; and this notwithstanding the fact that, only two months after its pastor's premature death, the bereaved church had solemnly voted that "the Fifteenth day of August next be a day set apart for solemn fasting and prayer to God for his Direction in order to the settling a Minister among us." At last, on the 16th of September, 1745, the Rev. Lemuel Briant, of Scituate, was unanimously chosen pastor, and on the 11th of the following December formally ordained. The salary of the new minister was fixed at "fifty pounds per year in bills of credit on this province of the last emission" during the first two years of his settlement, to be thereafter increased by a further annual sum of "twelve pounds and ten shillings in bills of the like emission." This salary was nominally much smaller than had been paid either to Mr. Hancock or to Mr. Fiske, but it was payable in bills of credit of the last emission. How clergymen and the few others who, in Massachusetts, were dependent on fixed incomes contrived to live in those days must always remain a mystery. At the time of Mr. Hancock's death, bills of the tenor in use when he was settled passed in circulation for about sixteen per cent. of their nominal value; in other words, silver was worth nearly forty shillings "old tenor" per ounce, instead of six shillings seven pence, as it should have been. In 1745 there were in circulation bills of the "new tenor," of the "middle tenor," and of the "old tenor;" and those of the two former emissions, being of greater value than those of the latter, were hoarded. Apparently, in 1746, Mr. Briant's salary of sixty pounds "new tenor" was equivalent to about fifty-four pounds in silver, or to six hundred pounds in " old tenor," and in purchasing power was not less than what had been paid to his predecessor. Nevertheless, owing to what the young pastor in his letter of acceptance not unhappily described as " the Fluctuating State of our Medium," it was in subsequent years found necessary to make frequent additions to his stated salary; though it may well be doubted whether even these additions, parsimoniously doled out after the custom of the period, placed Mr. Briant, as he had in the same letter expressed his confidence would be the case, "above the fear of wanting any good thing among you, however insufficient to answer all the Purposes of Life what you have already Voted may be judged by those who are best Acquainted with Living in the World."

A graduate of Harvard College in the class of 1739, Mr. Briant, when he came to Braintree, was in his twenty-fourth year. His pastorate was brief, for he died before he was thirty-three; but it was as troubled as it was short. Intellectually, a noticeable man, he was an advanced religious thinker and born controversialist, and as such seems to have paid small regard to conventionalities. Had he lived he might have held his ground, and succeeded in advancing by one long stride the tardy progress of liberal Christianity in Massachusetts; on the other hand, not improbably he was too far in advance of his day, and a premature physical decline alone saved him from the loss of his pulpit and theological ostracism. Yet the story of his brief career is even now indisputably interesting.

In the year 1749, Mr. Briant published a sermon on moral virtue. Before its publication he seems to have preached it several times in different pulpits, and it had excited a good deal of remark. In his native town of Scituate, especially, it produced so great an impression that the minister of that place felt moved to controvert its teachings. This he essayed to do by means of a series of discourses, in regard to which it was at the time observed the main difficulty was to discern the " difference between his doctrine and that of Mr. Briant." The progress of religious thought has since been so great, that it is not easy now to see in the Briant sermon anything to excite criticism. In it moral and religious truisms seem to be set forth in plain, strong English, which at times rises into eloquence; while, throughout, it is marked by the better quality of plain speaking. The writer said what he meant; and he said it in a way not to be misunderstood. He drew his text from Isaiah lxiv. 6, — " All our righteousnesses are as filthy rags," — and he vigorously denounced the absurdities to which a lifeless, conventional religion had led. The distinctness with which he gave utterance to the truth that was in him startled those who had comfortably settled down in the uncomforting faith that Calvinism was not only the foundation of all things, but that it was a good foundation. Once more accepted formulas had been challenged, and declared to be pernicious cant.

Formulas rarely lack defenders. Several of his brethren at once entered the lists against Mr. Briant, and the theological rancor with which they did it was expressed even on the title-pages of the sermons in which they thought to confute him. The Rev. Mr. Niles, of the Middle Braintree Precinct, for instance, called his discourse a vindication of certain gospel doctrines and teachers " against the injurious reflections and misrepresentations " of the " Rev. Mr. Lemuel Briant; " and the Rev. John Porter, of Bridgewater, improved on this by entitling a sermon, — " The absurdity and blasphemy of substituting the personal righteousness of men in the room of the surety righteousness of Christ, in the important article of justification before God." Mr. Briant was not a man to be summarily suppressed. He was young, it was true, but so far his church was with him, and he had a vigorous pen. Accordingly, in 1750, he published, in the form of a letter, some " friendly remarks " on the Rev. Mr. Porter's effort, to which, in its printed form, had been appended an " attestation," as it was called, signed by five other clergymen, in which they expressed their hearty concurrence with their brother Porter, and dolefully lamented the " dreadful increase of Arminianism and other errors in the land."

This reply of Mr. Briant's must have been very irritating to his opponents, for he met them in a way they could not understand. They were narrow-minded men of no great intellectual strength, and, after the manner of such, they could not grasp a new idea even when it was plainly set before them. Because it was new, was with them sufficient proof that it must be unimportant or erroneous. Nevertheless, they were men thoroughly in earnest and of implicit belief. Briant in his reply trifled with them. Hardly troubling himself to conceal his contempt, he permitted a vein of irony to run through his answer, which, while it must have bewildered as well as exasperated his opponents, was out of place.

Naturally they were not slow to respond, and, as is the custom of men of their calibre, they forthwith proceeded to identify themselves with the sacred cause of which they were the self-appointed and incompetent advocates. They accused Mr. Briant of levity in the treatment of religious truths, and of prevarication; and they proceeded in their labored way to show that he was an Arminian and unsound. Mr. Briant had in his letter referred to the Rev. Mr. Foxcroft, the colleague of Dr. Chauncey in the First Church of Boston, as "a verbose, dark, Jesuitical writer," and, accordingly, Mr. Foxcroft now returned the compliment by accusing Mr. Briant of being not Arminian merely, but even Socinian. To this contribution to eighteenth century theological debate Mr. Briant replied in a way which demonstrated that in pointed controversy his opponents were no match for him, and he now fairly convicted them of having brought serious charges against him on the strength of conjecture and suspicion only; but the discussion had drifted away from great doctrinal issues to mere personalities, and it ceased to be of importance.

Yet it did not stop then. Mr. Briant had stirred the waters of local theology to their depth, nor did the agitation subside during the remainder of his life. At the time of his second letter he was not yet thirty; but he was already drawing to his end, and the closing months of that short and stormy pastorate must have been most trying; for, though not without warm sympathizers among the more liberal of his brethren, Mr. Briant's own people were no longer undivided. This state of affairs resulted in the intervention of one of those Ecclesiastical Councils which, in the language of Mr. Briant's most eminent successor in the pulpit of the North Precinct church, effected " as much as Councils ever effect, — that is nothing at all, except, it may be, to increase the difficulty in which they intermeddled." [1] Nevertheless such was the bitterness and harsh language engendered by this controversy, going even to the length of groundless charges against the pastor of "scandalous immoralities," that, on the 22d of August following the sessions of the Council, " Ebenezer Adams was Suspended from the Communion of the Church for the false, abusive and scandalous stories that his unbridled Tongue had spread against the Pastor, and refusing to make a proper Confession of his manifest Wickedness;" but that Ebenezer Adams pursued the course he did from conviction rather than malevolence may be inferred from the fact that, twenty years later, in 1773, the church, in the days of Mr. Briant's successor, made choice of him for deacon, in the place of Deacon, and Brigadier-General, Palmer. The probabilities are that Deacon Ebenezer Adams was merely a rigid, old-school Orthodox, whose theology, of no unusual kind, was not above seeking the aid of calumny.

[1] Lunt, *Two Discourses*, 141.

On the 22d of the ensuing October a precinct meeting was held to take action on the pastor's request for dismission. His health was failing. Mr. Briant did not survive his dismissal quite one year, dying at Hingham in the early autumn of 1754. At the time of his death he was but thirty-two, and, of all those who have served as pastors of his church, his remains and those of his eloquent successor a century later, William Parsons Lunt, alone do not moulder in the old North Precinct graveyard. Briant was buried in the neighboring town of Hingham in September, 1754, while, over a century later, Mr. Lunt, a tired wayfarer, died as he journeyed towards the Holy Land. Falling ill at Ezion-Geber at the northern extremity of the Red Sea, he sank away after two nights of fever. " Decently and reverently, on the morning of the 21st of March, 1857, his mortal remains were laid in the sands. A rude heap of stones marks the spot."

The last French war, that which resulted in the English conquest of Canada, had then already begun before Mr. Briant died, and while Washington was then reconnoitring on the Ohio, Lord Monckton was preparing for the removal of the Acadians; Braddock's defeat took place the following July. The Revolutionary struggle followed close on the French War. This rapid sequence of great events outside materially affected even the North Precinct church of Braintree, and a long period of doctrinal quiescence ensued, which amounted at last almost to torpidity. It was on the 22d of October, 1753, that Mr. Briant was dismissed, and just one year later, on the 8th of October, 1754, the parish extended a call to the Rev. Anthony Wibird.

Mr. Wibird, a graduate of Harvard in the class of

1747, was at the time of this call in his twenty-eighth year. He at first declined, apparently on the ground that the salary voted would not suffice for his support. It was small, being but eighty pounds a year, with a further sum of one hundred and thirty-three pounds, six shillings, and eightpence, "lawful money," for " a settlement." This it will be noticed was not so much as Mr. Fiske had received nearly a century before. Subsequently the parish modified its terms, offering a salary of one hundred pounds a year, with no sum at settlement, and this proposition Mr. Wibird accepted. He was ordained on the 5th of February, 1755. The Wibird pastorate, the longest in the annals of the parish, covered forty-five years, outlasting the century, and during it the colonies separated from the mother-country, and the North Precinct of Braintree became the town of Quincy. What with French and Revolutionary wars and reigns of terror, the downfall of the old and the upbuilding of the new, the world in those days moved rapidly; but amid all the turmoil without, — stamp-acts, tea-riots, Bunker Hill fights, Declarations of Independence, and elections of Presidents, — the Rev. Mr. Wibird seems to have pursued the even tenor of his way. He was about seven years older than John Adams, who saw much of him during the years the former was picking up a practice at Braintree, and in 1759 the active-minded young lawyer wrote of the divine that his soul was lost in " dronish effeminacy," though he had "his mind stuffed with remarks and stories of human virtues and vices, wisdom and folly, etc." On yet another occasion he observed upon Parson Wibird's popularity, — " He plays with babies and young children that begin to prattle, and talks with their mothers, asks them familiar, pleasant questions about their affection to their children; he has a familiar, careless way of conversing with people, men and women; he has wit and humor."

Before Mr. Wibird's pastorate closed he was, through bodily infirmity, disabled from preaching, so that on February 5, 1800, exactly four months before the pastor's death, the Rev. Peter Whitney was ordained as his colleague. Like all his predecessors in that pulpit, except Tompson and Flynt, Mr. Whitney was a Harvard graduate, belonging to the class of 1791, and at the time of his ordination he was thirty-two. His pastorate lasted through forty-three years, and during it the Unitarian movement under Channing took place in New England, and, as was fit and proper, the former Braintree church, — the church of Wheelwright and Briant, — fell readily into line on the side of liberal Christianity. One hundred and sixteen years elapsed between the Cambridge synod, which so summarily suppressed the heresies of Wheelwright, and the Braintree Ecclesiastical Council which deprecated the teachings of Briant. A period of fifty years followed during which the mind of New England was drawn wholly away from problems of theology, and concentrated first on questions of civil rights and afterwards on questions of government. Not until the earlier years of the present century was political order established; and then religious issues once more came to the front. New England Unitarianism assumed shape, and Channing foreshadowed Parker. John Adams, discussing in 1815 the principles of the new departure, found in them nothing that was not familiarly known to him, and bore testimony to the fact that sixty-five years before Lemuel Briant was a Unitarian.[1] So the change from orthodoxy to Unitarianism in the case of the first church of old Braintree came in the fulness of time.

Thus in Quincy that ecclesiastical domination which had ruled "the Mount" with hand of iron passed slowly and imperceptibly away, and in 1827 Mr. Whitney was able to record that "for the last thirty years this society has been more united, perhaps, than any other in our country. No 'root of bitterness' has in any measure sprung up to trouble them; none of that ill-will which sectarianism so often produces has been found among them, nor have any of those sources of division arisen which in so many of the towns of New England have cut the happiest societies asunder."

These words were written at the very time when the old epoch had come to a natural close, and the new one was about to begin. The silence of the West Quincy hills was now broken by the sharp ring of the sledge on the drill, and loud blasts told of quarries from which gangs of busy men were taking huge blocks of stone to be carried off on the newly-devised railway, which, opened only the year before, was daily examined by curious visitors from far and near. Forces destined in a few years to revolutionize the town were newly but actively at work. Though the Mass had not yet been celebrated in Quincy, and, indeed, no new religious society had been organized there for more than a century, the church and the town were no longer one. The separation had taken place three years before. Most significant of all, the old church edifice of 1732, in which three whole generations of townspeople had worshipped together as one

---

[1] Pattee, *Old Braintree and Quincy*, 222, note.

civil and religious family, — this plain, wooden meeting-house was even then being removed to give place to that more pretentious temple of stone which was in a few years to be known only as the place of worship of one, and not the most numerous, of the many religious societies into which the people of the town had divided.

## CHAPTER III.

### LAND TITLES AND THE TOWN COMMONS.

IN speaking of the town of Braintree, then newly incorporated, Captain Edward Johnson, in his "Wonder-working Providence," remarked, — " Some of Boston retain their farms from being of their Town, yet do they lye within their bounds, and how it comes to pass I know not." It will also be remembered that at the time of the incorporation two thousand acres had been "set apart at the Mount" for the use of Boston, "in the most convenient place unallotted." For several years thereafter Boston continued to make allotments in Braintree, until in January, 1644, a tract of three thousand acres was granted to John Winthrop, Jr., and others for the encouragement of some iron-works then projected. Thus a quarter of the entire township, large as it was, had been either reserved to Boston, or set aside as common lands, or given away to form large private estates. It has already been remarked that the actual settlers in Braintree seem as a rule to have been poor persons who received small allotments proportioned to the size of their families, usually four acres to "a head," or for each member. On those who had received these allotments fell the burden of the town's charges.

Town charges, it is true, were in the earlier period in much the largest part for the support of the church: but a contribution of £110 a year for that purpose,

which was the amount at first annually paid to Messrs.
Tompson and Flynt, was a heavy burden; for, even
though made in country pay, it represented, when
the relative numbers and wealth of the communities
are considered, more than the equivalent of an annual assessment of a hundred thousand dollars upon
those now occupying the territory of the original town.
Naturally, also, in the case of early Braintree, the
exemption of the Boston allotments from their share
of the charge was from the beginning a source of
jealousy and contention. The arrangement of 1639,
therefore, was one which could not be permanent.
Accordingly, an order was passed by the Braintree
freeholders, as early as 1641, that no house or land in
the town should be sold to any one not an inhabitant
until it had first been offered to " the men appointed
to dispose of town affairs;" and, in case they did not
see fit to purchase, it could then be sold " only to
such as the townsmen shall approve on." Nor could
any one not received as an inhabitant build within the
town limits without permission.

In the seventeenth century the word "inhabitant"
carried with it a strict legal significance, very different from the loose meaning it has now; for it included those only who as householders, or through the
occupancy of the land, were interested in the management or well-being of the locality : but it included all
such, whether actually residing there or elsewhere.
By passing a vote, therefore, which strictly limited
the sale or transfer of land to such as " the townsmen
shall approve on," the freeholders made their town
something very like a close corporation. Similar restrictions are found not only in the early records of
the Massachusetts towns, but they can be traced back

to the Teutonic mark system and the Salian, or Frank, law of the fourth and fifth centuries; and, indeed, their ultimate origin would probably have to be looked for, not in any village or tribal usages no matter how primitive, but imbedded deep in the animal instincts of developed man.[1]

But, while rigid restrictions on inhabitancy were common to all the original Massachusetts towns, and may indeed be considered a fundamental principle of their polity, if not a necessary incident to their origin as commercial enterprises, yet in the particular case of Braintree it may further with confidence be surmised, that the inhibition of further non-resident landownership, and the strict limitation of the incoming of new settlers, had a fourfold object. In the first place, it was an outgrowth of the Antinomian excitement and its alien law.[2] Above all things, the peace of the church was not again to be disturbed; and to that end every element of civil and religious discord was to be excluded. Church and town were one; and it was thus reserved for the members of the church to say who might be inhabitants of the town. The Lord's people were to be hedged in securely against intruders. Next, and second in importance only to religious considerations, came the fact that the legal inhabitancy of the town carried with it certain rights and privileges in the common lands, then supposed to be of value. Further on, these rights and privileges will be more particularly referred to. Third, came in the question of the support of the poor and the helpless. Under that system of English law and custom which the settlers had brought over with them, every

---

[1] See paper in *Proceedings of Mass. Hist. Soc.* Series II. vii. 202.
[2] *Supra*, 459.

one had a right to insist on being kept from starving and freezing. That right was established by legal residence. From the beginning, therefore, it has been matter of deep concern with all Massachusetts towns to prevent the poor and dependent from becoming legal inhabitants within their limits; and this is still the case. The ancient records contain cases in which a married man is ordered to send his father-in-law, and a father and mother their married daughters, out of the town, and the answer was made that the parties ordered "would willingly be ridd of" the incumbrances referred to, but "considering the relation that is between them . . . could not turne [them] out of doars this winter time."[1] The Braintree town order of 1641 was to provide against this common liability. Fourth, and finally, the order was intended to meet in a certain degree the vexatious question, peculiar to Braintree, of non-resident ownership. The people of the town wished to purchase among themselves all lands and tenements offered for sale, so that neither land nor tenement should in future be held by any one who did not actually live in Braintree and share in its town and parish burdens.

But the evil of absentee land-ownership could not be remedied in this way. Accordingly, in 1647 another attempt was made to correct it. Upon a commutation payment of £50 in five equal annual instalments, "to be made in merchantable corn, as wheat, rye, peas, and Indian, at fifty shillings in each of them," Boston agreed that all land owned by its inhabitants in Braintree should, when laid out and improved, be accounted as Braintree lands, and as such become liable to every common town charge. But this agree-

[1] *Fourth Report of Boston Record Commissioners*, 180–2.

ment, also, failed to settle the question. The unsurveyed and unimproved lands next became the bone of contention. Inhabitants of Boston, going back to the loose grants freely made in earlier times, claimed ownership. A vexatious and endless litigation seemed imminent. On a greatly reduced scale, it was the question which during that century and the next involved England and France and Spain in war upon war. A wilderness was in dispute, the ownership of which rested on paper titles often coming in conflict with actual occupancy. Fortunately the parties to the conflict in this case were not in a position to declare war on each other, or even to come to blows; but in January, 1698, seventy freeholders of Braintree formally and in writing covenanted one with another " to defend our ancient Rights, and oppose in a course of Law those and all those that shall by any means disturbe, molest, or indeavour to disposesse " any of their number; and they promised to bear as a common burden all charges which might arise out of the lawsuits expected to ensue.

This determined front naturally brought about a compromise, and in the year 1700 a body of the Braintree freeholders agreed to purchase all the waste land within the town limits, a title to which was claimed by inhabitants of Boston, paying therefor £700; a sum which seems small, and the equivalent of perhaps $12,000 only in our money, but to that territorial community no less a burden than the payment of $700,000 would be now. In order effectually to prevent a repetition of the non-resident experience, it was at the same time, and at a public meeting, further voted that no purchaser of these lands should make any conveyance of them to any outsiders, " thereby to let them have a foothold or interest in said purchase or any other way." The purchase-money was raised by voluntary subscription through the efforts of an association consisting of one hundred inhabitants of Braintree, and the Boston claims finally extinguished. It was noticeable, also, and characteristic of the time and of the people, that the committee of the town of Boston appointed to execute the deed for these lands, and to receive the purchase-money, was further instructed to lay out "the said money in some real Estate for the use of the Public Latin School."

Thus ended a controversy the importance of which to Braintree cannot be exaggerated. It involved a vital question, — that of a fixed rent-charge to be forever paid by the actual occupant of land to a technical owner. English and Irish experience had sought to repeat itself on new soil. From the time of King James' grants to the Virginia companies in 1606 downwards, one grantee after another of large tracts of American wilderness had thought to secure forever some annual return from them, just as English adventurers and court favorites had secured similar returns from the grants of William the Conqueror, Henry VIII., and Elizabeth. It was proposed to transplant the feudal system to America, and the future increase, at least, in land value, — what is now in the language of the political economist known as the unearned increment, — was to be appropriated; and the town of Boston, under the order of May, 1634, giving it "convenient enlargement at Mount Wollaston," was but taking the place of Lord Gorges under the Greenwich allotment of June, 1623.[1]

Thus the Greenwich scheme on a most grandiose

[1] *Supra*, 139–40.

scale, and the "enlargement" vote, with the subsequent lavish Boston allotments, on a plan of greatly reduced proportions, were attempts to introduce into New England something bearing a close resemblance to that land system which Strongbow had introduced into Ireland four centuries and a half before. That the first of these attempts failed was, it may safely be asserted, the making of New England; the failure of the last was essential to the prosperity of Braintree. The occupants of the soil became the owners of it. Paying no rent, what they would under another system have been forced to pay as rent remained with them; and it represented that slow accretion of substance which built up the community. The additional value which the laborer's toil gave to the land belonged to the resident toiler, and not to his absentee landlord.

This is not the place to discuss in detail the cause of the failure of either the Gorges scheme of 1623, or the "enlargement" scheme eleven years later; though now it is plain to see that the first was, from natural economic influences, doomed from the start. Landlordism depends on a monopoly of land; and the abundance of cheap lands, combined with the want of accumulated capital, made landlordism impossible in America. But, while this was true of the country as a whole and of the Gorges scheme, it was by no means equally true of "the Mount" and the Boston "enlargement" plan. The net of the law was thrown over "the Mount" in 1637, when provision was first made for a church there, and again in 1640, when a town was incorporated. From that net the people of Braintree had to extricate themselves. The agreement of January 10, 1698, was accordingly their declaration of

independence of landlordism. The contract of 26th
January, 1700, was the recognition of that independence.
The long struggle between the paper claimants
of the soil, on the one side, and its actual occupants,
on the other side, runs through sixty years of the town
records. It was only an episode in the history of an
insignificant New England village, and as such is beneath
the notice of history. Yet it had great historical
significance. In a natural way, all unconsciously
to those composing it, a single member in a community
of towns was asserting itself in the line of common
development.

But there was a vested right in the soil of New
England anterior to the title derived from the crown,
— the right of occupancy by the Indians. Every
grant made by the General Court was made subject
to this right, and it devolved upon the grantee to
extinguish it by purchase. The "convenient enlargement"
at the Mount was no exception to the rule, and
this fact led to a complication which now reads like a
burlesque on those national claims then so freely asserted
and so bloodily argued. While the controversy
with Boston was still dragging on, certain inhabitants
of Braintree on behalf of the whole secured, as a
muniment of title and out of mere superabundance
of caution, a deed of the township from some of the
Indian descendants of Chickatabot. This deed, duly
signed and sealed, with delivery "by turf and twig,"
conveyed to the grantees one of those Indian titles so
frequently met with in the early records of New England,
— titles the result of transactions which grave
historians have not hesitated to defend and even to
extol, but which in point of fact were a mockery of
law, and entitled to no more consideration than if

those defrauded through them had been infants or simpletons. Nevertheless, the so-called Wampatuck deed of 1665 professed to convey a title to Braintree township from certain ignorant savages, who never owned the soil, to eight grantees, among whom was one Richard Thayer. Seventeen years later, in 1682, Richard Thayer not only asserted his title to the whole township by virtue of this deed, but actually petitioned the Privy Council to have the property put in his hands, he having been driven from it " to his bitter Ruine."

This occurred in the latter years of the reign of Charles II., — a period during which Massachusetts was not in favor at court. It was not possible to know what secret, or even corrupt, influences might be at work behind a distant and all-powerful tribunal like the Privy Council, and the freeholders were greatly stirred when tidings reached them of this new assault. An address to the King was at once prepared, and " subscribed by an hundred and thirty-four hands out of this small town;" after which it was duly forwarded to Joseph Dudley and John Richards, the agents of the colony in London, and by them filed with the Privy Council. The document and the accompanying letter of transmittal, presumably the work of that " true New England man," as Sewell describes him, Colonel Edmund Quincy, were characteristic of the time, and in it the claimant's history, methods and belongings were set forth with primitive directness. Thayer, it was alleged, had come to New England some forty years before, one of " eight poor children " of a very poor father, whose shop, for he was a cobbler, " would now hardly containe (the claimant) with his arms a Kimbow. And

of a mushrome hee's swolne in conceipt to a Coloss
or giant of State, and dreams of a Dukedome." The
body of the town, it was further stated, looked upon
themselves "as basely traduced by Thayer's reports;
whose cards, had they been good, hee had the less
need of cheating, fraud and falsehood to helpe him
out;" but "he hath been dealing so much for Indian
deeds and titles to land, and by these ways, having
made himself one of the forlorn hope among men
of desperate fortunes, he hath left himself little or
nothing but such imaginary vexatious claims to his
neighbors lands and possessions." Nothing more is
recorded of Richard Thayer and his claim; but the
Wampatuck deed of 1665, preserved doubtless among
the papers of Edmund Quincy, has long hung in the
Braintree Town-hall, an interesting reminder of a class
of fictitious or fraudulent conveyances which for over
half a century threw a cloud on colonial land titles.

The wrangle over land titles and absentee ownership
thus occupied sixty years, but the questions and quarrels
which arose out of the possession of the commons
required in their settlement twice that space of time.
In the original Braintree there were three descriptions
of these common lands; they included a little less than
2,000 acres, and were known as the South and North
Commons, the ministerial land and the school land.
When it is said that the settlers of Massachusetts
were as a body common people of the purest English
blood, much naturally follows. The English are a
tenacious race, not easily adapting themselves to new
conditions. They brought to New England, therefore,
together with their language and families and
household stuffs, a mass of customs and usages which
dated back to the Saxon days of King Ceawlin and

Ine, but were little applicable to the new surroundings. Of these usages and customs many yet remain in the more remote towns, strange relics of the almost forgotten communal system of early German life. Antiquarians from time to time come across them, and when they do so they are apt to expatiate, as if it were matter of surprise that the first settlers, in bringing with them their Saxon tongue, also brought their Saxon village ways.[1] Yet such was the fact. They not only brought those ways, but, after their natures, they were slow to see that in many respects such ways did not fit into their new life. In the matter of common lands, for instance, the original settlers came from a country in which almost every hamlet had its common and its rights of commonage, and in which also public institutions, whether religious or educational, were endowed, and thus, to a large extent, self-sustaining. Accordingly, almost as a matter of course, provision was very generally made in the Massachusetts towns to reproduce the system to which the settlers had been accustomed at home. The church and the school were provided for, and the inhabitant to a certain extent relieved of the burden of supporting them; while the town commons, either through the rental derived from letting them or the direct value of the rights enjoyed in them, were intended to supply a revenue which should go far towards meeting the miscellaneous expenses of the town. All descriptions of public charge would to a large extent in this way be

---

[1] Doyle, *English in America; the Puritan Colonies*, i. 74; Adams, *Germanic Origin of New England Towns*, Johns Hopkins University Studies, i.; Andrews, *Theory of the Village Community*, Am. Hist. Association Papers, v. 47; Remarks of Messrs. Chamberlain and Goodell, *Proc. Mass. Hist. Soc.* Series II. v. 272, 320.

provided for; and, in point of fact, as will presently be seen, more than a century after Braintree was incorporated the annual taxation of its inhabitants was little more than nominal, the revenue derived from the school lands and the town commons, badly managed as both were, materially contributing to the reduction of direct public charges.

While, therefore, the original settlers in Braintree undoubtedly brought with them from England the traditional idea of commons, yet, under the primitive system, half political and half commercial, with which they, like others at that time, organized their town, such an idea would also naturally have suggested itself. In a country yet unoccupied, those preparing to occupy it merely made provision out of the unappropriated domain to relieve themselves individually of a portion at least of those few public charges which were then incident to every civil community; while, at the same time, as a body of proprietors, — stockholders they would now be called, — they reserved an undivided interest in a tract of territory of present or prospective value. Apart from all question of tradition and usage, the proceeding, under the circumstances, indicated merely that ordinary forethought to be looked for in a thrifty, provident race.

The plan was not only natural, it was well devised; but, unfortunately for its practical success, the settlers did not make due allowance for changed conditions. Coming from a country in which all the desirable land was occupied, they were beginning the settlement of a wilderness, wherein, except in favored spots, land hardly repaid the cost of fencing. The occupant of it certainly could not afford to pay rent. Yet to get free from the English traditions and grasp this new fact seems to have required the lifetime of more than a generation of settlers. While existing in a wilderness still infested with forest animals and inaccessible for want of roads, the earlier generations were haunted with the fear of outsiders coming in. Such, instead of giving value to what then had no value, would seek, it was thought, to share a privilege the utter worthlessness of which, with the characteristic stolidity of their race, the original settlers failed to realize.

It was the common case of traditions and theories in conflict with realities; and consequently the Braintree commons, like those of most other towns, early proved a source of quarrel and vexation. The privilege of taking stone, timber and thatch from those commons, as well as pasturing cows upon them, was long regarded as valuable. It was one of the advantages pertaining to the commercial side of the organization. As early as 1646 a vote was passed, authorizing legal inhabitants to take timber off the commons for any use in the town, but imposing a penalty of five shillings a ton on any sold out of the town. For years votes of a similar character were from time to time recorded, especially in regard to stone for building material. Then, not satisfied with the commons they had within their own limits, with genuine Anglo-Saxon land-hunger, a number of the Braintree freeholders petitioned the General Court in 1666 for a grant of 6,000 acres elsewhere. The reason they assigned was that the town lands held in commonage were limited in quantity, only 2,000 acres, and "very poor and barren" as well as "much worn out;" that the inhabitants were multiplying and "already much straightened," as a great part of the township was held by "Gentlemen and friends of other Towns" which the townspeople were "inforced by their wants to hire of them at dear rates:" but the petition was, in fact, an outbreak of the general and indiscriminate land fever which then and ever since has prevailed in America. In this case the General Court listened to the prayer addressed to it, and "on consideration of the reasons therein expressed" made a grant of 6,000 acres "in some place, limited to one place, not prejudicing any plantation or particular grant;" and, a few years later on, this practice of granting to towns tracts of land at a distance for settlement became common.

Territorial questions, and the issues arising out of the disposition to be made of a public domain, were thus brought before the Braintree town-meeting. In the first place the grant had to be definitely located, and this proved a long and difficult process, so that King Philip's war broke out and wholly absorbed the mind of the General Court before anything definite was accomplished. At last, after that war was brought to a close, Braintree in 1679 again petitioned the Court that, "since the *Lord* out of his rich grace had made them *lords* of the heathen land, they might have an opportunity to have ratified the former grant;" and in answer to this quaint request leave was granted the petitioners "to lay out their sixe thousand acres in any vacant place" within the Massachusetts jurisdiction. The matter now seems to have lain dormant for thirty-four years, until in June, 1713, a committee was appointed to find and lay out the 6,000 acres, who were to receive "for their so doing Thirty Pounds if the thing be effected, otherwise nothing." The grant was now, in 1715, confirmed, and the land assigned in that part of Worcester County since incorporated as

New Braintree. In other words, it was much as it now is when a territory is organized, out of which a new State is ultimately to be created. But it was at this point the real trouble began, for it became necessary to devise some definite policy for dealing with the public domain. Was that domain to be held? — or was it to be disposed of? — and, if disposed of, was it to be for the benefit of individuals, or of the community? — If for the benefit of individuals, to whom did it belong, and how was it to reach the beneficiaries? — If for the benefit of the community, how and to what public uses was it to be applied? — The Congressional discussions of the future were anticipated in the wearisome town-meeting wrangles which, through long years, took place within the walls of the old stone meeting-house of Braintree.

Accordingly, in 1714 it was voted that the grant should be sold; and the year following it was voted it should not be sold. The question was then agitated as to whom the land in question belonged; and a committee appointed, in 1719, to consider the matter, in due time reported that, in the opinion of those composing the committee, the land " belonged to the Persons that were [at the time the grant was made, in 1667] Freeholders and to their Posterity." This conclusion the town refused to adopt; and then, after first voting neither to sell nor lease the grant, it finally, in apparent despair of any other solution, voted " that the said Land should be sold, the produce thereof to be disposed for the use of the Town for ever;" but " against this vote Ephraim Thayer entered his dissent." This decision was reached in 1720; but it did not prove final. And so the vexed question dragged along, — the action in the town-meeting of one year being reversed in the town-meeting of the next, — the grant remaining a useless and apparently a worthless bone of contention, until at last in 1727, — sixty years after the General Court acceded to the prayer of the original petitioners, — it was finally voted that, " for the more Peaceable settlement " of the matter, the land should be equally divided, as nearly as might be, between the two precincts, " to be henceforward managed, improved and further Divided or Disposed of, as shall be agreed on and ordered by each Precinct Respectively from time to time for ever hereafter."

This was one phase — what might be termed the territorial phase — of the public domain question. The other phase of the same question related to the communal lands within the township, — the so-called Braintree commons, which the inhabitants used " to pasture upon for the Summer time those cattle which they [were] necessitated to raise and keep." These lands, it has already been said, included some 1,800 acres within the town limits, lying in two different parcels and known as the North and the South Commons. Each year and at almost every town-meeting, the freeholders were called upon to take some action looking to what was called the improvement or to the defence of the town lands, and no less than 180 votes relating to this subject are found in the records. Almost endless provision of an unavailing sort was made to prevent waste, — votes looking to the preservation of the boulders scattered over the granite hills, or the trees on the scanty soil which overlaid them. Through a long series of years portions of the common lands were periodically fenced in, and litigation ensued. The lands were then leased, and the rent applied to the support of the school: but this plan of improvement failed in its turn, the lessees complaining bitterly of trespasses and encroachments, and finally throwing the lease up. In their memorial they particularly referred to one open way which had been recently laid out through these lands; and they add that, "although we repeatedly attempted to fence against the same by a sufficient stone wall, yet we were as often prevented by certain unknown evil-minded persons, who, as fast as we built up the wall by day, did in the night-time throw the same down again."

Under these circumstances both the lessees and the town were discouraged. However it might be in England, the remains of the communal land system, beyond the limits of a training-field and burying-ground, were not productive of satisfactory results in Massachusetts. It was accordingly proposed that the commons should be sold; and this question divided the town for years, just as it has since divided the Parliament of Great Britain and the Congress of the United States. The problem which Burke and Benton debated on a large scale was, on a smaller scale, and before they were born, discussed in the Braintree town-meetings. "The Difficulties and Disputes Relating to said Commons" seem to have culminated about the year 1750; for they then occupied the attention of the town-meetings almost to the exclusion of other business, and the meagre records still bear evidence to the heat with which the subject was wrangled over, for each article of the warrants relating to it is disposed of only after "considerable" or "great debate," and the question would be "voted and contested, Polled and determined." At last, in 1753, the issue was fairly raised whether the town would set a price on the commons with a view to their sale; and, a little later in the same year, after refusing to appoint a committee " to consider what method would be best to Regulate the Towns Commons by Dividing, selling, or Letting," it was voted to divide them, and a committee of fifteen, at the head of which were John Quincy and Josiah Quincy, was appointed to report a method of division. A month later this committee made to the adjourned meeting a report which, in brevity at least, was a model document. It was in these words: — " At a meeting of the Committee appointed by the Town to Consider and Report, what may be the most proper method of Dividing the Towns commons, The subject being fully considered and Debated, upon the Question being put whether it was best for the Town to Divide the same by Poles or Estates, the Committee was equally divided in their opinion thereon." This report was presented on the 16th of April, and a number of freeholders present at the meeting recorded their dissent " against dividing the commons by Poles," but, at a subsequent adjourned meeting held a month later, " after considerable debate " the division by polls was voted, and a new committee of five, " they serving the Town Gratis," was appointed to consider " who may and ought to be interested " in the division decided upon, and "to produce an exact list of all such persons." The name of Quincy did not appear among those composing this committee, which a month later made its report and submitted a list of those entitled to share in the division, both of which documents were "Lodged with the Clerk." Yet, though the course now recommended was approved and adopted, and "all votes that have heretofore passed Respecting the Division of the Towns commons [were] Ratified and confirmed," the commons still remained undivided.

In so far as the public domain sufficed for so doing, every freeholder had voted himself a farm; but the farm remained in the common possession, and was not conveyed to the individual. Such a method of division might commend itself to the average voter, but it was not practicable.

Accordingly, the next year the question of leasing again presented itself, and was referred to a committee; and, at an adjourned town-meeting held on the 6th of March, 1755, a number of open ways were laid out through the commons. Then, on the 24th of the same month, a special meeting was called to reconsider these votes, " as they were passed when there was but a small number of the Inhabitants by reason of the extraordinary snow;" and "the Question was put whether the Town concur with any of the votes passed at the adjournment voted and Polled, concurred, 83, non Concurred, 91." But, though nothing more seems to have been done to bring about a division in severalty among the inhabitants of the town, the contention still went on until in 1762 the lessees of the commons found themselves so annoyed and molested in the manner which has already been described, that they formally declined to fulfil any longer the conditions of their leases. The name of "Mr." John Adams now appears for the first time in the records; heretofore it had always been with the prefix of "Lieutenant" or "Deacon." Having graduated at Harvard in the class of 1755, John Adams was now twenty-seven and had been practising law in Braintree about four years; though, apparently, he had held no office, for his name does not appear in the records, he had, as a matter of course with a New England young man of that period, felt a lively interest in town politics. As the action of the lessees of the commons involved a legal issue, the matter was referred to a special committee, at the head of which was "Mr. John Adams." It was his entrance into public life, and the disposition to be made of the Braintree commons was the first of many issues involving questions of state policy with which he was destined to find himself confronted. Years afterwards he briefly told the story of what ensued: —

"In 1763 or 1764 the town voted to sell their common lands. This had been a subject of contention for many years. The south parish was zealous, and the middle parish much inclined to the sale; the north parish was against it. The lands in their common situation appeared to me of very little utility to the public or to individuals; under the care of proprietors where they should become private property, they would probably be better managed and more productive. My opinion was in favor of the sale. The town now adopted the measure, appointed Mr. Niles, Mr. Bass, and me to survey the lands, divide them into lots, to sell them by auction, and execute deeds of them in behalf of the town."

This was done, and so the strifes, contentions, litigations and ill feelings which the commons had through a century and a quarter engendered between neighbors, friends and freeholders were ended; nor that only, for at the same time a great element of corruption was removed from town politics, for jobbing out the commons could no longer be used in the interest of candidates at the annual elections.

## CHAPTER IV.

### THE HIGHWAYS.

LIKE most primitive settlements which are not themselves seminal, — such as Boston, Salem and Plymouth, — Braintree grew up naturally at certain more favored or fertile points on the line of a main thoroughfare between considerable local centres lying beyond its own limits. In this case the thoroughfare connected the Massachusetts and the Plymouth colonies, and the line followed by it was dictated in advance by the lay of the land, the points of ferriage or fording, and the course of the brooks. The construction of a great coast road from Newbury, on the Merrimac, to Hingham — the northern and southern limits of the Massachusetts Bay Colony — was ordered by special vote of the General Court in November, 1639, two months after the Braintree church was gathered. Those deputed to lay out the new road were empowered to do so wherever it might " bee most convenient, notwithstanding any man's propriety, or any corne ground, so as it occation not the puling downe of any man's house or laying open any garden or orchard." Its width was not specified, except in the common lands or where the soil was wet and miry; it was there to be six, eight and even ten rods wide. At first designed to connect all the outlying coast towns of the Massachusetts Bay with Boston, it naturally was almost immediately continued along the shore to Plymouth. South of Boston it doubtless closely followed the old Indian trail, seeking the fords, avoiding morasses, clinging to the uplands, and skirting the rough, wooded heights. This trail in due course of time was succeeded by the blazed way, axe-marks on the bark of trees supplying for the settler those more subtle indications which had pointed out a path to the savage. The blazed trail was shortly succeeded by the bridle-path, which was little more than the blazed trail made passable to such extent that only at certain points were horsemen forced to dismount and lead their steeds over difficult ground. The highway was beginning to take shape. Naturally, these incipient roads were far from straight, and in following them many fences and gates had to be passed. They were, in fact, little more than a succession of farm lanes running through cleared and fenced lands, and open only through the commons. Gradually these farm lanes were fenced in, and the bars and gates removed, until at last the lanes were more or less straightened out, and made public ways. But the genesis of the Massachusetts town roads can best be studied in the history of one of them, and the original main thoroughfare through Braintree, connecting it with Boston, is fairly typical.

In a direct line the centre of the North Precinct was but little more than seven miles from Boston stone; and the devious character of the colonial ways is well illustrated by the fact that the great coast road of 1639 increased this seven miles to ten. It followed in some degree the line of the bay shore in order to escape the difficult Blue Hill formation; and yet it was forced to make a long detour to avoid the creeks and marshes which everywhere indent the coast: but the Neponset River was the great obstacle to be overcome; and for more than twenty years that puny stream seems to have defied every colonial effort to secure a crossing which could always be depended upon. Indeed, the futile attempts to supply one afford perhaps as clear an insight as can be obtained into the process through which the road development of New England was gradually worked out.

The matter of a public-way crossing of the Neponset which could be depended on by travellers under any circumstances and at all seasons first received the attention of the General Court in 1634, the year in which Boston had "enlargement at Mount Woolliston." Mr. Israel Stoughton was then granted liberty to build a mill, weir and bridge at the river's lower falls. Five months later, at the next session of the court, an exclusive mill privilege on the Neponset was granted to Stoughton, who, on the other hand, agreed to "make and keep in repair a sufficient horse-bridge over the said river," which here was even at that time probably not one hundred feet in width: but the building of this bridge was an important event in the history of the colony, — as important as the building of the St. Louis bridge across the Mississippi in the history of the nation more than two centuries later; and, indeed, the earlier effort taxed much the more severely of the two the resources of the community which attempted it. Father of a son more famous than himself, and whose name in connection with the simple but venerable hall which perpetuates his memory is a household word among the graduates of Harvard College, Israel Stoughton was a man of enterprise and substance. In the summer of 1634 he built on the Neponset the mill at which was ground the first bushel of corn ever made into meal by water-power in Massachusetts. This prototype of all the busy water-wheels in New England stood at the foot of Milton Hill, on the Dorchester side of the stream, in the midst of a wilderness; for it was four miles from any settlement on the north, while to the southward, Wessagusset was the nearest inhabited place. There was no road to it, and in 1634 the bridge at Stoughton's mill was probably little more than a succession of logs thrown from rock to rock, affording passage across the tumbling stream to people on foot only. In the autumn of that year the blazed trail seems to have been converted into a bridle-path; for the town of Dorchester then ordered a road to the mill, and voted the sum of five pounds with which to make it. This amounted to a little over one pound a mile for a road through a wilderness, and it was the scheme apparently to make a trail passable for horses, so that those having corn to be ground could get access to the mill by land as well as water. Such was the beginning of the Plymouth road through Dorchester.

Mount Wollaston was now annexed to Boston, and a number of allotments made there, so that the need of a land route between the two places began to make itself felt. Accordingly, in 1635, John Holland, a wealthy and enterprising Dorchester man, was authorized to keep a ferry lower down the river and not far from its mouth, charging fourpence for the carriage of each passenger, or threepence each in case there were more than one passenger. There were not passengers enough to make the business of carrying them a paying one; so this ferry was soon discontinued, and another established higher up the river, subsequently known, from the rate of fares established for it, as the "penny ferry." It was intended for the conveyance of foot passengers; and, indeed, owing to the flats in the river's bed, could have been used only when the tide was partially up. Like its predecessor further down the stream, it soon proved a failure, and was discontinued.

Years passed away, and the problem of crossing the Neponset was still unsolved; yet the difficulty was one sure to force its own solution in time, for the river had to be crossed by every one journeying the length of the great coast road. Under the order of 1639 any town guilty of a default in the construction of so much of this road as lay within its limits rendered itself liable to a fine of five pounds; and, in view of its long neglect to build a bridge, measures were taken to enforce this penalty against Dorchester. The town then petitioned the Court for a remission of the fine. This was allowed in May, 1652, but only on condition that the bridge should be constructed in pursuance of law, within three months, " and, if not, the said fine to take place according to the court order, the making of such bridges over such river, being no more than is usual in the like case."

Dorchester was stimulated by this pressure to action, but it seems to have been very loath to go into bridge-building; so the town bethought itself of the clause in the exclusive grant to Israel Stoughton, in 1634, one condition of which was that the grantee should "make and keep in repair a sufficient horse-bridge" over the river. Israel Stoughton was then dead, but his widow owned and worked the mill; so proceedings were begun against her. She in her turn, had recourse to the General Court, and petitioned to be discharged from her liability. After some investigation the prayer of the widow Stoughton was granted in part; and, in view of the fact that near the mill there was a good fording-place with a gravel bottom, she was excused from building a horse-bridge on condition that she should maintain a good foot-bridge, with a sufficient hand-rail. Satisfied with this concession, the widow seems to have adopted a policy of masterly inactivity, and the next spring the attention of the Court was called to the fact that, so far from a new foot-bridge having been built, the old bridge during the winter had been wholly ruined. Then at last, in May, 1655, the matter was taken energetically in hand. It was time. Massachusetts now numbered a population of over twenty thousand, dwelling in more than a score of towns, while Plymouth had five thousand people in five towns; and a little river only seven miles from Boston, on the main road between the two colonies, was still unbridged, and in times of freshet must for days together have been impassable. The construction of a cart-bridge "neere Mrs. Stoughton's mill" was now, therefore, pronounced both a necessity and a county matter, and ordered to be undertaken at once; a committee of six, among whom was Deacon Samuel Bass, of Braintree, was appointed, with full powers to fix the place of the structure and to contract for building it, the cost to be duly apportioned among the several towns. The committee seem to have done their work effectively, and nothing more was heard of a bridge across the Neponset. Indeed, for a whole century and a half the travel between Boston and the south shore followed the old Plymouth road across Roxbury Neck through Dorchester, and over Milton Hill by the bridge at Stoughton's mill.

The first attempt to fix the line of the coast road through Braintree was in 1641; but not until 1648 was the final location made. Starting from the Milton line and running at the base of the hills, crossing brooks at the points where uplands were nearest each other, the coast thoroughfare divided, in the way already described, at the stone meeting-house, immediately beyond the bridge over the little brook known as the Town River; coming together just south of the meeting-house, the two forks became one road, which again took the best line, or line of least resistance rather, to the foot of the next range of upland, always avoiding the swamps: then, crossing a spur of the granite hills by a sharp ascent and decline, it approached the Monatiquot, which, like the Neponset, proved an obstacle not easy to overcome. As early as 1635 a ferry had been established across the Monatiquot between Mount Wollaston and Wessagusset, the toll being one penny for each person and threepence for each horse. The ferryman was one Thomas Applegate, of whom not much is known, except that he was married to a wife, Elizabeth, who would seem to have been an unamiable woman, inasmuch as in 1636, "for swearing, railing, and reviling," she was sentenced by the magistrates to stand with her tongue in a cleft-stick. Applegate did not long have charge of the ferry; for, in March, 1636, six months only after he was licensed, Henry Kingman, of Weymouth, was put in his place. A year later Kingman was authorized to keep a tavern in connection with his ferry, and the toll in March, 1638, was raised to twopence a person; but Applegate appears to have remained in Kingman's employ, for this year in crossing the ferry he upset a canoe in his charge, and into which he had crowded nine persons, three of whom were drowned. For this misadventure he was summoned before the General Court, and Richard Wright, a prominent personage at "the Mount," was commissioned "to stave that canoe, out of which those persons were drowned." The matter ended with the appearance of Applegate and five others before the March General Court of 1639, which discharged them with an admonition not in "future to venture too many in any boat." But in consequence of this mishap the use of canoes at ferries was interdicted.

At its September session the General Court of 1639 changed the location of the Kingman ferry, and at the same time reduced the toll to a penny. Two months later the act providing for the construction of the coast road was passed, and, as the road was laid out in 1641, the ferry undoubtedly was a link in it. It was many years before, at last, John Hubart of Boston built, probably at his own expense, a wooden bridge across the Monatiquot, which was not replaced by one of stone until 1752.

The section of the coast road within the limits of Braintree was about five miles in length, the church being not far from midway. It was the backbone upon which the growing settlement formed itself. At first it had but three lateral branches,— two to points upon the shore, and one to what subsequently became the Second Precinct of the town. From this simple beginning the system of modern town-ways gradually developed, the lane and farm-way regularly, at the proper time, becoming the village road and town street, fierce contests sometimes arising over questions of prescriptive right. But from 1641 to 1803 the old coast road remained the single thoroughfare from Braintree, and Quincy, to Boston.

During Braintree's first century it is questionable whether the roads were kept in systematic repair. That they, in common with those of all the other Massachusetts country towns, were very bad, and, at the season of the year when the frost comes out of the ground, well-nigh impassable, may safely be inferred; for there was no tax imposed for constructing or keeping them in order, and such work as was done upon them was done by commutation or in kind. That is, at certain seasons of the year every one was called upon to labor on the highways, bringing with him his horses or his oxen, if he had them, his cart and his tools. The principles of road construction were not understood, and, needless to say, the labor and time thus expended were largely thrown away.

As early as 1730 " the affair of mending or repairing the Highways " in the usual method, by surveyors, or by a town rate, had, in the Braintree town-meetings, been the occasion of " some considerable Debate." In 1734 the question was again agitated, and now "the vote was thought by some not to be clear, after which it was decided by the Poll in the negative." In 1756, "large Debate being had thereon," the town decided in favor of a rate; but, a few days later, this action was promptly reconsidered, and "the usual method of surveyors" substituted therefor. It may be inferred that the condition of the ways was now very bad; for, in 1761, when the question of repairing them by special tax or as theretofore came up, "after considerable Debate thereon Coll. Josiah Quincy made a Present of Fifty Dollars to the Town to be expended in mending the ways;" whereupon the town at once voted its thanks to " the Collo. for his noble and Generous Grant; " fifty dol-

lars represented the labor for one month of two men
and one horse and cart at the rate of wages then paid.
As will presently appear, John Adams was chosen
Surveyor of Highways at the town-meeting in which
Colonel Quincy made his offer, and very possibly it
was Colonel Quincy's gift of fifty dollars that the
young surveyor used in ploughing, ditching, blowing
rocks and building bridges during the ensuing season;
for, as no tax was levied, it is not apparent from
what source other than this the money spent could
have been derived.

In any event the change of system as respects the
highways, which had then been more than thirty years
under discussion, took place about the year 1764, and
John Adams was instrumental in bringing it about.
Two years before he had settled the vexed question of
the town commons, and now he turned his attention
to the town roads. He long afterwards recounted his
experience in this connection, saying that in March,
1761, being then a young lawyer in Braintree, he had
heard himself suddenly nominated in town-meeting
as surveyor of highways. At first he was very indignant, remarking that " they might as well have chosen
any boy in school;" but, after thinking the matter
over, he concluded that it was best for him to accept
the situation quietly, and give the town at least an energetic administration of the office.

"Accordingly, I went to ploughing and ditching and
blowing rocks upon Penn's Hill, and building an entire new
bridge of stone below Dr. Miller's and above Mr. Wibird's.
The best workmen in town were employed in laying the
foundation and placing the bridge, but the next spring
brought down a flood that threw my bridge all into ruins.
The materials remained, and were afterwards relaid in a

more durable manner; and the blame fell upon the workmen, not upon me, for all agreed that I had executed my office with impartiality, diligence, and spirit."

Yet this not unusual outcome of amateur, though official, zeal seems to have set the Braintree road surveyor reflecting, for he goes on to say: —

"There had been a controversy in town for many years concerning the mode of repairing the roads. A party had long struggled to obtain a vote that the highways should be repaired by a tax, but never had been able to carry their point. The roads were very bad and much neglected, and I thought a tax a more equitable method and more likely to be effectual, and, therefore, joined this party in a public speech, carried a vote by a large majority, and was appointed to prepare a by-law, to be enacted at the next meeting. Upon inquiry I found that Roxbury and, after them, Weymouth had adopted this course. I procured a copy of their law, and prepared a plan for Braintree, as nearly as possible conformable to their model, reported it to the town, and it was adopted by a great majority. Under this law the roads have been repaired to this day, and the effects of it are visible to every eye."

The use made of New England country town roads throughout the colonial period, down even to the year 1830, was comparatively light. There was no internal commerce worthy of the name, and the pleasure travel amounted to nothing. Travellers journeyed chiefly on horseback. In the winter-time, when the ground was hard with frost or covered with snow, clumsy carts and sleds, drawn mainly by oxen, were kept busy bringing loads of cordwood from the woodlots, or carrying corn, potatoes and other farm produce to market at Boston. Manure was hauled merely from the barn-yard to the neighboring field; lumber and material were carted only when some dwelling or out-building was to be raised. The stage-coach period was wholly of the present century. Though the first regular line of these coaches, that from Boston to Providence, was established in 1767, making part of the inside, or land and water route to New York, yet, strange as it now seems, it was more than one hundred and seventy years after the settlement before even a baggage wagon, adapted also to the carriage of passengers, was run between Boston and Braintree or Quincy, so trifling was the intercourse and traffic between the two places : and, indeed, it was not until 1840, two full centuries after the incorporation of the original town, that the stage-coach movement along the ancient coast road began to tax its strength as a highway.

Consequently, during the first two centuries of the settlement, the country roads in Braintree and Quincy, however poorly made or kept in repair, were quite equal to the light work exacted of them. Of what that work was in the earlier and colonial days we get glimpses here and there in such records as that of Tutor Flynt's journey to Portsmouth in 1755, and John Adams' drive with his wife to Salem in 1766 to visit their "dear brother Cranch." There being then no stages at all in the colony, "a single horse and chair without a top was the usual mode of conveyance. A covered chair, called a calash, was very seldom used." In the case of Tutor Flynt, he and his companion, leaving Cambridge after breakfast, "oated" and had "a nip of milk punch" at Lynn, and then towards sunset "reached the dwelling of the Rev. Mr. Jewett, of Rowley, and Mr. Flynt acquainted him he meant to tarry there that night." They reached Portsmouth the following evening. John Adams, some ten years later, leaving Braintree in the morning, dined in Boston and passed the night at Medford, getting to Salem at noon the following day. A few years later, while riding the circuit, he described how he

"Overtook Judge Cushing in his old curricle and two lean horses, and Dick, his negro, at his right hand, driving the curricle. This is the way of travelling in 1771, — a judge of the circuits, a judge of the superior court, a judge of the King's bench, common pleas, and exchequer for the Province, travels with a pair of wretched old jades of horses in a wretched old dung-cart of a curricle, and a negro on the same seat with him driving."

An eye-witness gave a somewhat similar description of Dr. Chauncey, pastor of the First Church in Boston, as he drove about the town making his parochial visits at a period about fifteen years later: —

"In a heavy, yellow-bodied chaise, with long shafts, a black boy perched on the horse's tail, the old divine was seated, in his dignified clerical costume, with three-cornered hat, gold cane and laced wrists, bowing gracefully to citizens as he passed. His grinning young driver in the meanwhile exchanged his compliments with young acquaintances of his own color by touching them up with his long whip from his safe perch."

This was after the Revolution, but the simple ways of the fathers were still in vogue. In November, 1700, the widow of Colonel Edmund Quincy died. Judge Sewall went out to Braintree to her funeral from the old Quincy house, and he describes how, "because of the Porrige of snow, the Bearers rid to the Grave, alighting a little before they came there. Mourners, Cous. Edward and his Sister rid first; then Mrs. Anna Quincy, widow, behind Mr. Allen; and

Cousin Ruth Hunt behind her Husband." A few years later yet, in 1712, Judge Sewall further tells of a journey he made from Plymouth, where he had been holding court, to Boston. It was early in March: —

"Rained hard quickly after setting out; went by Mattakeese Meeting-house, and forded over the North River. My Horse stumbled in the considerable body of water, but I made a shift, by God's Help, to set him, and he recovered and carried me out. Rained very hard, that went into a Barn awhile. Baited at Bairsto's. Dined at Cushing's. Dryed my coat and hat at both places. By that time got to Braintry, the day and I were in a manner spent, and I turned in to Cousin Quinsey. . . . Lodged in the chamber next the Brooke."

## CHAPTER V.

#### DWELLINGS AND MODES OF LIFE.

WHEN Judge Sewall thus turned in at its gate on that rainy March day, the portion of the Quincy house in which was "the chamber next the Brooke" was comparatively new;[1] for it had, after a fashion not uncommon then, been built on to the older dwelling, which, afterwards relegated to menial uses, had already stood there for nearly seventy years. The entire building still remains, a noticeable specimen of the best domestic architecture of colonial times. Its comparatively broad hall in the centre of the house; the easy, winding staircase with carved balustrade; the low-studded but fairly large rooms opening to the south and west; the broken line of the floors and ceilings which tell of enlargement at different times; the little ship-like lockers and other like attempts to economize space while space is everywhere wasted, — all these things bespeak the dwelling-place of gentry. Time has only hardened into something very like iron the solid timbers of hewn oak still bearing upon them the marks of the axe; and one room yet has on its walls the queer, old Chinese paper which tradition says was hung there in 1775 in honor of Dorothy Quincy's approaching marriage to John Hancock; though the ceremony, owing to political exigencies,

[1] 1706, June, "14 We raised Mr Quinzeys house." Marshall's *Diary, Proc. Mass. Hist. Soc.* Series II. i. 138.

## THE MANSION. 681

was after all performed, not in the house of the bride's father in Braintree, but at Fairfield, in Connecticut.[1]

Nor in the last century was the Edmund Quincy house the only specimen of this order of dwelling in Braintree North Precinct. Colonel John Quincy occupied another such house at Mount Wollaston, which he had built in 1716, and which stood there, though reduced to baser uses, until the year 1852. Here during his long public life he often entertained friends and acquaintances coming by boat across the bay from Boston to visit him, and there are traditions of strawberry parties held on the Half-Moon Island before the upland top of that now submerged gravel ridge had been wholly washed away. The house of Leonard Vassall, built by him in 1731 and later owned by his son-in-law, was bought by John Adams in 1787. Another of these residences, it was the summer resort of a West India planter, and still contains one room panelled from floor to ceiling in solid St. Domingo mahogany. Originally a small dwelling, constructed on a plan not unusual in the tropics, with kitchen and all domestic arrangements behind the house and in a separate building, in itself it contained only parlors and sleeping-rooms; but gradually it was added to, until the original house is now lost in the wide front and deep gabled wings of the later structure. In this house John Adams died.

These houses and houses like these were the homes in Braintree of the landed gentry, during the long time in which there was in the community little property other than land. They were the New England manor houses. Close to them stood the stable, the barn, the corn and wood and cart sheds, the cider-mill

[1] *Proc. Mass. Hist. Soc.* Series II. vi. 396.

and all the other buildings belonging to the broad-acred farm, which lay behind and about them. Nor were those farms merely the costly luxury of gentleman farmers. On the contrary, the owner of the house drew from the adjacent land his chief support. He lived upon its produce; for the more prolific soil of the West had not then beggared New England agriculture. From wood-lot to orchard the fruits of each acre were carefully gathered, and what was not sold was used in rude plenty at home. Yet the primitive simplicity of those early homes can now hardly be realized. They had none of the modern appliances of luxury, and scarcely those now accounted essential to proper cleanliness or even decency. As dwelling-places during the less inclement seasons of the year, the houses were well enough, though existence within them was simple and monotonous to the last degree; but in winter there was little comfort to be had. John Adams towards the end of his life used to wish that he could go to sleep in the autumn like a dormouse, and not wake until spring. The cold of the sitting-rooms was tempered by huge wood fires, which roasted one half the person while the other half was exposed to chilling drafts. The women sat at table in shawls, and the men in overcoats. Writing on the "Lord's Day, January 15th, 1716," Judge Sewall notes, "An Extraordinary Cold Storm of Wind and Snow. . . . Bread was frozen at the Lord's Table: . . . Though twas so Cold, yet John Tuckerman was baptized. At six o'clock my ink freezes so that I can hardly write by a good fire in my Wive's Chamber. Yet was very Comfortable at Meeting." And to the same effect, four years later, Cotton Mather says, " 'Tis dreadful cold, my ink glass in my standish is froze and splitt in my very stove. My ink in my pen suffers a congelation." Such was the indoor temperature at times in rooms artificially heated; while, as for the unventilated bedrooms, water was not left in them overnight for the simple reason that in the morning it might not improbably be found solid ice; and entries, which could not be heated, had the temperature of modern refrigerators.

Such were what might be called the mansions of the colonial gentry; and such in Braintree they continued to be until long after 1830 when the gradual introduction of coal and new appliances for heating revolutionized modes of life. The dwelling of the farmer was of another class. It was the simplest form of domestic architecture. A huge stack of brick chimneys was the central idea, as well as fact, in it, and about this the house was built. It was one room only in depth, and two stories in height. The front door opened on a narrow space, with rooms on either side, while directly behind the door, and some four or five feet away, were the crooked stairs, supported on the chimney. Behind this outer shell was a lean-to, or leanter as it was pronounced and is sometimes found spelled, the sloping roof of which, beginning at the rear eaves of the house, descended to within a few feet of the ground. In this were the kitchen and wash-room; and here, on all ordinary occasions, the family took their meals and the household work was done. Of the front rooms, one was the ordinary sitting-room, and the other, the best parlor, formal, unventilated and uncomfortable, was entered only upon the Sabbath or great occasions, such as a funeral or a wedding or a christening. About these houses, which as a rule stood facing towards the south and as near as might be to the road, though rarely square with it, were the out-houses, sheds and barns necessary for carrying on farm or household work.

The wearing apparel and household furniture, as revealed through the Braintree inventories, speak also of a modest and almost Spartan simplicity. There seem to have been a few beds, — possibly one of feathers, but generally of wool or of corn-husks, — some bolsters, blankets and coverlids; but, except in the cases of the more wealthy, there is no mention of bed linen. Col. Edmund Quincy's two carpets were appraised at one pound. There was one table, and possibly two; a few chairs, perhaps half a dozen, and, in the case of the rich, a scattering of cushions and covers to chairs, but stools were chiefly in use. Knives and forks are not mentioned in the probate inventories until a comparatively recent time, but pewter and earthenware is generally valued at from a few shillings to as many pounds. The kitchen utensils seem to have consisted of a brass and iron pot or two, and some pans. There would be a Bible in the house, and possibly a few other books; an old musket and sword; a looking-glass now and then. The dress was of homespun, and worn and reworn until there was nothing left of it. In the division of personal effects, "Benjamin Had a pair of Shoes," and "David Had a Beaver Hat," while "I Had one wosted Cap and a pair of old Shoues." A hat would thus descend from father to son, and for fifty years make its regular appearance at meeting. The wearing apparel of a whole family would be stored away for generations, fashions never changing; and accordingly it is a noticeable fact that wearing apparel constitutes the first and generally one of the largest items of the inventories, while in the wills, especially of the female heads of large families, every article of raiment, especially finery, was devised to individuals with long considered impartiality.

The food and drink of dwellers in Braintree during the first century or two of town life were as simple as their furniture. Indian-corn meal was the great standby; and, even as late as the earlier years of the present century, flour was bought by the pound, and used only in the houses of the gentry. As bread made wholly of meal soon became dry, rye was mixed with it; and Governor Hutchinson told George III. in their interview immediately after the arrival of the former in London, in July, 1774, that, from long use, the people of Massachusetts had at that time learned to prefer the coarse bread made of rye and Indian-corn meal mixed to flour or wheaten bread, "and some of our country people prefer a bushel of Rye to a bushel of Wheat, if the price should be the same."[1] Fresh meat was rarely seen, but the well-to-do in the autumn of each year were in the custom of salting down a hog or a quarter of beef, bits of which later on were boiled in the Indian porridge. During a period of fourteen years, including the last years of the seventeenth century and the earliest years of the eighteenth, a man named John Marshall, who lived in Braintree, kept a diary, in which he jotted down homely items which were to him of interest. This diary has been preserved, and the material portions of it published.[2] In it Marshall notes that in January, 1704, a hog weigh-

---

[1] Hutchinson's *Diary*, i. 171.
[2] A portion of it is in the appendix to Lunt's *Two Discourses*, 108–11, and another portion in *Proc. Mass. Hist. Soc.* Series II. i. 148–64.

ing two hundred and sixty pounds cost him fifty shillings, or about $8.33, and a quarter of beef, seventy-four pounds, cost him twelve shillings, or $2; and he at the same time mentions that provisions were then "more plenty and cheap than is frequently known, beef for six farthings per pound, pork at twopence the most, the best two and a half pence, Indian [meal] two shillings per bushel, mault barlay at two shillings." Naturally the constant use of salted meat created thirst; and this thirst, the necessary consequence of what it is the custom to call a simple mode of life, led to that intemperance which was the bane of New England. The use of tea and coffee as beverages was not general until about the middle of the last century, and prior to that time the people drank water, milk, beer, cider and rum. The excessive use of the last, and its demoralizing consequences, it will be necessary to speak of presently. Meanwhile it will be noticed that Marshall in his short price-list mentions "mault barlay" as the staple next in importance to corn-meal. A brewery was one of the earliest Braintree institutions, second only to the mill. The first was established by Henry Adams, the town clerk, shortly after 1640, and was afterwards carried on by his son. Later, cider seems to have supplanted beer as the every-day and all-day beverage, and the quantity of it drunk by all classes down to a late period in this century was almost incredible. In the cellars of the more well-to-do houses a barrel of cider was always on tap, and pitchers of it were brought up at every meal, and in the morning and evening. To the end of his life a large tankard of hard cider was John Adams' morning draught before breakfast; and in sending directions from Philadelphia to her agent at Quincy, in 1799, Mrs. Adams takes care to mention that "the President hopes you will not omit to have eight or nine barrels of good late-made cider put up in the cellar for his own particular use."

There were no shops, in the modern sense of the word, in Braintree or in Quincy prior to 1830. At the village store the more usual and necessary dry and West India goods, as the signs read, from a paper of pins to a glass of New England rum, could be obtained. For everything else people had to go to Boston, which they did on foot, on horseback, in chairs or carts, and by water. Marshall in his diary speaks of going to Boston as no unusual occurrence. In October, 1705, his father died; in September, 1708, he lost an infant son; and in October, 1710, his mother. In each case he speaks of going to Boston the next day "to get things for the funeral." He was himself a mason and plasterer, but like most men of his time he seems to have turned his hand to anything by which he could earn a few shillings, for he was a farmer, a carpenter, a tithingman, a coroner, and town constable; and, acting probably in the latter capacity, he notes that on April 3, 1700, he "went to Boston with a Roge that ran away from me." The boot-maker, the cobbler, the mason and the carpenter were all recognized mechanics, and earned a living by their trades. The usual wages of skilled laborers were from sixty-five cents to a dollar a day, those of ordinary, unskilled laborers two shillings or thirty-three cents; and, fluctuations of currency apart, these wages seem to have generally ruled until the end of the eighteenth century. The busiest man in the community was the blacksmith, for not only were all the horses and oxen shod at his forge, but he was the general wheelwright, and maker and repairer of farm tools. Everything made of iron soon or late passed through his hands, and his shop, standing on the main street, was a central point in the life and movement of the town. For the rest, the peddler and the fishman were the chief purveyors both of news and of merchandise, and their horns were regularly heard on Braintree roads during the first two centuries of town life.

## CHAPTER VI.

### POPULATION AND WEALTH.

AT the time the original Braintree church was gathered, the town numbered about eighty families, representing a population of not far from five hundred souls, living mainly within the limits of what afterwards became the North Precinct. In 1640 the English emigration to New England had already ceased, and for many years thereafter the coming of new families into Braintree was systematically discouraged. In 1682 the population of the town was limited to "about ninety or a hundred families at the most." Assuming that there were 143 families in the entire town in 1707, and the enumeration then made was undoubtedly thorough,[1] during the next half century the population seems to have increased less than threefold, for, in the census of 1765, Braintree was returned as containing 357 families. Franklin, as the result of careful computations, reached the conclusion that the inhabitants of America, from natural increase, doubled their numbers during this period in twenty-five years: and Governor Hutchinson, than whom no one was better qualified to form an opinion on such a point, thought the estimate not excessive; though, he said, the increase was greater in the southern than in the northern colonies.[2] The New England family was unquestionably larger then than now, and, according

[1] Pattee, *Old Braintree*, 208.  [2] Hutchinson, *Diary*, i. 170.

to the census of 1765, it averaged in Braintree almost exactly seven persons. If the same average held good for the earlier period, the population of Braintree did not fall much short of 700 in 1683, and had increased to 1,000 in 1707. During the next fifty-eight years it grew to 2,433, a rate of increase only half of that computed as natural by Franklin: yet the figures do not indicate anything larger, and the data are fairly trustworthy. The conclusion would seem to be that, judging by the experience of Braintree, the population of New England, with almost no immigration, increased during the century which preceded the revolutionary troubles at the rate of about fifty per cent. in each twenty-five years.

Between 1765 and 1790, — twenty-five years, — the increase was abnormally small, about fourteen per cent.; but during the next fifty years it was 220 per cent., for the period of rapid modern growth had then set in. Yet, in the one hundred and ninety years which elapsed between the incorporation of the town and the year 1830, the number of persons living within the limits of the original North Precinct of Braintree increased only fivefold; while, during the next sixty years, it was destined to multiply sevenfold. Making allowance for a positive decrease of population during the period of revolutionary troubles, the population of the North Precinct apparently increased in the eighteenth century from 500 in 1707, to 1,081 in 1800, or about twofold; during the next ninety years it increased from 1,081 to 16,711, or over fifteen fold. In other words, in the matter of population and in the case of Braintree, the development of the eighteenth century was to the nineteenth positively as 580 is to 15,630, and relatively as two is to fifteen.

There are few data upon which to base an estimate of the accumulated wealth of any of the New England towns before the beginning of the present century; or, in fact, during it. It is not difficult to take the figures of the census and, dividing the aggregate of returned wealth by the total of the population enumerated, to assert that the accumulated wealth of a community amounts to so many hundred dollars per head; but the result is merely one more statistical falsehood. The valuations thus used were made for purposes of taxation only; and, as is perfectly well known, a sworn probate appraisal would show very different results. Such is the case now; and it was much more so in the last century, for the appraisals as then made were merely nominal. For instance when, in 1792, Quincy was set off from Braintree and became an independent town, the whole amount of real estate in it was appraised by the assessors at £12 7s. 4d., and the personal property of the inhabitants at £3 7s. 8d.,[1] or a total of $52.77 as the assessed valuation of a town returning one hundred and ninety-two poll-tax payers with a population of not less than 2,000 souls. The assessors of those days were citizens of the town, and as such not devoid of worldly wisdom. They probably realized the fact that the newly incorporated Quincy would in due time be called upon to pay a state and a county tax, as well as to provide for its own needs; and, as those taxes were apportioned on assessors' returns, they saw no advantage likely to result from a valuation unduly inflated. They seem to have acted accordingly. The first name on the list of resident property holders is "Hon. John Adams." Mr. Adams was then a man of fifty-seven, and filling the office

[1] Pattee, *Old Braintree and Quincy*, 622.

of Vice-President of the United States. He owned in Braintree three houses situated on two independent farms, both well supplied with farm buildings and implements. Among the larger tax-payers of the town he was the fourth, his wife's uncle, Norton Quincy, being the first, and as such called upon for a tax of £12 2s. 11d., or $40.50. John Adams' real estate was valued by the assessors for purposes of taxation at 9s. 6d., or $1.60, and his personal property at 3d., or about four cents; a total estate of $1.64. Yet upon this estate he was called upon to pay a tax of $28.50, for the total town levy of 1792 was £350, though the valuation was but £15 17s. Of the £350 the sum of £72 was derived from one hundred and ninety-two polls taxed 7s. 6d. each; £220 2s. 10d. from real estate valued at £12 9s. 4d.; and £58 17s. 2d. from personal property appraised at £3 7s. 8d.

Such figures read like a burlesque; but they have their use as illustrating the value of the statistics upon which many of the conclusions of historical writers are based. Working from data of this sort, it is manifestly impossible to reach results of any value, either positively as respects the past, or comparatively as respects the past and the present. But, while this is the case as respects accumulation and the aggregate of wealth, it is not the case with the scale on which expenditure is conducted: and, dealing with the New England towns, it is possible to make a comparison of periods which will be not altogether deceptive by taking as data the annual town levies and certain salaries paid through a long series of years; and such a comparison may have a curious interest as well as some statistical value.

In the case of Braintree, for instance, the amount

paid to the two ministers in 1657 was £110, and besides this, and the county tax, there were probably other small sums disbursed of which no record remains. At the beginning of the next century the salary of Mr. Fiske was £90 a year. In 1798, when the century was drawing to its close, the question of a suitable salary for a colleague to Mr. Wibird was much discussed. A committee gave it " as their most mature judgment" that it would be best for the town to pay its minister annually such a sum " as will enable him to maintain himself and family comfortably and with such decency as will do honor to the society that supports them." And the opinion is then expressed that the sum of $500 will afford a minister and his family "a decent support." Accordingly, in 1799, Mr. Whitney was settled in the town on a salary of $550. As respects the total amount levied through taxation for both town and parish purposes, it may be said, approximately, that the North Precinct levy was in 1656 not far from £100, and, more than a century later, in 1770, the expenses of both town and parish had not increased to over £350. Thirty years afterwards, in 1800, the entire amount raised for town and parish purposes was $3,000. In 1810 it was $3,200, and in 1820 it had increased to $4,000. These figures reveal most strikingly the stability and evenness of the scale of expense through the long period covered by them. Between 1640 and 1820 the minister's salary increased from $300 to $750, and the total town and parish levy from $350 to $4,000. Ten years later, in 1830, the total town levy, then exclusive of any salaries paid to the clergy, was $4,556.24; in 1890 it was $196,717.87. The increase of salary through the first period of one hundred and eighty years was less than threefold, and that of town levy less than twelvefold; while in the second period of sixty years, the increase of levy was over forty-three fold.

That, except during periods of war, the eighteenth century Braintree community increased its belongings does not need to be said. Any community, every available member of which is brought up to do something, while its more active members work all day long every day in the week except Sunday, wasting nothing, utilizing everything, schooled from infancy in the severest economy and eternally striving to better its condition, — any community such as this, dwelling in a region not actually icebound or a desert, must accumulate from generation to generation. So the Braintree people accumulated. As each generation passed away it left more acres under cultivation, more houses, barns and farm-buildings, more furniture and household comforts, more cattle, tools and appliances. Yet this was all. Prior to 1830, except clothes and household effects, and little hoards of silver money, there was no personal property. Whatever the people had was tangible and in sight. There were no bonds or stocks locked away in safes. A few persons, — and they were very few, — having ready money amassed in trade, may, after 1800, have held some bank or turnpike shares; but the people of country towns had even then scarcely as yet begun to be educated in this respect, and their whole idea of property was the ownership of land and buildings. Money was made in trade; and the moneyed man was he who, having amassed some ready cash, put it into goods, or loaned it to others on good security, usually bond and mortgage.

## SLOW ACCUMULATION.

Thus the whole accumulation of the hundred and ninety years from 1640 to 1830 in a community like that of Braintree and Quincy was at home and on the surface. It showed for all it was worth. Accordingly, when John Adams returned to Braintree in 1788, after a ten years' absence in Europe, he spoke of the increase of population as "wonderful," and was amazed at the plenty and cheapness of provisions; but "the scarcity of money," he wrote, "is certainly very great." And, again, John Quincy Adams, coming back to Quincy to his father's funeral in 1826, after years of absence, spoke with deep feeling of the changes he noticed as he sat in his father's place in the old meeting-house, but he added "it was a comforting reflection that the new race of men and women had the external marks of a condition much improved upon that of the former age." Yet it may well admit of question whether the entire accumulation of that village community in those two centuries, lacking only ten years, amounted to over a million and a half of dollars. Allowing for the goods and money which the original settlers brought over with them, this estimate supposes an average annual accumulation in the case of Braintree of only some $8,000 a year. For an industrious, saving community of from 500 to 2,000 souls this seems small; and yet it is difficult to see how in the aggregate it could have been larger. In 1830 there were not over four hundred families in the town. The official valuation of their wealth exceeded $800,000. For reasons which have already been given, this valuation is entitled to no weight as respects accuracy; but, assuming that a fair valuation would have shown an aggregate of twice that sum, or $1,600,000, — approximately the amount just estimated as the entire accumulation of the town, — each family would then have had, on the average, property of some sort worth $4,000. In view of the fact that absolutely no one in Quincy was in 1830 more than well-to-do, and many families had nothing, living from hand to mouth, it does not seem possible that this average could have been exceeded.

Nor, in the case of a Massachusetts coast-town like Braintree, are the sources of accumulated wealth during the colonial period at once apparent; for there do not seem in those towns to have been any recognized and established branches of trade or manufacture. The people were landowners and laborers, the latter class including, of course, all skilled workmen and mechanics ; and they in greatest degree lived on themselves and each other. Almost nothing, from a modern point of view, seemed to come in from without, or to go out from within. Works, in which bog-ore was made into iron, were established at an early day in Weymouth, and also in West Quincy; but they did not prosper: shipbuilding, also, was carried on, though to a limited extent, from a period before the close of the seventeenth century. But industries of this character amounted to little in the aggregate ; and, while the people had almost nothing to sell, they had to buy something in the way of clothes, furniture, utensils and the few articles of luxury they used. The question naturally arises, therefore, — From whence did they derive even the small amount of ready money requisite for these purchases ?

It must in the first place always be borne in mind that these purchases were of the smallest possible description. Almost every house was in itself a factory, in which lap-stone and spinning wheel were in use;

and, what was not produced at home, people, in so far as possible, did without. The life of the period was hard and self-denying. But, in the case of Braintree, as of all the other New England towns east of Narragansett Bay and north of Cape Cod, more careful investigation uniformly reveals the fact that the fisheries were the basis of colonial commerce, and consequently the beginning of wealth. Though communities might not themselves be actively engaged in the fisheries, they yet made their exchanges through them, and got such accumulation as they had from them. The Navigation Acts of Great Britain were monuments of legislative ignorance intended to secure English commerce to English shipping; but in them the American colonies were treated as part of the British empire and fared accordingly. The way in which those particular trade restrictions worked is a matter now little understood and upon which the historian, rarely having himself been engaged in trade, fails as a rule to throw clear light: but, so far as New England was concerned, the better opinion is that the much denounced Navigation Acts, loosely administered or wholly evaded through the greater part of the colonial period, in point of fact stimulated rather than depressed commerce.[1] Illicit trade was free trade; and on free trade New England throve. Exports were practically unhampered, and those to the West Indies were large. Vessels adapted to the business were built at every convenient point along the coast, and these vessels, laden mainly with fish, and after fish with surplus farm produce, pipe-staves, lumber and live-stock, went out from the shipping-ports, chief among which was

[1] Channing, *The Navigation Laws, Proc. Am. Antiquarian Society*, October, 1889.

Boston, and, when not sold in England, as they often were, came back presently loaded with sugar, molasses, cotton, indigo, and bringing also some bags of coined Spanish silver. There was, moreover, a prosperous trade with Spain, Portugal and the Canaries, — the Catholic fast-day countries, — in the course of which fish was exchanged for wine and specie; and this also was a source of steady gain.[1] And thus a slow, steady accretion went on; Boston, with its foreign commerce based on fish, lumber, farm products, such as corn and live-stock, and rude manufactured articles like pipe-staves, being the mart to which everything the neighboring towns had to sell, was brought by wagon, ox-team or packet; while from Boston was carried back to the neighboring towns the wet and dry goods, the finer manufactured articles of necessity or luxury, and finally the small balance of coin which represented the hard-earned and carefully hoarded excess in value of what was sold over what was bought. Except in the case of a few families, therefore, composing the gentry, who, like the Quincys, were engaged in foreign trade, or, like the Vassalls, were West India planters, the entire accumulation of Braintree until the end of the last century was represented in the dwellings of those inhabiting within its limits, and in their farms, — more and better buildings, clothing, furniture and utensils; larger and more commodious barns, new acres under cultivation; more oxen, horses, cows, sheep and swine; and, behind it all, the little but ever, though slowly, growing hoards of silver money.

[1] Weeden, *Economic and Social History of New England, passim.*

# CHAPTER VII.

### SOCIAL LIFE.

WHILE speaking of the Braintree community prior to 1792, and of the Quincy community between 1792 and 1830, constant reference has been made to the class of landed gentry, whose presence influenced in a marked degree the character and development of the town. This class, it has been observed, was the legitimate offspring of the old English landowners; and in early Braintree there was one family more curiously typical of it than could elsewhere be found in New England: and, indeed, the record of the Quincy family is probably unique even in the larger field of American history. Dwelling at the close of two centuries and a half on the same land which the original ancestor in this country bought of the Indian sachem who ruled over the Massachusetts Fields when Standish first landed at Squantum, the Quincys have in every generation maintained the same high public level. Never perhaps rising to the topmost prominence, either official or intellectual, the family record has yet in both respects been exceptionally uniform and sustained. That record is part of the history of the town which took its name from one scion of the stock.

As their name implies, the Quincys were of Norman blood. The probability is that an ancestor came over with William the Conqueror and fought at Hastings;

and a century and a half later the signature of a "Saer de Quincy" was affixed to the great charter of King John. When in the early years of the seventeenth century the Puritan movement spread through England, Edmund Quincy and his wife, Judith, were living on an estate which the husband had inherited from his father, another Edmund Quincy, at Achurch, near Wigsthorpe, in Northamptonshire. Edmund Quincy, the son, was a Puritan; and when another Edmund was born in 1627, the local record shows that the child was "baptized elsewhere and not in our Parish Church." In 1633, being then in his thirty-second year, Edmund Quincy came to New England, a companion of John Cotton, landing in Boston on the 4th of September. He was almost immediately made a freeman, and afterwards his name is not infrequently met in the records of Boston. He died in 1637, shortly after the allotment " at the Mount " had been made to him. He and Governor William Coddington were of nearly the same age, and the grant of land to the two lay undivided for two years after Quincy's death. It may, therefore, be surmised that they were personal friends, and not impossibly it was Edmund Quincy's premature death which alone, in the Antinomian frenzy, prevented his sharing Coddington's troubles, and perhaps his exile. Though this Edmund died young, he left his name to a son and the name of his wife to a daughter. A descendant of the latter married into the Sewall family, and in her memory the stormy, western cape of Narragansett Bay was called Point Judith.

The second Edmund Quincy, born in England in 1627, unlike his father, lived to a full old age. He is the "Unckle Quinsey" of Judge Sewall's diary, whose death is recorded on the 8th of January, 1698, as that of "a true New England man, and one of our best Friends." It was the dead of winter. His funeral took place four days later, — there having been frost "one and near two feet thick" encountered in digging his grave, — and he was "decently buried — three foot companies and one troop at his funeral." The pall-bearers "had Scarves," and Judge Sewall drove out from Boston to be present, picking up Madam Dudley on the way, who "seem'd to be glad of the Invitation and were mutually refreshed by our Company." It was this Edmund Quincy who built at Braintree the old colonial house still standing,[1] and between the years 1670 and 1692 he repeatedly represented the town in the General Court. A magistrate and the lieutenant-colonel of the Suffolk regiment, he reproduced the type of the English country gentleman in New England; and just as the former had gone up to the Long Parliament ripe for rebellion against Charles I., and half a century later had joined William of Orange in the overthrow of James II., so Edmund Quincy, when Andros was "bound in chains and cords, and put in a more secure place," became naturally one of that Committee of Safety which carried on the government of the province until the charter of William and Mary was granted.

This Edmund Quincy left two sons, — Daniel, the child of his first wife, Joanna Hoar, sister of the president of the college, and Edmund, whose mother, Elizabeth Gookin, was the widow of John Eliot, Jr. Daniel Quincy was the father of that John Quincy, of Mount Wollaston, in whose honor the town of Quincy subsequently received its name. Of him it will be

[1] *Supra*, 680.

proper, therefore, presently to speak at length. Edmund, his younger half-brother, inherited the father's house and farm, and married Dorothy Flynt, already referred to as the common origin of that remarkable progeny, in which statesmen, jurists, lawyers, orators, poets, story-tellers and philosophers seem to vie with each other in recognized eminence. More distinguished than either his father or grandfather, the third Edmund Quincy passed nearly his whole life in the public service. Graduating in 1699, in 1713–14 he represented Braintree in the General Court, and became afterwards a member of the provincial Council. Colonel of the Suffolk regiment, he was in 1718 made one of the judges of the Superior Court, and in 1737, at the age of fifty-six, he was selected as the agent of the province to represent it before the English government in the matter of the disputed New Hampshire boundary. Reaching London in December, in the following February he was a victim of prevention, for he died from inoculated small-pox. He was buried in the graveyard which holds the dust of Bunyan; and the General Court of Massachusetts caused a monument to be there erected to him as lasting evidence that he was "the delight of his own people, but of none more than of the Senate, who, as a testimony of their love and gratitude, have ordered this epitaph to be inscribed."

Judge Edmund Quincy had two sons, Edmund and Josiah. A portion of the land at Braintree came into the possession of Josiah, and it was he who perpetuated the family, though the old mansion passed into other hands. A Boston merchant in his earlier life, this the first Josiah, so named after his grandfather, Parson Josiah Flynt of Dorchester, suddenly acquired what was for those days a handsome competence through the happy audacity of the captain of a vessel belonging to the firm of which Quincy was a member. One of his descendants has given a lively account [1] of this "rather singular adventure," as he terms it, as a result of which, during King George's war, a large Spanish ship, a part of the cargo of which was one hundred and sixty-one chests of silver and two of gold, was frightened by mere bravado into surrendering to a Yankee merchantman armed with fourteen iron guns and six of wood. The Spanish captain mistook his adversary for an English sloop-of-war, nor did he discover his mistake until too late.

Wisely retiring from business in consequence of this happy chance, the first Josiah Quincy passed his later years at Braintree, dwelling for a time in a house which stood on the "Hancock lot." This house was burned in May, 1759. In it John Adams, when a man of twenty-three, was wont to spend many evenings, and it was by mere chance he did not marry one of its daughters.[2] The methods of passing the time there may have partaken of the somewhat rude New England sociability of the period, or the young lawyer may have been suffering from a passing attack of spleen; but, after coming away from Colonel Quincy's on one occasion, he wrote: — "Playing cards the whole evening. This is the wise and salutary amusement the young gentlemen take every evening in this town. Playing cards, drinking punch and wine, smoking tobacco, and swearing. . . . I know not how any young fellow can study in this town."

In his turn Josiah Quincy was colonel of the Suf-

---

[1] Edmund Quincy, *Life of Josiah Quincy*, 3.
[2] John Adams, *Works*, ii. 70.

folk regiment, and he was also through many years a warm personal friend and correspondent of Dr. Franklin. A man of active, inquiring mind, his only experience in public life was in 1755, the year of Braddock's defeat, when he served as a commissioner of the province in arranging joint military operations with the sister province of Pennsylvania. He left three sons, the youngest of whom, named after himself and known in history as Josiah Quincy, Jr., rose rapidly to distinction; and, had he not died at the early age of thirty-one, could hardly have failed to be one of the prominent political characters of the Revolution. With John Adams he defended Captain Preston after the so-called "Boston Massacre;" and, in 1774, when scarcely thirty years of age, he was the confidential agent in London of the patriot party. Dying on shipboard, almost within sight of his native New England coast, Josiah Quincy, Jr., left behind him an infant son, whose long and honorable life, beginning before the Revolution, lasted far into the War of the Rebellion.

Recurring to the other seventeenth-century branch of the family, Daniel Quincy, the elder son of the second Edmund, was, on the maternal side, a grandson of Joanna Hoar, the widow of Charles Hoar, who was, during the reigns of the earlier Stuarts, for a time sheriff of the city of Gloucester, in England. About 1640, after the death of her husband, Joanna Hoar came to Massachusetts with her five children, and died in Braintree in December, 1661; where she sleeps in the old burying ground in a common grave with her son, the third president of Harvard College, and Bridget, the widow of that son and daughter of John Lisle by his wife, known in English history as the Lady Alice Lisle;[1] whose tragic fate, made familiar through the page of Macaulay, furnishes one of the historic incidents deemed worthy to be immortalized by the artist's hand on the walls of the entrance to the chambers of Parliament. The threads of human destiny are apt to interlace in a way calculated to excite surprise; and it is interesting in the old burying ground of a New England town thus suddenly to come upon an inscription which tells him who stops to decipher it that the daughter of her whom Jeffreys caused to be put to death for succoring the fugitives from Sedgmuir, there lies buried.

But Joanna Hoar may well herself be remembered as the common origin of an offspring at once numerous and notable; for, besides the family bearing her own name, than which none has developed more strikingly or through longer periods the sterling characteristics and some of the peculiarities of New England manhood, — besides this family, honorably perpetuating her own and her husband's name, from her through one daughter, who married Henry Flint, is descended the remarkable progeny already referred to; while from another daughter, herself bearing the mother's name, came the elder branch of the Quincys, issuing in Abigail Adams, and her son, John Quincy. Among Joanna Hoar's other descendants are numbered, also, the family of Evarts, and the Baldwins and Terrys of Connecticut, including among their members the brilliant advocate who defended Andrew Johnson and the brave soldier whose name is associated with the gallant storming of Fort Fisher. Indeed, it may fairly be questioned whether in the whole wide field of American genealogy there is any strain of blood more

---

[1] VI. *Mass. Hist. Soc. Coll.* v. 104, n.

fruitful of distinguished men than that which issued from the widow of the seventeenth century sheriff of Gloucester, who himself never crossed the Atlantic.

Daniel Quincy, the eldest of the two sons of the second Edmund, was the grandson of Sheriff Hoar through his daughter, who also bore her mother's name, Joanna. In due time, Daniel Quincy married Anna Shepard, the granddaughter of the Rev. Thomas Shepard, of Cambridge. The marriage ceremony took place on the 9th of November, 1682, and the following account of what then occurred is found in the pages of Sewall: —

"Cousin Daniel Quinsey Marries Mrs. Anna Shepard Before John Hull, esq. Sam'l Nowell, esq. and many Persons present, almost Captain Brattle's great Hall full; Captain B. and Mrs. Brattle there for two. Mr. Willard began with prayer. Mr. Thomas Shepard concluded; as he was Praying, Cousin Savage, Mother Hull, wife and self came in. A good space after, when had eaten Cake and drunk Wine and Beer plentifully, we were called into the Hall again to Sing. In Singing Time Mrs. Brattle goes out, being ill; Most of the Company goe away, thinking it a qualm or some Fit; But she grows worse, speaks not a word, and so dyes away in her chair, I holding her feet (for she had slipt down). At length out of the Kitching we carry the chair, and Her in it, into the Wedding Hall; and after a while lay the Corps of the dead Aunt in the Bride-Bed: So that now the strangeness and horror of the thing filled the (just now) joyous House with Ejulation: The Bridegroom and Bride lye at Mr. Airs, son-in-law to the deceased, going away like Persons put to flight in Battel."

There were two children born of this marriage, a daughter, Ann, in 1685, and a son, John, in 1689. The year following the birth of the son, Daniel Quincy died. He seems always to have lived in Boston, where he followed the trade of goldsmith, the banker of those days, and in Boston John Quincy was born; but circumstances seemed to draw the Quincys towards Braintree. When William Coddington left Massachusetts he gradually disposed of his property there, and in 1639 the greater part of his allotment at Mount Wollaston was purchased by William Tyng, a Boston merchant. Thomas Shepard married a daughter of this William Tyng, and the farm at Mount Wollaston, in 1661, passed by inheritance into Mrs. Shepard's hands. In 1677, five years before Anna Shepard married Daniel Quincy, her father, Thomas Shepard, died, but her mother, William Tyng's daughter and the owner of Mount Wollaston, lived until August, 1709. Mrs. Daniel Quincy, it has already been seen, married the Rev. Moses Fiske in 1701, and died in July, 1708; accordingly Mrs. Shepard, surviving her daughter, left the farm at Mount Wollaston in 1709 to her grandson, John Quincy, who had graduated from Harvard College one year before.

Coming into possession of the property at this early age, John Quincy, in 1715, married Elizabeth Norton, daughter of the Rev. John Norton, third pastor of the Hingham church, and on Tuesday, October 4th, of that year, Judge Sewall records that he gave him a "Psalm-book covered with Turky-Leather for his Mistress." At about this time, being already major of the Suffolk regiment, John Quincy built his house at Mount Wollaston, and went there to live. Two years later, in 1717, he was first sent to represent Braintree in the General Court, and he continued to represent it at intervals through forty years. From 1719 to 1741 his service was consecutive, and from

1729 to 1739 he was Speaker of the House. Paul Dudley was then chosen to the place, but Governor Shirley negatived him, and John Quincy was rechosen. In 1742 he became a member of the Council, and again in 1746, continuing in it until 1754, after which he again became a delegate for three years. He was now sixty-eight years old, and seems to have retired from active life to pass the remainder of his days at Mount Wollaston. We there get a glimpse of him through the memoranda of John Adams, who, on Christmas-day, 1765, says he " drank tea at grandfather Quincy's. The old gentleman inquisitive about the hearing before the Governor and Council; about the Governor's and Secretary's looks and behavior, and about the final determination of the Board. The old lady as merry and chatty as ever, with her stories out of the newspapers." The hearing here referred to which excited the old councillor's interest was that before Governor Bernard on the memorial of the town of Boston, at the time of the Stamp Act riots, that the courts of law should be opened.

For a number of years John Quincy was colonel of the Suffolk regiment, but in 1742 he lost that position through the intrigues of Joseph Gooch. John Adams has left a lively description of this affair, in which at the time he felt a boy's keen interest; for his own father was in the regiment, and was offered a captain's commission by Gooch, — an offer which " he spurned with disdain; would serve in the militia under no colonel but Quincy." Early appointed a magistrate, for years and years the name of John Quincy — or Col. John Quincy, Esq., as the form of those days went — appears in the Braintree records as moderator of every town-meeting. In the parish also he was the leading man. After the usage of the period, he was noted for "a strict observance of the Lord's day, and a constant attendance upon the public ordinances of religion." John Adams describes him "as a man of letters, taste, and sense," as well as "an experienced and venerated statesman;" but it is a curious fact of one so prominent that not a letter or paper of his, or even a book known to have belonged to him, now remains in the possession of his descendants.

Among those of his own day John Quincy "was as much esteemed and respected as any man in the province." Enjoying what was then looked upon as an ample fortune, "he devoted his time, his faculties, and his influence to the service of his country," studiously avoiding "an ensnaring dependency on any man, and whatever should tend to lay him under any disadvantage in the discharge of his duty." He filled almost every public office to which a native-born New Englander could in the colonial days aspire. Colonel in the militia, Speaker of the House, member of the Council, he also negotiated Indian treaties, and in 1727 the remnant of the Punkapog tribe, abused and defrauded, petitioned that he might be appointed their guardian. For nearly twenty years he held this trust, then resigning it "by reason of his distance" from his wards. Finally, in all positions he approved himself "a true friend to the interest and prosperity of the province; a zealous advocate for and vigorous defender of its liberties and privileges."

This detailed sketch of John Quincy is a necessary feature in the history of a typical Massachusetts town of the colonial period; for John Quincy was a typical man of that period. He represented, perhaps more completely than any other member even of the remarkable family to which he belonged, a political and social element in New England life which has since disappeared. He belonged to the class which in England produced John Hampden, — the educated country gentlemen, the owners of the broad acres on which they dwelt. Following no profession, but going up to Parliament year after year, they were the loyal, ingrained representatives of the communities of which they were a part. Of these men Washington was a Virginia offshoot. He represented them in their highest phase of development under Southern surroundings, — plain, true, straightforward, self-respecting, gifted with that perfectly balanced common-sense which in its way is one sort of genius. Favorable circumstances, always availed of, brought Washington to the front, and have made of him an American immortality. Yet in America at that time, as in the Stoke-Pogis churchyard, there were doubtless many men who contained within themselves the possibilities of a Hampden, a Milton or a Cromwell. That John Quincy contained those elements cannot be asserted, for of him nothing now remains except a name and a few dates. His grave, even, is not marked, nor its place known; but, none the less, throughout a long life lived in the land he was a good specimen of the sturdy, common-sensed, high-toned class of English gentlemen in the shape New England reproduced them in colonial days. What under other circumstances he might have proved, it would be idle to surmise. Born and dying a colonist in a small provincial community thickly crusted over with theology, and in freedom of thought and fancy hardly more than childish, he and those of his time had scant room for development. The stage was small, and its atmosphere was icy.

In one respect, however, John Quincy was singularly fortunate. Though scarcely a line of his writing remains, though his public services are forgotten, though his grave is unknown and his only son died childless, yet his name survives. When, in 1792, the original town of Braintree was subdivided, the Rev. Anthony Wibird " was requested to give a name to the place. He refusing to do so, a similar request was made to the Hon. Richard Cranch, who recommended its being called Quincy, in honor of Col. John Quincy." [1] Nor was this the only form in which the name was perpetuated. Colonel Quincy had two children, a son named Norton in honor of his mother's family, and a daughter, who became in time the wife of William Smith, of Weymouth. Among the children of this couple was one who, in October, 1764, married John Adams. In July, 1767, as old John Quincy lay dying at Mount Wollaston, this granddaughter of his gave birth to a son; and when, the next day, as was then the practice, the child was baptized, its grandmother, who was present at its birth, requested that it might be called after her father. Long afterwards the child thus named wrote of this incident: — " It was filial tenderness that gave the name. It was the name of one passing from earth to immortality. These have been among the strongest links of my attachment to the name of Quincy, and have been to me through life a perpetual admonition to do nothing unworthy of it."

In the year 1791, Miss Hannah Adams, the historian, in writing to John Adams, made reference to the " humble obscurity " of their common origin. Her correspondent, in reply, while acknowledging the kin-

[1] Whitney, *Hist. of Quincy*, 27.

ship, went on energetically to remark that, could he "ever suppose that family pride were any way excusable, [he] should think a descent from a line of virtuous, independent New England farmers for a hundred and sixty years was a better foundation for it than a descent through royal or noble scoundrels ever since the flood." The "virtuous, independent New England farmers" thus alluded to were not less important as a social and political element in colonial days than the gentry. They represented the free yeomanry of England under the new conditions, just as the gentry represented the landholders; with the distinction, already noticed, that the New England farmer, as a rule, did not pay rent. He was the owner of the land on which he lived and a freeholder, — the equal of any one. This holding of the fee it was which gave him his individuality. He ceased to be the cultivator of another's ground and himself had a stake in the country. Accordingly, he became an influence second to none other in the shaping of New England development. His influence, too, was immensely conservative. Not quick of thought, he was the reverse of receptive of new ideas; and, when money entered into the question, he was mean. Accustomed in his struggle for subsistence to extort everything he got from a niggard soil, he watched public expenditure with a cold, saving eye, and in town-meeting could be safely counted upon to raise his voice against anything which was likely to impose a burden on his acres. Subsequent history showed this clearly. Questions of taxation appealed to him at once, and a freedom from all imposts not voted by himself most nearly embodied his idea of independence. In the sphere of his narrow village life, far removed from great cities, he saw round about him but two classes of men to whom he in any way looked up, — the clergy and the gentry, the minister and the magistrate. So far as means and mode of life were concerned, those composing these classes were not very different from himself; they, as well as he, led simple lives. All mingled in the streets, at church and in town-meeting, with an equality which was not the less mutually respectful because it was real. In the gentry and clergy, therefore, the farmer saw nothing to which he might not aspire for his own child. There was no privileged class; no suggestion of caste, or rank, or nobility. If the small farmer chose by dint of severe economy to send his son to college, that son would be a minister or a lawyer, and might marry into the gentry. Accordingly, the farmer was very apt to send one son at least to college.

As Edmund and John Quincy were in Braintree typical of the gentry, so Deacons Samuel Bass and John Adams were typical of the farmer class. Through the whole colonial period the deacon was held in high respect; on the Sabbath he sat on his own bench before the pulpit, and on the week-day he and the magistrate and the officers of the militia were the titled men of the village. Speaking of a kinsman of his, Oxenbridge Thacher used to say, — "Old Col. Thacher, of Barnstable, was an excellent man; he was a very holy man; I used to love to hear him pray; he was a counselor and a deacon. I have heard him say that of all his titles, that of a deacon he thought the most honorable." Braintree's first deacon, Samuel Bass, has already been referred to as the progenitor of a numerous offspring, for at the time of his death he had seen one hundred and sixty-two descendants. Born in

1601, he came over to New England in 1632, and first settled at Roxbury; from whence, in 1640, he removed to Braintree, there purchasing lands which for over two centuries remained in the hands of his descendants. He was received into the communion of the church in July, 1640, and chosen deacon, which office he held until his death, in 1694. A small two-handled cup of plain silver in the communion service of the First Church yet bears his name and title inscribed upon it as one of its givers. Active also in civil life, Deacon Bass represented the town in no less than twelve General Courts between 1641 and 1664. In 1645 he was on the committee to see that the town-marsh should "be improved to the Elders' use," and for several years he was one of three, empowered by the court to "end small cases in Braintree under twenty shillings." In 1653 he received fifteen votes out of a total of forty-one for the position of ruling elder in the church, and two years later he was one of the commission appointed by the General Court to build a cart-bridge over the Neponset. Thus —

> "His virtues walk'd their narrow round,
> Nor made a pause, nor left a void;
> And sure the eternal Master found
> His single talent well employ'd."

In 1657 a son of Deacon Bass, John by name, married Ruth Alden, the daughter of John and Priscilla Alden, of Plymouth and Mayflower fame. By her he had a daughter, Hannah, born in June, 1667. This Hannah Bass presently married Joseph Adams, of Braintree, and on the 8th of February, 1692, she gave birth to John Adams, afterwards in his turn deacon of the North Precinct church. This John Adams, therefore, was the great-grandson of the original Deacon Bass, and one of the hundred and sixty-two descendants born to him before his death. John Adams was in his turn a typical New England yeoman. He lived on his farm, through which ran the main street of the town, dying in 1761, "beloved, esteemed, and revered by all who knew him," having had seven children, the eldest of whom, also named John, he had sent to college. The life of the elder John Adams well illustrates what has been called [1] " the sturdy, unostentatious demeanor of those who filled the minor places of usefulness" in early New England. For nearly forty years his name regularly appears in the records of the town. He passed through all its grades of office; for in 1722, he being then by occupation a "cordwainer," or maker of shoes, was chosen "sealer of leather." In 1724 he was tithingman, and in 1727 constable, or collector of taxes; in 1734 he was an ensign in the militia, and also selectman; and a little later, having become lieutenant, he volunteered to take care of the town powder, providing a chest for it in his own house, which he thus converted into a magazine. Between 1740 and 1749, being still Lieutenant Adams, he was nine times selectman. It was in one of the earlier of these years that his military life came to an end as the result of Joseph Gooch's intrigues to supersede Col. John Quincy. Loyal to his commanding officer, Lieut. John Adams, it will be remembered, refused "with disdain" the offer of a captaincy from Gooch. But in May, 1747, he had taken his place among the deacons on the bench before the pulpit, and in 1752 he reappears in the records among the selectmen as Deacon John Adams, and is chosen through four successive

---

[1] Hobart, *Centennial* (1876) *Oration at Braintree*, 22.

years, and again in 1758; fourteen years in all, did he fill the office, "almost all the business of the town being managed by him." He was now in his sixty-seventh year, and his name is found but once more in the records, and then only in connection with a way through his land. He died in a season of epidemic three years later. Long after, in referring to him, his son wrote that he could not adequately express the exalted opinions he had " of his wisdom and virtue," and that he was "a man of strict piety and great integrity; much esteemed and beloved wherever he was known, which was not far, his sphere of life being not extensive." Still later his grandson, then President of the United States, while philosophizing in his diary over the difference of fortune in life between those of his kindred educated at Harvard College and those not enjoying that advantage, wrote as follows of the generation of his family to which the first John Adams belonged: — " If my grandfather himself had received the same education, he would have been distinguished either as a clergyman or as a lawyer.

"'But Knowledge to his eyes her ample page,
Rich with the spoils of time, did ne'er unroll.'

And the summit of his political distinction was the office of a selectman of Braintree." [1]

If the Quincys — Judges and Colonels — furnish perfect types of the colonial gentry, as Deacon Bass and Lieutenant John Adams do of the colonial yeomanry, so an equally perfect type of the colonial skilled workman and non-commissioned officer is furnished in John Marshall, sometime treasurer of the North Precinct in Braintree, whose diary memoranda have already been referred to. Born in Boston in 1664,

[1] J. Q. Adams, *Memoirs*, vii. 143.

Marshall passed the greater portion of his working life in Braintree. His regular trade seems to have been that of mason; but, when work in that line was dull, he made a living by turning his hand to almost any occupation, seeking a job wherever it could be found. So, without apparently owning any land, he at times farmed on a small scale, made laths in winter, painted houses, did carpenter work, burned brick, bought and sold live-stock, and acted as a messenger. He was also a non-commissioned officer in the Braintree company of the Suffolk regiment, and an active member of the church, being for a time precinct treasurer ; his name appears frequently in the town records, usually as constable, but sometimes as tithingman or surveyor of highways. John Marshall died in October, 1732, having been during his sixty-eight years of life " much esteemed" in his station, and, as the record sometimes expressed it, " Improved in the Town in many Offices of publick Trust."

Some of Marshall's diary jottings have now become curious as affording glimpses of the daily life and modes of thought of a laboring man in the New England of two centuries ago. He lived on what he could earn, and his usual wages as a mason were four shillings, or sixty-seven cents, a day, about the equivalent of $3.50 a day now. He found his more regular employment in Braintree, but sought odd jobs in Boston and on Castle Island, as well as in Hingham, Weymouth, Milton, Dorchester and elsewhere. He was very religious, and his diary contains entries like the following : —

" This is written October 1st in the evening, and to-morrow is my birthday. I am now forty years old, and cannot but be ashamed to look back and consider how I have spent my lost time; being at a great losse whether any true grace be wrought in my soul or no: corruption in me is very powerful; grace (if any) is very weak and languid. I have reason to pray as the spous, awake o north wind, and come thou south wind and blow upon my garden, to stir up myself to take hold of God, to engage my cry to the Lord and my whole man in his service, which the Lord enable me to doe."

He notes how he made laths, — six hundred in two days, — "watched with Mr. Quinsey," — dug and bricked Mr. Quincy's grave, — "went to Boston to lecture," and "mended Doctor Hoar's monument." Early in 1690 Marshall seems to have been clerk and accounting officer of the Braintree company, and he wrote, " it was then ordered by the malitia that a military watch be kept in this towne of half a company a night. Our company watched the 6 and 7 of Aprill. In the two nights we spent in drink 6s. 4d., in candles 8d., one shilling taken between father and self." In 1699, the Earl of Bellomont reached New England, the newly appointed Governor of the Province, and Marshall went to Boston, apparently with his company, to take part in the reception, for which great preparations were made: —

"Ther was I think twenty companys of souldiers, of which three were troops, and such a vast concourse of people as my poor eys never saw the like before: the life-guard went to Roadisland to wait on him: two troops went to Dedham to meet him their: and when he came to Boston we made a guard, from the end of the town to the South meeting house. The life guard rode foremost then came some oficers: next his Lordship and Countess: then the troops and other gentlemen: the drums beat, the trumpets did sound, the Coullors weer displayed: the Cannons and ordinance from the ships and fortifications did roar : all manner of expressions of Joy : and to end all Fireworks and good drink at night."

Marshall then notes his contributions to the support of the church, — three shillings in 1700, five shillings and fourpence in 1702, three shillings and eight pence in 1703; — he mentions the death of the Rev. Mr. Ichabod Wiswall of Duxbury, " a man of eminent accomplishment for the service of the sanctuary," and in December, 1701, reviewing the occurrences of the year, he says : —

" God frowned on the Land by the death of our governor the earle of Bellomont Last March And by the death of the Deputy Gouvernour Stoughton in July Last past, and sundry others of great worth dyed this year as the Rev$^d$. Mr. William Brimsmead, of Marlbourough. Yet among all these sad providences God remembered mercy for his poor people by speriting the remaining of our Councellors to their work. By which the Country was put into a posture of defence against enemyes."

A year later, speaking of an epidemic of small-pox which had then been raging for some time, Marshall wrote : —

" Through the great mercy of God we in Braintree weer in health thus far in this sick and dying time, only a few children weer sick. But at Boston many dyed allthough the feaver was not so bad now as in time past, yet the small pocks was very Bad. So that I may truly call to mind the words of the prophet, the Lords anger is not turned away. But his hand is stretched out still."

On June 13, 1704, " was a muster in Braintree to press men for the Country's survise, among whom I was impressed, for one : " next day he says, " I went to the Governour and got a clearance from the impress." Three years later, in March, 1707, Marshall agrees " to serve in the office of constable for Nath[l] Spear for three pounds money," and then, on the 31st of that month, he writes, —

"At home Gathering stones out of the lott, and so this cool, windy month of March is marched away. And indeed it was right march many weathers : sometime cold : then hot then cold, then wet, then dry : it was a time of genral health."

In June, 1709, another impressment was ordered of soldiers for the Canada expedition, and now Marshall "pressed James Puffer and Jabez," and then observes, — "we had our army in pay all this month; nothing done by them, only eat and drink and run the country in debt." In 1710 he remarks at the close of February, "the month ends well with them that are in health and have store of money." But in the following August he was again impressed and notes, "8–9 weer idle days seeking to hire a man;" and at the close of the month he says, "I was impressed to go forth in her majesties service. My circumstances not allowing me to go out myself, I therefore hired Nathaniel Owen in my room, who was well accepted by Major Taylor, muster-master. And I paid him ten pounds money."

Such was a country mechanic in Massachusetts in the latter part of the seventeenth century and at the beginning of the eighteenth. Such was his life and such his line of thought, leading him to comment on the Rev. Samuel Willard, vice-president of Harvard College, at the time of that eminent divine's death, as "a person of excelent accomplishments natural and acquired: an hard student, a powerful preacher of the word of God, an exemplary christian: a mirror of all that is good." [1]

[1] Lunt, *Two Discourses* (1839), 108–12; *Proc. Mass. Hist. Soc.* Series II. i. 148–62.

## CHAPTER VIII.

### THE VICIOUS, THE POOR AND THE INSANE.

WHILE the individuals whose lives have been sketched represented the gentry, the yeomanry and the artisans of the province, it must not be supposed those classes made up the whole of that community. Such was not the case. They were its distinctive types only. The body of that community, like those of all communities, was composed of laboring people; and, while in Braintree the richest were poor, there is ample evidence that the poorest did not live in abundance. On the contrary, besides the ordinary laborer who simply made his living, there was a curious pauper class, traces of which appear all through the records, living in hovels on the waste land and picking up a living in unknown ways. Those composing this class were not peculiar to Braintree, and it has been pointed out that the denizens of the groups of wretched hovels in places locally known by such names as "Purgatory" and "Hell-huddle," or the like, while in many instances the degenerate offspring of a sound New England stock, yet in other cases "show strong points of resemblance to that 'white trash,' which has come to be a recognizable strain of the English race;" and they have been classed with the "redemptioners," or immigrants, common in the middle colonies, but rare in New England, who voluntarily bound themselves to service for a stated time in order to defray the cost of their passage over from Europe.[1] While this may be generally true, yet, so far as traces of this class are to be met with in the Braintree records, they do not seem to call for much explanation. As an element in the community, it was merely the natural residuum of existing social conditions, — that inevitable, though varying, percentage of the vicious, the shiftless and the weak always to be found in every population, no matter how thrifty and energetic, or moral and temperate; and, while the inhabitants of colonial New England were as a race remarkable for thrift and energy, they were less conspicuous for morality and most decidedly intemperate.

Left to take care of themselves, the law of the survival of the fittest, though then not understood, worked slowly, but in that rugged climate with terrible certainty, on these transient denizens of the waste places. They died out. When Quincy was set off, in 1792, one of the first things the selectmen did was to warn fourteen adults, seven of whom had families, to "depart the limits of the town." Throughout the records of the whole colonial period, down even to the year 1830, the heavy proportion which the expense of maintaining the poor bears to all other public charges is most noticeable. It was far heavier than it now is, and it showed a continual tendency to disproportionate growth. In 1770 for instance, out of a total expenditure of only £245, or $820, no less than £90, or thirty-six per cent. of the whole, was spent in assisting the poor. The outlay on that account very nearly equalled that on account of the schools. A century later, though the amount spent on the care of the poor was considered so large that it excited criticism and

[1] Fiske, *Beginnings of New England*, 142-3.

led to a loud demand for reform, it was but eight per cent. of the total amount assessed and thirty per cent. of that expended on the schools. As compared with the aggregate of town expenses, the amount spent on the care of the poor was therefore, in Braintree, nearly five times as large in 1770 as it was in Quincy in 1870. And yet the charity of those earlier days was cold. Indeed, anything colder could not well be conceived. It acknowledged in the poor and the unfortunate a right to live; and that was all. On this point the record is instructive.

It opens with the town-meeting of December 24, 1694, when the earliest specific appropriation ever recorded in Braintree was made. The first item of it reads : — "Five pounds for John Belcher's widow's maintenance ; thirty shillings to Thomas Revell for keeping William Dimblebee." But the unfortunate Dimblebee had already gone to his rest, and this payment was for service performed, as a little further on seven shillings is appropriated " for Dimblebee's coffin." Before this entry of 1694 there is one other which throws a gleam of ghastly light on a subject which in recent years has been much discussed. It has been somewhat the fashion to assert that for certain reasons, traceable to local peculiarities of life or thought, insanity is in New England on the increase, and the census tables have been confidently appealed to in support of this startling theory. Those advocating it have seemed to forget that social statistics are of recent invention, and that the charitable systems of some communities are more perfect than those of others. To compare the showing as respects insanity of a community which now carefully gathers the demented together and tenderly cares for them in hospitals, with the showing of that same community before its demented were cared for at all, is sufficiently absurd: yet even this is far less absurd than it is to compare the record of such a community with that of some other community which still leaves its insane tied in attics and cellars, or wandering in the streets, or, at best, shut up in a poor-house; and then to argue that the first community, because it cares for the insane and numbers them, is afflicted with an epidemic of insanity from which the last community, because it neither cares for or numbers them, is exempt. It is a mistake to suppose that our age has been fruitful of new social or physical evils. There is a world of truth in Macaulay's remark, when treating of these questions, that the social and physical ills which so shock us now are, with scarcely an exception, old; "that which is new is the intelligence which discerns and the humanity which remedies them."

Here is the first record relating to the treatment of the insane poor of Braintree town, under date of 1689: —

"It was voted that Samuel Speer should build a little house, seven foot long and five foot wide, and set it by his house to secure his sister, good wife Witty being distracted, and provide for her, and the town by vote agreed to see him well payed and satisfied which shall be thought reasonable."

The wretched maniac was chained like a dog in a kennel which stood by her brother's house. Then again, in 1697, the "freeholders orderly convened" voted "five pounds for the healing of Abigail Neal, now underhand," and a committee of two, one of whom was the town treasurer, was appointed "to transport and take care of her." Where the poor creature was carried, or who contracted to "take care of her," nowhere appears, nor, among human affairs now nearly two centuries old, is it of much account; but, in 1700, the record reads again, in language hardly less significant of cold, merciless brutality than that used in the case of "good wife Witty Speer:" —

"Voted, That Mr. John Bayly, of Roxberry, should have five pounds monney for keeping Abigail Neale. Provided he give the Town noe further Trouble about her:" —

But Abigail Neal was not yet, nor in this way, to be got rid of; and the next year Dr. Bayley had to be voted eight pounds more, accompanied again with the condition that he should "take up therewith and give the Town no Farther Trouble." The year following Abigail cost the town thirty-eight shillings, and the year after that twenty shillings; and at last, in 1707, it was bargained with one "Samuel Bullard, of Dedham or Dorchester," that he should take the unfortunate creature and keep her for eighteen pence a week; and if he cured her he should have ten pounds, but, if he failed to cure her, only twenty shillings. The records contain no further trace of Abigail Neal. But at the same time "Ebenezer Owen's destracted daughter" had to be cared for, and the selectmen accordingly in 1699 are instructed to treat with Josiah Owen "and give him Twenty pounds money provided he gives bond under his hand to cleare the Town forever of said girle." Mary Owen was no more to be so disposed of than Abigail Neal, and in 1706 forty shillings a year was voted Josiah Owen for her care.

Such in those days — "good old days" — was the provision made for the insane, — a kennel in which to "secure" them, or eighteen pence a week for care, or twenty pounds provided bond was given "to clear the town forever of said girl." The poor were treated with consideration not much more tender. In 1710 for instance, "John Penniman of Swansey" having apparently obtained in some way a legal settlement in Braintree, it is voted that "Twelve pounds be raised" for him, "provided that the Town be forever cleared of him;" and eighteen months later, Samuel Penniman, in consideration of the "above named Twelve pounds money," binds himself "to find my Brother the above said John Penniman with good and sufficient meat, drink, apparell, washing and Lodging, and with all other things necessary and convenient in sickness and in health during the time and terme of his natural life." John Penniman, therefore, seems, at a not unreasonable public charge, to have been well fixed for the remainder of his existence. But some of the votes have a more human ring, as, in 1729, when William Taunt, " by breaking his legg and being long lame and uncapable of business, he was reduced to low circumstances; and therefore desired of the town the loan of five Pounds for a year," the town voted him the amount "for his relief not to be Repaid."

In old Braintree there was no almshouse, nor any regular system of caring for the poor, until shortly before the division of the town. Paupers were either aided at their own abodes, or the care of them farmed out on the lowest attainable terms, either for the time being, or, as in the case of John Penniman, with the condition that on payment of a lump sum "the Town be forever cleared of him." Occasionally some special provision was made for their housing, as when in 1701 it was voted that "Nathaniel owen should have five pounds allowed him next Town Rate Towards the errecting of a Room for the entertaining and taking care of his Father and mother. Provided the said owen will doe it." [1] At last, in 1786, only six years before Quincy was incorporated as an independent town, and at the close of a century and a half of corporate existence, an almshouse was built in the Middle Precinct as the result of an agitation on the subject which began at least as early as 1740, and in the course of which the adjoining town of Milton had at one time proposed that such a house should be built on common account. This proposition was declined; but twenty years later, the spirit of conservatism was so far overcome that it was voted " a Power be lodged in the Hands of the Overseers of the Poor to hire a House if they see cause." At last the erection of a species of barrack "sixty-eight feet in Length, fourteen feet wide, with two Stacks of Chimneys," was ordered, as a " receptacle for the Poor," and the following year, 1787, it was voted that no relief should be given to any except " to such as are or may be deposited in the Towns Hows Built for that purpose." The appointment of an overseer of the poor having been agitated during thirteen years, Capt. Jonathan Thayer was now chosen to the position, and subsequently allowed £3 12s. for a year's services, or about one dollar a month; certainly not an inordinate salary if measured by nineteenth century standards: nor would there seem to be any occasion for surprise that, when again chosen "overseer of the Towns Poor " in March, 1787, Captain Thayer asked to be excused. He was excused accordingly, and Captain Silas Ward chosen in his place; to whom a year later the sum of £6, or twenty dollars, was voted, " for his

[1] See Bliss, *Colonial Times on Buzzard's Bay*, 96–100, 203–6.

trouble in providing necessarys for the Poor and looking after and taking cair of them the year past, and Up to this day."

Throughout the eighteenth century the providing for the needs of the town poor — entailing as it did the duty of hunting them up at the places where they made their abodes — was one of the most important and irksome duties of the selectmen. It was also a fruitful source of jobbery. John Adams describes how, the moment a selectman was elected, he was importuned for "the privilege of supplying the poor with wood, corn, meat, etc." He then had to visit them, and, if he found they had a legal settlement in another town, return them to it. After the division of the original town in 1792, Quincy adopted the practice of putting the care of its poor up at public auction, to be knocked down to those who would undertake it at the lowest price. In 1813 this price averaged "$1.42 each per week, exclusive of sickness and funeral charges." In 1806, also, it was voted that "the medical care of the poor be let out by the selectmen to the physician who will undertake that charge at the lowest price." Naturally this method of dealing with pauperism put a premium on its increase, and, instead of improving, affairs steadily grew worse; so that, strange as it now seems, during the six years between 1808 and 1813, both inclusive, out of $18,200 levied by taxation to meet necessary town and parish expenses, $6,205, or more than one third of the whole, went to the support of the poor; and in 1816, while $800 was spent on the schools, the poor cost $1,600. Even at that late day, forty years after independence was achieved, the support of the town poor cost more than either church or schools. As will presently be seen, the matter was then vigorously taken hold of, and the abuse reformed. Nevertheless, the evidence all points to the conclusion that, in proportion to the total of all expenses, the cost of maintaining the poor prior to 1820 was several times what it now is in any well-regulated town, and in Quincy it still amounted, as in 1770, to nearly one half of the town expenses, those of the parish being deducted. When, seventy years later, in 1889, the town was incorporated as a city, it was less than one tenth. Carelessness and want of system in extending relief undoubtedly had much to do with this excess; but, making every proper allowance, it is difficult, judging from the facts as recorded in the Braintree records, to avoid the inference that there is proportionally much less extreme poverty in the modern than there was in the colonial New England town. Pauperism has distinctly decreased. This is not generally supposed to have been the case; should it prove to be so, a partial explanation, at least, of the fact will probably be found in the more temperate habits of the people.

In Braintree and Quincy, as in all the other Massachusetts towns, these social problems, of which pauperism was one and the care of the insane another, were, until a comparatively recent date, disposed of in what is commonly known as the plain, practical, businesslike way. Unfortunately the problems were complex; so the plain, practical way of disposing of them proved not to be the right way. Insanity and pauperism could not be permanently hustled out of sight by a town-meeting vote; nor could the charge of the poor and insane be disposed of beyond the current year to those who would take the job at the lowest rate. Though excellent for certain purposes, it had yet to be made plain that the town-meeting was not adapted to every purpose; least of all could it work to results through what is now known as a scientific method. As a means for dealing with complex social problems, government by town-meeting is, therefore, not a success. It can in fact no more deal successfully with these problems than it could make discoveries in chemistry or astronomy. But poverty, intemperance, ignorance and vice are found everywhere; the town government is found only in New England: and it is the object of the present work to deal rather with those institutions which are peculiar to New England than with problems common to all mankind. It is of interest here, therefore, only to show how those problems were dealt with through the machinery of New England town government. That the plain people were not scientists is obvious; but it is equally obvious that, though intensely conservative, and very slow of movement, they did, through their failures and under the pressure of circumstances, grope their way to some results. Those results may not have been great, nor always correct; but, such as they were, they were at least the results of those who worked them out: and, in working them out, these people learned to depend on themselves. This educational work at least was always going on; and it was all-important. In comparison with it the systematic regulation of the poor, or even the proper care of the insane, were things of little moment.

## CHAPTER IX.

### THE MEETING-HOUSE.

WHEN John Adams was minister of the federated States at the English Court, a certain Major Langbourne, of Virginia, one day dined with him, and in the course of their table-talk noticed, rightfully enough, the difference of character between Virginia and New England. John Adams then goes on : —

"I offered to give him a receipt for making a New England in Virginia. He desired it; and I recommended to him town-meetings, training-days, town schools and ministers, giving him a short explanation of each article. The meeting-house and school-house and training-field are the scenes where New England men are formed. . . . The virtues and talents of the people are there formed; their temperance, patience, fortitude, prudence and justice; as well as their sagacity, knowledge, judgment, taste, skill, ingenuity, dexterity and industry."

Mr. Adams spoke from actual observation, for he, and his ancestors before him, had for a century and a half been part of that which he described. Long afterwards he wrote that it was notorious he had himself " been a church-going animal for seventy-six years from the cradle," and his memory went easily back to the time when the oldest men sat on the fore-seats; for, he added, " I shall never forget the rows of venerable heads ranged along those front benches which, as a young fellow, I used to gaze upon." In the study of early New England life and manners, there are few things more noticeable than the difference which existed between church usages and town-meeting usages. An absolute, almost rude political equality prevailed in town-meeting, and was rigidly enforced by custom amounting to a common law. It is not easy to conceive of anything more democratic. On the other hand, by virtue of another common law usage, a degree of deference now almost unknown was on the Sabbath day systematically paid within the walls of the meeting-house, not only to age and official standing, but to social and family distinctions. Harvard College, as its seal still indicates, was founded more especially to insure for Massachusetts a sufficient supply of learned and pious ministers, — it was the seminary of the established church of a Puritan commonwealth. For nearly a century and a half after the college was founded, and until 1773, the names of the undergraduates were arranged in the catalogue, not alphabetically or in recognition of proficiency as students, but according to the social standing of the families of which they were members. The principle that prevailed in seating the meeting-house was thus carried into the college.

When, during the early half of the eighteenth century, John Wesley felt a call to inspire the conventional Church of England with new evangelical life, in so doing he sought always to revert to the primitive customs of those assemblies seventeen hundred years before, in which "Paul the tent maker or Peter the fisherman presided," and two of his cardinal tenets related to the seating of the congregation, — the men and women were to be separated, and no one should claim any pew as his own. During the whole of the first half century of the Braintree church, this primitive custom prevailed with it. There were no pews in the original stone edifice " over the old Bridge," and the congregation sat on benches, the men on one side and the women on the other; so, when in town-meeting the vote was doubted, "the moderator, that it might be clearly decided, Divided the Polls by desiring those who were for it to go into the womens seats, and those that were against it to go into the mens seats." Naturally, with the recognized social distinctions which prevailed in those days, certain places at Sabbath meeting were by a sort of tacit, common consent conceded to particular persons, and by the year 1693 this had developed into a formal assignment of seats. The division of the floor-space into pews naturally followed; but, in the case of the first church of Braintree, this came about slowly and involved almost a history of itself, quaintly illustrative of the period.

The first move towards a regular seating of the congregation was made in 1694, when the town formally authorized the selectmen to " seat the meeting-house." The task necessarily involved many difficult questions of precedence, and evidently the selectmen were not forward in the matter, so nothing seems then to have been done; but in March, 1698, a special committee of five, including the two deacons, was appointed to attend to the neglected business. " They did the work," though, as might naturally be supposed, " not to general satisfaction; " and at last on "the first Sabbath in April people took the places (assigned to them) as many as saw good so to do." Even then, doubtless owing to jealousies excited by the action of the committee, it had the year before been voted " that upon the drawing up or uniting the men's seats with the

## THE PEW INNOVATION. 735

women's in the present alley, any Roome being left after alterations, any person with consent of the Selectmen may at their own proper charges mak pews for themselves and familys." At the same town-meeting it was also voted "that Mr. William Rawson should have priviledge of making a seate for his familie, between or upon the two beams over the pulpit, not darkening the pulpit." What means of access existed to this pen on the rafters nowhere appears; nor, if indeed it was ever constructed, can it now be learned whether it was reached by staircase or ladder : but three years later, in 1700, Mr. Fiske, then the pastor, was voted "liberty to Build a Pew by South East window in the meeting house He leaving convenient passage." Bit by bit the floor space of the common house of worship seems then to have been parcelled out in severalty.

It was, in fact, at first much the same with the meeting-house floor as with the soil ; there was thought to be plenty for all, and possession was not greatly prized until every desirable place, whether for seeing, being seen or to listen, had become the exclusive property of some one. Permits to build pews seem consequently to have been issued almost as a matter of course, and on the most liberal terms. Captain Wilson, for instance, was allowed to construct in whatever convenient place he should elect; and in 1712 Joseph Crosby was actually granted leave to move the east entrance some four feet to the northward, so that he might get for himself satisfactory space. To do this he stoned up the old doorway, tearing down sufficient wall to make a new one. But, so far, the pews were at least confined to the wall space, and the centre of the floor remained free to the great body of churchgoers, who still sat in the " mens seats " or the " womens seats ; " and now these began to grow jealous, and when, in 1725, David Bass sought to be allowed to squeeze in one more pew in a small space still unoccupied near the east window, the vote passed in the negative. The galleries at first were not appropriated, except in so far as, by New England prescriptive right, they belonged to the village youth; but this implied much. In Boston, for instance, as early as 1643, by a formal vote of the selectmen, " Sergeant Johnson and Walter Merry are requested to take the oversight of the boyes in the galleryes;" and strict order was subsequently made for the arrest of " any young person" who might be "found without either meeting-house, idling or playing during the time of publick exercise on the Lords day." So it was also in Braintree: but, as there is no duty without a right, if duty compelled boys to go to church, rights were secured to them in the gallery while in church. In 1720, the whole wall space on the floor of the meeting-house having been appropriated to individual use, John Saunders and Samuel Savil thought to possess themselves of a portion of the gallery; and, in compliance with their request, the precinct voted to them " the Two hindermost short seats in the gallery, in the southwest side of the meeting-house, extending to the Beams, for a Pew for their wives and children." While the church-going duty of the boys remained the same, their prescriptive gallery rights were by this vote distinctly impaired; and consequently the Saunderses and Savils in due time found their pew unmeet for occupancy, the material of which it was constructed having apparently been reduced to rubbish. At a subsequent precinct meeting the matter came up for consideration, and the question was "put by the Moderator, whether [the Saunderses and Savils] would Relinquish their Right to their Pew, which was broken, to the Precinct. They then did both thereupon Resign their Right to the Precinct." The galleries of the old stone meeting-house do not seem again to have been invaded by the pew-builder.

Though in Braintree, as elsewhere in New England, the system just described, under which the floor-space of the common place of worship was parcelled out into boxes like the proscenium of a theatre, grew out of the usage of "seating the meeting-house," yet from the beginning it seems to have been founded on a wholly different principle. Money, and not recognition, whether personal or family, was at the basis of it. The finer and more ennobling principle was then by degrees lost sight of. For instance, it has been seen that the first vote in relation to the matter passed by the Braintree church in 1697 provided that persons might " at their own proper charges " make pews for themselves and families; but when thirty-five years later Mrs. Mary Norton gave to the same church " a Velvet Cushion of Considerable Value," the precinct formally invited her " to tak the upper end of the fore seet for her seet in the new Meeting-House." When the John Hancock meeting-house of 1732 was built, it was decided that it " should be accomidated with Pews as conveniently as may be ; " but the great body of the floor space was still reserved for the "men's seats" and the "women's seats," and on the front benches of the first were ranged those " venerable heads " on which John Adams gazed with eyes of boyish awe; while, at the " upper end of the fore-seat " of the latter, was the place formally and by vote reserved for

"Madm. Norton." The pews, little, irregular square-shaped boxes, were mainly set against the walls, and were disposed of in lots and for money to those who could or would pay most for the better place, the prices varying from seven to twenty-five pounds, or from about $25.00 to $85.00; but it was not until after 1760 that the common public seats disappeared wholly from the body of the floor. From that time forth the control of money superseded age, and recognition of private worth or public service or family consideration, in securing precedence in the house of the Lord; until, at length, in 1800 it is voted that "the vacancy where the old stairway was in the church, be appropriated for the use of the black people to sit in."[1] In establishing such an order of precedence and making this provision for the poor, the lowly and the despised, those composing the church could hardly have had in mind that dread day of judgment, the thought of which was so constantly with them, when, according to the scripture, the King sitting " on the throne of his glory" should thus answer their prayer: — "Verily I say unto you, Inasmuch as ye did it unto one of these my brethren, even these least, ye did it unto me." If the language of holy writ was to be accepted, through formal and recorded parish action the Master had in Quincy been relegated to " the vacancy

[1] "At a Town meeting holden at Hingham, on the fifth day of May, 1684, It is ordered by the Town, that the Negro Servants, men and Boys and also Indians shall sit in the new meeting house in the short seats, between the Door and the Gallery Stairs, at the northward end of the meeting house. And the English Boys under twelve years old to set at the northward end of the meeting house behind the mens seats. And Caleb Beal and John Prince are appointed by the Town to look to the Boys in the time of meetings, and to do their best endeavors to keep them from playing at meeting and to continue in that place till new be chosen."

where the old stairway was." In the primitive church of old, as in John Wesley's chapels, the thing was differently ordered ; and it is somewhat noticeable that equality in the worship of a common Creator has ever been as little observed in democratic New England as in any country classed as civilized ; if, indeed, it has not been there less observed.

The " old stairway " had been in the west corner of the edifice, — the point furthest removed from the pulpit whence the Word was preached, and the vacant space created by its removal was immediately in the rear of the " men's hind seats," in which, some years before, those persons that had " Ben at Pains and expense to Gain Instruction in the use of Psalmody," had by vote been invited to " acomidate " themselves. But the choir itself was then a modern innovation, dating no further back than 1764 ; for, during a whole century and a quarter prior to that time, the original congregational custom had been continued in the Braintree church, under which the psalm was slowly lined out, and then repeated by the congregation after such fashion that, in the words of Cotton Mather, " in length of time their singing (had) degenerated into an odd noise that had more of what we want a name for than any regular singing in it." The North Precinct records show that, in 1723, " Major Quincy was fairly and clearly chosen by written votes to the office of tuning the Psalm ; " while at about the same period his kinsman Judge Sewall filled the similar office at the Old South in Boston, where on one occasion, he wrote, " I intended Windsor and fell into High Dutch ; and then assaying to set another Tune, went into a Key much too high. The Lord humble me and Instruct me that I should be occasion of any Interruption in the Worship of God." There is nothing in the records of the North Precinct of Braintree to indicate that Major Quincy in " tuning the Psalm " was ever the " occasion of any Interruption in the Worship of God," but there is evidence that at the time he performed this service the church of the Middle Precinct, over which the Rev. Samuel Niles then ministered, was torn by dissension through " Disorders occasioned by Regular Singing," so that Judge Sewall having, as one of a church council, attended a " publick hearing of the Matters " in the Middle Precinct meetinghouse at Braintree, was moved when he "got safe home a little after sunset" to write in his diary, — " O Lord restore Peace and Truth and Holiness to that divided Flock."

The difficulty was illustrative of the period. The Rev. Mr. Niles seems to have been an adherent of " singing by rote," while the major part of his flock were in favor of " singing by rule." As they persisted in their practice, regardless of his admonitions, he suspended several, and, at last, himself seceded from his flock, performing on Sunday, December 1, 1723, " the Duties of the Day at his Dwelling House, among those of his Congregation who (were) opposers of Regular Singing. The Regular Singers met together at the Meeting House, and sent for Mr. Niles, who refused to come unless they would first promise not to sing Regularly ; whereupon they concluded to edify themselves by the Assistance of one of the Deacons, who at their Desire prayed with them, read a sermon, &c." It was not until the following April that this breach was healed. The church council then met again, and an accommodation was proposed, which was so far effective that the suspended brethren made some general acknowledgment, and were restored. And now Judge Sewall wrote in his diary:—"O Lord Pardon the Sin, and heal the Distemper whereby the minds of that people are alienated from each other."

But, returning from these experiences of the Middle Precinct of Braintree to those of its North Precinct, in 1761 the church voted "to sing Dr. Watts hymns and spiritual songs on Sacramental occasions," and three years later the choir came into recognized existence: but not until 1804 was it voted "to procure a bass viol for the use of the congregation;" while about the year 1812 we are told "the voices of the choir in the front gallery were assisted by a discordant assemblage of stringed and wind instruments," most prominent among which were "Hezekiah Bass with his large bass-viol, John Pray with his fiddle (and) Captain Josiah Bass with his noble voice to lead the singing."

During the early years of the century Quincy was still a retired village, in which few changes had taken place since the Revolution; and the young wife of Josiah Quincy, third of the name and subsequently President of Harvard College, used afterwards to describe the meeting-house of that period as an ancient wooden edifice, the pews in the centre of which, "having been made out of long open seats by successive votes of the town, were of different sizes, and had no regularity of arrangement, and several were entered by narrow passages, winding between those of the neighborhood. The seats, being provided with hinges, were raised when the congregation stood during the prayer, and at its conclusion thrown down with a momentum which, on her first attendance, alarmed Mrs. Quincy, who feared the church was falling.

The deacons were ranged under the pulpit, and beside its door the sexton was seated, while, from an aperture aloft in the wall, the bell-ringer looked in from the tower to mark the arrival of the clergyman."[1]

But the colonial period was then fast drawing to its close. New England's individuality was passing away; and, in the meeting-house, the gradual introduction of the pew, the choir and the stove had step by step marked the change. How great that change had been can be inferred from a few scattered entries in the ancient records of church and town, indicating a condition of affairs, which, in view of the inclemency of the New England climate, is now not easy to understand. The meeting-house would for a long period have seemed to be not only out of repair, but, both Sundays and week-days, actually open both to animals and the elements. For instance, in 1695 a committee was appointed " to stop the leaks in the south side of the meeting-house; " and in 1730 the precinct clerk, Joseph Parmenter, was allowed twenty shillings — a large sum at that time, and equivalent to pay for the labor of one man during ten days — for his services as clerk, and for " clearing the meeting-house of snow the year past, there having been cart-loads of snow blown in by a terrible storm."

Nor, in the New England mind, did any religious sentiment or idea of consecration attach to the church edifice. That the meeting-house and its furniture, such as it was, underwent hard treatment from numerous secular and political gatherings, scarcely needs to be said. In Braintree not only were those gatherings frequent, but the deliberations and debates which took place at them were sometimes long and exciting, while

[1] *Memoir of Mrs. Quincy*, 92.

among those assembled there was not a little disorder and drunkenness. The Middle Precinct meeting-house stood directly opposite the Eben Thayer tavern, where a sort of open house was kept on all election and other public days, and in 1766 John Adams records that a certain candidate on the ticket with himself was defeated because "the north end people, his friends, after putting in their votes the first time, withdrew for refreshment." Accordingly, it is small matter of surprise that the record contains formal votes to the effect that " it shall be considered as a disorder and treated as such for any person who shall get on the Seats with their Feet in any part of the meeting House." Indeed, the Middle Precinct meeting-house seems to have served for a time not only as a town-hall, but apparently also as a magazine; for in 1746 the selectmen were instructed by a formal vote to build a " Closite on the Beams of the Middle Precinct meeting-house (if it be allowed of) as a suitable place to keep the powder." Nor was this use of the church edifice peculiar to Quincy. On the contrary, only six years after the above vote was passed, on the 23d of April, 1752, the meeting-house of the neighboring town of Weymouth, in which Parson Smith, the future father-in-law of John Adams, then ministered, by some chance caught fire. Three barrels of the town powder were at the time stored for safe and convenient keeping in the loft of the building ; and these at the proper moment brought the conflagration to a crisis, making, as the minister of the church at the time duly recorded, " a surprising noise when it blew up."

It has been asserted that in the earlier days it was the custom in some communities for each family to bring its dog to church on days of great cold and to make use of it as a foot-warmer;[1] whether this was so or not, at a Braintree North Precinct meeting held in December, 1729, those assembled "having Debated upon the Disturbance made by Dogs in the meeting-house on Sabbath Days, to Prevent the same, they then voted that Joseph Parmenter should have twenty shillings, provided he would take care and pains in that matter, by beating and keeping of them out, until the Precinct meet next March." This provision, it will be noticed, was made for the winter months, and it was in strict accordance with a vote of the whole town passed in April fifteen years before, instructing the selectmen to " draw up a by-law for the prevention of Dogs coming into the Meeting-houses, in the time of Publick worship." But, from the other provisions of this vote, directing that a " meet " penalty should be imposed " on the owners thereof," it would seem probable that the "dogs," following the vehicles of their owners to the meeting-house, found their way into it among the entering members of the congregation; and coming in contact with each other as they smelt their way down the benches, an occasional dog-fight would, as a natural consequence, lead, in the language of Judge Sewall, to an " Interruption in the Worship of God;" an interruption doubtless of deep and abiding interest to the nascent manhood of the gallery, but the reverse of edifying to those spiritually minded.[2]

[1] Earle, *The Sabbath in Puritan New England*, 95, 242.
[2] In the Johns Hopkins University Studies (I. iv.) there is a curious and interesting paper by Herbert B. Adams on Saxon Tithing Men in America. In the course of it Mr. Adams says, — " But more usually one tithingman sat at each door of the meeting-house to keep out dogs, and one often sat in the gallery to keep in boys; " and he adds in a note, — "'The 'Dog Whipper' was a regular institution in certain old English towns, notably in Exeter and Congleton (in Chester). Mr.

## DOGS AT CHURCH.

In other and more conventional matters pertaining to church-going, the people of Braintree differed, probably, in nowise from the people of other New England country towns; and of New England church-going sufficient has been written and said. For gen-

Edward A. Freeman has called our attention to a curious law of Edgar (see Thorpe's *Ancient Laws and Institutes of England*, ii. 251), whereby parish priests were to see to it that no dog should enter church, nor yet more a swine, if it could possibly be prevented!"

In his *Colonial Times on Buzzard's Bay*, Mr. Bliss enumerates "the appointment of dog-whippers to beat out dogs in meeting time" among the New England town customs which "were an inheritance from the parishes of Old England" (p. 103). And Mr. Richard Grant White in his edition of *Shakespeare* (vii. 426) quotes the following from Greene's *A Looking Glass for London and England*: — "A gentleman! good sir, I remember you well, and all your progenitors; your father bore office in our town; an honest man he was, and in great discredit in the parish, for they bestowed two squires' livings on him, the one was on working days, and then he kept the town cage, and on holidays they made him the sexton's man, for he whipped dogs out of the church." In his story of *Woodstock*, Sir Walter Scott, also, describes Sir Henry Lee of Ditchley as being always accompanied to church by his deerhound, Bevis, who, "bating an occasional temptation to warble along with the accord, behaved himself as decorously as any of the congregation."

In the Dedham (Mass.) town records is the following entry under date of "12-11-1673:" — "Agreed with Nat Heaton to whip doges out of the Meeting House, and to goe upon errands for the reverend elders, referring to the church: and to take care of cushin and glass, till further order be taken and for his paynes herein he is to receive of the Towne ten shillings for an whole year."

In Charlestown, Thomas Brigden, senior, was employed in 1666, at a yearly compensation of four pounds, "to look unto the Meeting House and clear it, to ring the bell to meetings, and to keep out doggs in meeting time." Frothingham, *Hist. of Charlestown*, 157.

Paige in his *History of Cambridge* (p. 130) says: — "On the 12th of May, 1729, it was, 'Voted, that so often as any dog or dogs is or are seen in the meeting-house on the Lord's day in the time of public worship, the owner or owners of the said dog or dogs shall for every such offence pay one shilling, half to go to the officer appointed to regulate said dogs, the other half part of said fine to be for the use of the poor of the town.'"

erations all those dwelling in Braintree, of both sexes and of every age, — on foot, in carriage, wagon or chair, or on horseback, — as regularly as the Sabbath dawned, gathered towards the plain, wooden structure standing on the training-ground. While the services were conducted within, the horses stood patiently without in the neighboring meeting-house sheds, or, in summer, hitched to the fence-posts; and, in Quincy, until the year 1827, the old horse-block, for the convenience of the pillion-riding goodwife, stood close to the main entrance. In the galleries sat the boys, under the vigilant eye of the tithingman, though in the earlier days of the old stone church it had once been voted "that the uppermost westerley gallerry be from henceforward a seat for womenkind." Before the pulpit were the deacons. And here doubtless in the early days not unfrequently in midwinter was it so cold that "the Sacramental Bread was frozen pretty hard, and rattled sadly as broken into the plates."

# CHAPTER X.

### THE CHURCH, AND CHURCH DISCIPLINE.

It remains to speak of the church as an educational, directing and restraining force during the colonial period, and of what is known as church discipline. As will presently be seen, prior to the year 1693 the church organization was in Braintree the organization which had assumed most definite shape. Up to the time when the charter of King Charles was superseded by that of William and Mary, and the Colony became a Province, church-members only were freemen, and the church must practically have governed the town, no division into precincts yet having taken place. Nor, in the case of Braintree, was this arrangement otherwise than natural, for the meeting-house was the town-building, the bulk of the tax levy was for church purposes, and the minister was the central figure in the community. After 1693 the political machinery as distinguished from the religious organization assumed a more and more definite shape; and in 1708 the process of development in Braintree was greatly stimulated by the establishment of a second precinct, — the practical separation of church from state then took place, in so far as those composing the body of inhabitants belonged to different precincts and contributed to the support of independent churches. This separation lasted until 1792, when, on the incorporation of Quincy as a distinct municipality, church and town were again merged, and they remained merged until April 12, 1824. On that day the parish was finally, under the laws enacted in pursuance of the provisions of the amended constitution of 1821, separated from the town, and became merely the Congregational Society of Quincy. Two generations of men have since then passed away, and the church as it existed prior to 1824 has ceased to be more than a tradition; and even as a tradition it has become vague. Yet the church of 1824 was in its influence and power the mere shadow of the church of the earlier day; and while, during the fifty years of town life between 1640 and 1690, under the colonial charter, the church organization was in Braintree all in all to its people, yet probably it was in the provincial period, and during the first half of the eighteenth century, that what is known as the discipline of the church made itself most distinctly felt; in any event the record of the larger portion of the earlier period, so far as Braintree is concerned, long since disappeared, and its traditions even have faded wholly away.

Six names, besides those of the pastor and teacher, were appended to the original Braintree church covenant of September 16, 1639, and, during the ministry of Mr. Flynt, extending over twenty-nine years, the church contained two hundred and four adult members. During the Fiske, Marsh and Hancock pastorates, down to the close of the first century of church life in 1739, this number was increased to five hundred and fifty-eight, and on the 16th of September of that year the pastor made a note of the fact that the church, "both males and females, solemnly renewed the Covenant of their Fathers, immediately before the participation of the Lord's Supper," — that covenant under which "poor unworthy creatures, who have sometimes lived without Christ and without God in the world, . . . by the help and strength of Christ renounce the devil, the wicked world, a sinful flesh, with all the covenants of Anti-Christian pollution wherein sometimes we have walked, and all our former evil ways, . . . and we give up ourselves also one to another by the will of God, . . . and we also manifest our joint consent herein this day in presence of this assembly, by this our present public profession, and by giving to one another the right hand of fellowship."

During those hundred years which ended on the 16th of September, 1739, it is not too much to say that the church was the life centre of Braintree. Nor, when its second century began, had that life centre as yet begun to lose its vitality; on the contrary it then glowed with a brighter, a more feverish heat than ever before, — a heat which preceded the gradual waning of the old theological fire about to begin. It was the period of religious revivals, — the "Great Awakening," as it was called, in New England. Already, four years before, in 1735, the famous Northampton revival had taken place, when, in the words of Jonathan Edwards, who engineered and presided over it, "the noise among the Dry Bones waxed louder and louder," and "Souls did as it were come by Flocks to Jesus Christ." Two years later, in 1741, George Whitefield preached on Boston Common to an audience of "about fifteen thousand," computed as not far from three quarters of the whole population of the town. In May, 1744, Mr. Hancock died, and with him ceased the records of Braintree church discipline; for, whether from indolence or because they saw no advantage in so doing, the ministers who succeeded Mr. Hancock made no mention of anything pertaining to the church's life or action beyond what was contained in the book regularly kept by the precinct clerk. But, among the still remaining archives of the society, there is one small volume both curious and valuable. Bound in smooth dark leather, the paper of which this volume is made is of that rough parchment character in such common use during the last century, and the entries in it, in the handwritings of five different ministers, while deciphered only with the utmost difficulty, throw vivid gleams of light on social habits and modes of existence which long since wholly disappeared. Beginning in 1673, these entries end in 1741, and the material out of which any direct knowledge can now be derived of Braintree church life during colonial times is confined to those sixty-eight years.

During those years, as during the years which preceded and followed of which no record remains, the church of Braintree, like the churches of other New England communities, was a social centre as well as a religious organization. The life of the town radiated from it. The people dwelt on farms, at some distance from each other in most cases, and usually at considerable distance from the meeting-house. Local and parental authority, church discipline, public opinion, enforced church attendance. Fashion, habit, choice, the love of company, the desire to see people and hear the news, all concurred in bringing every one to meeting. To many it was sometimes impossible and often inconvenient to return home between services. The result was that the inhabitants of the town, old and young, male and female, were every week thrown and kept together for several hours, during which they could not avoid that social intercourse which they naturally craved. Church attendance was thus a more effective, educational and controlling influence than town-meeting; for not only did it occur far more frequently, but it included all ages of both sexes. On pleasant Sabbaths, especially in the spring and autumn, neighbors and acquaintances would gather together in knots, and the young would stroll off among the trees or along the brook-side. In bad weather or in winter they would remain in the meeting-house, or find shelter and warmth in the dwellings nearest to it. John Adams had reason, therefore, for defining the colonial New Englander as "a meeting-going animal," for the meeting-going habit produced results upon the character of that people than which none were more marked. In the absence of newspapers and of travel, the Sabbath was the day for hearing and telling the news, and the meeting-house became a sort of central bazaar where local gossip could be interchanged. The church thus became a club, as the door of the meeting-house served as a bulletin board.[1] It was a club, too, from which exclusion placed an inhabitant of the town under a ban, and made of him a pariah.

To be a "child of the covenant," as the expression runs in the records, was to be born of those who were members of the church, and the pastor would not baptize a child unless one of its parents had entered into

---

[1] See on this subject Upham, *Salem Witchcraft*, i. 207–8; and Bliss, *Colonial Times on Buzzard's Bay*, 121. While I am most indebted to the first, the description contained in the last is the more life-like and entertaining. Also, Earle, *The Sabbath in Puritan New England*, 109–10.

the covenant; nor would he always baptize it even then.[1] The method pursued in admitting a new member to church fellowship was well established. The pastor was what the name implied, — the shepherd of the flock. As such it was his duty to keep a faithful oversight of it, which extended as well to those who were merely attendants at meeting as to those who partook of the sacrament. This oversight was inquisitive, — pastoral. It took in the home and included the catechism. Such as, not yet of the covenant, gave evidence "in a godly walk" of being under religious influence, or hopefully pious, were those for whom pastor and deacon, brother and sister, were most concerned; but all candidates for admission to the church were to offer themselves individually and under conviction, and this conviction was to be avowed. A conference with an officer of the church then followed, and if this was satisfactory the candidate was "propounded" before the whole congregation for admission into the select body those composing which were in covenant, — the church. This was a trying ordeal, for, though objection was rarely made, any member of the congregation was free to rise up and demur, and in so doing might ask questions of a most embarrassing character relating to all sorts of incidents in the past life of the candidate. The records of the older churches of Massachusetts contain many individual experiences "the rehearsal of which is not now viewed as edifying." After a suitable time from the "propounding" had elapsed, — a fortnight or a month, — the candidates, rising from their seats at the call of the pastor, in full congregation and at a recognized point in the Sabbath services, gave an oral or written relation of their

[1] *Proc. Mass. Hist. Soc.* Series II. vi. 493–4.

individual religious experience.[1] A survival of the confessional, but now made in public, this relation of experiences, while eagerly entered upon by some, could not but have been a severe ordeal to others, and entries like the following are met with in the records : — "The wife of our brother Hinsdell being fearful and not able to speake in publike, but fainting away ther, coming to the church in private gave good satisfaction; which being publikly testified and declared, and she confirming the same relation to be so, was received." The person seeking admission, man or boy, girl or matron, stood, the object to which all eyes were directed, and was then expected to reveal in public those things which in the church of St. Peter were whispered in the ear of the hidden confessor.

The practice, of course, degenerated in time into a mere form; but it must always have remained an ordeal for the timid, while for the conscientious it was a cruelty. Nor were the confessions, especially those of a certain class in which women were involved and concealment was impossible, of an improving character. So in 1722 "some persons of a sober life and good conversation," dwelling in the North Precinct of Braintree, signified their unwillingness to join the church unless they might be admitted " without making a Public Relation of their spiritual experiences, which (they said) the church had no warrant in the word of God to require." It was therefore proposed that the church should no longer require a relation from " any person who desires to partake in the ordinance of the Lord's supper with us; and after the case had been under debate at times among the breth-

---

[1] Ellis, *The Puritan Age in Massachusetts*, 206-8; *Dedham Church Records*, 20-1.

ren privately for the space of three weeks, the question was put to them January 28th, being on a Lord's Day Evening, in the meeting-house;" and "it passed in the negative by a large majority."

But this action was confined to the relation of the individual experiences of those seeking admission into the church. The confessions of shortcomings on the part of church-members were still made, and discipline was enforced after 1722, as apparently it had been from the beginning. Some of these cases, as they stand recorded,[1] are interesting as well as curious, revealing strange touches of human nature. One of them, the first of its kind, in the handwriting of the Rev. Mr. Fiske, bears date of March 2, 1683. Temperance, the wife of one John Bondish, had fallen into error and her offence was manifest: —

[She was accordingly] "called forth in the open Congregation, and presented a paper containing a full acknowledgment of her great sin and wickedness, [in which she] publickly bewayled her disobedience to parents, pride, unprofitableness under the means of grace, as the cause that might provoke God to punish her with sin, and warning all to take heed of such sins, begging the church's prayers, that God would humble her, and give a sound repentance, etc. Which confession being read, after some debate, the brethren did generally if not unanimously judge that she ought to be admonished ; and accordingly she was solemnly admonished of her great sin, which was spread before her in divers particulars, and charged to search her own heart wayes and to make thorough work in her Repentance, etc., from which she was released by the church vote unanimously."[2]

---

[1] *Proc. Mass. Hist. Soc.* Series II. vi. 480-90.

[2] In the *Dorchester Church Records* under date of February 5, 1681, (p. 87) is the following entry relating to the case of Mary Modesly, her offence being similar to that of Temperance Bondish: — "She was

## "A PRODIGIE OF PRIDE." 755

The case of Samuel Tompson was of a different character from that of Temperance Bondish. This individual, though he bore the same surname, does not seem to have been related to the first clergyman of the town. Apparently he was the son of Deacon Samuel Tompson, who, born in 1630, was promoted to a seat on the bench in front of the pulpit in 1679, while his name appears on almost every page of the earlier records of the town. Though the son of one of the deacons of the church, Samuel Tompson, Jr., was, as elsewhere appears in this narrative, a man constitutionally otherwise minded, and he saw fit not only to nourish but openly to proclaim a bitter personal animosity to his minister. He was accordingly subjected to discipline in the manner following : —

"Samuel Tompson, a prodigie of pride, malice and arrogance, being called before the church in the Meeting-house for his absenting himselfe from the Publike Worshipe, unlesse when any strangers preached; his carriage being before the Church proud and insolent, reviling and vilifying their Pastor, at an horrible rate, and stileing him their priest, and them a nest of wasps; and they unanimously voted an admonition, which was accordingly solemnly and in the name of Christ applied to him, wherein his sin and wickedness was laid open by divers Scriptures for his conviction, and was warned to repent, and after prayer to God this poor man goes to the tavern to drink it down immediately, as he said, &c."

Then, under date of 27th August, 1697, a month later, Mr. Fiske proceeds : —

"He delivered to me an acknowledgment in a bit of paper called to answer for her sin. She did appeare but being put to it to speak by way of acknowledgment of the sin, she gave noe answer but wept whether for the shame or the sin that was not known, and the Church was dismissed for that time."

at my house in the presence of Leift. Marsh and Ensign Penniman, who he brought. 'T was read before the Church at a meeting appointed 12.8. They being not willing to meet before. Leift. Col. Quincy gave his testimony against it, and said that his conversation did not agree therewith."

The next entry, also in the same handwriting, is dated 25th December, 1697: —

"At the church Meeting further testimony came in against him: the church generally by vote and voice declared him impenitent, and I was to proceed to an ejection of him, by a silent vote in Public. But I deferred it, partly because of the severity of the winter, but chiefly because his pretended offence was chiefly against myself, and [he] had said I would take all advantages against him, I deferred the same, and because 4 or 5 of the brethren did desire that he might be called before the church to see if he would own what they asserted: and having [notified] the church, he came, brought an additional acknowledgment. Of 15 about 9 or 10 voted to accept of it, &c."

This occurred on the 11th of April, 1698; and on the 17th, Mr. Fiske proceeds, —

"After the end of the public worship his confession was read publickly, and the major part of the Church voted his absolution."

Samuel Tompson, Jr., seems thus through a divided vote of the church-members to have escaped excommunication, and it exemplifies either the power of the organization, or the efficacy of an accepted faith in hell-fire, that a man of this character, a frequenter of the tavern and a chronic dissenter in town-meeting, did not dare set the church at defiance and ignore its action. He publicly confessed. Joseph Belcher was less fortunate. His case came before the church in October and November, 1677: —

"Joseph Belcher, a member of this Church though not in full communion, being sent for by the Church, after they had resolved to inquire into the matter of scandal, so notoriously infamous both in Court and Country, by Deacon Basse and Samuel Tompson, to give an account of those things; they returning with this answer from him, — that he would consider of it and send the Church word, the next Sabbath, whether he would come or no ; on which return by a Script, whereunto his name was subscribed, which he also owned to the elder, in private the weeke after, wherein he scornfully and impudently reflected upon the officer and church, and rudely refused to have anything to doe with us. [So], after considerable waiting, he persisting in his impenitence and obstinacy, (the Elders met at Boston unanimously advising thereto) the Church voted his not hearing of them, some few brethren not acting, doubting of his membership but silent. He was proceeded against according to Matthew 18, 17,[1] and rejected."

The case of Isaac Theer, a child of the covenant and a member of the church, but not in full communion, came up shortly after that of Mrs. Temperance Bondish was disposed of. He it seems had been convicted of "notorious scandalous thefts multiplied," for some of which he "suffered the law." Not content with this, he was now proceeded against in a church way, and the brethren labored with him in private "to bring him to a thorough sight and free and ingenuous confession of his sin ; as also for his abominably lying, changing his name, &c." Then comes in the language of the record a scene vividly illustrative of the olden time. As the words are read the simple village meeting-house, crowded on that

---

[1] "And if he shall neglect to hear them, tell it unto the church: but if he neglect to hear the church, let him be unto thee as an heathen man and a publican."

May afternoon with plainly dressed, hard-featured, Massachusetts men and women, comes back out of the past. In the pulpit is Parson Fiske; before it on their bench sit the gray-haired deacons; on the right of the minister as he faces his congregation are the men, on the left are the women; the boys look down with eager interest from the gallery. Then presently, after the services are ended, Isaac Theer

" was called forth in public, moved pathetically to acknowledge his sin, and publish his repentance, who came down and stood against the lower end of the fore-seat after he had been prevented (by our shutting the east door) from going out; stood impudently, and said indeed he owned his sin of stealing, was heartily sorry for it, begged pardon of God and men, and hoped he should do so no more, which was all he could be brought unto, saying his sin was already known, and that there was no need to mention it in particular, all with a remisse voice so that but few could hear him. The Church at length gave their judgement against him, that he was a notorious, scandalous sinner, and obstinately impenitent. And when I was proceeding to spread before him his sin and wickedness, he (as 't is probable) guessing what was like to follow, turned about to goe out, and being desired and charged to tarry and hear what the church had to say to him, he flung out of doors, with an insolent manner, though silent. Therefore the Pastor applied himself to the congregation, and having spread before them his sin, partly to vindicate the church's proceeding against him, and partly to warn others; sentence was declared against him."

In 1690 Ebenezer Owen, the son of parents who had long been in full communion, had gone as one of the thirteen men impressed from Braintree as the town's quota in the Quebec expedition of that year. The small-pox broke out and Owen died of it, being one of four from Braintree thrown overboard off Cape

Ann. He left a widow and a brother Josiah, who, to the great scandal of the church, he being "a child of the covenant," "obtained by fraud and wicked contrivance some marriage" with her. The two were living together when they were visited "at his cottage by the Pastor of the Church with Major Quinsey and D. Tompson," who informed them of the "appointment of an open confession of their sin in the congregation." Josiah Owen, the record goes on to say, was "affectionately treated" by the church emissaries, and

"after much discourse finding him obstinate and reflecting, he was desired and charged to be present the next Sabbath before the Church, to hear what should be spoken to him, but he boldly replied he should not come. And being after treated by D. Tompson and his father to come, and taking his opportunity to carry her away the last week, after a solemn sermon preached on I Cor. 5. 3, 4 and 5,[1] and prayers added, an account was given to the church and congregation of him, the Brethren voting him to be an impenitent, scandalous, wicked, incestuous sinner, and giving their consent that the sentence of excommunication should be passed upon and declared against him, which was solemnly performed by the Pastor of the Church according to the direction of the Apostle in the above mentioned text: this 17 of January 1691/2."

And so Josiah Owen and the widow of his brother Ebenezer, who was "thrown overboard at Cap an," rise up distinctly enough for an instant out of the Braintree church records of two centuries ago; and

[1] 3. "For I verily, as absent in body, but present in spirit, have judged already, as though I were present, concerning him that hath so done this deed.

4. "In the name of our Lord Jesus Christ, when ye are gathered together, and my spirit, with the power of our Lord Jesus Christ,

5. "To deliver such an one unto Satan for the destruction of the flesh, that the spirit may be saved in the day of the Lord Jesus."

then flit back into oblivion in company with Parson Fiske, "Major Quinsey," Governor Phips and the Quebec expedition of 1690.

A few years later James Penniman causes much trouble. A member of the church though not in full communion, he was a man of "notoriously scandalous life," noted for his "unchristian carriage towards his wife, and frequent excessive drinking." When called before the congregation and allowed to speak in his own vindication, "he behaved himself very insolently, and was far from discovering any signs of true repentance." Unanimously voted guilty, he was laid under solemn admonition. This was in 1713; but, as the years went on, James Penniman did not walk more correctly, so in April, 1722, it was proposed to excommunicate him. This seems to have thoroughly frightened the worthless fellow, and the record goes on: —

"Sabbath day, April 4, 1722. This day he presented a confession which was read before the Congregation, and prayed that they would wait upon him a while longer, which the Church consented to, and he was again publicly admonished and warned against persisting in the neglect of Public Worship, against Idleness, Drunkenness and Lying; and he gave some slender hopes of Reformation, seemed to be considerably affected, and behaved himself tolerably well."

"May 26, 1723. The brethren of the Church met together to consider what is further necessary to be done by the Church towards the reformation of James Penniman. He being present desired their patience towards him, and offered a trifling confession, which was read, but not accepted by the brethren, because he manifested no sign of true repentance thereof: they came to (I think) a unanimous vote that he should be cast out of the Church for his incorrigibleness in his evil waies, whenever I shall see good to do it, and I promised to wait upon him some time, to see how he would behave himself before I proceeded against him.[1]

"January 26, 1723/4, Lord's-day. In the afternoon, after a sermon on I Cor. v. 5,[2] James Penniman persisted in a course of Idleness, Drunkenness, and in a neglect of the Public Worship, &c., had the fearful sentence of excommunication pronounced upon him."

In 1723 Joseph Parmenter was the town clerk, and as such the town voted him the sum of twenty shillings, worth about $1.25 in silver, for his services as such during the year. Possibly there may have been two Joseph Parmenters in Braintree at that time, as a little earlier there were certainly two Samuel Tompsons, but the record says that on the 9th of September, 1722, " Brother Joseph Parmenter made a public Confession, in the presence of the Congregation, for the sin of drunkenness," and at a church meeting held twelve days later to consider his case,

"the question was put whether they would accept his confession to restore him ; it passed in the negative, because he has made several confessions of the sin, and is still unreformed thereof: the Brethren concluded it proper to suspend him from communion in the Lord's Supper, for his further humiliation and warning. He was accordingly suspended.

"March 3d, 1723. Sabbath Evening. Brother Parmenter having behaved himself well (for aught any that appears) since his suspension, was at his desire restored again by a vote of the brethren, *nemine contradicente.*"

[1] See the similar case of Consider Atherton, *Dorchester Church Records*, 96-7.

[2] 5. To deliver such an one unto Satan for the destruction of the flesh, that the spirit may be saved in the day of the Lord Jesus.

It will be noticed that the action last recorded took place on the 3d of March, 1723. The next day the annual town-meeting was held, at which "the inhabitants of Braintree being Lawfully Assembled then chose John Quincey Esq. moderator for that day. They then chose Joseph Parmenter clerk for the year ensuing by lifting up their hands."

The last public confession recorded as made before the North Precinct church was on the 20th of January, 1740; and the last recorded case of discipline, except that of Ebenezer Adams already referred to,[1] was on the 25th of October, 1741, when Eleazer Veazie was suspended by formal vote from the communion "for his disorderly unchristian life and neglecting to hear the Church."

The facts which have been stated and the examples given suffice to illustrate the power of church discipline in the colonial period, and the way it was made to enter into the every-day life of that people. It was a direct inheritance from the original church and the mother country, for Pepys notes down in his diary for a Sunday in 1665 how he went by coach "to church four miles off, where a pretty good sermon and a declaration of penitence of a man that had undergone the church's censure for his wicked life."[2] The practice was continued much longer in other parts of Massachusetts, but it wholly died out in Braintree under the easy-going pastorate of the Rev. Anthony Wibird before the revolutionary troubles began. Just in the degree the political machinery assumed new and larger functions, the ecclesiastical machinery fell into disuse. So far as Braintree was concerned,

[1] *Supra*, 640.
[2] Bliss, *Colonial Times on Buzzard's Bay*, 142, 155.

the change was clearly defined, and it took place in 1744, at the close of the Hancock pastorate. Before that, the church was greater than the town-meeting; after that, church discipline ceased to make itself felt, and the fervor of religious feeling cooled rapidly under the reaction which followed " the Great Awakening."

## CHAPTER XI.

#### THE TRAINING-FIELD AND THE SCHOOL-HOUSE.

IN mentioning the muster-field among the great formative influences of New England, it may well be questioned whether John Adams did not give to that field an undue importance. Certainly there are in the Braintree records few traces of it as an active educational force. Whatever else they were, the New Englanders were not a military race. On the ocean they were at home; and the hardy mariners who, as Burke expressed it, pursued their gigantic game "among the tumbling mountains of ice," and "drew the line and struck the harpoon on the coast of Africa," — these same men, skilful, alert and venturesome upon their element, have never failed to assert a brilliant supremacy in maritime warfare. But, though repeatedly in the course of its history engaged in conflicts the brunt of which was sturdily assumed, New England proper has never yet produced any considerable military genius. Church and Pepperell, Putnam, Allen, Knox, Stark, Lincoln, and even Greene, are names of only local note; while during the war of the Rebellion the great leaders from the New England stock were born and bred far in the interior of the continent. Not one New England soldier achieved renown.

As a people the New Englanders do not take kindly to camp life. When forced to it, they have always fought in a dogged, intelligent sort of way, just as they fought at Lexington and Bunker's Hill; impelled, as it were, by a consciousness that the situation was one of their own making, and they proposed to see the thing through. But to disband a New England army has never proved a difficult or delicate task; for, once the work in hand is done, the camp quietly and joyously dissolves of itself. An army of Yankee mercenaries sounds like a contradiction in terms. Accordingly, though the Suffolk regiment existed as a military organization through a century of colonial life, and the Braintree companies were always a part of it, there is no reason to suppose that it was ever an effective force. Commissions in it were eagerly sought, and were intrigued for, and the titles of captain, lieutenant and ensign are continually met with in the records: but, except in time of military excitement, the training-days were few and far apart; and partook apparently more of the character of a rough country jollification than of war. Certainly, when Washington took command of the provincial army at Cambridge, neither its discipline nor its equipment bespoke a martial race. It was little more than a mob of intelligent men, organized by localities, and, as sportsmen, accustomed from youth to the handling of guns.

The training-field may have been overestimated as a factor in the making of New England, but to overestimate the influence of the school in that making would be difficult. It stands next below the church in the earlier period, and above it in the more recent. Prior to 1830 it was below it. There are entries in the Braintree records which indicate that a public Latin school was established in the town at a very early period, in the neighborhood, indeed, of 1645, though the exact date cannot now be fixed; yet in 1735 the records refer to "a Free Latin School" which had then been kept by the town "for about ninety years;" and in 1645 Winthrop made note of the fact that "divers free Schools were erected, as at Roxbury, . . . the charge to be by yearly contribution, either by voluntary allowance, or by rate of such as refused, &c., and . . . other towns did the like, providing maintenance by several means." In 1719 Roxbury and Braintree were classed together among the towns of Suffolk county as "noted for their Free-Schools,"[1] and Braintree may, therefore, have been one of the "other towns" referred to by Winthrop, though it is certain that even two years later, in 1647, to use the language of the famous colonial law of that year, the Lord had not increased the inhabitants of the town "to the number of one hundred families," necessitating the setting up of "a grammar school, the master thereof to be able to instruct youth so far as they may be fitted for the University, . . . to the end that learning may not be buried in the graves of our forefathers." Indeed, it may well be doubted whether at that time Braintree yet numbered even those "fifty households" prescribed by the same law as the point at which every township should designate some one "to teach all children to read and write." None the less, the town records indicate that even then, with a population of scarcely three hundred souls, Braintree did maintain within its limits some sort of a school in which youths were prepared for college when those might be admitted who were "able to read Tully, or such like classical author, extempore, . . . and decline per-

[1] Neal, *Hist. of New England*, ii. 229.

fectly the paradigms of nouns and verbs in the Greek tongue:" but at this point the record stops, throwing no light on the source from whence "the maintenance" of this institution was drawn; though in 1740 an annual rent of £142, worth in the currency of that day a quarter part of that amount in silver money, was then derived from the Coddington schoolland,[1] and it was stated that from the rent of this land the town had "reaped great benefit in good schools for many years past." It is a fact worthy of notice, also, that during the first century of the town's history, which was also the distinctly formative colonial period, extending from about the time of Winthrop's death (1649) nearly to the beginning of the final French wars (1744), — during this century no less than forty-nine young men, prepared either at the "Free Latin School" or elsewhere, are said to have entered college from Braintree, forty-seven of whom were from the North Precinct church. Considering the extreme poverty of the period, and the fact that even at its close the town scarcely numbered a population of 1,500 souls, having begun with about 200, such a record of those seeking a university education is significant. In those early days also, in proportion to its means, Braintree town was more than a liberal, it was a munificent benefactor of the college; for when, in 1669, the condition of the seminary was critical and apparently hopeless, — when its buildings were pronounced "ruinous and almost irreparable," and it was declared that without a new building its situation was desperate, — in this great emergency Braintree was one of the towns which responded most liberally to "the loud groans of the

[1] *Supra*, 546.

sinking College," contributing to "erecting a new College" the sum of £87 14s. 6d.,[1] an amount than which four places only in the province gave more. Nor is it easy now to understand what could have induced those composing a community the size Braintree then was to make so large a gift, or how they could have afforded to do so. In proportion to population, supposing the wealth per capita to have been as large then as it is now, such a contribution was the equivalent of $9,000 from the Quincy of to-day; but in reality it is not unsafe to say that in proportion to accumulated wealth the gift of $90,000 would mean less to those now inhabiting the four towns into which the Braintree of 1669 has been divided than the poor $292.43 meant then. That people gave of their little.[2]

[1] Quincy, *Harvard University*, i. 29, 30, 508.
[2] As there is no reference made in the town records to any gift of this nature, it must apparently have been made through the church, or as the result of voluntary individual action. The proportion given in the text between the original gift and a corresponding gift at the present time seems so excessive that it is only proper to give the data on which the estimate is based. The population of Braintree in 1669 was about 550, and the gift to the college ($292.43) represented as near as may be fifty-five cents to an inhabitant, or one and two thirds days' labor, the ordinary wages then being two shillings, or thirty-three cents a day. The population of the same territory now is 28,000, and the ordinary day's wages may be computed at $1.75. The wages for one day and two thirds of a population of 28,000 would, therefore, be $81,665.00.

Again, in 1669 the entire town and parish assessment of Braintree did not exceed £150, or $500, which was raised only with extreme difficulty, being paid partly in money, partly in kind. The gift to the college amounted, therefore, to sixty per cent. of one annual tax levy. In 1889–90 the annual tax levy of the four towns into which old Braintree has been divided, amounted to over $310,000.00, paid in money, and without apparent inconvenience to the people paying it. Sixty per cent. of this amount would have been $186,000, a sum far larger than the estimate in the text.

## THE SCHOOLMASTER.

The earliest village school-house in Braintree, which must have been a structure of the humblest description, stood at the side of the Plymouth highway, or main thoroughfare of the settlement, and not far from the meeting-house. When it was built nowhere appears, but in 1679 it was referred to as a landmark, and does not then seem to have been new; in the still earlier days, such teaching as the children got they must have received at home, or in the house where some temporary teacher lodged. At last in 1679, thirty years after the gathering of the church, the town agreed with Benjamin Tompson that he should be schoolmaster, receiving for his services the rent of "the Towne land," estimated at £15 a year, and a further sum, to be paid out of the town rate, sufficient to secure him an annual salary of £30, or a third part of the Rev. Mr. Fiske's contract stipend, which was payable to the latter at that time " in countrey pay at countrey prise." Unlike the clergyman, the schoolmaster in this case did not look for sustenance merely to his salary; but, having graduated at Harvard sixteen years before, he had since been endeavoring to support himself as a physician, and sought by teaching to eke out an insufficient professional income. Yet even this school was not free, for part of the agreement with Tompson was "that every child should carry into the school master halfe a cord of wood beside the quarter money every yeare;" and twenty years later, in 1700, the nature of the contract was more specifically defined by a vote providing that "every schollar shall pay for his entry Into the school one shilling and so successively for every quarter for the whole year if he shall goe more than one quarter, and this shall be a part of the school sallary to be paid unto the schoolmaster, and he to give an account of all that came to the Selectmen." A year later yet more definite provision was made, for, the salary still standing at £30, the town voted that any "parent or master" sending a child to school pay the town treasurer for the support of the school five shillings a year, and proportionally for any part thereof; but, if such "parent or master" lived in another town, the payment in such case should be twenty shillings. The selectmen were further empowered to abate any part or the whole of this payment on the application of "any poor persons in this Town who shall find themselves unable to pay," and any deficiency over and above "the Rent of the Town Lands and the head money of the Schollars shall be raised by a Town Rate equally proportioned upon the Inhabitants." And this, the vote passed in 1701, sixty-one years after the incorporation of Braintree, seems to have been the initial step in the introduction there of a free public school system. Prior to that time, schooling was apparently paid for in money or in produce by those immediately deriving advantage from it; for, not only in Tompson's day, but thirty-five years later, in 1715, the town voted "that all Parents or masters of all children or servants going to schools shall deliver into the present Schoolmaster, for the use of the Schoolhouse, three foot of cord wood to be the proportion of each child or servant for this year;" a change from the vote of 1710, under which the master was "impowered to demand a Load of wood of each boy that comes to school this winter." The explanation of so liberal a provision of fuel is probably to be looked for in Samuel Maverick's statement that, during the earlier colonial period, Braintree subsisted " by raising provisions, and furnishing Boston with wood," — wood, in other words, was "countrey pay at countrey prise," and those furnishing it paid in this way for the schooling of children and servants; no scholars, until the year 1701, being exempted from any payment at all. But, from and after 1701, the other policy prevailed, the cases of exemption increased, and a steadily growing part of the total school expenses was "Raised by a Town Rate equally proportioned upon the Inhabitants."

Benjamin Tompson, Braintree's first schoolmaster and son of its earliest minister, has since been referred to as "an eminent and learned man," and, though this judgment may be open to question, there is little doubt he was what is known as "a character," — he also, like his father, was subject to "sullen fits," and in them was apt to be "full of matter." Born in 1642, and graduated from Harvard in 1662, he seems, with intermissions during which others filled his place with more or less acceptance on the part of the town, to have kept the Braintree school from 1678 to 1704, a period of twenty-five years.[1] In 1699 he got into a controversy with the town in reference to the payment of his salary, and presently, after appointing a committee to defend in case of prosecution, the inhabitants

---

[1] Benjamin Tompson had previously (1671–74) kept the school at Charlestown, and is spoken of by Mr. Frothingham in his history of that town (p. 177) as "a celebrated teacher." The following were the terms on which he taught: —

"1. That he shall be paid thirty pounds per annum by the town, and to receive twenty shillings a year from each particular scholar that he shall teach, to be paid him by those who send children to him to school.

"2. That he shall prepare such youth as are capable of it for the college, with learning answerable.

"3. That he shall teach to read, write, and cypher."

voted to allow "Mr. Benjamin Tompson" five pounds for a discharge in full, "and also that John Ruggles, Sen., and Lt. Samuel Penniman should go and make the tender thereof unto him." The committee performed the duty assigned to them, and, "that all may issue in love," Tompson, accepting the five pounds tendered him, signed "a mutual and everlasting discharge." Remaining in Braintree until as late as 1710, Tompson was the town clerk as well as its physician and schoolmaster, and the records, written in no unscholarly hand, were kept by him from 1690 to 1710; yet his wife witnessed her signature with a cross. An erudite man, he was fond of Latinity, and in 1693 made entry of the births of all his nine children, going back to 1670, and piously added these words: — "Quos omnes, Deus omnipotens, pro unigeniti filii sui ac salvatoris nostri meritis, vita eterna dignetur."[1]

A successor in the office of town clerk recorded of Mr. Tompson, that, a "Practitioner of Physick for above thirty years, during which time hee kept a Grammar School in Boston, Charlestowne and Braintry, having left behind him a weary world, eight children, twenty-eight grand children (he) deceased April 13th, 1714, and lieth buried in Roxbury, Atatis sue, 72." In the epitaph inscribed on his tombstone he is also referred to as "ye Renouned Poet of N. Engl." Born under a New England sky and amid Calvinistic surroundings, Benjamin Tompson was a contemporary of Dryden, Addison and Pope; but, unfortunately, though addicted to versification, the results of his labor were to the full as devoid of imagination as they are of metre.

[1] "Whom all, may Almighty God, through the merits of his only begotten Son and our Saviour, deem worthy of life everlasting."

Halting badly, even the best of his lines are suggestive both of paucity of thought and of the exigencies of rhyme. When Cotton Mather published the Magnalia, Tompson wrote to him some verses of a complimentary character, which are now printed with it. They contain one good line, in which, referring to the "ancient names," among them his father's, recorded in Mather's pages, the writer says they are

> "Like gems on Aaron's costly breast-plate set."

Tompson's other contribution to the Magnalia consisted of a long copy of rhymed and more or less metrical lines in honor of the Rev. Samuel Whiting, of Lynn, an eminent seventeenth century divine, of whom it is recorded he wrote two books, in one of which he developed thirty-two distinct doctrines out of Abraham's prayer in the eighteenth chapter of Genesis; while in the other, more successful yet, he developed no less than forty-two such distinct doctrines out of the promise of the Lord contained in the fourteen verses of the fifty-eighth chapter of Isaiah. Of him Benjamin Tompson, "ye Renouned Poet of N. Engl.," wrote: —

> "Such awful gravity this doctor us'd
> As if an angel every word infus'd.
> No turgent stile, but Asiatic store;
> Conduits were almost full, seldom run o'er
> The banks of Time: come visit when you will,
> The streams of nectar were descending still.
> Much like Septemfluous Nilies, rising so,
> He watered Christians round, and made them grow."
> . . . . . . . .
> "Should half his sentences be truly numbered,
> And weighed in wisdom's scales, 't would spoil a Lombard:
> . . . . . . . .
> "The loss of such an one would fetch a tear
> From Niobe herself, if she were here."

But, returning to Benjamin Tompson, the building

in which he taught, and within the walls of which all the children of the town gathered, measured twenty feet by sixteen, "and seven foot between joynts." In 1715 it had grown old and was pronounced unfit to repair, and the town, evidently much agitated over the issue, voted to erect two new houses, one "for the acomidating of a grammar School" not far from the North Meeting-house, and the other "a convenient School house for writing and reading" near the meeting-house, "in the south end of this town;" then "the use of the old School house" was given to "Mr. Benjamin Webb" (excepting the stone and brick) "for the securing of his hay till the first of May next. . . . after which the said old house was sold by the committee to the said Benjamin Webb for three pounds, paid to the Treasurer."

The history of the Braintree schools, no less than that of the church, shows in a clear, striking way how slow was the process of development during the colonial period, and how that period, — the New England chrysalis stage, — instead of ending with the Revolution, lasted down even to the year 1830. It is not too much to say that for one hundred and ninety years — through the lives of six generations of those born on the soil — the same identical system was pursued with regard to the schools and in them, the difference being only in degree and detail. First population spread, the original town becoming the North Precinct, and the original town school the grammar school; then an elementary school, in which reading and writing were taught, was provided for the outlying districts. Two generations passed away while this phase of development was working itself out. The precinct meanwhile grew, and in due process of time became a town; but this process required eighty years, and during those eighty years the old system was continued, almost unchanged. About the year 1720, the practice of exacting payment from the parents or master of each child taught was abandoned, the whole expense of maintaining the schools becoming a charge upon the town; but the selectmen still engaged the teacher, over whom and whose methods no supervision seems to have been exercised. In 1720 the master was paid thirty-four pounds a year; he had been paid thirty pounds in 1680, and he was paid only seventy-five pounds in 1792. The school-house of 1697 measured twenty feet by sixteen; the school-house built nearly a century later, in 1793, "on the training-field" and opposite the meeting-house, contained one large school-room only, measuring twenty-eight feet by twenty, and its cost was estimated at ninety pounds. In 1815 this building was burned, and another was constructed in 1817 to serve both as town-hall and school-house. It measured twenty-five feet by fifty, and cost a little more than $2,000. It was the last structure of the colonial period, — the chrysalis stage was near its end, and the integument was soon to be rent.

The first symptom of differentiation in school matters took place in 1717, when provision was made for elementary instruction, independent of the grammar school, in the South Precinct. Two years later, as population spread yet more, the experiment of making this school peripatetic in character was attempted, and it was voted that it "may be moved into more than one place." In 1757 the same experiment was tried with the grammar school, which it was provided should the ensuing year "be kept the one half of the time in the North Precinct, the other half in the Middle Precinct;" while "an Equal sum as shall be necessary for the maintaining a Grammar School be Employed under the Direction of the Selectmen for writting and Reading Schools in the several parts of the North and Middle Precincts." In 1739 a species of special school committee had been provided, at the head of which Col. John Quincy was placed, which was "Impowered to provide a School Master," and "to order the time and place when the school shall be kept in each precinct;" but, the very next year, "after some debate thereon," it was ordered — "That the affair of the Schools be regulated by the Selectmen, In all things as heretofore." And so the thing went on from year to year through nearly a century, every possible crude experiment and makeshift being tried in turn, — what was attempted one year being abandoned the next, while the grammar school served as a sort of a shuttlecock, as it shot about here and there under the impacts of local jealousy and sectional requirement. It was this chronic condition of affairs which, as will presently be seen, was at last the immediate and ostensible cause of the disruption of the original town.

Even after the separation took place, and the necessary remedy for the old condition of affairs was thought to have been applied, the school facilities of the new town long remained of the most primitive character. For eight years, and until 1800, the ancient precinct feeling controlled the policy of Quincy so that all children whose parents desired them to be taught had to find their own way to the centre. In a town the size of Quincy, this implied a daily walk measured in many cases by miles. For the smaller children such a walk was generally found too severe, and provision was made for local or "dame" schools, for which specific sums varying from four dollars to forty dollars were annually appropriated. Yet in the year 1820 the whole amount voted for the support of the centre school, "including ink and fuel," as well as the pay of both a male and a female teacher, was but $692. It is now, therefore, small matter for surprise that a committee then reported the school-room so crowded that the scholars, two hundred and four in number, "were obliged to wait one for the other for seats, notwithstanding the master gave up his desk, and used every other means in his power to accommodate them." Still the town had not yet reached the stage of differentiation. With the innate conservatism of a community grown up under majority government, it clung to the primitive customs; and the committee went on to submit a plan for certain alterations, at an estimated cost of $200, by which two hundred and fifty scholars were to be brought together in one room and under one master, "with an assistant when necessary." Then in 1825 the master was censured for not attending more faithfully to his duties; whereupon he replied that he was not paid enough ($450 per annum) to support him, but if the town would increase his salary to $500 he would devote all his time to the schools. This addition to the master's salary increased the total appropriation to $745, leaving $245 with which to pay the female assistant and defray all other school charges. At last, in 1829, the condition of affairs had become intolerable, and provision was made for the district system. The chrysalis stage was over.

It is needless to speak at length of the old town school of Braintree, and the system of instruction pursued in it, for the schools of Braintree were like the schools of most other Massachusetts towns similarly placed, and those schools have been often described. They were wholly primitive, and the New England Primer, with the Rev. John Cotton's Spiritual Milk for American Babes, affords for modern eyes a sufficient glimpse of them. In the pages of that odd little volume, — a volume used as a text-book by six generations of Massachusetts progeny, — besides the singular results achieved by native artists in their efforts to portray to the physical eye the experiences of Elijah, Job, Lot, Obadiah, Timothy, Zaccheus and other Hebrew characters of Biblical fame, may still be studied the intellectual nutriment once deemed most appropriate for New England infants who were acquiring a knowledge of the alphabet. They were cheered and inspired by being taught verses like these : —

> "There is a dreadful fiery hell,
> Where wicked ones must always dwell;
> There is a heaven full of joy,
> Where goodly ones must always stay;
> To one of these my soul must fly,
> As in a moment, when I die."

And doctrine of this character was then emphasized and brought home to the childish imagination by ditties like the following : —

> "In the burying place may see
> Graves shorter there than I,
> From death's arrest no age is free,
> Young children too must die :
> My God, may such an awful sight
> Awakening be to me."

The infant mind having through such agencies as this been brought into a thoroughly receptive condition, the Rev. John Cotton then took the matter in hand, and thus administered to the babes what was regarded as milk " for their Souls Nourishment, drawn out of the Breasts of both Testaments : " —

" Q. What is done for you in the Lord's supper?

" A. In the Lord's supper, the receiving of the bread broken and the wine poured out is a sign and seal of my receiving the communion of the body of Christ broken for me, and of his blood shed for me, and thereby of my growth in Christ and pardon and healing of my sins, of the fellowship of the Spirit, of my strengthening and quickening in grace, and of my sitting together with Christ on his throne of glory at the last judgment.

. . . . . . . . . . .

" Q. What is the reward that shall then be given?

" A. The righteous shall go into life eternal, and the wicked shall be cast into everlasting fire with the devil and his angels."

This is followed in the Primer by a familiar rhymed "dialogue between Christ, Youth and the Devil," — a sort of closing spiritual and educational divertisement, in which Death is again introduced as saying to the terrified child, —

"Thou hast thy God offended so,
Thy soul and body I 'll divide:
Thy body in the grave I 'll hide,
And thy dear soul in Hell must lie
With Devils to Eternity.

"THE CONCLUSION.

"Thus end the days of woful youth,
Who won't obey nor mind the truth ;
Nor hearken to what preachers say,
But do their parents disobey :
They in their youth go down to hell,
Under eternal wrath to dwell.
Many don't live out half their days,
For cleaving unto sinful ways."

Such in those days was the milk adjudged meet for babes;[1] and this was the old-time primer of which it is asserted that there never has been printed in this country a book laying no claim to inspiration, whose influence has been so extended and enduring as a manual of religious instruction for the young, while societies were formed the sole purpose of which was to introduce it into schools!

No print or black-board or map or motto adorned the grimy, blackened walls of those primitive colonial school-houses, in which the New England Primer was the earliest text-book, but within their narrow limits were crowded scores of children of both sexes and of every age. Ranged twos and threes on benches, behind rude rows of desks cut and hacked and mutilated by the jackknives of successive generations, the larger scholars, among whom were full-grown young men and women, sat at the rear, the sexes on opposite sides, while the smallest of the little children occupied low benches close to the teacher's chair. Great logs of wood blazed in the fireplace, or later in stoves, one of which was at each end of the room, and before these the scholars read and ciphered and wrote. The period was not one of either refinement or sentiment, and both at home and in the school the rod — " the rawhide " — was freely used; nor did either sex or age afford immunity from corporal punishment which would now excite indignation if inflicted on dogs. In the matter of instruction, the public records of the two preceding centuries, as compared with those of the present cen-

[1] For the singular and morbid effects produced on infant minds by the terrorism of the colonial theology, see the curious passages in the Sewall Diary of January 13, 1695-6 (v. *Mass. Hist. Soc. Coll.* v. 419-20), the *Magnalia*, B. 6, ch. 7, App. Ex. IV. and, above all, Jonathan Edwards' *Faithful Narrative*, 65-72.

tury, show clearly the increasing elevation of standard. The town and precinct clerks certainly were not then, any more than they are now, chosen for conspicuous illiteracy, and the records prior to 1800 are conclusive as evidence of the instruction in writing given in the public schools of the period; nor is there any reason to suppose the instruction in other respects was better, or the results attained more creditable. In point of fact the children were neither taught much, nor were they taught well; for through life the mass of them, while they could do little more in the way of writing than rudely scrawl their names, could never read with real ease or rapidity, and could keep accounts only of the simplest kind. As for arithmetical problems, the knowledge of them was limited to the elementary multiplication, division, addition and subtraction. None the less, after a fashion and to a limited extent, the Braintree school child, like the school children of all other Massachusetts towns, could read, could write and could cipher; and for those days, as the world then went, that was much. In itself, though the highest of the time, the standard was not high; nor does an examination of what has been handed down to us justify, or indeed afford any reasonable basis for, the laudation so frequently indulged in of late over the thoroughness of the ancient school methods, or the excellent results achieved by them. It is well to extol the simplicity and directness of what are known as the good old times, and the New England schools of the eighteenth century doubtless reflected the usages of the homes; but the further familiarity with those times is pressed, the less alluring do their details and actualities appear, and the more do they tend to make those living in the present contented with their lot.

Brutality, ignorance and coarseness have not yet vanished from the world, nor are they soon likely to vanish from it; but it is safe to say that, if by any chance the Braintree village school of 1790 could for a single fortnight have been brought back to the Quincy of 1890, parents would in horror and astonishment have kept their children at home until a town-meeting, called at the shortest possible legal notice, could be held; and this meeting would probably have culminated in a riot, in the course of which school-house as well as school would have been summarily abated as a disgrace and a nuisance.

## CHAPTER XII.

### INTEMPERANCE AND IMMORALITY.

WHEN John Adams enumerated to Major Langbourne the educational institutions of New England, there was one which he omitted to mention, which, for good and ill, was hardly a less influential element in New England life and action than town-meetings, training-days, public schools or church gatherings. That omitted institution was the country tavern. In the days before railroads, mails and newspapers the tavern was the common gathering-place of the town, where the news was circulated and the events of the day discussed. The modern caucus is a substitute for it, for there the politics of the village were arranged, and there the questions at issue between the colonies and the mother country were debated. From his early life John Adams detested the public houses. He declared that in them "the time, the money, the health and the modesty of most that were young and many old were wasted; here diseases, vicious habits, bastards and legislators were frequently begotten." Yet of their potency as a political educator and influence he was a living witness. More than thirty years afterwards he thus described one of these colonial tavern debates:—

"Within the course of the year before the meeting of Congress, in 1774, on a journey to some of our circuit courts in Massachusetts, I stopped one night at a tavern in

Shrewsbury, about forty miles from Boston, and as I was cold and wet, I sat down at a good fire in the bar-room to dry my greatcoat and saddlebags till a fire could be made in my chamber. There presently came in, one after another, half a dozen, or half a score, substantial yeomen of the neighborhood, who, sitting down to the fire after lighting their pipes, began a lively conversation upon politics. As I believed I was unknown to all of them, I sat in total silence to hear them. One said, 'The people of Boston are distracted.' Another answered, 'No wonder the people of Boston are distracted. Oppression will make wise men mad.' A third said, 'What would you say if a fellow should come to your house and tell you he was come to take a list of your cattle, that Parliament might tax you for them at so much a head? And how should you feel if he was to go and break open your barn, to take down your oxen, cows, horses and sheep?' 'What should I say?' replied the first; 'I would knock him in the head.' 'Well,' said a fourth, 'if Parliament can take away Mr. Hancock's wharf and Mr. Rowe's wharf, they can take away your barn and my house.' After much more reasoning in this style, a fifth, who had as yet been silent, broke out, 'Well, it is high time for us to rebel; we must rebel some time or other, and we had better rebel now than at any time to come. If we put it off for ten or twenty years, and let them go on as they have begun, they will get a strong party among us, and plague us a great deal more than they can now. As yet, they have but a small party on their side.' . . . I mention this anecdote to show that the idea of independence was familiar even among the common people much earlier than some persons pretend."

This is a reminiscence long after the event; but it only confirms what he wrote in 1761, describing what he then daily saw going on before his eyes: —

"If you ride over this whole province you will find that

taverns are generally too numerous. . . . In most country towns in this country you will find almost every other house with a sign of entertainment before it. If you call, you will find dirt enough, very miserable accommodations of provision and lodging for yourself and your horse. Yet, if you sit the evening, you will find the house full of people drinking drams, flip, toddy, carousing, swearing; but especially plotting with the landlord to get him at the next town-meeting an election either for selectman or representative."

Later in life John Adams was wont to say, it was in silently listening to these tavern talks among farmers as he rode the circuits that he first came to realize that American independence was both inevitable and close at hand. But the school, though effective, was dangerous. The intemperance of the colonial period is a thing now difficult to realize; and it seems to have pervaded all classes from the clergy to the pauper. In the earliest days, beer brewed from barley malt was the usual table beverage, the ordinary and free use of which had been brought over from England; and the price was regulated by law, that sold at 3d. a quart of a quality carrying six bushels of malt to the hogshead; that at 2d., four bushels; and that at a penny, two bushels. But cider was the natural beverage of the soil, and, though more expensive than beer at first, as orchards became common it grew sufficiently cheap, inasmuch as in 1728, when an ounce of silver, the equivalent of $1.20, was worth eighteen shillings in currency, twelve shillings in currency sufficed to buy a barrel of cider. Indeed, in barrel quantities, cider at that time cost less than either Indian corn or carrots. Tea and coffee did not come into common use as table beverages until a much later period, and all through the eighteenth century the "generality of the people with their victuals" drank cider. But the juice of the apple failed to satisfy that love of strong drink — that longing for alcoholic stimulant — which though the first settlers seem to have been temperate when compared with their descendants, the New Englander inherited direct from his Saxon ancestry. Craving something more potent, the West India trade soon supplied it. Here is an extract from a sermon of Increase Mather delivered in March, 1686, before a criminal awaiting execution for murder, which tells the story: —

"It is an unhappy thing that later years a kind of strong Drink called Rum has been common amongst us, which the poorer sort of People, both in Town and Country, can make themselves drunk with. They that are poor and wicked too, can for a penny or twopence make themselves drunk: I wish to the Lord some Remedy may be thought of for the prevention of this evil."

One hundred and ten years later, speaking of the work on his farm in Quincy, John Adams describes how one of the hands got drinking, and he adds: —

"A terrible drunken distracted week he has made of the last. A beast associating with the worst beasts in the neighborhood, running to all the shops and private houses, swilling brandy, wine and cider in quantities enough to destroy him. If the ancients drank wine and rum as our people drink rum and cider, it is no wonder we read of so many possessed with devils."

Not until after 1830 did the great temperance movement make its influence potently felt, and for a century and a half, therefore, it is not too much to say that "rum" was the bane of New England.

Braintree seems to have been scourged by it, even more than most of her sister towns. At the very time the town was incorporated, at the May General Court of 1640, Martin Sanders, who a year before had been "alowed to keepe a house of intertainment" at the Mount, and whose name was one of the eight subscribed to the church covenant there, was "alowed to draw wine at Braintree." In 1731 a new church edifice was "raised" and in the North Precinct records is the vote already referred to, authorizing the purchase for the occasion of "Bread Cheese Sugar Rum Sider and Beer at the cost of the precinct." In 1754 Tutor Flynt made the memorable journey from Cambridge to Portsmouth. In addition to being a tutor, Mr. Flynt was then also a fellow of the corporation, and acted as clerk of the overseers. He had for his companion an undergraduate, and was in his seventy-eighth year. There are few more amusing and instructive pictures of the manners and methods of travellers in eastern Massachusetts during the eighteenth century than that contained in the account of this journey written by Tutor Flynt's companion;[1] but in that account there is nothing that sounds more singular to the reader of to-day than the way in which the venerable preceptor, travelling with the youthful student, took his "nip of milk punch" after they pulled up at the public house: and when, "in full view of Clark's Tavern" near Portsmouth, the old gentleman was tumbled headlong out of the chaise, nearly breaking his neck, he was revived by "two or three bowls of lemon punch, made pretty sweet," which, as they "were pretty well charged with good old spirit" made him "very pleasant and sociable."

[1] *Proc. Mass. Hist. Soc.* 1878, pp. 5–11.

## INTEMPERANCE AND IMMORALITY.

In 1758 Samuel Quincy and John Adams were admitted to the province bar. After the oath had been administered on motion of Gridley and Pratt, the leading lawyers of their day, the two young men "shook hands with the bar, and received their congratulations, and invited them over to Stone's to drink some punch, where the most of us resorted, and had a very cheerful chat." It is not easy to imagine leading counsel of to-day drinking with students in a tap-room. Again, in 1778 Count d'Estaing came to Boston with the French fleet. Mrs. Adams visited it, and could not sufficiently express her admiration of the bearing of officers and men, which she said ought to make Americans "blush at their own degeneracy of manners." What delighted her most was, that "not one officer has been seen the least disguised with liquor since their arrival."

So bad had the condition of affairs become about the year 1750 that John Adams declared that several towns within his knowledge had "at least a dozen taverns and retailers." Suffolk County he asserted was worse than any other, and in Braintree, within a circuit of three miles, there were "eight public houses, besides one in the centre." Within three quarters of a mile on the main road there were three taverns, besides retailers, or those who supplied the "neighborhood with necessary liquors in small quantities and at the cheapest rates." These houses, frequented as they were by a "tippling, nasty, vicious crew," had become "the nurseries of our legislators," for there were many who could "be induced by flip and rum to vote for any man whatever." Aroused to the necessity of doing something to restrain this growing evil, the young village lawyer had an article looking to a reduction of the number of licensed houses inserted in the warrant for the May town-meeting of 1761. A full debate took place upon it, and a vote was passed, which is chiefly curious now as indicating what the condition of affairs must have been for which this measure was regarded as one of reform; for in it, after reciting "the present prevailing Depravity of Manners, through the Land in General, and in this Town in particular, and the shameful neglect of Religious and Civil Duties," it was ordered that in future no persons should be licensed to sell spirituous liquors by retail in Braintree; but one innholder, suitably selected, was to be "approbated by the selectmen" in each precinct. These three innholders were then to have a monopoly of the business on condition that they "oblidge themselves by written Instruments, under their Hands and Seals, to retail spirituous Liquors to the Town Inhabitants, as they shall have occasion therefor, at the same price by the Gallon or smaller Quantity, as the same are usually sold, by Retail, in the Town of Boston."

It hardly needs to be said that such a measure of reform was productive of no considerable result. Revolutionary troubles then shortly ensued, and John Adams was called away to larger fields of usefulness. Long afterwards, referring to this experience, he wrote: —

"Fifty-three years ago I was fired with a zeal, amounting to enthusiasm, against ardent spirits, the multiplication of taverns, retailers, and dram-shops and tippling-houses. Grieved to the heart to see the number of idlers, thieves, sots and consumptive patients made for the use of physicians, in those infamous seminaries, I applied to the Court of Sessions, procured a committee of inspection and inquiry, reduced the number of licensed houses, etc. But I only acquired the reputation of a hypocrite and an ambitious demagogue by it. The number of licensed houses was soon reinstated, drams, grog and sotting were not diminished, and remain to this day as deplorable as ever. You may as well preach to the Indians against rum as to our people."

When John Adams made his futile attempt at temperance reform, and for seventy years thereafter, the town in which he lived was as respects intemperance no better and no worse than her sister towns. In every store in which West India goods were sold, and there were no others, behind the counter stood the casks of Jamaica and New England rum, of gin and brandy. Their contents were sold by the gallon, the bottle or the glass. They were carried away, or drunk on the spot. It was a regular, recognized branch of trade; and when during the Revolution Mrs. Adams sent a list of current prices to her husband, she always included rum, looking upon it as no less a farm staple than meat or corn or molasses. Three shillings a gallon, or ninepence a quart, was a high price; and John Adams wrote back to her from Philadelphia, "Whiskey is used here instead of rum, and I don't see but it is just as good."

Rum or whiskey for home and farm consumption were here spoken of; for among laboring men rum was served out as a regular ration, and during the early years of the present century a gallon of it a month was considered a fair allowance for each field hand. It was used especially during the haying season and at hog-killing; for the latter it was mixed with molasses and known as "black-strap," while, compounded for the former with cider, the result was called "stone-wall." It seems, indeed, to have been

## THE CORN-HUSKING.

an essential ingredient in every form of rural festivity as well as labor. Take for instance the autumn corn-huskings. These occasions are generally associated in popular tradition with the idea of red ears of corn and somewhat promiscuous consequent osculation. The following is a more authentic account of the favorite indulgence at one of these harvest festivals from a diary of events in the year 1767, the locality being Dedham, a neighboring town to Braintree, and the day the 14th of October: —

"Made an husking Entertainm't. Possibly this leafe may last a Century and fall into the hands of some inquisitive Person for whose Entertainm't I will inform him that now there is a Custom amongst us of making an Entertainment at husking of Indian Corn whereto all the neighboring Swains are invited and after the Corn is finished they like the Hottentots give three Cheers or huzza's but cannot carry in the husks without a Rhum bottle; they feign great Exertion but do nothing till Rhum enlivens them, when all is done in a trice, then after a hearty Meal about 10 at Night they go to their pastimes." [1]

But recurring to the regular use of spirits in connection with all agricultural work, it is not easy now to get any correct idea of what must have been the physical condition of the average farm laborer during the New England haying season of a century ago. He worked with scythe or fork from ten to twelve hours of the July day, and the unnatural heart action necessarily incident to exertion of this kind was then stimulated by draughts of cider reinforced by an infusion of New England rum. How, with blood naturally fevered by heat, and throat and tongue artificially

---

[1] *The Ames Diary, Dedham Hist. Reg.* ii. 98. See, also, Pattee, *Old Braintree and Quincy,* 65.

coated by alcoholic stimulants, the laborer of those days slept at all, after a day in the haying field, is difficult to understand. Every rule of health or principle of physiology, as now understood, was not only disregarded but habitually set at defiance. Under the midday heat of an almost vertical sun, men worked with hardly an intermission, while such meat as they ate was strongly impregnated with salt, and the craving of thirst was assuaged by draughts of a fiery stimulant. Even as late as 1838 it was voted in Quincy town-meeting that "the paupers be allowed a temperate use of ardent spirits when they work on the road or farm;" while at about the same time a distinguished Massachusetts divine gave as his reason for joining actively in the temperance movement that among his brethren in the ministry "he knew forty-four who drank so much as to affect their brains, and he had assisted in putting four to bed on occasions like ordinations."[1]

Upon the main street of the Braintree North Precinct, in its most thickly settled part, there were during a large portion of the colonial period three taverns standing at convenient points. They were buildings of a type still not uncommon in the more remote and older New England towns. Two stories high, they faced the road, and before them was the hitching-rail; while stables and covered standing-sheds stretched away on either side or to the rear. A piazza or gallery ran along the front, on which sat in summer those who most frequented the house; while in winter they gathered before the bar-room fires. The village topers were as much recognized characters as the minister and the magistrate. They remained so in Quincy

[1] *Groton Historical Series*, No. XVIII. 15.

down to the beginning of the railroad period. The children all knew them, nor as they reeled through the streets did they attract more than a passing glance. Prematurely old, they drank themselves into their graves; and another generation of the same sort succeeded them.

At a later period great numbers of the more energetic youth of the town went out to California and the West, a portion of the New England migration. It was astonishing and lamentable to note the destruction then wrought by this inherited vice. Failure was the rule; and in the majority of cases the failure was due to drink. In this matter it is easy to charge exaggeration, and neither the gravestone nor the registry bear witness to the facts. Those who remember the old condition of affairs also are fast passing away. Yet any man of middle life, who has talked of his townspeople and of their families with a Massachusetts man or woman born near the close of the last century, has been exceptionally placed if he has not heard the same old tale of lamentation. As the name of one after another is recalled, the words " He drank himself to death " seem so often repeated, that they sound at last not like the exception, but the rule.

While it does not follow that in communities where there is no intemperance crime is unknown, it may safely be asserted that where there is drunkenness there is vice. In New England the enforced industry, the religious training, and the law-abiding habits of the people during the colonial period modified to some extent the evils of drinking. The New Englander was neither an Irishman nor an Indian; and so he did not in his cups become fighting drunk like the first, or sodden drunk like the last. The habits and traditions and ingrained training of a race assert themselves even through rum. Consequently, a Donnybrook fair was in Yankee inebriety as unknown a feature as a Mohawk war-dance. When they were sober the people were not quarrelsome or lawless or shiftless; and consequently when they were drunk they did not as a rule fight or ravish or murder: but that the earlier generations in Massachusetts were either more law-abiding or more self-restrained than the latter, is a proposition which accords neither with tradition nor with the reason of things. Where, in a small community, every class of which has been brought up in a school of the severest economy, and with a profound regard for the austere conventionalities of local public opinion, the eyes of all are upon each, the general scrutiny is a potent safeguard of morals; but while the habits of those days were simpler than they now are, they were also essentially grosser. It becomes, then, a question of standards; for the standard of morality, such as it is in any given community, whether high or low, will always be observed there, and very generally lived up to.

Was the moral standard of the Massachusetts towns during the colonial period high or low, as compared with the standards at the same time in vogue elsewhere, or that now in vogue here? — The answer to this question is one by no means free from doubt. The great essentials of popular morality — the cardinal virtues in a community — are cleanliness, truthfulness, temperance and chastity. As respects cleanliness and that decency of living which distinguishes man from the brutes, though primitive if judged by modern standards, the colonial New Englander contrasted favorably with other communities of the same time, whether in America or in Europe. Decidedly less archaic, he was regarded as somewhat unnecessarily disposed in speech and act to ignore what others were accustomed to consider and treat as matter of course. Untruthfulness is an attribute of servility. The New Englander never was servile. On the contrary, he was noted rather for the disagreeable, even when innocent, assertion of his equality. Accordingly, when he had recourse to falsehood, which was not infrequently the case, he had recourse to it, not as a subterfuge or from fear, but in order to secure an advantage, or save himself from loss. In this respect, while the New England standard was not high in itself, it might have been much lower. To convict an opponent of falsehood — to brand him as a liar — was the result most carefully held in view in every controversy; and this fact in itself showed conclusively the high regard in which truthfulness was held. Nevertheless, as a race, the genuine and average New Englander probably felt more annoyance, or perhaps pain, at his detection in a falsehood, than remorse at the thing itself. In this respect he was in the earlier stages of moral development. Of the lack of temperance in colonial Massachusetts, at least during the whole of the eighteenth century, something has already been said, and more will have to be said presently; so that the question of chastity, or sexual continence, alone remains now to be considered.

The records of its churches tell the story of the moral life and moral standards prevailing in the towns of Massachusetts between the years 1650 and 1800. If made public, those records would reveal much which would now excite surprise, and, in some quarters, dismay; but in studying their pages it is necessary to bear several things constantly in mind, not least important among which is the fact that those pages deal in a concentrated form with exceptional cases only, spread over great periods of time during which the mass of mankind moved along with unnoticed regularity. This fact, indeed, cannot be too strongly emphasized if a correct historical perspective is to be obtained. During the Hancock pastorate (1726–1744) for instance, some twenty or more cases calling for discipline came before the Braintree North Precinct church.[1] They were usually cases of incontinence. Compressed in a series of brief entries covering a few consecutive pages of the little volume in which they are recorded, these cases read like the numerous counts in a formidable indictment; yet they cover a period of eighteen years! In a large rural parish, therefore, the cases of church discipline scarcely averaged one in a twelve-month.

The colonial church records, also, tell the story of an oversight and action severe and well-nigh all-pervading, such as would now be regarded as scarcely less impertinent than tyrannical, the patient submission to which in the times now under discussion is a thing in itself most significant. The church then took public cognizance of drunkenness, of domestic discord and the neglect and disregard of family duties, and, above all, of cases of incontinence. The continued and active existence of such an inquisitorial power is in itself strong evidence of the high average morality of those upon whom the power was brought to bear, and who moreover not only thus used, but, themselves, controlled it. The community was the church, and in that community there was practically but one class. No

[1] *Proc. Mass. Hist. Soc.* Series II. vi. 487–91.

## INCONTINENCE.

one was privileged: what was criminal in one was criminal in all; what was condoned to one was condoned to all. This was a fundamental fact, and it had a close bearing on the relations of the sexes; for in Massachusetts there were no lords of the manor and peasantry as in Europe, or masters and servile class, as in the South. There were well-defined social grades, it is true, but nothing which even approached to the distinctions of caste. Accordingly, domestic and social practices derived from primitive times and other countries, which under certain social conditions would have tended directly to general profligacy, were in New England comparatively innocuous. They left, none the less, a deep mark on the records.

Again, in colonial Massachusetts there was, outside of Boston, which was a seaport town of large commerce, no appreciable criminal class, whether male or female. There were enough and to spare of individuals with criminal tendencies more or less fully developed, — the weak and misled, or the inherently vicious, — and such there will always be in every community; but during the colonial period there was no considerable or recognized portion of the Massachusetts community those composing which made their avowed livelihood, such as it was, by vice or crime. In the absence of this class, many of the extraordinary confessions and cases of discipline revealed to us through the records implied consequences then very different from what similar confessions would imply now. They would under existing conditions, in which vice has been developed into a profession, involve for the maker a social degradation to the level of those in that profession; whereas, under the conditions then prevailing, the same offences were looked upon as lapses of a comparatively venial character, and were not only readily condoned, but seem to have been speedily forgotten. Critically examined, and judged by the more primitive, less conventional and coarser standards of the time, — standards the very existence of which implied the absence of what must be termed professional vice and degradation, — judged by these standards, the entries in the old church records are in no way either hard to understand, nor are they discreditable to the generations to which they relate. On the contrary, the very fact that the exceptional cases are recorded as matter for discipline, is conclusive evidence that those cases were exceptional.

When left to itself, the stern church discipline of the colonial period, though it reflected a severe morality, did not ignore the fact that those with whom it dealt were human. At times, especially in periods of so-called religious revival, or under the immediate influence of some strong individual nature, the church lost its head, and it would then seek to establish some code of morality at variance with human nature; but the bow, thus overdrawn, invariably broke. Such was the case with Jonathan Edwards, the greatest of American theologians, than whom no one could have been more devout, or purer, or more lofty minded. Edwards, with the most elevating ends in steady view, treated his church, composed of men and women, — and young men and young women, — as if it had been, or, at least could be, disciplined and purged of every unregenerate trait; and he did all in love. Jonathan Edwards flourished just one century after Governor William Bradford, of Plymouth, and during that century human nature had not greatly changed; but the Northampton divine had less of worldly wisdom than

the Plymouth magistrate, for the latter, lamenting in
1642 over the "notorious sins, espetially drunkenness
and unclainnes," of the community he had helped to
found and to foster, consoled himself with the reflection "that it may be in this case as it is with waters
when their streames are stopped or dammed up; when
they gett passage they flow with more violence, and
make more noys and disturbance, than when they are
suffered to rune quietly in their owne channels. So
wikednes being here more stoppd by strict laws, and
the same more nerly looked unto so as it cannot rune
in a comone road of liberty as it would, and is inclined, it seerches every wher, and at last breaks out
wher it getts vente;" and the writer then goes on
with these further words, than which none could better express the probable conclusion which any careful
investigator would reach who undertook to draw a
comparison between the morality of colonial Massachusetts and that of the present time, or of other countries of the same time: —

"Heer (as I am verily perswaded) is not more evills in
this kind, nor nothing nere so many by proportion as in
other places; but they are here more discoverd and seen,
and made publick by due serch, inquisition, and due punishment; for the churches looke narrowly to their members,
and the magistrats over all, more strictly than in other
places. Besides, here the people are but few in comparison
of other places, which are full and populous and lye hid, as
it were, in a wood or thicket and many horrible evills by
that meens are never seen nor knowne; whereas heer, they
are, as it were, brought into the light, and set in the plaine
feeld, or rather on a hill, made conspicuous to the veiw of
all." [1]

[1] Bradford, 385–6; see also the paper on Some Phases of Sexual
Morality and Church Discipline in Colonial Massachusetts, in *Proc.
Mass. Hist. Soc.* Series II. vi. 477–516.

# CHAPTER XIII.

### HEALTH, READING, DIVERSIONS.

As, in course of time, the striking exception only is remembered and is consequently assumed to have been the rule in matters of morality, so in regard to physical health and longevity, particular cases of old age in each family are long borne in mind, while the average death-rate is ignored. Some grandparent, uncle or aunt, who nearly completed a century, will cause a whole family to be reputed long-lived, though half those belonging to it have died before forty. The physical health of the people of colonial Massachusetts towns was far less good than it has since become. The average human life was not so long. As must naturally have been the case, the drinking habits of the last century generated a class of diseases of their own, besides *delirium tremens*. Men broke down in middle life, dying of kidney and bladder troubles, or living with running sores which could not be closed. It is singular to note how common it was for fathers or mothers to die at an age between forty and fifty. Rheumatism was more prevalent then than now. A closer and more scientific observation has given new names to old ills, tracing them back to their sources; but, referring to the frequent cases of Bright's disease brought to his notice during the latter part of his life, the last and shrewdest medical practitioner in Quincy of the old, country-doctor school was wont to remark that he had known the new disease for fifty years; but, he added, they "used to call it dropsy, and the patients died." Not only were visitations of the small-pox periodical, but in 1735 the diphtheria raged fearfully, and again in 1751. Indeed, in this latter year more than a hundred and twenty died of it in the neighboring town of Weymouth out of a population of only twelve hundred. In 1761 an epidemic raged among the old people of Braintree, carrying off seventeen in one neighborhood. In 1775, during the excitement of the siege of Boston, a chronic dysentery prevailed to such an extent that three, four, and even five children were lost in single families, and Mrs. John Adams, writing from amid the general distress, could only say, "The dread upon the minds of the people of catching the distemper is almost as great as if it were the small-pox."[1]

Notwithstanding such facts as these, it ever has been, and probably always will be, the custom to look back upon the past as a simpler, a purer, and a better time than the present; it seems more Arcadian and natural, sterner and stronger, less selfish and more heroic. As respects New England and Massachusetts, this idea is especially prevalent among those of the later generations; and, indeed, has been almost sedulously inculcated as an article of faith. The growing laxity of morals, the decay of public spirit, the vulgarity of manners and the general tendency of the age to deteriorate, have from the very beginning of

[1] The manner in which the population of colonial New England "was at once abundantly replenished and ruthlessly weeded," through large families and a prodigious infant mortality, is forcibly presented by Mr. John A. Doyle in his *English in America; the Puritan Colonies*, ii. 7–8. Appendix C.

New England been matters of common observation: for as early as the year 1659 one of the reasons formally assigned for " a generall day of Humiliation in all the Churches " was " the sad face of things in regard of the rising generation; "[1] and a century and a quarter later, shortly after the close of the Revolution, the papers were crying out against "the extravagances of the present day" and lamenting the vanished " simplicity in dress and manners, temperance in meat and drinks, which formed the virtuous characters of our illustrious ancestors." Thus each generation has observed these symptoms with alarm; and each generation has in turn held up its fathers and mothers before its children as models, the classic severity and homely, simple virtues of which a plainly degenerate offspring might well imitate, but could not hope to equal. Those fathers and those mothers were not for days like these.

Yet a careful study of the past reveals nothing more substantial than filial piety upon which to base this grateful fiction. The earlier times in New England were not pleasant times in which to live; the earlier generations were not pleasant generations to live with. One accustomed to the variety, luxury and refinement of modern life, if carried suddenly back into the admired existence of the past, would, the moment his surprise and amusement had passed away, experience an acute and lasting attack of home-sickness and disgust. The sense of loneliness incident to utter separation from the great outside world, the absence of those comforts of life which long habit has converted into necessities, the stern conventionalities and narrow modes of thought, the coarse, hard, mo-

[1] *Records of First Church of Dorchester*, 30.

notorious existence of the old country town would, to one accustomed to the world of to-day, not only seem intolerable, but actually be so. He would find no newspapers, no mails, no travellers, few books, and those to him wholly unreadable, Sunday the sole holiday, and the church, the tavern and the village store the only places of resort or amusement. Last week's politics at home and last month's abroad, the weather, the crops, the births, the deaths and the Sunday sermon would be the subjects of droning talk. Long after the North Precinct of the original town had been set off, and Braintree for over twenty years reduced to what had formerly been the Middle Precinct only, there was no post-office within the limits of the place, nor any public conveyance for letters, papers or persons; and "but for the occasional rumbling of a butcher's cart or a tradesman's wagon, the fall of the hammer on the lap-stone, or the call of the ploughman on his refractory team, our streets had well-nigh rivalled the grave-yard in silence." Yet in those silent streets of the time of the war of 1812, the same high authority [1] asserted there was, as compared with the time of the Slave-holders' Rebellion, far more "brawling, shameless intoxication, quarrelling, profaneness, vulgarity and licentiousness;" while "wine and spirits were imbibed at funerals to quiet the nerves and move the lachrymals of attendants," and "rowdyism and fisticuffs triumphed over law and order on town-meeting, muster and election days."

As it was in Braintree so was it in Quincy, though in the latter town a post-office was established in 1795; probably through the influence and at the request of John Adams, then Vice-President, whose

[1] Storrs, *Fiftieth Anniversary Sermon*, 32–3.

brother-in-law, Richard Cranch, was made postmaster. The postage on a letter from Quincy to Boston was then six cents; to Springfield, it was ten; to New York, fifteen. Before 1830 not a single copy of a daily paper found its way regularly to Quincy. As regards books the case was not much better. A library, in the sense in which the word is now used, was a thing unknown. Harvard College possessed one, it is true, and by 1830 the Boston Athenæum had reached a certain degree of growth; but in Quincy, only after 1800 was there even a poor collection of ordinary standard works of the day, which, owned by a social club, were allowed sluggishly to circulate among its members. About the year 1704 "the Venerable Society for the Propagation of the Gospel" had, indeed, sent over the gift of books already referred to for the use of the rector of Christ church in Braintree, and those volumes then, as now, loaded down the shelves of the vestry; but, wholly doctrinal, "their dark and ribbed backs, their yellow leaves, their thousand folio pages" repelled all but the professional student. Commentaries of Simon, Bishop of Ely, and of Hieronymus Zachius, the Help to Devotion of Thomas Comber and the Latin annotations of Grotius on the apostolic letters and the Apocalypse, — works like these, even when bearing the dates of 1613 and 1679 and made interesting by the quaint device on the seal of the mother society, were not mentally nutritious. More than eighty years later, and subsequent to 1788, John Adams had a library, large and interesting for those days, which at his death in 1826 he bequeathed to the town; but the works in it were little adapted for general reading, and the restrictions put upon its use were such as made it available only to scholars. Had it been otherwise, it would have made no difference. In his famous speech on conciliation with the colonies in 1775, Edmund Burke dwelt at length on the tendency to read, even then, as he asserted, almost universal in America; and probably he was right, having in mind the general condition in that respect then prevailing in Europe, and with which he was familiar: but, in point of fact and in comparison with the present, before 1830 the people of Braintree and Quincy, like their countrymen as a whole, never having been accustomed to books and reading, did not really know what a library was, or how to use it. Two generations of newspapers, railroads and bookstores were needed to convert even New Englanders into a really reading race.

Going back to the earlier period, the Bible, and that alone, seems to have been found everywhere; while in the houses of the gentry might be seen copies of Shakespeare and Milton, a few volumes of the classics, the Spectator and the Tatler, the philosophical works of Locke and of Bolingbroke, a number of sermons and theological works now wholly forgotten, and, if the owner was a lawyer, a doctor or a minister, a few professional books. As a young man, on a Sunday, John Adams, in the old house at the foot of Penn's Hill, read Baxter's Enquiry into the Nature of the Human Soul, and, for amusement, "Ovid's 'Art of Love' to Mrs. Savil."[1]

The sensations of John Adams when he came back to this vegetating existence after having for thirty years been part of great events have already been alluded to. In winter he longed to hibernate as a

[1] *Works*, ii. 37.

dormouse. Yet he at least knew what he went back to, and expected nothing else. It would be otherwise with a visitor bred to modern usages. In his case an illusion would be dispelled. If his experience chanced to fall on a Sabbath of the last century and during the season between November and March, he would pass a day of veritable torture. In order to escape the tedium of the dwelling, if for no other reason, he would be forced to spend weary hours in a meeting-house scarcely as weather-proof and far less comfortable than a modern barn, in which the only suggestion of warmth was in that promise of an hereafter which was wont to emanate from the orthodox pulpit. Most of the remaining hours of the dreary day he would pass seated in a wooden, straight-backed chair, from which perhaps he might, like Cotton Mather on a Sunday in January, 1697, curiously observe, as he shivered before "a great Fire, the Juices forced out at the end of short billets of wood by the Heat of the Flame on which they were laid, yett froze into Ice on their coming out." [1] If he conversed with a young lady, and she chanced to be of a "thinking mind," he might be confounded by "observations on actions, characters, events in Pope's Homer, Milton, Pope's Poems, any plays, romances, etc.," and struck dumb by being asked, — "What do you think of Helen? what do you think of Hector, etc.? what character do you like best? did you wish the plot had not been discovered in Venice Preserved?" [2] He would sit down to dinner at one o'clock, and his repast would be set before him in the following order: "first course, a pudding made of Indian corn, molasses and

[1] Wendell, *Cotton Mather*, 156.
[2] John Adams, *Works*, ii. 56.

butter; second, veal, bacon, neck of mutton, potatoes, cabbages, carrots and Indian beans; Maderia wine, of which each drank two glasses." [1] At two o'clock all would go to afternoon service. In his bedchamber the wayfarer to the last century would, were he treated as a member of the family, find no water for washing; for, if exposed overnight, it would be solid ice in the morning. If among personal virtues cleanliness be indeed that which ranks closest to godliness, then, judged by nineteenth century standards, it is well if those who lived in the eighteenth century had a sufficiency of the latter quality to make good what they lacked of the former. Prior to 1820 there certainly was not a bath-room in the town of Quincy, and it is very questionable whether there was any utensil then made for bathing the person larger than a crockery hand-bowl. The bath-room is a very modern institution; nor was the ordinary laundry wash-tub, of which it is an outgrowth, by any means in family requisition each Saturday night. In 1650 it is recorded that those dwelling in certain portions of the British Isles did "not wash their linen above once a month, nor their hands and faces above once a year." As compared with these the New Englander was cleanly, but even his ewers and basins were strictly in keeping with a limited water supply; and in 1627, Dr. Cotton Mather took pains to advise candidates for the ministry "daily to wash your Head and Mouth with Cold Water," as a "Practice that cannot be too much commended; If it were only for saving you from the Toothache." [2]

---

[1] Fearon, *Narrative of a Journey*, etc., in which is described a Sunday at the house of John Adams, in 1817.
[2] *Manuductio ad Ministerium*, 132.

When the temperature of a bedroom ranges below the freezing-point, there is no inducement for the person who has sought sleep therein to waste any unnecessary time in washing or dressing; so, when Monday morning came, the visitor to the good old days would huddle on his clothes and go down, blue and shivering with cold, to the sitting and breakfast-room, in which he would find a table spread with a sufficiency of food, neither well cooked nor well served. The salted meat and heavy bread made of Indian meal and rye he would wash down with draughts of milk or hard cider, though in a few houses tea might be offered him. All day he would look in vain for a newspaper, or a letter, or even a distant echo from the outside world. Weary with the monotony of in-door life, the nineteenth century exile might wander forth and watch for a time the hands on the farm as they hauled and split wood, husked corn, or tended the stock. Then he would find his way through the village. On the bare and dreary road he would meet only an occasional chaise or traveller on horseback, and an ox-cart or two loaded with cordwood or produce; a few children might be on their way to or from the half-warmed school-house in which they huddled together on the long, hard benches, shivering for hours. Coming at last to the tavern, and driven into it in search of warmth and comfort, he would understand at a glance why the New Englander was intemperate. There, gathered round about the great fire in the bar-room, would be a half-dozen or more rough, sinewy Yankees smoking their pipes, drinking flip and talking politics. The room might be dirty, the language coarse, the air foul with tobacco, and scenes of drunkenness might occur, but here was an escape from tedium, and a natural craving for society and excitement was gratified. It was the one form of sociability open to the average New Englander through the long, comfortless winter hours of enforced idleness.

With the tavern the circle would be complete, unless the stranger also stopped at the village store. There again he would find the occupationless lounger seated on the stools or leaning against the counter; and there also rum would be on sale, drawn by the glass or by the bottle from the barrels on tap at the rear of the room. The resources of the town would now be exhausted. It would only remain to return to the point of commencement, and, seated in the wooden chair, resume Baxter on the Soul, or the Tatler, or Paradise Lost, before the great wood fire. And so it went on as generation followed generation across the little stage. No change came; nor was change either expected or desired. To use again Burke's supremely happy phrase, it was the existence of a people "still, as it were, in the gristle, and not yet hardened into the bone."

## CHAPTER XIV.

### TOWN-MEETINGS.

As generally understood, the political record of an old New England town is the narrative of the connection of that town with the broad current of external events. Yet, when so treated, it cannot but lose in great degree both its individuality and its significance. The events of large historical moment which have occurred within the limits of any town are necessarily few, and those few belong to general history. In most cases the narrative connected with events of this character is already familiar, and to go over it in a purely local connection is but to repeat a story already sufficiently told. It only remains to develop whatever of individuality there may have been in a particular unit of a remarkable system. Having a family resemblance, just as the individuals composing a community resemble each other in a general way, each of the Massachusetts towns in the early days had also characteristics and peculiarities of its own. In making a portrait of the individual, the attempt of the artist should be to impress on his canvas the traits peculiar to that individual, — not those which he had in common with the mass of his neighbors. So in dealing with the New England town, the historical student should cut loose as far as possible from the general current of political events, and labor to bring into prominence that which made his particular town as an individual unit not altogether like its fellow units.

That which lends an especial interest to the New England towns, — the one thing which makes the careful study of them worth while, is the complete absence from their growth of all paternal or fostering care. The key-note is here struck. In the history of these towns, when closely studied and intimately known, all the phases of a natural development — social, political and economical — can be observed. No extraneous influences come into play to confuse action and obscure results. All is easily understood. For those towns there was no prophet, no chief, no lord, no bishop, no king. Those dwelling in them were all plain people. As such, they were neither guided nor protected from above. They stood on their own legs, such as they were; and there was no one to hold them up. They had no "saviours of society;" nor, in their dark and troubled hours, did they look or call for such. When in March, 1623, there were indications of a general conspiracy of the Indian tribes, the little community at Plymouth did not seek for aid from without, but " it being high time to come to resolution, made known the same in public court. . . . But in the end . . . because it was a matter of such weight as every man was not of sufficiency to judge, nor fitness to know . . . therefore the Governor, his Assistant, and the Captain, should take such to themselves as they thought most meet, and conclude thereof." And again, when in January, 1635, measures were taken at Whitehall preliminary to sending out to New England a Governor-General, the immediate representative of King Charles, the question was formally submitted to the clergy of the Massachusetts colony, sitting in solemn conference with the magistrates, — " What ought we to do if a Governor-General should be sent out of England?" And the answer came back quick and decisive, — " We ought not to accept him, but defend our lawful possessions, if we are able." That answer was prophetic. In it was condensed and made concrete not only a century and a half of history, destined to include the War of Independence, but also the essence, moral and social, of a civilization, instinct with stubborn individuality and self-reliance. Its strength came from within; and it came from within, because each town, like Plymouth in 1623 and Massachusetts in 1635, as an organized political body worked out its problems in its own way. Neither were those problems simple. On the contrary, it has already been seen that in the course of the first hundred and ninety years of municipal life Braintree and Quincy had to deal in a practical way with almost every one of those questions which are wont to perplex statesmen. Religious heresies, land-titles, internal improvements and means of communication; education, temperance, pauperism and the care of the insane; public lands, currency, taxation and municipal debt, — all these presented themselves, and the people assembled in town-meeting had to, and did, in some fashion work out a solution of them. Nor, being wholly unaided, did they fail to do so. There was fortunately no inspiration in New England. It is needless to say that the solutions worked out were often rough and superficial and wrong. None the less they were the best of which those people were capable; and so best for them. They were hammering out their destiny in their own way on the hard anvil of common-place current events; and they paid for their experience as they went along. Their so doing marked an epoch in history.

It is in the towns and town records of Massachusetts, therefore, that the American historical unit is to be sought. The political philosopher can there study the slow development of a system as it grew from the germ up. The details are trivial, monotonous; and not easy to clothe with interest: yet the volumes which contain them are the most precious of archives. Upon their tattered and yellow pages the hardly legible letters of the ill-spelled words are written in ink grown pale with age; but they are all we have left to tell us of the first stages of a political growth which has since ripened into the dominant influence of the new world: nor is it too much to imagine that when the idea of full human self-government, first slowly welded into practical form in the New England towns, and as yet far from perfected, shall have permeated the civilized world and assumed final shape, then these town records will be accepted as second in historical importance to no other description of archives.

The tendency of the antiquarian and the student of history, to find among the usages and customs of New England town life vestiges of primitive and well-nigh forgotten systems, — English, Saxon and Teutonic, — has already been referred to;[1] but in no connection has this tendency been more clearly or frequently seen than in what has been written and said of the town-meeting. That such should have been the case is, also, natural, for probably there is no single American institution which, since De Tocqueville made it

[1] *Supra*, 656.

famous half a century ago, has excited so much interest and admiration. Indeed, the New England town-meeting has been the one feature in American polity which no one, speaking with the slightest authority, has as yet seen fit to criticise adversely; while investigators have busied themselves to trace for the Massachusetts town a direct descent from the Germanic "tun," and the town-meeting has been derived sometimes from the English vestry and at other times from the Saxon folk-mote.

On the other hand, there are those who insist that in this, as in many other cases, resemblances, however striking, are no evidence of descent, and that it is easy to give altogether too much weight to similitudes and analogies; and those who take this view of the subject claim that both the Massachusetts town and town government, if not actually autochthonous, are products of New England, — the growth of an English germ planted in transatlantic soil.

So far as Braintree is concerned, its records by themselves throw little light on this mooted question, for Braintree was not an original town; and, for reasons which have already been set forth,[1] its history through six years, from September, 1634, to May, 1640, must be sought for in that of Boston, of which during that time it was a part. When its independent existence began, the process of further development naturally took place on the lines already marked out in the experience of the mother town. Yet in the volumes of the published records of the two places can be seen clearly enough how town and town-meeting were natural and slow developments from existing as well as preceding circumstances and conditions, legal and

[1] *Supra*, 646–53.

ecclesiastical, material, social and political; and, if
the records have been correctly studied, the opinion
of those who hold that both town and town government are genuine New England products would seem
to be much more nearly right than that of those who
trace them to remote and alien sources.[1] According
to this view the origin of the town was legal and corporate, not ecclesiastical or feudal. It did not come from
the "tun," nor was the town-meeting an adaptation
from the vestry or the folk-mote. That the English
of the great Massachusetts emigration brought with
them to New England their political and social usages
and modes of thought and action, together with their
speech and clothes, is a thing of course, nor does it
need to be repeated; but, in the matter of government, both colonial and town, the records seem clearly
to indicate that the usages and forms of procedure
followed were those then in vogue with the English
commercial associations of the day; and, accordingly,
they must be looked for in that charter of 1629 which
incorporated a business company to establish and
maintain a plantation on Massachusetts Bay. At an
early day convenience and necessity combined to cause
the creation of lesser plantations subordinate to the
mother plantation; and, following the ordinary physiological law, the descendants were of the same species as the progenitor. Under the terms of its charter
the Massachusetts Bay company had, like other business and commercial corporations before and since, an
organization consisting of a body of proprietors, or

---

[1] The question is discussed, and authorities are cited in the paper entitled The Genesis of the Massachusetts Town and the Development of Town-Meeting Government, in *Proceedings of Mass. Hist. Soc.* (Jan. 1892) Series II. vii. 172–211.

stockholders as they are now called, who at stated periods assembled in corporate meeting, or Great and General Court, and chose a board of directors, or assistants, to manage the affairs of the company.

The town, or plantation as it was likewise called, was merely a convenient, though vague designation of territory assigned to subordinate corporate bodies of proprietors, who, in turn, made allotments of land or held it in common, managing all local affairs through their own general courts, or meetings of proprietors, which originally, in the case of Boston and Braintree, confined themselves to the choice of a smaller body "Deputed for towne affairs," to whom the entire management of all matters of common, local concernment was intrusted. This smaller body held towards the freeholders, or inhabitants, of the town the same relation the board of assistants under the charter held to the freemen of the colony. Only very gradually in both Boston and Braintree did the town-meeting assume shape as a fully developed legislative body; indeed, in the case of Braintree, so far as the records show, this did not take place for more than half a century after the incorporation of the town, though in March, 1673, an order was passed at a "publike meeting" that twice a year thereafter, general town-meetings "of the whole inhabitants" should be held "to consult and agree upon all things that may concerne the good of the Towne and for the choice of all their publike towne Officers;" but, if such meetings were subsequently held, more than twenty years elapsed before a formal record of them was made. Indeed, so slow was the process of development, — so far were the early immigrants from having brought over the well developed practice of the English vestry with them, that in Braintree they were in their graves before the Massachusetts system assumed final form. Prior to 1693 the Braintree town book contains little but transcripts of contracts, or orders relating to ways, or votes affecting the title to lands.

The colonial charter of 1629 was vacated by the action of the English courts in 1686, and in 1691 the provincial charter of William and Mary was granted. Of what the constituent body composing the "Publike Towne meeting" prior to 1690 was made up can only be conjectured. The letter of the law conferred the right of voting in the town-meeting, as well as at the charter elections, on freemen of the colony only, though all inhabitants might participate in the deliberations or be compelled to fill offices; and the freemen were but a minority, and a small minority, of the freeholders. But, though the law was thus restrictive, there is reason to believe the practice in town-meeting was far more democratic, and that from a comparatively early day all who were accepted inhabitants or householders were by tacit common consent, if not otherwise, admitted to an equal voice. Thus it was in the town-meeting that Massachusetts found the vigorous political life which saved it from atrophy;[1] and in Braintree the famous town-meeting government of the eighteenth century had in 1690 developed at last into full being, — an outgrowth, not of the congregation, but of the body of proprietors, or stockholders, assembled in corporate form.

The active, recorded town-meeting government of Braintree practically began, therefore, with that Revolution of 1688 which terminated the Stuart dynasty; and the town sympathized heartily in the movement

[1] *Supra*, 577; *Proceedings Mass. Hist. Soc.* Series II. vii. 210.

which overthrew Andros, though its action exemplified the extreme slowness in New England of seventeenth century political procedure. It was on the 18th of April that the popular rising in Boston took place, and the captain of the Rose, a British frigate then at anchor in Boston harbor, was seized, the ensign of revolt being raised on Beacon Hill. The next day Sir Edmund Andros was confined, a captive, in the fort. Yet not until the 20th of May, more than a month later, were "the Inhabitants of Braintrey convened together to give their sentiments and minds about a present settlement of a Government." They then voted that the magistrates and deputy "chosen and Sworne in 86 bee reinstated." It was also voted "that the Hon$^{rd}$. Waitt still Winthrop be major Generall of the Millitia of the Colony of the Mattathusetts," while "Capt. Edmund Quinsey," already acting as one of the Committee of Safety, which formed the provisional government of the colony until the arrival of the charter of William and Mary, was authorized to "Signe our returne of the names of the representatives and the order therein given them In the name of the Inhabitants." A fortnight afterwards another town-meeting was held to take further action "about the emergencies that came under consideration" by choosing a representative to consult with the Committee of Safety thereon, and, so far as Braintree was concerned, the Revolution of 1688 was then complete; the freeholders thereupon at once turned their attention from large affairs of state to providing, as already mentioned,[1] a hutch in which to secure "good wife Witty," sister of "Samuel Speere," she "being distracted."

[1] *Supra*, 725.

It was not until five years after the Revolution of 1688 that a list of town officers appears in the record-book, but from that time forward the machinery of town government was complete. The old theocracy then ceased to exist by virtue of the provisions of the new charter; religious toleration was secured to those of all Christian sects except papists; the right of suffrage was bestowed on all adult male inhabitants, subject to a small property qualification; the chief executive officers of the province were thereafter appointed by the King. The franchise was thus greatly enlarged, while the town-meeting was left unrestrained in action. Though not so regarded at the time, the charter of 1691 was, therefore, from a wide and popular point of view, a vast improvement on that of 1629. Through its operation the last remnant of ecclesiastical organization was forced to give way to the purely political organization, — the shadow of theocracy disappeared, and the town-meeting as a developed reality took its place. The officers chosen in Braintree in 1693, the year in which the new charter went into operation, were five selectmen, a town clerk and a commissioner, two constables, five tithingmen, and eight viewers of fences. The next year surveyors of highways and field-viewers were also chosen, and the first specific appropriation was made. It amounted to £9 13s. in colonial money, the pound being $3.33, and it is instructive in its details. It reads as follows: —

" five pounds to John belsher's widow's maintenance, and thirty shilings to Thomas Revill for keeping William Dimblebee, and twenty-five shilings for the ringing of the bel and sweping the meeting-house in the year 1694, and eight shilings for mending the pound, seven shilings to William

Savill for dimblebe's cofin, and eight shilings to constables for warning the Town, and five shilings for the exchang of a Town cow to Samuel Speer, and ten shilings to Thomas Bas for dept for ringing the bell formerly, this to be raised by rate."

No provision was made for the payment of town officers, and, with the exception of the constables who notified town-meetings, they seem at first to have served gratuitously. Nor when, in lapse of time, compensation was voted them for their services, was it based on any scale open to the charge of extravagance. A town treasurer was first chosen in March, 1695; two years later he was voted one pound, or $3.33, for a year's services; and thirty-two years afterwards the amount had increased to only £3, and that in a paper currency depreciated more than one half. In 1717 the town clerk was paid the sum of $13.33 in full for his services through four years. For the work done by them as assessors in the apportionment of the town rate, the selectmen seem to have been first paid in 1716, — there were three of them and they received sums aggregating $7.67. Even as late as 1770, when the board had been increased to five, its members were allowed for their services only the sum of £9, or $6, each, while the town clerk had forty shillings, and the constable £3.

But in a general sketch such as the present it would not be profitable to enter into the petty details of municipal legislation through monotonous years. They repeated each other. Regular votes were passed in relation to the church, the commons, the school; and at times the dissent of certain freemen from the action had was noted. Certain large issues always loomed up as the engrossing questions of the time, upon the

## SEPARATION. 821

solution of which the common mind was fixed. Now it would be the matter of title, and determined resistance to the pretensions of Boston land claimants; and then the division of the town into precincts would force itself to the front. The village theatre of 1700 was in fact exactly like the national theatre of 1850, excepting only that it was not so large. As the tariff and bank issues in the latter were succeeded by the disunion issue, so in the former the question of title was followed by the demand for parochial division. The questions of title to the land and absentee ownership have already been sufficiently referred to, but a few words more may be given to the division of the town into precincts as illustrating the methods of the time. It has already been stated [1] that the freemen of the two sections were so wrought up over this issue that they by no means abstained from angry words, and almost came to blows. For a time the battle raged over the apportionment of the minister's salary. Then an overt act of secession followed, and the frame of a new meeting-house was raised. Finally a joint committee of eight, four being selected from each of the two precincts, was sent to " discourse with Mr. Fiske one with another, and bring report to the town whether there can be any proposals made that may and shall be complied with on either side that may be for the peace and satisfaction of both parts of the town." It was a committee of representative men, for Edmund Quincy served upon it, and it went on an errand of peace; but, as registered, it has now a warlike ring. Upon it were a lieutenant-colonel, two captains, one cornet, two sergeants, besides " Lieut. Deacon Savel." One only bore no military designation, plain " John Ruggles, senior." This was in March, 1708.

[1] *Supra*, 611-13.

Apparently the committee did not "discourse" in vain, or perhaps the Rev. Mr. Fiske proved a successful peacemaker; for steps were soon taken towards effecting a peaceful division. By December matters had been so far advanced that a special town-meeting was called, as the warrant ran, "then and there to consult and consider about, and if possible to fix upon a suitable and reasonable line of division, distinction, or limitation. . . . That said line be lovingly agreed upon and settled (if it may be)." Edmund Quincy was chosen moderator, and then ensued an angry and exciting debate, for the record reads that "after the warrants were read there were some immediately that did declare against the dividing of the town, and that they did refuse to Joyne with said Inhabitants in that affair, and requested that it might be entered with their names in the Town Book." The names were then recorded; and it is a significant fact that three at least of those names belonged to persons active in organizing the Episcopal church. They apparently desired no settlement of parochial disputes which did not cover their own case. But the division of the town into separate precincts was none the less effected, and this absorbing issue disposed of.

Town government was now thoroughly organized in Braintree; and, for purpose of illustration, the record of a single year will not be uninstructive. Take, for instance, that of 1710–11. During those twelve months, from March to March, three town-meetings were held, one in March, one in May, and one in November. At the March meeting town officers were chosen, and a special committee was appointed "to go and search the records at Boston with reference to the grant of the six thousand acres of land by the

General Court to the town of Braintree."[1] Twenty shillings were also voted to Joseph Bass as a suitable compensation for two years' service as town treasurer. At the May meeting the delegate to the General Court was chosen, and also a sealer of leather. At the November meeting a levy of thirty pounds was ordered to defray the town charges for the current year. Provision was next made for the increase of the town herds, and an appropriation of six pounds was made therefor. The schoolmaster, "Mr. Adams," was then "impowered to demand a Load of wood of each boy that comes to school this winter." It was also further voted that "twelve pounds be raised for John Penniman, of Swansey, provided that the Town be forever cleared of him." Finally, the further order was passed by the North Precinct freeholders that Mr. William Rawson should have "liberty to build a Pew for himselfe and Family where the three short seats of the women's be, and so to joyn home to the foreseat of the women's in the old Meeting-house at the southwest end." To this same Mr. Rawson, it will be remembered, there had ten years before been conceded "the privilege of making a seat for his family between or upon the two beams over the pulpit, not darkening the pulpit."

Reference has been made in an earlier chapter[2] to the difference which existed in early New England life, between church usages and town-meeting usages, and to the rude political equality which was such a striking feature in the latter. In the case of Braintree, this was well illustrated by an incident which occurred in 1758. It was the duty of the annually elected town constable to collect all taxes. The office, there-

[1] *Supra*, 659.  [2] *Supra*, 733.

fore, was avoided; for not only did it entail much work, but, until after the year 1740, this work was wholly unremunerated. It was looked upon as a public duty to be performed by every one in turn. Nor was this all, for under the law as it then stood the constable had to account for the taxes included in the levy which he had failed to collect, as well as for those he actually received. A dangerous liability, therefore, attached to the office; and not without reason was it argued in the town-meeting of 1766 that " collecting taxes had laid the foundation for the ruin of many families." So much was the office avoided that as early as 1710, the meeting-house bell being cracked, one Daniel Legaree offered to mend it " upon condition of his being freed from being chose a Constable;" and the precinct accepted the offer, providing that "if anything should happen whereby [the bell] should be melted or broken, that [Legaree] will return the same weight of the same metal that he receives." At the March town-meeting of 1761, John Adams says, "when I had no suspicion, I heard my name pronounced in a nomination of surveyors of highways. I was very wroth, because I knew no better, but said nothing. My friend Dr. Savil came to me and told me that he had nominated me to prevent me from being nominated as constable. 'For,' said the doctor, 'they make it a rule to compel every man to serve either as constable or surveyor, or to pay a fine.'" This was quite true; nor could John Adams well have failed to know it. He had probably thought that, as a college graduate and student of law, he would be exempted from the common rule. If he did think so, he should have known better. There were no exemptions allowed; and, indeed, it was one of the rough towr meeting jokes to elect men constables who had never served, and make them pay the fine. For instance, in 1734, Josiah Quincy, then a young man of twenty-five, was elected; and the record reads, "Mr. Josiah Quincy refused to serve, and paid his fine down, being five pounds." So John Borland, belonging to one of the few wealthy families in the town, a member of the Church of England society and subsequently a Tory, was chosen constable in 1756, though then excused from serving; but in 1757 he was chosen again and appears to have served. In 1774 General Joseph Palmer, being then fifty-eight, a man of fortune and a deacon, was duly chosen constable at the annual March meeting over which he was at the time presiding as moderator. But he "refused serving as incompatible with his church office." In 1728, Moses Belcher was chosen; and he declaring non-acceptance, William Fields was next chosen. Fields also declaring his non-acceptance, "John Adams being by a majority of votes chosen, he declared his acceptance." In 1735 no less than twenty-five pounds were paid in as fines for non-acceptance, and those fines were looked upon as so considerable a source of revenue that in 1730 it was voted that the money paid in on this account should be for the benefit, not of the town as a whole, but of the particular precinct in which the person who paid it might live. Colonel John Quincy's only son, Norton, was graduated from Harvard in 1756, and two years later, at a town-meeting held on September 11th, he was duly chosen constable. A week afterwards another town-meeting was held. Colonel John Quincy was then a man of nearly seventy, and for almost fifty years he had been the most prominent personage in the town. He was looked up to with that respect which in the popular mind always accompanies advancing years associated with high public office. The old man seems to have thought the choice of his son as town constable an act derogatory to himself; so he went into the meeting, and, as the record says, "desired his son might be excused from serving constable." Among those to whom this request was addressed there could not have been many who remembered a time when the man who made it had not, as a matter of course, presided at town-meetings. They were not wanting in deference to years and standing; and, if they would defer to any one, they would surely defer to him. But, clearly, they thought that Colonel Quincy was now demanding for himself and his an exemption from public service which amounted to little less than a denial of equality. Such an assumption of superiority was inconsistent with the spirit of town government. And so, the record proceeds, "after reasons offered," the request to be excused was "passed in the negative," and the town treasurer was directed "to call on said Norton Quincy for his fine." Apparently the old man felt this slight, as he regarded it, deeply, for his name does not again appear in the town records, though it was nine years yet before he died. But young Norton Quincy accepted the rebuke in the true spirit. He paid his fine; and the next year, when the town again chose him constable, he quietly accepted the office and performed its duties.

## CHAPTER XV.

#### COLONIAL WARS AND TOWN CONTENTIONS.

IT is a noticeable fact that there is no trace whatever of the Indian wars to be found in the Braintree records, and yet it does not need to be said that Braintree could not have escaped its share of the burdens of that severest New England trial when, and when only in New England history, the enemy was at almost every door. The long struggle with the French was carried on at a distance, and, so far as Massachusetts was concerned, entailed heavy drafts for men and money; but no camp-fire smoke was seen or hostile shot heard within the colony's limits. The forays of the Revolution were limited to the coast and one short memorable march to Concord. The war of 1812 caused for Massachusetts nothing more than needless alarms along the shore. The Rebellion was fought out at a distance. Not so the Indian wars. The struggle then, where it was not actually over the hearthstone, was at the threshold. Braintree was one of the more fortunate towns. Though a few wretched Indians lingered within its limits down even to the middle of the next century, the great plague of 1616 had in the vicinity of " the Mount " done its work thoroughly. Rum and smallpox finished what little pestilence had left. Accordingly, Braintree was never called upon, until King Philip's war, for anything more than men and money.

The first draft of this kind was in August, 1645. A

war with Passacus and the Narragansetts was then threatening, and Major-General Gibbons, he who had been a companion of Morton's at the Mount Wollaston of the old May-pole days, was sent out in command of a force of two hundred men. Braintree, Weymouth and Dorchester were ordered to furnish three horses, with saddles and bridles, " to be at Boston by seven o'clock in the morning, the 18th of this 6th month," to accompany General Gibbons ; and it was Mr. Tompson, of the Braintree church, who was selected " to sound the silver trumpet along with his army." Among the commissary stores of this expedition were included — " Bread, tenn thousand ; beif, six hogsheads ; fish, tenn kintalls," etc., — " strong water, one hogshead ; wine at your pleasure ; beere, one tunn." These preparations proved too much for the savages and, it has already been said, they succumbed before a blow was struck.

Again in 1653, the commissioners of the confederacy of New England colonies " conceived themselves called by God to make a present war against Ninigret, the Niantic sachem," and the next year it fell to Massachusetts to raise one hundred and eighty-three soldiers, foot and horse, to go forth in that cause. Braintree's quota was four men. Simon Willard, of Concord, was in command, and he mustered his force at Dedham on the 9th of October, 1655, and led it off through Providence to the shores of Long Island Sound. In fifteen days he was back at Dedham, having accomplished a military promenade.

Twenty years later came King Philip's war, and Braintree is said now to have received a scratch from the wildcat's claw. An insignificant Indian raid occurred, and four persons were killed, — " three men and a woman. The woman they carried about six or seven miles, and then killed her and hung her up in an unseemly and barbarous manner by the wayside leading from Braintree to Bridgewater." In consequence of the alarm occasioned by this raid, a sort of frontier post was established on the Bridgewater road, and Richard Thayer, the same who a few years later posed as claimant of the whole Braintree township by virtue of the Wampatuck deed, was put in charge of it. Thayer was evidently a man of a type by no means uncommon in Massachusetts at all periods of its history, men in whom the elements of the braggart and the impostor are compounded, and who, having an unbounded assurance, seek to live by their wits. So now Thayer, who had been "impressed" as one of Braintree's quota, was conspicuous for spreading noisy, false alarms, and afterwards claimed the glory of capturing one John Indian; though his participation in this last exploit was by others denied, while the poor savage was, furthermore, represented as being at the time he was made a captive "so feeble and weake that he came creeping under the fences, and not able for any action, being without arms." Nevertheless Thayer afterwards brought in a bill for services and disbursements, amounting to thirteen pounds, which the "Military Committee of Braintree" promptly disallowed. In 1675 the town was called upon to furnish nineteen men for active duty, seven of them mounted. These figures now have an inconsiderable sound, and convey but a slight idea of the stress of war; yet a call for nineteen men was to Braintree of 1675, with its ninety families, as heavy a draft as a call for 600 men from those inhabiting the same territory during the war of the Rebellion, a little less than two centuries later.[1]

[1] Assuming the population of Braintree to have been 500 in 1675, —

In 1690 came the French war, and Braintree was called upon to furnish thirteen men for the ill-fated Quebec expedition under Sir William Phips. The fate of these men was hard. The town records tell it in a way not to be improved upon: —

" The 9th of August there went soldiers to Canada, in the year 1690, and the smallpox was abord, and they died six of it; four thrown overboard at Cape Ann, Corporal John Parmenter, Isaak Thayer, Ephraim Copeland and Ebenezer Owen, they; and Samuel Bas and John Cheny was thrown overboard at Nantaskett."

Two more of the thirteen, making eight in all, died shortly after reaching home: yet, according to the Rev. Cotton Mather, "during the absence of the forces the wheels of prayer in New England had been continually going round." From the beginning this expedition had not been popular in Braintree. The young men refused to be impressed, and Col. Edmund Quincy, on whom had fallen the duty of supplying the contingent called for, had been forced to write to old Governor Bradstreet, then the head of the provisional government, that there were among those impressed in Braintree "but two or three who will go. I can do no more, without there be some sent for, and made example to the rest. To behold such a spirit is of an awful consideration."

The French and Indian war was followed by a long period of quiet; and after the division of the Braintree church had been effected there was little about which

and in 1683, it consisted of " about ninety or hundred families at the most" — a levy of nineteen men in that year would have been equivalent to a levy of 256 men from Quincy alone in 1861-5, when the population was returned at 6,748. The largest number of men who enlisted from Quincy in any one year of the Rebellion was 304 in 1861.

the town was under any call to agitate itself, though in point of fact there was one matter which seems to have stirred the local waters to their lowest depth: indeed it may well be questioned whether during the ninety years which elapsed between the close of King Philip's war and the passage of the Stamp Act Braintree was ever so excited over any emergency in public affairs, as it was in 1736, over a controversy with one Thomas Vinton concerning the obstruction caused to the passage of alewives up into the Braintree ponds by the dam in the Monatiquot at the old iron-works. Vinton had, in 1720, purchased the land on which the iron-works stood. The attempt to manufacture iron there had years before been finally abandoned as unprofitable; but the dam which furnished water-power was still standing, and it seems to have obstructed for no sufficient cause the passage of the fish up the river during the spawning season. It is singular now in studying the course of earlier town-life on the Massachusetts seaboard, to notice the importance of the alewives. "Their annual return ' with such longing desire after the fresh-water ponds ' — as an old chronicler writes — was the most important event of the year."[1] Long now unheard of and unthought of in Braintree, a century and a half ago these "historic fishes" not only vexed town-meetings, but because of them the whole community was wrought to such a pitch of excitement that it took the law into its own hands. There was never any other similar experience in the town's history. The matter must long have been under discussion among the people, and there was much feeling in regard to this vested private right which ran counter to a public right in no way

[1] Bliss, *Colonial Times on Buzzard's Bay*, 196–9.

less vested. At last the issue was brought up for action by an article in the warrant for a town-meeting called for the 10th of March, 1736. The article read: — " To consider and determine on some effectual means of giving the Fish free passage up the River at the Iron works &c; " and, after warm debate, a committee was appointed to treat with Mr. Vinton for the surrender of his rights. At a special meeting called a month later to receive the report of this committee, its chairman, Lieut. Joseph Crosby, stated verbally: —

" That they had been with Mr. Thomas Vinton and had asked of him, on what terms he would quit his Claim to the River aforesaid, To which (they said) he made no answer, and Mr. Vinton being present at the meeting, The moderator [Benjamin Neal] put the Question to him, whether he would part with his Right in the River, To which he made answer, that he would not sell his Right therein on any tearms whatsoever. The moderator then put the Question to the meeting whether they would defend their Rights in said River against the claims of all persons, whatsoever, It passed in the affirmative, against which John Hunt entered dissent. Then the Question was put Whether they would raise money to defrey the charge that may arise in defending their Rights, It passed in the affirmative, against which Ensign John Hunt and Benjamin Ludden dissented.

" Then Voted, That One Hundred Pounds shall be assessed on the Town (if need be) to defrey the charge of defending their Rights abovesaid.

" Then the Question was put, whether they would chuse a Committee To Take care that the River be kept clear of all obstructions to the passage of the Fish, and to prosecute in the Law all such as shall hinder or obstruct their passage in Said River. It passed in the affirmative."

The committee now appointed was especially authorized to submit the whole matter in dispute to a reference of "indifferent men," if Vinton would consent to so doing. He would come to no terms; and apparently the committee was afraid to do anything. In any event, its action certainly was not energetic enough to meet the views of the townsmen, and another meeting was held on the 23d of August. A vote was then passed that "all such things as obstruct the Passage in Monaticut River, in any part thereof be removed." It was further voted not to continue the former committee, nor to add to it other "meet Persons;" but a wholly new committee was chosen, at the head of which was "The Honble. Leonard Vassal, Esq." This committee appears to have had recourse at once to high-handed measures. They pulled the dam down; thus summarily abating what the town regarded as a public nuisance. In consequence of this action another town-meeting was held on the 14th of September, at which Mr. Benjamin Neal, a member of the committee, was chosen moderator. It was then voted that the committee should be empowered to defend all individuals against any action which Mr. Vinton might bring, "excepting any charg Mr. Vinton shall or may recover of any person or persons by making out a Riot."

Three weeks later still another special meeting was called, and a vote was passed offering Vinton three hundred pounds in bills of credit if he would quitclaim to the town all his right in the river, and discontinue legal proceedings against those who had been concerned in the pulling down of the dam. "Mr. Vinton being present, declared his acceptance of the Towns offer, and promised to comply with their demands, concerning a Deed of his Right in said River."

It was then voted that, after the committee had done what they should see cause to do about clearing the river, Mr. Vinton should be at "liberty to take away the remainder of the stuff, at any time at his leisure." Yet another meeting was held before this matter was fully disposed of. There seems to have been a strong feeling that the town had dealt too liberally with Vinton. Accordingly, the meeting had hardly come to order and chosen its moderator when "Peter Marquand appeared and declared that he had no warning to the meeting, and therefore desired his desent might be entered against the meeting and all that might be therein Transacted." Nevertheless, the town proceeded to tax itself to the amount of the three hundred pounds which it had agreed to pay Mr. Vinton. But its action did not pass without a strong protest from the minority. No less than twenty-four persons insisted upon having their names recorded in opposition.

In the record for the year 1757 there is another passage which shows in a curious way how thoroughly the parliamentary system had become a part of political habit. In the rough town-meeting they evinced as much respect for precedent as was shown at Westminster. They had their customs, with all the force of law. The question was on the election of selectmen. The record is as follows: —

"The votes being called for brot in and examined it appeared that Coll. Josiah Quincy, Mr. Jonathan Allen, Mr. Benjamin Porter were chosen by a majority of votes, Capt. Richard Brackett and Capt. Eben Thayer, Junr., were chosen according to the usual custom of said Town as having more votes than any others, and were Declared Selectmen by the Moderator according to the custom of said

Town. Upon which and much Dispute Respecting the Legallity of the aforesaid choice, Messrs. William Penniman, Samuel Bass, Peter Adams, Jonathan Rawson, Ebenezer Adams, John Adams, John Hunt, Samuel Bass, Junr., Josiah Capen, and John Clark Entered their Dissent against the proceedings of the said meeting. After much Debate Respecting the Legallity of Capt. Brackett and Capt. Thayers choice as Selectmen the Question was put by the Modr. whether the Town would then confirm said choice. Voted and passed in the affirmative."

The last struggle with the French and Indians was at this time already two years old. Braddock had been defeated before Fort Duquesne in July, 1755, and in May, 1756, war between Great Britain and France was formally declared. It was the great administration of William Pitt, and the province resounded with warlike preparations as expedition on expedition went forth; but, through all the din, Braintree seems to have pursued the absolutely even tenor of its ancient ways. In the records of the town there is no trace of famous events. The usual town-meetings were held, but even less than the usual interest attached to them. Questions of commons and ways were discussed; fines were imposed or remitted; schools were provided for; and from £60 to £150 was annually ordered to be levied to meet current expenses: but of the stress of war in the form of calls for men, supplies and money there is no indication. Yet these must have come and been felt, and that severely, for a partial examination of the provincial muster-rolls has shown that between 1756 and 1760 more than two hundred Braintree men did military service. Some were impressed; the greater number volunteered. Twenty-eight took part in the unfortunate Crown Point expedition of 1756, serving during that season only. Hutchinson says that "when the main body of the enemy went back to Canada, the provincial army broke up and returned to the government in which it had been raised. Many had deserted and more had died while they lay encamped. Many died upon the road, and many died of the camp distemper after they were at home."

The following year the capitulation of Fort William Henry to Montcalm and the subsequent massacre of its garrison by savages spread a panic all through New England. Those living west of the Connecticut were ordered to destroy their wheel carriages and to drive in their cattle, while the authorities hoped to hold the line of that river. Nearly the whole military force of the colony was called to arms, and, from Braintree, Capt. Peter Thayer's company was marched as far as Roxbury. They lay there in camp for some days; and then, the alarm having subsided, returned home. Some seven or eight Braintree men are known to have been in the garrison of Fort William Henry at the time of the surrender.

The next year, in response to the strong, personal appeal of Pitt, Massachusetts put forth what she then supposed to be her utmost efforts. A levy of seven thousand men was ordered. Forty-five hundred only could be raised by voluntary enlistment, and the remainder had to be drafted. They composed part of the force intended to operate against Ticonderoga, at the head of which Lord Howe was killed. In it were at least thirty men from Braintree; and during the same season twelve more enlisted on the ship of war King George. The year ensuing (1759) saw the fall of Quebec, and brought the war to a practical close. While Wolfe, with his regulars moved against

Quebec, the provincial levies relieved the garrisons of Nova Scotia. To this force Braintree contributed a quota of some forty men, while more took part in the operations under Amherst which resulted in the fall of Ticonderoga and Crown Point.

The terms of enlistment during this war were short, and the name of the same man often appears more than once on the rolls. But during those three years it is probably safe to say that Braintree furnished, apart from the promenade of Captain Thayer's company in August, 1757, one hundred different men for actual service. The population of the town was then about two thousand, of whom some five hundred were males above sixteen. From this it would appear that at least one man in each five of those belonging to the town, who, during the war, were capable of bearing arms, was put into the field.

## CHAPTER XVI.

#### THE REVOLUTIONARY EPOCH.

WITH the close of the French war a new generation came on the Braintree stage. The last recorded appearance of John Quincy at the town-meetings was in September, 1758, and Deacon John Adams, though a selectman in 1758, was not again chosen to that office, and died two years later. But in 1761, though his name does not appear on the records, the younger John Adams has asserted that he was chosen surveyor of highways, and from this time forward his presence in the town made itself perceptibly felt. The active, inquiring mind was at work impelled by all the nervous energy of youth.

Meanwhile new issues began to take shape. The report in favor of selling the north commons, and thus finally disposing of a matter of long standing controversy, was presented at the town-meeting of April 1, 1765, just ten days before Parliament passed the Stamp Act. When the news of the passage of that act reached New England it caused prodigious excitement everywhere. In Braintree John Adams took the matter up at once. He says, —

"I drew up a petition to the selectmen of Braintree, and procured it to be signed by a number of the respectable inhabitants, to call a meeting of the town to instruct their representative in relation to the stamps."

The town met in the Middle Precinct meeting-house

on the 24th of September. Norton Quincy was chosen moderator. Mr. Adams then goes on, —

"I prepared a draught of instructions at home and carried them with me. The cause of the meeting was explained at some length, and the state and danger of the country pointed out; a committee was appointed to prepare instructions, of which I was nominated as one. We retired to Mr. Niles' house; my draught was produced, and unanimously adopted without amendment, reported to the town, and accepted without a dissenting voice. These were published in Draper's paper, as that printer first applied to me for a copy. They were decided and spirited enough. They rang through the state and were adopted in so many words, as I was informed by the representatives of that year, by forty towns, as instructions to their representatives."

These instructions were printed in the Boston Gazette of October 14, 1765, and in comparing them with some of an opposite nature coming simultaneously from the town of Marblehead, a correspondent of the Evening Post picked out at the time one paragraph as "worthy to be wrote in letters of gold." It was the following: —

"We further Recommend the most Clear and explicit assertion and vindication of our Rights and Liberties to be entered on the Public Records that the world may know in the Present and all future Generations, that we have a clear knowledge and a just sense of those Rights and Liberties and that with submission to devine Providence, we never can be slaves."

The authorship of this paper brought the young Braintree lawyer into popular prominence, and upon the 18th of the following December the town of Boston retained him to appear with Gridley and Otis before the Governor and Council in support of the memorial praying that the courts of law might be opened. It was a week later, on Christmas day, that he and his wife "drank tea at Grandfather Quincy's" at Mount Wollaston, and found the "old gentleman inquisitive about the hearing." A few days after, referring to the dangers of the times, he wrote in his diary, — "Let the towns and the representatives renounce every stamp man and every trimmer next May!" That slow and familiar process of popular education through which a whole people is gradually worked up to the war pitch was now going on. It was the same process in 1765 which had been witnessed in England one hundred and thirty years before, and which was again to be witnessed in America ninety years later, — the process by which, as the necessity for action becomes gradually apparent, the spirit of conservatism, expressed through doubts and fears and efforts at compromise, is slowly overcome. During the winter of 1765-6, young John Adams probably felt some anxiety in regard to the attitude of Braintree, for the North Precinct, he afterwards declared in a letter which has been printed, was at that time "a very focus of Episcopal bigotry, intrigue, intolerance and persecution." The local Episcopal influence was certainly great, and one of its prominent representatives was on the board of selectmen. On the other hand, so intense was the popular feeling, that politics had now fairly taken possession of the orthodox Massachusetts pulpit. For instance, the Rev. Ebenezer Gay, of Hingham, had preached a Thanksgiving sermon in which he inculcated distinctly submission to authority and a resource to "prayers and tears, not clubs." This discourse greatly disturbed the Hingham people, who persuaded themselves that their worthy pastor had the stamps in his house, and they even threatened to go and search it for them. The feeling was not allayed when, the next Sabbath, Parson Smith, of Weymouth, preached a sermon in the Hingham pulpit in which he recommended obedience to good rules and a spirited opposition to bad ones, interspersed with a good deal of animated declamation upon liberty and the times. A month later Parson Wibird alarmed his parishioners by announcing the following as the text of his discourse: — " Hear, O heavens, and give ear, O earth! I have nourished and brought up children, and they have rebelled against me." John Adams goes on : —

" I began to suspect a Tory sermon on the times from this text, but the preacher confined himself to spirituals. But, I expect, if the tories should become the strongest, we shall hear many sermons against the ingratitude, injustice, disloyalty, treason, rebellion, impiety, and ill policy of refusing obedience to the Stamp Act. The church clergy, to be sure, will be very eloquent."

Major Miller was then one of the board of selectmen. The Millers, the Veaseys and the Cleverlys were all churchmen, and their names will presently be found in the town records as those of political " suspects ; " but none the less we get from John Adams' diary not unpleasant glimpses of those thus composing a little knot of Church of England loyalists and conservatives in a Massachusetts country town of the pre - revolutionary period. Here, for instance, is a pen-and-ink sketch of him who was subsequently the teacher of the deserted and fallen church : —

"December 26, 1758. Tuesday. Being the evening after Christmas, the Doctor [Savil] and I spent the evening with Mr. Cleverly and Major Miller. Mr. Cleverly was cheerful, alert, sociable and complaisant ; so much good sense and good knowledge, so much good humor and contentment, and so much poverty, are not to be found in any other house, I believe, in this province. I am amazed that a man of his ingenuity and sprightliness can be so shiftless."

And again, at the time of the resistance to the Stamp Act : —

"December 29, 1765. Sunday. The church people are, many of them, favorers of the Stamp Act at present. Major Miller, forsooth, is very fearful that they will be *stomachful* at home, and angry and resentful. Mr. Veasey insists upon it, that we ought to pay our proportion of the public burdens. Mr. Cleverly is fully convinced that they, that is Parliament, have a right to tax us; he thinks it is wrong to go on with business; we had better stop and wait till Spring, till we hear from home. He says we [the patriots] put the best face upon it; that letters have been received in Boston, from the greatest merchants in the nation, blaming our proceedings, and that the merchants don't second us. . . . He says that things go on here exactly as they did in the reign of King Charles I., 'that blessed saint and martyr.'"

Then a few days later : —

"January 10, 1766. Friday. Mr. Cleverly here in the evening. He says he is not so clear as he was that the Parliament has a right to tax us; he rather thinks it has not. Thus the contagion of the times has caught even that bigot to passive obedience and non-resistance; it has made him waver. It is almost the first time I ever knew him converted, or even brought to doubt and hesitate about any of his favorite points, as the authority of Parliament to tax us was one. Nay, he used to assert positively that the King was as absolute in the plantations as the Great Turk in his dominions."

As the day in March approached when town officers for 1766-7 were to be chosen, Braintree was alive with excitement and intrigue. The church party was anxious not to lose the degree of influence it still had, and its members accordingly professed to have seen new light. This fully accounted for the fact that Mr. Cleverly was not so clear as he had been that Parliament had the right to tax the colonies; and, indeed, was inclined to think it had not. For selectmen the Episcopal faction proposed a combination ticket, — Colonel Josiah Quincy and Major Ebenezer Miller, the former being a stanch patriot. At last the day for the town-meeting came, and John Adams, who long afterwards spoke of it as " the first popular struggle of the Revolution in the town of Braintree," thus at the moment described what took place : —

"My brother Peter, Mr. Etter, and Mr. Field, having a number of votes prepared for Mr. Quincy and me, set themselves to scatter them. The town had been very silent and still, my name had never been mentioned, nor had our friends ever talked of any new selectmen at all, excepting in the South Precinct; but as soon as they found there was an attempt to be made they fell in and assisted, and although there were six different hats with votes for as many different persons, besides a considerable number of scattering votes, I had the major vote of the assembly the first time. Mr. Quincy had more than one hundred and sixty votes. I had but one vote more than half. . . . Etter and my brother took a skillful method. . . . Many persons, I hear, acted slyly and deceitfully; this is always the case. . . . Mr. Jo. Bass was extremely sorry for the loss of Major Miller; he would never come to another meeting. Mr. Jo. Cleverly could not account for many things done at town-meetings."

This was the meeting at which the popular party achieved only a partial victory, owing to the fact that "the north end people," after voting for "Cornet Bass" once, "withdrew for refreshment," and while they were congregated before the bar of Ebenezer Thayer's tavern, just across the road, another vote was taken, and their candidate defeated. A fortnight later, on the 18th of March, the newly chosen selectman met Major Miller, who, though a Tory then and afterwards, was a worthy man and useful member of his church and town. The successful candidate gave this account of the interview: —

"Went to Weymouth; . . . on my return stopped at Mr. Jo. Bass's for the papers. [This was the tavern at the centre of the North Precinct.] Major Miller soon afterwards came in, and he and I looked on each other without wrath or shame or guilt, at least without any great degree of either, though I must own I did not feel exactly as I used to in his company, and I am sure by his face and eyes that he did not in mine. We were very social, etc."

Six weeks later Mr. Adams wrote: —

"May 4. Sunday. Returning from meeting this morning, I saw for the first time a likely young buttonwood tree, lately planted on the triangle made by the three roads, by the house of Mr. James Bracket. The tree is well set, well guarded, and has on it an inscription, 'The Tree of Liberty, and cursed is he who cuts this tree!' . . . I never heard a hint of it till I saw it, but I hear that some persons grumble, and threaten to girdle it."

Planted at a point almost exactly midway between the site of the old stone meeting-house of the previous century and the place where Christ church then stood, — a point where the Plymouth road, winding Boston-ward, turned sharply to the north, and was joined by the town-way leading to the landing on the river, — a more prominent spot on which to set a

Liberty Tree could not have been selected in Braintree. John Adams must have gone by it each Sabbath as he walked or drove with his young, newly married wife from the old dwelling at the foot of Penn's Hill to the meeting-house, shortly before they came to Bracket's tavern, after passing the Episcopal church. Whether that "likely young buttonwood" remained there and throve, or, neglected during the troubled years that ensued, was allowed to languish and die, does not appear. No other mention of it is recorded; and, so long ago that no tradition of it lingers, it vanished away from what is now the busy centre at which four crowded thoroughfares meet.

On the 16th of May, 1766, news of the repeal of the Stamp Act reached Boston and was the cause of general rejoicing. For some reason the event was not noticed in Braintree, which John Adams pronounced "insensible to the common joy," declaring that a duller day he did not remember to have passed. Yet there was a town-meeting held, and Ebenezer Thayer was chosen representative. Two more town-meetings were held that year, at each of which the question of granting compensation from the treasury of the province to the sufferers by the August riots of 1765 in Boston came up for discussion. Like many other towns, Weymouth for instance, Braintree at first instructed its representative to vote against the proposed indemnity. The inhabitants desired " att all times to bear their testimony against such unlawful and abusive practices, but as they were in no wise accessary to the mischief committed they do not judge they can be justly charged with the Damages." At another meeting held in December, Mr. Thayer was instructed to vote for indemnity.

In the following March, Norton Quincy and John Adams were again elected selectmen, and Major Miller appears at the head of the fence-viewers and surveyors of highways; but the next year John Adams, who was then in active law practice in Boston, asked to be excused from further service. Not only did the town excuse him, but it passed a formal vote thanking him "for his services as selectman for two years past." There is no other case of such a vote of thanks, and the occasion for it does not appear. Mr. Adams may have declined to receive pay for his services; but if he did, the fact was not stated. Though fast rising into professional eminence, he was at the time a man of only thirty, and there seems no reason why a town which for generations had seen colonels and judges and counsellors serving it as selectmen should have been especially grateful to the son of Deacon Adams because he filled for a brief period the office to which his father had been thirteen times elected. It would seem probable, therefore, his services were, for reasons which do not now appear, known to have been of peculiar value.

After the repeal of the Stamp Act there was a lull in political agitation, — the action of Parliament "hushed into silence almost every popular clamor, and composed every wave of popular disorder," and it was asserted that the people of Massachusetts were then "as little inclined to tumults, riots, seditions, as they were ever known to be since the first foundations of the government."[1] The calm did not last long. It was in March, 1766, that the Stamp Act was repealed, and in May, 1767, Charles Townshend brought before the House of Commons the first of those Revenue

[1] John Adams, *Works*, ii. 203.

Acts which culminated seven years later in the Boston Port Bill. The popular alarm over Townshend's initial measure is next reflected in the record of town-meetings, and the warrant for that in Braintree at which John Adams declined reëlection as selectman contained an article for the town to agree upon "some effectual Method to promote Economy, Industry and Manufactures, thereby to prevent the unnecessary importation of European commodities, which threaten the country with poverty and Ruin."

This was in March, 1768, and a few months later the rumor crept abroad that regiments of British soldiers were to be brought from Halifax and Ireland to overawe the Massachusetts colony. Boston again took the lead in agitation, and a formal committee from its town-meeting waited on Governor Bernard, asking, in view of the well-authenticated character of the rumor, that the General Court should be called together. It was not supposed that this request would be complied with; but the refusal to comply with it gave the popular leaders a pretext for taking the next step to which they now saw their way, and the town of Boston by circular letters invited all the other towns to choose delegates to a convention. As Hutchinson said, this act "had a greater tendency towards a revolution in government than any preceding measure in any of the colonies. The inhabitants of one town alone took upon them to convene an assembly from all the towns, that, in everything but in name, would be a house of representatives." This was the exact state of the case. The appeal was direct to the New England town system. In that system, acting through town-meetings called in a strictly legal way, the popular leaders saw the material for a complete political organization. The units being of one mind, the way was open to a reorganization of the whole; and the slow growth of a hundred and thirty years was now to produce its results. Without having recourse to any suddenly improvised political machinery, with no noise or confusion, but acting quietly through their accustomed local organizations, the people of Massachusetts were in the most natural manner conceivable about in one moment to take the management of their affairs into their own hands.

In this work Braintree only did its share. John Adams had removed to Boston, and was now busy with his law books; though both this year and the year after he drew up the Boston instructions to its representatives. When the Braintree town-meeting was held, on the 26th of September, Colonel Josiah Quincy and Ebenezer Thayer were chosen to represent the town in the proposed convention. A letter of instructions to them was at the same meeting read and approved, and ordered to be spread on the records, two pages of which are covered by it.

These instructions — and during this period many similar papers were entered in the records of the town — are no longer interesting reading. Though historically of value, they relate to issues long since decided, and set forth principles which few now take the trouble to dispute. Generally well written, though in the somewhat turgid style of the day, they almost always show a clear idea in the mind of him who prepared the paper, not only of what was wanted, but of the means through which it was proposed to get it. That such papers should have emanated at once from so many towns in the province shows the generally high standard of political thought then prevailing.

Nor were these papers the work of a few leaders in advance of the people. The whole popular column was moving together. The instructions, prepared by committees, were read, discussed and understood in town-meeting. Those of Weymouth were cast in the same mould as those of Braintree. It was one voice; and it emitted no uncertain sound. It was the voice of an intelligent people moving by an accustomed path towards a given end which they distinctly saw. Hence there was nothing strange, irregular or mob-like in their action. Even when engaged in a revolution they elaborately argued every measure, and took each new step in careful conformity with law and precedent.

Between September, 1765, and September, 1776, there are seven of these state papers, as they may properly be called, entered at length on the Braintree records, filling eighteen closely-written folio pages. The town's instructions to its representative in relation to the Stamp Act come first in the series; the last in it is the Declaration of Independence. Between these are the instructions to Colonel Quincy and Ebenezer Thayer, delegates to the Boston convention of September, 1768; the resolutions of March 1, 1773, in response to the circular report of the committee of correspondence of the Boston town-meeting of October 28, 1772; the report and resolves on taxation without representation of March 11, 1774; the brief instructions of January 23, 1775, to Deacon Joseph Palmer, town delegate to the Provincial Congress held at Cambridge; and, March 15th, the full covenant for non-importation, non-consumption and non-exportation then recommended by the Continental Congress.

Events now moved rapidly. On the 18th of the

following December, the tea was thrown into the docks of Boston, Deacon Palmer's son from Braintree aiding in the work. On the 1st of the following June, Governor Hutchinson sailed away into life-long exile, and the same day the Boston Port Bill went into effect. During June, also, the General Court appointed five delegates to represent the province in the first Continental Congress; and August 10th, John Adams set off with his colleagues for Philadelphia, having previously moved his wife and family back to Braintree from their home in Queen Street, Boston. On the 22d of August Braintree appointed Deacon Palmer, Colonel Thayer and Captain Penniman its delegates to the county convention, and likewise its committee of correspondence; a larger body of six, at the head of which was Norton Quincy, was likewise instructed to act as a sort of committee of public safety.

For this latter committee there was then supposed to be special need in Braintree. The town powder was stored in a small building on the common in the North Precinct, and some anxiety was felt as to its safety. Owing to the presence of the Church of England people, the North Precinct was looked upon as a Tory hot-bed. Party feeling there certainly ran high, "and very hard words and threats of blows upon both sides were given out." In the course of the month of September, General Gage sent two companies of soldiers over to Charlestown, and secured some ammunition stored there. This led to a tumultuous gathering the next day at Cambridge, and the excitement soon spread through the neighboring towns. Mrs. John Adams then tells the story of what occurred in Braintree: —

"The report took here on Friday, and on Sunday a soldier was seen lurking about the Common, supposed to be a spy, but most likely a deserter. However, intelligence of it was communicated to the other parishes, and about eight o'clock Sunday evening there passed by here about two hundred men, preceded by a horse-cart, and marched down to the powder-house, from whence they took the powder, and carried it into the other parish, and there secreted it. I opened the window upon their return. They passed without any noise, not a word among them until they came against this house, when some of them, perceiving me, asked me if I wanted any powder. I replied, ' No, since it is in such good hands.' The reason they gave for taking it was that we had so many Tories here they dared not trust us with it; they had taken Vinton [1] in their train, and upon their return they stopped between Cleverly's and Etter's and called upon him to deliver two warrants. Upon his producing them, they put it to vote whether they should burn them, and it passed in the affirmative. They then made a circle and burnt them. They then called a vote whether they should huzza, but, it being Sunday evening, it passed in the negative. They called upon Vinton to swear that he would never be instrumental in carrying into execution any of these new acts. They were not satisfied with his answers; however, they let him rest. A few days afterwards, upon his making some foolish speeches, they assembled to the amount of two or three hundred, and swore vengeance upon him unless he took a solemn oath. Accordingly, they chose a committee and sent it with him to Major Miller's to see that he complied; and they waited his return, which, proving satisfactory, they dispersed. This town appears as high as you can well imagine, and, if necessary, would soon be in arms. Not a Tory but hides his head."

[1] Captain John Vinton, afterwards of the Continental Army; but then deputy sheriff. (*Vinton Memorial*, 57-61.)

The powder was removed on Sunday, September 4th, and the alarm caused among the Episcopalians by such proceeding was naturally great. Their sympathizers were almost wholly confined to Boston, and accordingly exaggerated rumors soon began to get currency there of the dangers to which Mr. Winslow and the members of the Braintree society were exposed. Lexington and Concord were still six months in the future, and public feeling had not yet reached the pitch of intolerance to which it subsequently rose; accordingly these rumors so scandalized the law-abiding sentiment of Braintree, that early in October the matter was brought to the notice of an adjourned town-meeting, which passed a vote declaring the report " Malicious, false and injurious, and calculated to defame this Town . . . we being as ready to allow that right of private judgment to others which we claim for ourselves."

Three years more passed away before the persecution of the Tories in Braintree became open and pronounced, and during the intervening time they were certainly treated with no little forbearance. Even after the Declaration of Independence had been read from the North Precinct pulpit and entered in the records of the town, Mrs. Adams, on the 29th of September, 1776, wrote to her husband: — " The church is opened here every Sunday, and the king prayed for, as usual, in open defiance of Congress." In reply, he expressed his surprise at "prayers in public for an abdicated king," and declared that nothing of the kind was heard anywhere in the country except New York and Braintree. " This practice," he added, " is treason against the state, and cannot be long tolerated." Outwardly, and in other respects, Mr. Winslow was probably more discreet, but it has already been observed that he felt bound by his ordination oath to conform literally to the ritual; and he did so, until at last the long-suppressed popular feeling found open expression. In June, 1777, a town-meeting was called for the purpose of agreeing upon a list of those persons dwelling in Braintree who were "esteemed inimical" to the popular cause. The names of nine persons were reported, among them being those of the rector, Mr. Winslow, Mr. Cleverly, — John Adams' neighbor, — and Major Miller, a few years before one of the selectmen, and to these nine names the town by vote added four others. All of the persons named it was then voted were "esteemed inimical," and William Penniman was chosen to procure evidence of their disloyalty and lay it before the court.

The coming event had cast its shadow before, and on the 2d of April, Mrs. Adams wrote: — "The Church doors were shut up last Sunday in consequence of a presentiment; a farewell sermon preached and much weeping and wailing; persecuted, be sure, but not for righteousness' sake." The action of the town two months later was in the nature of a formal indictment of the whole society, for among the names of those recorded as "inimical" were its rector, its wardens and all its leading members. Yet Mr. Winslow alone would seem to have left the town, his occupation being gone. Against the other members of the society proceedings do not seem to have been pressed, and afterwards they all became good citizens of the United States, their names again appearing in the Braintree and Quincy records, and, at last, on the stones in the little Episcopal graveyard. Later, a certain amount of property in Braintree was seized and sold because of Tory ownership, but it belonged chiefly to non-residents. Thus the Tory persecution in Braintree, though it unquestionably made the lives of those suspected miserable enough at the time, seems, so far as actual residents in the town were concerned, to have resulted only in the expatriation of Samuel Quincy and the Rev. Edward Winslow. The other suspects, quietly accepting the situation, made the best of it; and, as is not unusual in such cases, found it in the close far less unendurable than, doubtless, they had gloomily anticipated.

Returning to the autumn of 1774, after the seizure of the powder on the 4th of September Braintree was alive with rumors and military preparation. On her way home from a visit to Salem, Mrs. Adams stopped at her house in Boston, and thence wrote to her husband on September 24th : —

"'In time of peace prepare for war' (if this may be called a time of peace) resounds throughout the country. Next Tuesday they are warned at Braintree, all above fifteen and under sixty, to attend with their arms; and to train once a fortnight from that time is a scheme which lies much at the heart with many."

She then goes on to speak of a conspiracy among the negroes in Boston, which, it was supposed, had just been discovered, and she adds, —

"There is but little said, and what steps they will take in consequence of it I know not. I wish most sincerely there was not a slave in the province; it always appeared a most iniquitous scheme to me to fight ourselves for what we are daily robbing and plundering from those who have as good a right to freedom as we have. You know my mind on this subject."

In the form of covenant "very unanimously" adopted in the Braintree town-meeting of 15th March following the date of this letter there appears this clause, —

"We will neither import, or purchase any slave imported since the first day of December last, and will wholly discontinue the slave trade; and will neither be concerned in it ourselves, nor will we hire our vessels, nor sell our commodities or manufactures to those who are concerned in it."

The two utterances, taken together, are significant, for Mr. Adams returned from Philadelphia in October, 1774, and, having passed the winter at home, it was he, doubtless, who drafted the covenant. As soon as the covenant was adopted he came forward with another report as chairman of a committee on minute-men, in accordance with the recommendations contained in which, it was voted to raise three companies, one in each precinct, to be composed of forty-one men each, including officers. Provision had already been made in January for military drill, and payment for attendance thereat; and now the minute-men in prompt attendance were to receive "one shilling and four pence per day for one day in every week, and the selectmen were directed to supply the officers of the three companies with money to pay off said men day by day;" and if there were no funds in the treasury they were to borrow on the town's credit. The affair of Lexington and Concord occurred on the 19th of April, and on the 24th the adjourned town-meeting directed the selectmen to "dismiss Mr. Rice, their Grammar School master, as soon as their present engagements are expired." Evidently it was thought there was no money for anything but men and munitions; and ten days later Mrs. Adams wrote to her husband : — " Mr. Rice is going into the army as captain of a company. We have no school. I know not what to do with John." This John was her oldest son, John Quincy, then a boy of seven, to whom, eighteen months later, she again refers as having " become post-rider from Boston to Braintree."

It was the general belief, after the affair of Lexington and Concord had tightened the lines about Boston, that the need of supplies would oblige General Gage to send out boat parties along the shore under protection of the fleet. As one of the salt-water neighborhoods, the North Precinct was accordingly in great and perpetual terror of forays. On the 4th of May, Mrs. Adams wrote : — " There has been no descent upon the seacoast. Guards are regularly kept." The widow of Josiah Quincy, Jr., who had died only a few weeks before, was then at the house of her father-in-law in the North Precinct, — the house, already referred to, in which President Josiah Quincy, of Harvard College, subsequently lived and died. On Saturday, April 29th, Mrs. Adams went to see her there, " and in the afternoon, from an alarm they had she and her sister with three others of the family, took refuge with [Mrs. Adams] and tarried all night." A little later Colonel Quincy arranged with Deacon Holbrook, of the Middle Precinct, for a place of retreat, if he needed one ; and Mr. Cranch, who lived at Germantown, did the same with Major Bass. Mrs. Adams herself secured a refuge at the house of her husband's brother.

So things went on from day to day, the now inevitable conflict drawing always nearer. At last, on Sunday morning, May 21st, Braintree had a veritable alarm, — the enemy was actually at its door. Three sloops and a cutter had come out from Boston harbor and dropped anchor in Weymouth fore-river, not far from Germantown. Before six o'clock alarm-guns were heard, and shortly after the bells began to ring. Then at tap of drum the minute-men fell in on the training-field. The panic was great, especially in Weymouth, and men, women and children came flocking over the Plymouth road and down Penn's Hill to Braintree. The wildest rumors were circulated. Three hundred men had been landed! They were marching into Weymouth village! They were coming to Germantown! Meanwhile the companies of minute-men came rapidly in, showing sufficiently well what a hornet's nest the region was. They came from distances of twenty miles and more, but those from Braintree were naturally among the first on the ground. Elihu Adams, a younger son of Deacon John Adams, who afterwards died of dysentery contracted in camp during the siege of Boston, was in command of the Braintree company, and also one of the party which went out to drive the marauders away from Sheep Island, where they were foraging. This they succeeded in doing without loss to themselves.

Through all these events Mrs. Adams wrote that her house, being on the main road, was a scene of lasting confusion. "Soldiers coming in for a lodging, for breakfast, for supper, for drink, etc. Sometimes refugees from Boston, tired and fatigued, seek an asylum for a day, a night, a week." More than fifty years afterwards, while, during his term as President, John Quincy Adams was passing a few of the summer weeks at Quincy, an elderly gentleman named Cary, a resident of Bridgewater, called on him one day in relation to some appointment to office, and Mr. Adams noted in his diary, —

"Cary asked me if I remembered a company of militia who, about the time of the battle of Lexington in 1775, came down from Bridgewater, and passed the night at my father's house and barn, at the foot of Penn's Hill, and in the midst of whom my father placed me, then a boy between seven and eight years, and I went through the manual exercise of the musket by word of command from one of them. I told him I remembered it as distinctly as if it had been last week. He said he was one of that company."[1]

A few weeks after this scene in the Penn's Hill barn John Adams was writing to his wife from Philadelphia: — "Let me caution you, my dear, to be upon your guard against the multitude of affrights and alarms which, I fear, will surround you;" but a little later he exclaims, — "Oh, that I were a soldier! I will be! I am reading military books. Everybody must, and will, and shall be a soldier!"

All this was in May. At last, on the morning of Saturday, June 17th, a heavy cannonading to the northward awoke the town at early dawn. The British ships of war in Boston Harbor were firing at the breastwork which had been thrown up the night before on the crest of Bunker's Hill. The only records which have come down to us showing how that day was passed by those dwelling in Braintree are found in a letter from Mrs. Adams to her husband, and in the later recollections of her son.[2] Restless with excitement and suspense, unable to shut out the noise of the distant cannon, the mother, then a woman of a little more than thirty, taking with her the child of eight, went out to the neighboring Penn's Hill, and climbing to its summit, looked towards Boston. It was a clear

---

[1] *Memoirs*, vii. 325.
[2] *Memoir of Eliza S. M. Quincy*, 209.

June day of intense heat, and across the blue bay they saw, against the horizon, the dense black volume of smoke which rolled away from the burning houses of Charlestown. Over the crest of the distant hill hung the white clouds which told of the battle going on beneath the smoke. There was withal something quite dramatic in the scene; but, as the two sat there silent and trembling, the child's hand clasped in that of the mother, thinking now of what was taking place before their eyes, and now of the husband and father so far away at the Congress, they little dreamed of the great future for him and for the boy to be surely worked out in that conflict, the first pitched battle of which was then being fought before them.

Nearly sixty years later, when recalling those events to memory, the son spoke of "the deep and awful agitation of that day;"[1] but, with that same "deep and awful agitation" still surging in her breast, the very next day, in the country quiet of a June Sunday, the mother wrote : —

"The battle began upon our intrenchments upon Bunker's Hill Saturday morning, about three o'clock, and has not ceased yet, and it is now three o'clock Sabbath afternoon. Charlestown is laid in ashes. It is expected they will come out over the Neck to-night, and a dreadful battle must ensue. Almighty God, cover the heads of our countrymen, and be a shield to our dear friends ! How many have fallen we know not. The constant roar of the cannon is so distressing that we cannot eat, drink, or sleep. My bursting heart must find vent at my pen. 'The race is not to the swift, nor the battle to the strong; but the God of Israel is He that giveth strength and power unto his people. Trust in him at all times, ye people, pour out your hearts before him; God is a refuge for us.'"

[1] *Memoirs*, viii. 545.

There were no services held that Sunday in the North Precinct meeting-house, nor had there been on the Sunday before. "They delight in molesting us on the Sabbath," wrote Mrs. Adams. But at last, on the 25th of June, " we have sat under our own vine in quietness; have heard Mr. Taft. The good man was earnest and pathetic; I could forgive his weakness for the sake of his sincerity." Nor did her own pastor fully meet the spiritual needs of this lady, for presently she speaks of him as " our inanimate old bachelor," whom she " could not bear to hear;" and then says that he " made the best oration (he never prays, you know) I ever heard from him." Two companies of soldiers were now stationed in the town, — that of Captain Turner, at Germantown, and that of Captain Vinton, at Squantum. Presently they were engaged in small affairs in the harbor; but, before this, their presence led to a town-meeting episode which showed how the lessons of history were ingrained in the people: the descendants of the Puritans bore freshly in memory the fact that Cromwell had with his soldiery dispersed the Long Parliament. The town was to choose a representative. Colonel Palmer and Mr. Thayer, dwelling in different precincts, were opposing candidates, and Captain Vinton's company was largely composed of men from Mr. Thayer's precinct. The meeting was held on the 12th of July, and again Mrs. Adams tells what took place: —

"Colonel Palmer is the man. There was a considerable muster upon Thayer's side, and Vinton's company marched up in order to assist, but got sadly disappointed. Newcomb insisted upon it that no man should vote who was in the army. He had no notion of being under the military power;

said we might be so situated as to have the greater part of the people engaged in the military, and then all power would be wrested out of the hands of the civil magistrate. He insisted upon its being put to vote, and carried his point immediately."

During the night of the 9th of July, a body of three hundred volunteers put out in whale-boats from Germantown and crossed over to Long Island, where they seized some cattle, sheep and prisoners, and brought them off without being discovered from the vessels lying near. Their emulation being fired by this achievement, a few days later another party put off from Moon Island, opposite Squantum, in open day, and fired the house and barn which the previous party had spared. Though exposed to a sharp fire from the enemy's ships, the whole force returned in safety, and only one of the covering party on the Moon was killed. Then all the companies guarding the south side of the bay were ordered to go to Nantasket, and cut and bring away the ripened grain. While there, and under the eyes of several men-of-war, they crossed over in their whale-boats and set fire to the light-house. Returning, they were fired upon and pursued, but got back without loss. General Gage thereupon sent a force of carpenters, under guard of thirty marines, to repair the building, and caused a new lamp to be set up. In consequence of this, on Sunday evening, the 29th, a body of men went off from Squantum in the whale-boats, surprised and overcame the guard, killing the lieutenant in command and one man, and completely destroyed the buildings. Returning with their prisoners they were hotly pursued, but escaped with the loss of one man killed; who, two days after, was buried from Germantown. These were the only military operations undertaken from Quincy Bay during the siege of Boston; and though, as Mrs. Adams wrote, they were in themselves but trifling affairs, yet they served "to inure our men and harden them to danger."

The summer was hot and dry. There was meat to be had in abundance, but at one time it seemed probable the corn crop would prove a failure, and famine might thus be added to war. Tea, coffee and sugar became very scarce, but "whortleberries and milk we are not obliged to commerce for." The camps about Boston, swarming with raw, untrained levies, were not properly policed, nor were the food and mode of life such as the men were accustomed to. As a matter of course sickness ensued. The state of continual excitement and alarm in which the people of the neighboring towns had long been living naturally predisposed them to disease, and when the camp sickness took the form of dysentery it soon became epidemic and spread rapidly. Then followed some weeks of terrible trial. It was a time of pestilence. In Braintree Mr. Wibird was stricken down, and all through August and September the Sabbath services were not observed. There was almost no house which did not count some dead; and two, three, and even four funerals would take place in a day.

"The small-pox in the natural way was not more mortal than this distemper has proved in this and many neighboring towns.... Mrs. Randall has lost her daughter. Mrs. Bracket hers. Mr. Thomas Thayer his wife. I know of eight this week who have been buried in this town. . . . In six weeks I count five of my near connections laid in the grave. . . . And such is the distress of the neighborhood that I can scarcely find a well person to assist in looking after the sick.

Mr. Wibird lies bad, Major Miller is dangerous, and Mr. Gay is not expected to live. . . . We have fevers of various kinds, the throat distemper, as well as the dysentery prevailing in this and the neighboring towns. . . . Sickness and death are in almost every family. I have no more shocking and terrible idea of any distemper, except the plague, than this. . . . So mortal a time the oldest man does not remember."

So wrote Mrs. Adams to her husband. His brother Elihu, who had just taken a commission in the army, was among the earliest victims. Returning home at that time, John Adams had started back to Philadelphia on the 26th of August, and between that day and the 8th of September there were eighteen persons buried in the Middle Precinct alone. The disease was supposed to be contagious, so that watchers and nurses could be obtained only with difficulty; and the sustained physical strain upon the well soon made them sick. Mrs. Adams' own house was a hospital. A servant was first taken down; she herself was then seized; another servant followed, and then one of her children; a third servant fell sick, and had to be moved to Weymouth, where she afterwards died. Thither Mrs. Adams followed her to be by the bedside of her own mother, and from thence, on October 1st, she wrote, in an agony of grief, to her husband, —

"Have pity upon me! have pity upon me, O thou my beloved, for the hand of God presseth me sore. Yet will I be dumb and silent, and not open my mouth, because Thou, O Lord, hast done it. How can I tell you (O my bursting heart!) that my dear mother has left me! After sustaining sixteen days' severe conflict, nature fainted, and she fell asleep. At times I was almost ready to faint under this severe and heavy stroke, separated from *thee*, who used to be a comforter to me in affliction; but, blessed be God! his ear is not heavy that He cannot hear, but He has bid us call upon Him in time of trouble."

Ten days after this letter was written Col. Josiah Quincy watched, from an upper window of his house, the ship that bore General Gage down the harbor on his way home to England. The pane of glass is still preserved on which he then scratched a record of the incident. But six months more were to pass before the evacuation of Boston. During that time the apprehension of attack along the Braintree shore was continual; but those dwelling there had become accustomed to it, and took the alarms more quietly. Colonel Quincy wrote, —

"Although we have five companies stationed near us, yet the shells thrown from the floating batteries and the flat-bottomed boats which row with twenty oars, carry fifty men each, and are defended with cannon and swivels, keep us under perpetual apprehension of being attacked whenever we shall become an object of sufficient magnitude to excite the attention of our enemies. Our circumstances are truly melancholy, and grow rather worse than better."

Towards the end of October the sickness abated, and as the winter came on the situation became in every way more endurable. Money, it was true, had already become scarce. Paper currency was at a discount of ten per cent., and a silver dollar was a great rarity. Prices had begun to rise. Those of foreign goods had doubled. Molasses was an article in common household use; its ordinary price had risen from twenty-five cents a gallon to forty. Of the domestic products, corn was sixty-five cents a bushel, rye eighty, hay twenty dollars a ton, and wood three dollars and a half a cord. Meat was abundant. The condition of the people was, therefore, in no way unbearable; and, though Boston was in a state of siege only ten miles away, with the exception that the greater part of the able-bodied men were away in camp, life went on in Braintree much as usual.

This continued until March, the war and its incidents being, meanwhile, the great subject of discussion. Rumors of what was going on in camp and in Congress were abundant. Among others, there came a story, which was industriously bruited about, that Hancock and John Adams had both left Philadelphia, and sailed for England from New York, on board an English man-of-war. In other words, they had proved traitors. In the morbid condition of the public mind, even this absurd story gained credence. Angry disputes took place in Braintree taverns, and "some men were collared and dragged out of the shop with great threats for reporting such scandalous lies." Norton Quincy, then one of the selectmen, seems to have been especially excited over the calumny. Though a man of indolent temper, he went so far as to offer his own life as a forfeit for that of the husband of his niece, should the report prove true; but, a mere war rumor, it was soon forgotten. Indeed, the beginning of new military operations soon drove all such wild ideas out of the people's heads.

On the 3d of March the sound of heavy cannonading from the direction of Boston warned the people of Braintree that new movements were on foot. The militia were all mustered, and marched away with three days' rations. Scarcely a man was left in town, and the place of those serving as seacoast guards was filled by others from the interior.

"I have just returned," wrote Mrs. Adams, "from Penn's Hill, where I have been sitting to hear the amazing roar of cannon, and from whence I could see every shell which was thrown. . . . I went to bed about twelve, and rose again a little after one. I could no more sleep than if I had been in the engagement; the rattling of the windows, the jar of the house, the continual roar of twenty-four pounders, and the bursting of shells. About six this morning there was quiet. I rejoiced in a few hours' calm. I hear we got possession of Dorchester Hill last night."

Three days later, she speaks of the militia as all returning, and of her great disappointment that nothing more was effected than the occupation of Dorchester Heights. "I hoped and expected more important and decisive scenes. I would not have suffered all I have for two such hills." A fortnight later the evacuation of Boston had been decided upon. "Between seventy and eighty vessels of various sizes are gone down and lie in a row in fair sight of this place, all of which appear to be loaded." The fear of marauding parties was so great at this time that the shores had to be guarded nightly, and the town, while authorizing the selectmen to pay the public moneys in their hands over to the provincial treasurer, added the words, — "He removing his office Ten miles at least from Boston or any other Seaport Town." To the same effect, under date of the 18th of March, when an adjourned town-meeting was to have been held, the following entry appears in the records: —

"The inhabitants being obliged to guard the shores to prevent the threatened damages from the ships which lay in the harbor with the troops aboard, the meeting was adjourned to 25th instant, at one o'clock P. M."

Three days later, Colonel Quincy reported as follows to General Washington: —

"Since the ships and troops fell down below, we had been apprehensive of an attack from their boats, in pursuit of live stock; but yesterday, in the afternoon we were happily relieved by the appearance of a number of whale-boats, stretching across our bay, under the command (as I have since learned) of the brave Lieut.-Col. Tupper, who in the forenoon had been cannonading the ships, with one or more field-pieces, from the east head of Thompson's Island, and I suppose last night cannonaded them from the same place, or from Spectacle Island. This judicious manœuvre had its genuine effect; for, this morning, the Admiral and all the rest of the ships, except one of the line, came to sail, and fell down to Nantasket Road, where a countless number is now collected."

At the same time Mrs. Adams wrote, —

"From Penn's Hill we have a view of the largest fleet ever seen in America. You may count upwards of a hundred and seventy sail. They look like a forest. . . . To what quarter of the world they are bound is wholly unknown; but it is generally thought to New York. Many people are elated with their quitting Boston. I confess I do not feel so. 'T is only lifting a burden from one shoulder to the other, which is perhaps less able or less willing to support it. . . . Every foot of ground which they obtain now they must fight for, and may they purchase it at a Bunker Hill price."

And in reply John Adams exclaimed, —

"We are taking precautions to defend every place that is in danger, the Carolinas, Virginia, New York, Canada. I can think of nothing but fortifying Boston Harbor. I want more cannon than are to be had. I want a fortification upon Point Alderton, one upon Lovell's Island, one upon George's Island, several upon Long Island, one upon the Moon, one upon Squantum. I want to hear of half a dozen fire-ships, and two or three hundred fire-rafts prepared. I want to hear of row-galleys, floating batteries built, and booms laid across the channel in the narrows, and *Vaisseaux de Frise* sunk in it. I wish to hear that you are translating Braintree commons into the channel."

Though the body of the English fleet took its departure for Halifax during the month of March, a few vessels lay at anchor in the outer harbor or cruised about the bay for several weeks longer. They seemed reluctant to give up all pretence of maintaining a hold on Boston. At the end of May, Mrs. Adams wrote: — " We have now in fair sight of my uncle's [Norton Quincy's house, at Mount Wollaston] the 'Commodore,' a thirty-six gun frigate, another large vessel, and six small craft." At last military movements were made under orders from the patriot authorities looking to the occupation of the islands, and on Friday, the 14th of June, Ezekiel Price wrote in his diary : — " I went to Squantum, and spent the day there, where I had the pleasure of the agreeable sight of the harbor of Boston being wholly cleared of those pirates and plunderers, which this day completed two years since they had shut up the port and harbor of Boston. The Continental troops were assisted by the Colony troops and the militia of the neighboring towns ; all of which behaved with their usual bravery, courage and resolution."[1] In consequence of these movements the last remnant of the fleet, " 'Commodore' and all," put to sea upon the day named, and " not a transport, a ship, or a tender [was next day] to be seen." Braintree, in common with her sister-towns on Boston Bay, was thereafter allowed to rest in peace.

So far as Massachusetts was concerned, the War of Independence now entered upon a new stage. Neither

[1] *Proc. Mass. Hist. Soc.* Nov. 1863, p. 257.

any longer was the enemy on the hearthstone, nor was the struggle a novelty. The glow of excitement which stimulated and made easy the first patriotic movement had passed away. In its place came a consciousness of the drag and drain of a seemingly endless war. In this respect the experience of one generation is but a repetition of that of another. The ugly details of the past are forgotten, while whatever there was of heroic about it stands out clean-cut and prominent. On the other hand, the selfish, venal spirit of the present makes itself painfully apparent, and is supposed always to be of recent development, — one of the characteristics of a race degenerate. A careful examination of the record reveals a different story. The years between 1860 and 1865 will lose nothing by contrast with those between 1776 and 1782. In each case the conflict opened on a people wild with patriotic ardor. All were burning to do something; many could not do too much. Money was poured out like water: regiments formed as if by magic. Self-sacrifice was the order of the day, and life in the presence of trial assumed an unknown charm. For the time being a whole people had become heroic.

Then came the reaction. The realities of war began to be felt. Enlistments fell off in 1776, as they did in 1862. It grew harder to procure men just in proportion to the more pressing need of men. Values were unsettled. Prices rose. The poorer and more selfish natures began to show the baseness of which they were capable. The voice of the croaker was loud in the land. The contractor grew rich; the patriot poor. It seemed as though the war would never end; not a few were forward to express the wish that it had never begun. The weak, the craven and the mean longed for quiet and the flesh-pots.

Even while the town clerk of Braintree, in obedience to the mandate of the Provincial Council, was entering the Declaration of Independence on the records, "there to remain as a perpetual memorial," — only three months after the last British ship had been driven from Boston Harbor, — even thus early Mrs. Adams wrote as follows to her husband: —

"I am sorry to see a spirit so venal prevailing everywhere. When our men were drawn out for Canada, a very large bounty was given them; and now another call is made upon us. No one will go without a large bounty, though only for two months, and each town seems to think its honor engaged in outbidding the others. The province pay is forty shillings. In addition to that, this town voted to make it up six pounds. They then drew out the persons most unlikely to go, and they are obliged to give three pounds to hire a man. Some pay the whole fine, — ten pounds. Forty men are now drafted from this town. More than one half, from sixteen to fifty, are now in the service. This method of conducting will create a general uneasiness in the Continental army."

She then goes on to speak of the rage for privateering which prevailed, and adds that "vast numbers" were employed in that way.

Before entering further into the burden which the war then imposed on Braintree, in common with all other Massachusetts towns, it will be well to try to form some idea of the strength which was there to bear the burden. What was the population of the town during the Revolution? — and what was its wealth? The census of 1765 gives the population at 2,433, that of 1776 at 2,871, and that of 1790 at 2,771. During the war, therefore, taken as one period, the population of Braintree ran up to close upon 3,500 souls, for in the course of seven years nearly the quarter part of a full generation grew up, the child of eleven becoming the adult of eighteen. Of these 3,500, the males above sixteen years of age must have numbered not less than 875. Experience has always shown that, for the practical purposes of war, men above forty years of age are useless. As members of a home-guard and during short periods of service, they can be made more or less effective; but the bivouac, long marches and unaccustomed fare break them down. They are not equal to campaign exposure. Consequently not more than two thirds at most of the men above sixteen in any community are properly capable of bearing arms. Those above forty years of age, and the halt, the lame and the blind, must be exempted. During the years 1776 to 1782, therefore, the whole arms-bearing population of Braintree did not exceed 600 at the outside. It probably fell considerably short of that number.

As respects available wealth, it is far more difficult to fix on any safe basis for estimate. This subject has already been considered. It has been stated that the Braintree people during the colonial period had substance, but very little of what would now be called quick capital. In other words, they had nothing which could readily be turned into money. They owned the houses in which they lived, their farms, farm buildings and stock. They had clothes and some furniture. A few had money out at interest; and others were in debt. To this general rule of no available means there were, of course, in an old town like Braintree, a few exceptions. Such were Colonel Quincy, Major Miller, General Palmer, and, possibly, Mr. Thayer. John Adams was not an exception to it.

He had nothing except his house in Queen Street, Boston, and the farm at Penn's Hill. The farm his wife tried to manage. Few men were more capable, and yet in September, 1777, she wrote to him, — "Unless you return, what little property you possess will be lost. . . . As to what is here under my immediate inspection, I do the best I can with it. But it will not, at the high price labor is, pay its way." This was the common experience. The Penn's Hill farm also affords a basis on which to make an approximate estimate of the wealth of the town. One part of that farm consisted of thirty-five acres of arable land, with a house, barn and other buildings. With this part went eighteen acres of pasture. Bought in 1774 the cost of the property was £440, or $1,450. In 1765 there were 327 houses in Braintree, occupied by 357 families, and ten years later, at the time of the war, the number of houses may have increased to 400. That bought by John Adams was one of the better sort. Judging by the sum paid for it, an estimate of $1,000 to a house and a family would seem to be liberal, and is probably excessive; for in the town there were some paupers and many poor people, who, living from hand to mouth only, never accumulated anything. The owners of farms were accounted the rich men. The sum of $400,000 would thus represent the aggregate accumulated wealth of Braintree in 1776.

Such being the strength, — 600 men capable of bearing arms, with an accumulation of $400,000 behind them, — it remains to consider the burden. This is no less difficult correctly to estimate than the other. The rolls show, for instance, that Braintree furnished 1,600 men for military duty in the course of the war, besides a large number (of which there is no record) who served on the water. And, again, in one single year (1781) it assessed itself $600,000 to buy beef for the army and pay the town expenses. But the $600,000 were paid in paper currency, and the term of service of the men was apt not to exceed three days. Such figures only serve to falsify. During the Revolution Braintree did not contribute either 1,600 men or a million dollars, for the simple reason that her inhabitants did not number the one or have the other. The drain was doubtless heavy enough, but it was at least limited by the total resources.

In considering, then, the Braintree enlistments, those for short periods must be left out of the account. A service of one or two days in guarding the shore may have been a summer picnic, with an agreeable spice of danger, but in no sense was it war. The men engaged in that service were not soldiers. They were mere members of a *posse comitatus*. The shorter enlistments also should hardly be taken into account. Indeed, experience has shown that in actual war there is no more cruel way of wasting blood and treasure than sending to the field men enlisted for a few weeks or months. Almost never are they of any real service.

A Mr. Partridge, of Duxbury, one of a committee who waited on Washington in October, 1776, asked him whether enlistments for one year would not suffice. He exclaimed in reply, — " Good God! gentlemen, our cause is ruined if you engage men for only a year. You must not think of it. If we hope for success we must have men enlisted for the whole term of the war." This course was too Spartan; the weaker, the more wasteful and more murderous one of short enlistments was pursued. Accordingly, men were enlisted in Braintree for the Canada expedition in 1776, for the Rhode Island expeditions in 1777 and 1778, and for the Penobscot expedition of 1779; others went down to garrison the castle in the harbor, or were stationed at Hull. Furnishing and equipping these men went far toward exhausting the town; but it was playing at war. The long term Continentals were the men who did the work. They were at Long Island, and they were at Stony Point; they forced Burgoyne's intrenchments, and captured Rahl's Hessians; they bore the heat of Monmouth, and stormed the redoubt at Yorktown. This was war. The question is always, — How many of these men did the town put into the field? Picnics and summer promenades do not count.

So also as regards taxes and supplies. That the stress on the towns during the Revolution was great is indisputable. They were called on for money and they were called on for men, for clothes and for meat. But the figures are apt to be expressed in Continental currency. There was no financial, as there was no military, folly which the New England people did not commit during the Revolution. Throughout they showed that the town-meeting is ill adapted to war. They tried to make patriotism a substitute for the provost-guard. They issued false money. They regulated prices. They mobbed those who preferred not to exchange good merchandise for worthless paper. It was not in them to do what Frederick II. did in Prussia, — take the men they needed and the supplies they needed, and finish up the work in hand. That would have been war; and to war with this grim visage the government of the people by the people is distinctly averse. Even in 1757, when it was a question of protecting the hearthstones of New England against tomahawk and the Frenchman, — even then, when there came down from Fort William Henry " almost every day despatches from the General to the New England colonies, urging for troops and assistance," — even at that supreme moment the Braintree town-meeting instructed its representative " to use his best endeavours to prevail with the General Court to Project and pursue some better and less oppressive Method of raising soldiers . . . than that of Fine and Impress." As it was in 1757, so was it in 1777 and again in 1862. What New England did was to campaign interminably, under town-meeting inspiration, with infinite and unnecessary loss of life and waste of money.

As respects Braintree's contributions to this waste of money during the War of Independence, the records are suggestive, but exasperatingly vague. Though full of votes alluding to reports and statements at the time made, but since lost, they contain almost no exact figures, and, even when supplemented by the state archives, they fail to piece out the story. One thing stands out in them hard and apparent: the early, eager zeal soon vanished. Not only during the years which followed could few recruits be obtained from among the townsmen, but the town would not submit to a draft; and in September, 1777, and again in June, 1780, and July, 1781, the Braintree town-meeting formally voted to indemnify the militia officers for any fine they might incur by omitting to draft men when required so to do by the General Court. Committee after committee was then appointed to fill up the quota by going out to hunt up men in other towns. The inhabitants were finally divided into classes, and each class was called upon somewhere to secure its recruits. The poorest and worst material in the community was thus collected together and swept into the ranks of Washington's army. In 1781, for instance, Captain Joseph Baxter, one of the town recruiting committee, had a long wrangle with the selectmen of Boston over a wretched bounty-jumper named Williams. Both parties claimed him as one of their quota. The Boston agents had given him fifteen guineas, and Captain Baxter "was drove to every extremity to prove the justness of his claim to said Williams, but finally obtained him;" though a year later Braintree had to pay over to Boston the sum of £21 "to refund to them the money paid by them" to this particular exemplar of Revolutionary patriotism: and a large portion of the heroes of '76 were men of this stamp, whose names, and after them those of their widows, were inscribed for nearly a century on the indiscriminate pension-rolls of an overgrateful people. But recurring to the matter of enlistments, the records of the year 1780 indicate the most severe stress. They read as follows, the meeting being held in the Middle Precinct meeting-house on the 27th of June. The motion was

"To make an offer to such persons as will engage to go into the Service.

"After a considerable debate upon the matter, it was

"*Voted*, To give each man One Thousand Dollars as a Bounty, also Half a Bushel of Corn for Every Day from the Time they march to the time they are discharged or leave the army; and also half a bushel of Corn for every Twenty miles they shall be from home when discharged; and also

"*Voted*, That the town will pay them the Forty shillings

per month promised by the State, in hard money, if the soldiers enable the Town to Receive the said 40/ from the State. Unless it will best sute the soldiers to Receive it from the State themselves.

"*Voted*, The Selectmen should give Security to the persons that shall engage pursuant to the foregoing vote; and also the Selectmen Procure the Corn at Harvest, and Store it for the men until they return.

"General Palmer generously gave into the hands of the moderator One Thousand and Eighty Dollars, to be equally divided among the thirty-six men that shall first engage in the six months' service as a Reinforcement to the Continental Army. For which the thanks of the Town were voted him.

"The Familys of such men as shall engage for the Term of six months shall be supply'd by the Selectmen with Corn, Wood, or such other articals as they stand in need off, which is to be charge and Reducted from the wages of that person, which is to be paid him in Corn upon his Returning home."

At an adjourned meeting held the next day it was further voted to exempt from tax all notes issued by the town for money loaned it to procure men. Two days later the town again met, and then

"The Committee Reported that they had Inlisted thirty-one men, and that there was a prospect of Inlisting the other five men which is wanting to complete the first 36 men called for, and likewise a part or all the nine men Required.

"General Palmer generously made the same offer to the nine men as he did to the 36 men, — that was thirty dollars each; for which the Thanks of the Town was again Voted him."

At an adjourned meeting, held on the 5th of July, it was,

"after a Long Debate, Voted that the officers' pay, including the State's pay, be made equal to a Private."

At another adjourned meeting on the 10th, "the Votes that was past on that day (5th) Concerning the officers' pay being all disannul'd and void, *Voted*, To give each officer that shall go from this Town for the three months' service Five Hundred Dollars, being the same sum as was Voted the soldiers as a Bounty; also voted the officers the same pay from the Town, Exclusive of their other pay, as the soldiers Receive. Cap. Newcomb appeared to go upon the encouragement."

The calls for men were incessant until 1782. A new crop of fighting material had then matured, for the boy not yet twelve when the skirmish at Concord bridge took place was eighteen at the surrender of Yorktown. Between 1775 and 1782, as nearly as can now be estimated, Braintree sent into the field about 550 men, enlisted for periods of six months or over. The number of men, as well as the length of enlistment, varied with the different years. In 1775, for instance, besides militia to guard the coast, the town sent not less than 150 men, enlisted to the close of the year, into Washington's army about Boston. In 1776 about 120 men were furnished. In 1777 some seventy were enlisted for three years. In no year were less than forty sent, except in 1781, when the enlistment appears to have been for four months only. Under this system the same men in the course of a seven years' war may have enlisted several times. It is impossible, therefore, to even estimate the portion of Braintree's 600 arms-bearing men who actually served in the Continental army, though it is probably safe to say that the number did not fall below 300. For shorter terms and in the militia every man in town capable of bearing them bore arms. The average force of Continentals which the town kept in the field would seem to have been about seventy men. There is no record of the number of those who were wounded, or who died in battle or in camp; nor do the figures which have been given include those who served on the sea. Indeed, it is only through incidental mention in the letters of Mrs. Adams that we even know that privateering was all the rage among the young men of Braintree. Yet not only did she so describe it in 1776, but five years later, in December, 1781, she sent to her husband at the Hague the names of no less than twelve Braintree boys captured in the British Channel on the privateer Essex, from Salem, and then confined in Plymouth jail. "Ned Savil," "Job Field" and "Josiah Bass" were unmistakable North Precinct names, and doubtless several score of others saw service in this same way. Nor was it a service lightly to be spoken of. The supplies and munitions of war picked up by the Yankee privateers went far toward keeping Washington's army in the field.

So far, therefore, as men were concerned, it seems probable that the Revolutionary land and sea service combined kept at least a fourth part of the effective arms-bearing force of Braintree continually employed from 1775 to 1782. They were drawn away from all peaceful occupations, and, in place of being producers, they became consumers; and what the consumption of the war amounted to now remains to be considered. During the three years prior to Lexington and Concord — that is, between 1772 and 1774 — Braintree raised annually by taxation the sum of £150 provincial money, or $500, to meet current town expenses; the precinct or church levy being a distinct charge. In 1776 the sum of £1,176 was raised under three separate votes. This, too, was in hard money, for even as late as December of that year silver was but ten per cent. premium. The next year the amount raised was £1,500. Indian corn was still only five shillings a bushel, its ordinary price being four shillings; but rye had doubled, selling for twelve shillings, while rum had gone up from three to eight shillings, and molasses was not to be had. In May, 1778, the sum of £4,000 was ordered to be assessed immediately, for in April a requisition in kind of shirts, shoes and stockings had been made on the town. A similar requisition for blankets had been made in January, 1777. In June, 1779, another requisition of shirts, shoes and stockings was made, the town to furnish "a number of these articles equal to one-seventh Part of the Male Inhabitants above the Age of sixteen years;" from which possibly it might be inferred that Braintree then had nearly one hundred men in service. In January the selectmen had been ordered to procure one thousand bushels of grain for the town, and in November a levy of £6,000 was voted "toward defraying the charges of the same." The currency was now fast losing its value, — how fast may be inferred from the fact that in place of the former allowance of twopence a head for killing old blackbirds, in May, 1780, the sum of thirty shillings was voted, while the three shillings a day for labor on the highways became seven pounds ten shillings. Indeed, there were no longer any quotable prices. Calico was from thirty to forty dollars per yard, molasses twenty dollars a gallon, sugar four dollars a pound. In May, 1780, the selectmen were ordered to secure corn, so as to be prepared to give those who enlisted half a bushel of it a day instead of money. In July a requisition came for shirts, shoes, stockings and blankets, and another for horses; in September a third for 23,400 pounds of beef, and in December yet a fourth for 44,933 additional pounds of beef. In August it was voted to raise £120,000, and in October £60,000 more. At the same time the selectmen were directed to "wait on Colonel Quincy and know of him whether he will lend the Town a sum of hard money." It nowhere appears whether he did so; but he would, even if he had the "hard money" in hand, have been quite justified in declining further money transactions with the town, as his last experience in that way had afforded convincing proof that the same spirit Mrs. Adams noticed in August, 1776, not only prevailed, as she asserted, "everywhere," but it pervaded the financial no less than the military systems. The New England town organization was in 1776 no more exempt from jobbery than the Continental government then, or the government of the United States ninety years later. For years ugly stories circulated in the town in regard to a "hard money" loan made to it by Colonel Quincy during the fervid period of 1775, until at last, though not before 1796, the facts of the transaction were made public. It then appeared that the whole sum borrowed was £150, of which £101 only had reached the treasury of the town, the remaining £49 having been retained for their own use by three of the selectmen of 1775, respectively bearing the titles of Colonel, Deacon and Major, all of whose names were given, though two of them were then dead; and the brief report closed with the statement that this sum of £49 "has not as yet been accounted for."

The debts due from the town to those who "advanced money for the purpose of hiring men in the years 1775, etc.," were not paid until after 1791; and in the mean time those who had thus loaned to the community in the time of its need became objects of reproach and popular odium, and they are referred to in the Braintree records as "certain Persons who call themselves sufferers by shifting their securities for money Lent to the Town:" these "certain persons," it appears, not unreasonably declined to allow the town to discharge its debts in a currency for which the town-meeting had formally authorized its collectors to receive "one Dollar of the New Emission in Lieu of Forty Dollars of the old Emission or one Dollar in Silver in the Lien of one Hundred and twenty."

The position in which the collectors of taxes found themselves placed was, also, scarcely less difficult than that of the holders of public obligations. It has already been stated that in those days and under the laws then in force, after the warrant for the tax levy was delivered to the constable he became personally liable for the amount specified in it. It was a debt from him to the town; and, if he failed to collect any part of it, for that part he became responsible, and must make it good or go on record as a defaulter. Looking over the mysterious entries in the Braintree town records now, — and those entries will be found duplicated in the records of all the Massachusetts towns, — it is difficult to see how during the Revolutionary period any constable could have performed his duties, or any town treasurer kept his accounts. The confusion was inextricable. It seems at last to have settled itself on some basis reached by compromise, and deemed "about right."

But in 1780 the Massachusetts towns had received

their lesson on the subject of "fiat" money, though they had not yet paid in full for it. The country was flooded with counterfeit bills, the regular issues were discredited, and but half of the £200,000 assessment of 1780 was ever collected. In 1781 the sum of £1,400 in specie was raised, and the town as usual was called on for beef and clothing in kind. In 1782 only £700 were raised, but the requisitions for men and supplies still came in. In March, 1783, the old record-book, which had served for fifty-two years, was full, and when the town clerk bought a new one he noted on its first page that its price was "Five Silver Dollars;" and "a Days Work on Highways," instead of being "sott" at £7 10s. per day, was fixed at three shillings. The paper-money delusion was then over, and effectually disposed of for two generations. Indeed, for long years it was supposed to be finally killed in English-speaking America, as to say that a thing "was not worth a continental" passed into the speech of the people as the proverb expressing complete absence of value; but later years have proved again that nations learn slowly, and that few sleights of hand have more lasting fascination for the average man than what has been happily termed "the currency juggle."

In view of the requisitions in kind, and the utter confusion of the currency, it is impossible to say what was the real money cost of the War of Independence. Braintree went into it in excellent financial condition,—a condition, indeed, which theoretically was almost ideal, for, as the result of the sale of its common lands, it had interest-bearing securities in its treasury from which it derived an income sufficient to defray three fourths of its whole annual expenses. The inhabitants of the town were, therefore, as nearly exempt from taxation as people dwelling in a civilized community can hope to be, for the total annual municipal levy exacted from 2,500 souls was but $270, or less than eleven cents each; nor was there any system of indirect taxation. Of course such a state of affairs could continue only so long as the lessons of thrift and economy which generations of hard, close living had ground into the lives of the people, lasted and were binding as unwritten laws upon them. The time inevitably must have come when the absence of any sense of public burden would have led to extravagance and corruption; but in 1770 that time was far distant. The town then was a capitalist, — a very considerable money-lender for that day, — holding in its treasury the bonds of many of its more prominent inhabitants, bearing interest and secured by the mortgage of real estate. In the course of the Revolutionary troubles all this accumulation disappeared, and, when peace came at last, Braintree was heavily in debt. The annual tax levy, which before the war was only £150, after it became £1,000. The cases of individual hardship must have been many; but, fortunately, there were in those days few who lived on fixed incomes. Indeed, the minister was almost the only such person who could be suggested. All others were dependent for support on their hands, or the produce of their fields. Taxes and the increased price of labor more than used up the whole profits of industry, and, during the entire Revolutionary period, the people were eating into their accumulated substance. Braintree, it has been seen, kept an average of at least seventy men in the Continental army, besides the indeterminate number employed in the Massachusetts service on its uniformly unfortunate independent expeditions to Maine, Rhode

Island or the like. While it is impossible even to approximate the cost, expressed in hard money, of the men employed in the enterprises last referred to, it would certainly not seem out of the way to average the daily charge of those serving in the Continental army at three shillings, or fifty cents, per day, which would include food, clothing and munitions, as well as pay; any possible margin of excess in this allowance serving as an offset for expense incurred on all accounts not included in the Continental service. Estimated on this far from extravagant basis, the War of Independence could not have cost the inhabitants of Braintree less than $100,000 in money. It has been seen that this sum was probably equivalent to a quarter part of the entire accumulation since the settlement of the town. That one fourth part of the whole substance of the community should have been thus consumed in distant military operations seems incredible; and the statement of the fact should cause in subsequent generations a realizing sense of the obstinate spirit of independence which nerved the patriot side. In 1786 the population was not yet so large as it had been ten years before, in 1776, and a long period of terrible depression followed the return of peace. The stress had indeed been great, and the loss of men and means oppressive; but none the less Braintree had been fortunate, — the war had never once crossed the boundary of the town.

The military contribution of Braintree to the War of Independence was limited to men and supplies. She furnished no officer who rose to high command, or evinced marked soldierly qualities. Deacon Joseph Palmer was commissioned brigadier-general; but, though a man of active nature and full of enterprise

of a certain sort, Palmer was then sixty years of age.
His campaigning days were past. Full of zeal, he
was at Bunker Hill, and subsequently very active during the siege of Boston; but his largest experience
was as commander of the Massachusetts contingent in
the unfortunate "secret expedition" of September,
1777, planned to drive the British from Rhode Island.
It is claimed that the wretched failure of the expedition was not to be laid at General Palmer's door; but
Mrs. Adams could not refrain from saying in a letter
to her husband, — "I know you will be mortified, but
if you want your arms crowned with victory, you
should not appoint what General Gates calls dreaming
deacons to conduct them."

During the later years of the struggle John Adams
was absent from the country. In November, 1777,
he came home from Philadelphia, and then, while
still at Braintree, was selected to represent the Congress in Europe. All arrangements having been made,
the frigate Boston reported in Boston Harbor to carry
him abroad, and in February it lay at anchor in Nantasket Roads. On the morning of the 13th, Mr.
Adams left his house at Penn's Hill, and accompanied
by his son John Quincy, a boy of ten, drove down to
Norton Quincy's, at Mount Wollaston, on the Germantown road. His wife did not accompany him;
most probably she did not feel equal to it. Hardly
had he got to Norton Quincy's when a boat from the
frigate pulled up to the beach. In it was Captain
Tucker, of the Boston. Coming up to the house he
joined Mr. Adams, who, after writing a few hurried
lines to his wife, walked down to the shore, and, bidding good-by to Norton Quincy, the party was rowed
across the bay to the frigate. As the father and the

young lad drew away from the familiar land, they could not but have cast homesick glances back to it; for it was midwinter, and the British were masters of the sea. But "Johnny," his father wrote, behaved "like a man."[1]

Mr. Adams returned after an absence of eighteen months, reaching Braintree on the 2d of August, 1779. He came home on the French frigate La Sensible, and, strange to say, he and his young son were landed on the very beach of the Mount Wollaston farm, close to Norton Quincy's house, from which they had embarked in Commodore Tucker's barge a year and a half before.[2] To those dwelling in the monotony of the quiet Massachusetts town it was as if the returned, ocean-tossed wanderers had suddenly dropped from the skies. A week later a town-meeting was held for the purpose, among other things, of choosing delegates to the convention which was to meet at Cambridge, on the 1st of September, for the purpose of framing a state constitution. It was voted to send only one delegate, and "the Honble. John Adams, Esq., was chosen for that purpose." The convention met, and while in attendance upon it, with the draft of the instrument the preparation of which had been committed to him[3] still incomplete, Mr. Adams was again sent abroad, and left Braintree on the 13th of November, shortly before the setting in of what his wife afterwards wrote to him was "the sublimest winter I ever saw. In the latter part of December and beginning of January there fell the highest snow known since the year 1740;

---

[1] *Familiar Letters of John Adams and his Wife*, 326; J. Q. Adams, *Memoirs*, xii. 277.

[2] J. Q. Adams, *Memoirs*, ix. 12.

[3] *Proc. Mass. Hist. Soc.* Nov. 1860, pp. 88–92.

and from that time to [the close of February] the Bay has been frozen so hard that people have walked, rode and sledded over it to Boston. It was frozen across Nantasket Road so that no vessel could come in or go out for a month after the storms." But, like most steadily severe winters, unbroken by rain or thaw, that of 1780 was healthy, the people of Braintree suffering only for need of fuel; in that respect sharing to a small extent in the hardships of Washington's army in its New Jersey cantonments, where, in the coldest winter of the century, the snow lay two feet deep about soldiers insufficiently supplied with either food or clothes, and the term of enlistment of a large part of whom expired with the year.

It was not until the summer of 1788, when the war had been closed for more than five years, that Mr. Adams returned to Braintree, and in July, 1784, his wife had joined him in London. Fifty-six years later Josiah Quincy, then a man verging upon seventy, described how he, a boy of twelve, went with his mother in June to bid Mrs. Adams farewell before she left the house at the foot of Penn's Hill, not again to return to it, for her voyage across the Atlantic. "I remember her a matronly beauty, in which respect she yielded to few of her sex, full of joy and elevated with hope. Peace had just been declared, Independence obtained, and she was preparing to go from that humble mansion to join the husband she loved at the Court of St. James." [1]

[1] Whitney, *Commemorative Discourse*, 1840, p. 53.

## CHAPTER XVII.

#### EXHAUSTION.

It was in November, 1779, four years and a half before his wife left Braintree to join him in London, that John Adams left with James Bowdoin and Samuel Adams, his associates on the committee of the Cambridge convention, his unfinished draft of the Massachusetts Constitution of 1780. On the 22d of the following May "the freeholders and other inhabitants of Braintree qualified to vote in the choice of a Representative" — so the record ran — met in the Middle Precinct meeting-house and made choice of Richard Cranch to the General Court; at the same time "the male Inhabitants of said Town of the age of Twenty-one Years and upwards" were assembled to consider of the form of government agreed on by the convention. "The Form being Read, The Town thought proper to choose a Committee to take the same under consideration and Report upon the adjournment." A committee of fifteen was accordingly selected, with General Palmer at its head. This was by no means the first time in recent years that the inhabitants of Braintree had met to consider questions of fundamental law; and, indeed, nothing could be more characteristic than the formal and deliberate manner in which they uniformly approached the subject. They seemed fully impressed with its importance. In February, 1778, the Articles of Confederation and Perpetual Union then drawn up by the Continental Congress had been submitted. The Braintree record states that in the town-meeting these articles were " distinctly and Repeatedly read and maturely considered." They were approved except in one point. The action of the town upon this was significant, as showing how jealous the ordinary New Englander was of his local independence, and what a vast educational work then remained to be done before a stable Federal constitution had any chance of adoption. It was provided in the Articles of Confederation of 1778 that Congress should " have the sole and exclusive right and power of determining on peace or war." For this necessary provision the town of Braintree formally submitted the following absurd substitute: — " The United States in Congress Assembled shall first obtain the approbation of the Legislative Body of each of the United States, or the major part of them, before they shall determine on peace or war."

At this same time the General Court having seen fit, as Bancroft expresses it, to form themselves into a constituent convention, submitted a draft of a state constitution for approval by the people. It was considered in a Braintree town-meeting held on the 13th of April. Having been read, it was referred to a committee of fifteen to take the same " under Consideration and Report upon the adjournment." Capt. Peter B. Adams, a younger brother of John, was chairman of this committee. A month later it reported that those composing it " did not approve " of the proposed government, and " it being put to the members present, thirteen was in favor of the form, seventy-four against it."

It has been asserted that the history of the world

contains no record of a people which, in the institution of its government, moved with the caution which during 1779 and 1780 marked the proceedings of Massachusetts,[1] and the truth of this statement was certainly exemplified in the case of Braintree. The committee of fifteen, of which General Palmer was chairman, included among its titled members one general, two colonels, two majors, one captain, one lieutenant, two deacons and a judge, and for two weeks it had the draft of the proposed constitution under careful advisement. It was understood to have been framed in large part by their own fellow townsman; but when, on the 5th of June, the committee reported the instrument back to the town-meeting, it recommended " sum alterations and amendments, which being read to the Town was Voted and axcepted." General Palmer was then chosen a delegate, in place of John Adams, to attend the convention which was to perfect the draft. The first election under the Constitution was held on the 4th of the following September, and in Braintree 106 votes were cast for governor, of which John Hancock received 95, and James Bowdoin 11.

In 1780 the war, so far as Braintree was concerned, entered on the dreary, dragging stage which preceded its close two years later. It was in May of this year that Charleston was captured by the British forces, and in August Gates was defeated at Camden by Cornwallis; while the next month occurred the treason of Arnold and the execution of André. In May the Braintree town-meeting fixed the price of a day's work on the highways " at seven pounds, Ten shillings and all other Labour in the usual proportion," and

[1] Bancroft (ed. 1876), vi. 309.

Mrs. Adams wrote to her husband, — " Our poor old currency is breathing its last gasp." This was the year already referred to as that of the most severe stress, when forty-five men were called for from Braintree, or what practically amounted to one man out of each eight who were still left capable of bearing arms. The difficulty found in raising that large quota of recruits has been described, as well as how the town practically nullified the action of the General Court by voting " to Indemnify the militia Officers from any Fines that may be lay'd on them for Ommitting or neglecting to Draught the men when Required." Mrs. Adams was quite justified in writing, — " The efforts are great, and we give, this campaign, more than half our property to defend the other. He who tarries from the field cannot possibly earn sufficient at home to reward him who takes it." In September, at the very time of Arnold's treason, a " Silver money Tax " was imposed, and in October Mrs. Adams wrote telling how flour was a dollar and a half a pound, and mutton nine dollars, — " Money scarce ; plenty of goods; *enormous* taxes." As if to make matters worse, the General Court had passed a legal tender act intended to bolster up the rapidly vanishing value of the paper money, and during the first month of the following year, 1781, Mrs. Adams again wrote to Mr. Adams, — " A repeal of the obnoxious tender act has passed the House and Senate. The Governor, as has been heretofore predicted, when anything not quite popular is in agitation, has the gout, and is confined to bed. A false weight and a false balance are an abomination, and in that light this tender act must be viewed by every impartial person. Who but an idiot would believe that forty were equal

to seventy-five? But the repeal gives us reason to
hope that . . . the heavy taxes which now distress all
orders will be lessened. . . . Yet our state taxes are
but as a grain of mustard seed, when compared with
our town taxes."

So affairs continued, until, on the 28th of January,
1783, exactly two years from the day on which Mrs.
Adams wrote the words just quoted, her husband put
his name at Versailles to the preliminary articles of
peace. The long, seemingly endless war was at last
over, and now the people of Braintree, in common
with the rest of the State, began to feel the full effects
of the reaction which followed. The financial collapse was complete; business and enterprise seemed
dead, and labor in little demand. The discontent
was general, and an inferior set of political leaders
cropped out. It was the time before Shays' insurrection. Yet, so far as the record shows, the town of
Braintree had now fallen back into the accustomed
ways; the regular town-meeting was held, and the
usual action taken at it, the great question of the day,
of course, relating to finances, for they were in dire
confusion. The valuation for work done on the highways had fallen from the nominal paper price of $40
a day in 1781 to fifty cents in 1782, and in the collection of taxes a dollar in silver was ordered to be accepted in lieu of $120 in Continental currency. The
schools had been reopened; and, though the Committee of Safety was still in existence, its work had
ceased. But there was one subject, besides the town
debts and the badness of the times, which now worried Braintree. The General Court had passed an
act determining the legal limits of the Sabbath. Accordingly the warrant for the March meeting of 1783

contained an article "that the town may advise thereon and act as they shall think most agreeable to the Sacred Law of God." When the meeting had assembled, Deacon Holbrook, of the Middle Precinct, was chosen moderator, and a vote was passed " that it should be deemed a disorder for any person to go upon the seats in the meeting-house with their feet." Finally the article relating to the Lord's Day was referred to a committee of seven, of which Joshua Hayward was chairman. The report of this committee was presented at an adjourned meeting, and, after two readings, was accepted and approved. No extract can do justice to it. As the criticism of an individual town-meeting upon a solemn legislative act, it is unique and characteristic. After stating that under the terms of the act in question the Sabbath was curtailed six hours on the ground that there were " deferant opinions among the sober and Consciencious Persons of the same," the report proceeded as follows : —

"A very slender excuse indeed to whom ought we to hearken to the Great Governor of the world or to the Voice of the sober and consciencious People, a semmilar excuse once was given by a King of Gods antient People for his disobedience of a special command because he feared the people but the inspired Profits Introgative Answer was hath the Lord as great dilght in burn offerings and sacrifice as in obeying the Voice of the Lord behold to obey is better than sacrifice and to hearken than the fat of Rambs. We cannot conceive that the diference of opinion or the fear of the People ought to cause an abolition of that sacred command ye fourth Commandment but that it ought to have it due extent at one end or the other, perhaps in some future day this sober and Conscientious party may request

an other part of six hours more to be abolished and so on,
untill that Great and most Interesting command becomes
null and void, not by the traditions of men, but by the Law
of the State."

The next formal instructions approved by the town
were three years later, when, in the summer of 1786,
Massachusetts was seething with that spirit of discontent which a few months afterwards culminated in
Shays' rebellion.

There can be no question that individually the New
England community then felt poor. Those who could
had borrowed at usurious interest to pay taxes, and
now no one had any ready money. Under these circumstances, seeing no way out of the evil which surrounded them, the people of Braintree seem to have
shared to the full in the general discontent, and in
May, 1786, after choosing a representative, a committee
of nine was appointed to prepare instructions for him.
This committee was further directed to present these
instructions to the town " for their approbation previous to their being delivered to the representative."
Accordingly, at the adjourned meeting three weeks
later the instructions were submitted, and, in the words
of the record, " were debated upon untill it was dark in
the house, and the inhabitants Dispersed without passing any Vote whatever." Ten days later a special
town-meeting was summoned to further consider the
instructions, and a new committee of five was appointed.
The town was now clearly bent on action, for it gave
its committee thirty minutes only in which to consider
the subject. At the end of that time the moderator
called the meeting to order, and the committee submitted its report. The town's representative was
thereupon instructed to use his efforts to secure the
following results : —

"1st. To remove the Court [State Legislature] from Boston.

"2dly. To Tax all Public Securities.

"3dly. To Tax money on hand and on Interest.

"4thly. To Lower the Sallery of place men.

"5thly. Make Land a Tender for all debts at the Price it stood at when the debts were contracted.

"6thly. To take some measur to prevent the growing Power of Attorneys or Barristers at Law." [1]

This was in July. In September following, three months before Shays' outbreak, these instructions were more fully matured at another town-meeting. In their final shape they breathed the full communistic spirit of the time, and contrast singularly with the better papers of ten years before. A new set of men had come forward in town affairs who could neither write English nor grasp principles of political action. Braintree accordingly now indulged in the following rhetorical bombast : —

" The clouds are gathering over our heads pregnant with the most gloomy aspects, we abhor and detest violent measures. To fly to Clubs or Armes, to divert the impending Ruin the consequences of which would render us easy victims to foreign and inveterate foes. No as Loyal Subjects and Cytizens inflamed with true Patriotism we feel ourselves chearfully willing to lend our aid at all times in supporting the dignity of Government, but in as much as there are numerous Grievances or intolerable Burthens by some means or other lying on the Good Subjects of this republic, Our Eyes under Heaven are upon the Legislature of this Common-

---

[1] See the articles in warrant for town-meeting held in Groton at this time, *Proc. Mass. Hist. Soc.* Series II. i. 299–300 ; and the causes of public discontent enumerated in the published memorial of the Worcester county convention which met at Leicester, August 15, six weeks after the town-meeting in Braintree. Barry, *Massachusetts*, iii. 225.

wealth and their names will shine Brighter in the American annals by preserving the invaluable Liberties of their own People than if they ware to Cary the Terror of their Armes as far as Gibralter."

Then followed in ten specifications a statement of the grievances complained of, and the remedies suggested therefor. These it is needless to repeat. What the people really objected to was paying their debts. The machinery through which debts were collected was consequently peculiarly obnoxious to them. In regard to it they expressed themselves as follows : —

" 2dly. That the Court of Common Pleas and the General sessions of the Peace be removed in perpetuam rei Memoriam.

" 6thly. We humbly request that there may be such Laws compiled as may crush or at least put a proper check or restraint on that order of Gentlemen denominated Lawyers the completion of whos modern conduct appears to us to tend rather to the distruction than the preservation of this Commonwealth."

Yet in this matter, also, the town-meeting would seem to have served as a safety-valve. The discontent, for which some ground did exist, there found expression; and the people felt better for it. The spirit of dissatisfaction at least had its say, and afterwards, when the time for decisive action came, the town arrayed itself on the right side. In December the disturbances in the western counties occurred, and courts, confronted by bayonets and hickory clubs, had to be adjourned. On the 12th of January Governor Bowdoin's appeal to law-abiding citizens was issued, and the Suffolk militia were called out. In a few hours a company was organized at Brackett's Corner, in Braintree North Precinct, and on the 19th of January it marched away towards the Connecticut, as part of Colonel Badlam's regiment. It was composed of thirty-eight men besides the officers, and upon the roll are found all the old Braintree names. On the 22d of the following February these men were disbanded at Northampton, and the expense incurred by the State on their account was £154 9s. 4d.

The vigorous action of the authorities had put down the rioters; but the depth of discontent may be inferred from the popular odium which seems to have attached to the authorities for so doing. Take Braintree, for instance. In April, 1786, Governor Bowdoin had received there 41 votes, — all that were cast. One year later, having in that year actually saved civil government to the State, he received 40 votes, and General Lincoln, his military agent in the work of suppression, 3, while his opponent, Hancock, had 181. Yet time, in which to let matters adjust themselves, was all that now was needed. Twelve months later, when John Adams returned from England, after nine years of absence, he spoke of the increase of population as "wonderful." As compared with what he had seen in Europe, he was amazed at the plenty and cheapness of provisions, though the scarcity of money was certainly very great. The industries of the country he found in a much better condition than he expected. Politically the state of affairs was less to his taste, and he wrote that "the people in a course of annual elections had discarded from their confidence almost all the old, staunch, firm patriots who conducted the Revolution, and had called to the helm pilots much more selfish and much less skilful." On this point the Braintree records bear lasting testimony to the correctness of his judgment.

## CHAPTER XVIII.

### RECUPERATION.

DURING the next few years no matters of considerable importance would seem to have engaged the attention of the town. The people were hard at work repairing the losses of war. The complaint was loud over the crushing weight of taxation, and it was heavy as compared with the halcyon days already referred to before the Revolution, when the tax-gatherer hardly made his presence felt; yet even now the burden was absolutely light. In Braintree, for instance, the levy was about $3,300 a year, whereas in the later colonial years it had been but a little over $250; this seemed a large increase, but, after all, $3,300 a year amounted only to $1.20 to each individual in the town, while a century later the regular annual levy was $12 to each individual. Apportioned in this way among the entire population, the taxes levied to pay the war debts of the Revolution were at the time of Shays' insurrection not one tenth part of what has since become customary.

And now, the pressure of war being no longer felt, the old questions which had for years lain dormant again presented themselves. The division of the county and the annexation to the town of contiguous territory included in other townships were agitated once more. Standing subjects of debate sixty years before, it seemed as though the town-meeting would never hear the last of them. How best to take care of the town poor was another matter of contention; for the poor the town had always with it. One party adhered to outdoor relief, — helping the indigent at their homes, the way which had always been pursued; another party wished to build a poor-house, and provide only for those who were paupers, and in it. It was the old familiar question, and Braintree was slowly working out a solution of it. At last, in 1785, the party of innovation carried its point, and the town ordered that an almshouse should be built "in the form of a Barrack, to be thirty-three feet in length and sixteen feet wide." But the other party succeeded in having this vote reconsidered at another meeting, held during the same month. The next spring, the almshouse people found themselves again a majority, and they not only voted the building but clinched the matter by adding that this vote should not be reconsidered at any future meeting unless one hundred and seventy-three members of the town were there present. This was a new principle introduced into the conduct of town business. No such restriction on the power of a town-meeting had ever been attempted before, and it is a matter of surprise that no one recorded his dissent to it now. But under this vote the almshouse was built, and the town poor moved into it; the overseer receiving £3 10s. for his services the first year, and his successor £6 for the second year.

The need of a reorganization of the schools also began to make itself felt. In 1790 an attempt was made to divide the town into districts. A committee was appointed to consider the matter, but its report, when it made one, was rejected, and the town decided to go on in the ancient way, having "a Gramer School keept nine months, three in each precinct beginning in the North and so on to the Middle and South." This action seems to have caused great discontent in the North Precinct. Those living there felt that they were numerous enough and sufficiently prosperous to have a school of their own. They naturally did not like sending their children, during three of the nine months' yearly schooling, two miles away to the Middle Precinct, and, during another three months, four miles away to the South Precinct. Yet the only alternative to so doing, under the arrangement which the town had voted, was to give the children but three months' schooling a year; and this was what the vote really meant. Accordingly, the question of political separation suddenly awoke from long sleep. The century was drawing to a close, and this question had been agitated during its earlier years, — at a time which no man now active in town affairs could remember. Sixty years before it had come up for serious consideration, and been referred to a committee of eight of which John Quincy was chairman. The report of this committee was unanimous and favored the proposed division; but the reception it met with in town-meeting was emphatic. The townsmen of that day had evidently come to the meeting prepared to take the matter into their own hands. The report having been read, the record proceeds as follows: —

"After which, upon a motion made the question was put whether the agreement of the committee should be voted article by article, and it passed in the negative.

"The question was then put whether all the articles thereof should be voted upon at once, it passed again in the negative.

"The Question was then again put whether they would accept of the Report of the said Committee. It passed again in the negative.

"After this, upon a motion made, the Question was put whether they would Reconsider their last vote, viz., of non-acceptance, and it was voted in the affirmative.

"Then again, the Question was put, whether they would accept of the Report of the Committee, and it passed in the negative.

"Upon which the meeting was dismissed."

This took place in January, 1729; and at another town-meeting held in the following May the report was again brought up, and the question was put whether the town would reconsider its former action; and it passed in the negative. It is almost needless to add that nothing more was heard on the subject of dividing the town. The people showed that they were not ready for it, and the customary leaders who seem to have worked the plan up, were compelled to drop it.

But even in the New England of the eighteenth century the passage of sixty years changed conditions somewhat; and now when in May, 1790, an article looking to a territorial division of the town was inserted in the warrant, the town-meeting dismissed it only after considerable debate. Then in the latter part of that year one hundred and twenty inhabitants of the North Precinct, and fifteen inhabitants of those portions of Dorchester and Milton lying immediately south of the Neponset, joined in a petition to the General Court that the regions in which they lived might be incorporated together as a distinct town. The petition came before the Senate for its action in January, 1791. While it was still pending a Braintree town-meeting was called to consider it.

The struggle between the precincts took place over the choice of moderator, and the record says that "after a long dispute it was finally voted to chuse the moderator by ballot, and Maj. Stephen Penniman was chosen by 93 votes out of 152." In other words, the Middle and South precincts were united against the North, and outnumbered it. A committee of six was then chosen to appear before the Legislature by counsel to oppose the division of the town, and its representative was instructed to use his influence to the same end. Nor did the other precincts desist from their opposition to the inevitable so long as opposition to it could be made. The dislike to anything which looks like political dismemberment seems ingrained; and, in the case of New England, it is difficult to say which the people most object to, — the surrender of local independence through consolidation, or the supposed loss of local influence through separation. Action towards either has never failed to awaken a conservative feeling, which saw nothing but political disaster in not keeping things exactly as they then were. This was the experience of Braintree in 1791; and in September of that year another town-meeting was held which voted to put forth one last effort before the legislative committee in behalf of the ancient limits. It was unavailing. On the 22d of February, 1792, one hundred and fifty-two years, lacking three months, after its original incorporation as Braintree, the North Precinct was set off, and ordered to be called by the name of Quincy. This act, also, was signed, as governor of the State, by John Hancock, who had himself been born, brought up and found a wife in the territory thus made a town.

It has already been explained [1] how the name of

---

[1] *Supra*, 711.

Quincy chanced to be selected. At the time, the choice was not wholly satisfactory. Governor Hancock was then at the height of that personal popularity which he enjoyed in Massachusetts to a degree which no other public man has since equalled, and there were those who did not forget that he was a native of the North Precinct. They wanted the new town to be named after him. Richard Cranch, who, it will be remembered, had selected the name of Quincy, was at this time, and in the absence of John Adams, the leading citizen of the town. He had married the eldest daughter of Parson Smith, of Weymouth, whose sister, Abigail, two years afterwards, in 1764, became the wife of John Adams. Consequently, Mr. Cranch and John Adams were brothers-in-law, and their wives were grand-daughters of Col. John Quincy. Hence, probably, the selection of the name. Subsequently a judge of the Court of Common Pleas, as well as Quincy's first postmaster, Richard Cranch is now remembered through his son and among lawyers, in connection with that series of reports which contain the early decisions of Marshall.

On the eighth of March, two weeks after the act incorporating it was passed, Quincy held its first town-meeting, and chose Major Ebenezer Miller at the head of its board of selectmen, thus showing that Major Miller's former Church and Tory proclivities were not remembered against him. At the meeting in May for the choice of a representative the question of the town name was brought up, and a strong effort made to have it changed to Hancock. After what is reported to have been a long and somewhat heated discussion, it was voted by a narrow majority not to take up the article in the warrant relating to the matter. This settled the question; and the name of Quincy, thus preserved, has since been multiplied and made familiar in connection with other and larger towns in regions which had then hardly been explored.

The political history of Quincy as recorded in the town-books during the thirty-eight years which next ensued shows few points of general interest. It was a period of peace. The people had in a great degree made good the losses of the war, and they were intent on bettering their condition. Year after year the town offices were filled, the regular appropriations made, new roads laid out, and local questions discussed. One generation went off the stage; another came upon it. An almshouse was built on the old Coddington farm in 1815 at a cost of $1,973.18; and when in the same year the town-hall and school-house was burnt down, the building which sufficed for both purposes was presently rebuilt at a cost of $2,100. Through long years the question of where the new building should stand — whether "adjoining the burying-ground," or "adjoining Mr. Quincy's sheds," or "north of Mr. Burrell's house," or "opposite the engine-house" — was earnestly discussed. Finally it was placed next the burying-ground. It was then only eight years since this had been inclosed. In it lay the bones and dust of four generations that had lived and died in the North Precinct. It stood by the side of the Plymouth road, an open and uncared for common, in which the swine ran at large and cattle grazed. Nor was there in this apparent desecration anything offensive to New England eyes. The gravestones were rooted up by hogs and trodden down by cows; the children played among them: but it had been so from the beginning, and that it should be so now wronged no one's sense of fitness.

On points such as these the fathers were the reverse of refined, and before the burying-ground was fenced in another generation had to grow up with a nicer sense of decency. At last, in 1809, a number of the inhabitants bought up the rights of passage, herbage and pasturage on the bit of ground in which their ancestors lay, and, through John Quincy Adams and Josiah Quincy, conveyed it to the town, to be thereafter " set aside as exclusively a place of human burial."

But incidentally the records of the Massachusetts towns of the earlier years of the nineteenth century are apt to be suggestive. They reveal conditions which have a species of middle-age flavor. For instance, in 1792 it was voted in Quincy " to have Hospitals in town for the purpose or benefit of those who chuse to have the smallpox." And again, in 1809, at a special town-meeting, the subject of vaccination was discussed, and, after prolonged debate, the majority decided against it. Piracy, or, as it was more delicately called, privateering, had strong attractions then for the more adventurous spirits. The United States was at peace with the world, but England and France were at war; accordingly, on August 12, 1793, just as the French reign of terror began, Benjamin Beale, Richard Cranch and Moses Black were made a standing committee " to see that there be not any privateers fitted out from this place by any of the Citizens of the United States or others against any of the beligerent powers, in order that a strict neutrality be kept between us and them." Having thus disposed of international questions, local affairs next occupied the attention of the town, and the hours were fixed at which " for the future the Bell tole on Sunday for beginning divine service." A few years later, in 1804, the singers are granted twenty-five dollars "to procure a bass viol for the use of the congregation;" and in 1818, Mr. Daniel Hobart is "authorized and directed to keep the boys in order in the meeting-house on Sundays." All, be it remembered, by formal votes of nineteenth century town-meetings.

The separation of the precincts had thus once more united town and parish, and the political and religious organization fell naturally back to just what it was a whole century before. The town again regulated every detail of church management. In 1810 the selectmen were "authorized to appoint a sexton and to mark out his duty;" and two years later it was made a part of the sexton's duty "to ring the bell at twelve o'clock at noon and nine o'clock at night." The nine o'clock evening bell was the New England curfew, and originated in a real and general need at a time when watches were an expensive luxury within the reach of the rich only, and cheap clocks had not yet been invented. Through seventy years after 1810 the nine o'clock curfew rang regularly in Quincy from the meeting-house tower.

The church singing was also matter of grave discussion. The introduction of Hezekiah Bass and the "great bass viol" into the choir in 1804 had not been unopposed. Indeed an ancient and conservative worshipper was so offended thereat that he rose from his seat and incontinently departed from the edifice, remarking as he went that "he did not want to go to God's House to hear a great fiddle." But the bass viol proved merely the edge of the entering wedge, and in 1821 the question was agitated whether it would not be well to have the selectmen hire a "professed Master of Sacred Musick."

The salary of the minister also engaged the attention of the town hardly less during this period than it had a century and a half before, in the days of Parson Tompson. Mr. Whitney had always received five hundred dollars a year, which sum — such was the immobility of that time — had for a hundred and seventy years been considered "a comfortable support in this part of the world."[1] To this stated, contract salary the town had, by annual vote, been in the custom of adding a further sum of one or two hundred dollars. In 1808 Mr. Whitney asked to have his stipend increased to eight hundred dollars; but the request was not complied with. In April, 1811, he addressed another letter to his parishioners on the subject asking that his salary be increased to $860. This letter was referred to a committee which in due time reported that the pastor's request was wholly reasonable, and that his "sallary was inadequate to his suitable maintenance;" but in view of "the uncertain and fluctuating state of our public affairs, the great embarrassment under which we at present suffer, and the threatening prospect of still greater," a postponement of the question was recommended. A vote of three hundred dollars additional salary for the current year was then passed. But from this correspondence it would seem not unfair to infer the change of values and the standard of living had been such that a salary of $900 in a Massachusetts town of 1810 was about the equivalent of a salary of £90, or $300, a century and a half before. This it would also be found[2] is not far from the proportionate increase in the cost of labor during the same period.

[1] *Mem. Hist. of Boston*, ii. 469.
[2] *Report (Mass.) on the Statistics of Labor*, 1885, 201–312.

The "threatening prospect" in public affairs here alluded to was the impending war with Great Britain of 1812-14. Quincy was a Federalist town. John Adams, true to his old patriotic and Revolutionary instincts, was an earnest supporter of the Madison administration, which his son, John Quincy, was then representing at St. Petersburg; but his townsmen were on the other side. Warm passages used to occur. Nearly seventy years afterwards a Quincy boy of that time gave the following entertaining account of one such incident. It is merely necessary to premise that the gentleman referred to in it was a near neighbor of Mr. Adams', and in his time the most useful citizen of Quincy: —

"I remember very well at a social dinner-party in time of the war, when the political element ran perhaps as high as ever it did, that I had the honor as well as pleasure to stand behind the President's chair as waiter. Directly on his left was seated Thomas Greenleaf, a violent Federalist, who was bearing down upon the old gentleman with more zeal than discretion. The President bore it as long as he could, when he raised his left hand and, instead of bringing it down on Mr. Greenleaf's head, which he might perhaps have done with as much propriety, he brought it down upon the table near him with a force that made the plates and glasses rattle, and exclaimed in a voice that could not be misunderstood, 'Tom Greenleaf, hold your tongue! you are always down on me when there is no occasion for it.' The scene which followed reminds me of that passage which says, 'There was silence in Heaven for half an hour.'"

But at this time Mr. Greenleaf represented much more nearly than the old ex-President what was the prevailing political sentiment in Quincy. At every annual election from 1812 to 1815, Governor Strong, the Federalist and anti-war candidate, polled nearly three votes to his opponent's one. His smallest majority was in 1812, when he had one hundred and twenty-seven votes to fifty-nine cast for Elbridge Gerry. The second war with Great Britain accordingly left no more marks than the old French wars on the town record-book; and, indeed, owing to the disloyal and almost treasonable action of the state government, the Quincy militia were called out but twice, marching once to South Boston and once to Cohasset. An absurdly large town bounty, in addition to the state pay, was voted to those called into service in June, 1814; but one short experience sufficed, and in December this vote was "so far repealed as not to operate in future." Yet at this time the uneasiness was great in the seaport towns. The British ships of war were always hovering on the coast, and in the autumn a flotilla ascended the Connecticut, destroying more than a score of vessels. Edmund Quincy, in his life of his father, President Josiah Quincy of Harvard College, has vividly reproduced the sensations in those days of the dwellers on Quincy Bay: —

"A general sense of personal insecurity prevailed all along the seaboard. . . . In these apprehensions the family at Quincy had good reason to share. For the estate bounds on the ocean, and the fears of boat attacks and foraging parties which had haunted the roof thirty years before returned again to disturb its repose. Every ship enters and leaves the port of Boston in full view of the windows of the house, and it may well be believed that a sharp lookout was kept up in the direction of the lighthouse. The first naval spectacle discerned from the post of observation, however, was a memorable and an auspicious one. It was the entrance of the 'Constitution' into the harbor, on the 29th of

August, 1812, after the capture of the 'Guerriere.' . . . Toward evening the frigate (recognized as the 'Constitution') came in under full sail, and dropped her anchor beside Rainsford Island — then the Quarantine Ground. The next morning a fleet of armed ships appeared off Point Alderton. As they rapidly approached, the 'Constitution' was observed to raise her anchor and sails, and go boldly forth to meet the apparent enemy; but, as the frigate passed the leader of the fleet, a friendly recognition was exchanged, instead of the expected broadside. They joined company, and the 'Constitution' led the way to Boston. It was the squadron of United States ships, then commanded by Commodore Rodgers, unexpectedly returning from a long cruise.

"A few days afterwards, Hull, who had just taken the 'Guerriere,' came with Decatur to breakfast at Quincy. . . . This breakfast is one of the earliest of my own recollections. I was a very little child, but I remember perfectly well sitting on Decatur's knee, playing with his dirk, and looking up at his handsome face, the beauty of which struck even my childish eyes, and which I still seem to see looking at me from out the far past. . . . As I have already related, every ship that enters or leaves the harbor can be seen from the windows of the house. And as the triumphant entry of Hull in the 'Constitution,' after his victory over the 'Guerriere,' had been discerned from the post of observation, so was the departure of Lawrence in the 'Chesapeake' on his fatal quest of the 'Shannon,' — doomed to 'give up the ship,' but only with his life; and, with the telescope, the 'meteor-flag of England' could be seen from time to time flying at the masthead of men-of-war that prowled about the mouth of the harbor, so that it was no idle fear which suggested the probability of a midnight visit from a party of foragers or pillagers to that solitary shore.

"One Sunday there was an alarm that the enemy had landed at Scituate, a dozen miles away. The news was announced in the meeting-house during Divine service. The congregation was dismissed at once, and the village was all astir with excitement. The bell rang, the drums beat to arms, and the volunteer companies marched to meet the enemy. It is unnecessary to say that they did not find him. . . . I suppose it was on the Sunday following this false alarm that the militia companies, in uniform, attended service to return thanks for their escape from the assaults of their enemies; though it may have been after some more real and nearer danger. But the circumstance made a deep impression on my young mind by the delightful variety it gave to the usual monotony of Sunday."

It was at this time that the town appointed a committee to confer with similar committees of the towns of Hingham and Weymouth, to devise " some measures for the safety and protection of this and those towns against the assaults of the enemy." But the enemy did not come; and the actual contribution of Quincy to the burden of the war of 1812 was practically limited to the sum paid in bounties, and a special state tax of nine hundred dollars. One coasting schooner also, owned in the town, while on her way from the Penobscot to Quincy, was boarded off Gloucester from an ambitious privateer out of that port, and, after some "ferocious conduct" on the part of the captors, was carried into Marblehead. What individuals from among the youth of Quincy may have served on the Niagara frontier, or fought in the naval battles of Hull, Decatur and Bainbridge, nowhere appears. The official record of the town in this war is unpleasantly meagre.

The sum raised by taxation for town expenses in 1815 was $4,000, which covered also the expenses of the church. The growth of the appropriation was very slow. In 1792 it had been £350, or $1,160, of which

£75 had been on account of the schools. Of these there was still but one, — the grammar school at the centre, — while the germs only of outlying district schools were to be found. During the first ten years of independent town life (1792–1801) the average annual levy by taxation was $1,680, or about $1.60 to an inhabitant on account of both town and parish; but by 1800 the annual appropriations had increased to $2,100, and thence to $3,300 in 1810. In 1820 they were $4,000. Four years later the town was separated from the parish, and accordingly the appropriation for that year fell to $2,800. In 1829 it was $3,500. Perhaps a fivefold increase in forty years. The long period of immobility was drawing to a close.

Up to 1824, the great items of expense were the church, the schools and the town poor; after 1824 they were the schools and the poor. These have both been elsewhere referred to. It has been seen that the cost of maintaining the town poor throughout the colonial period was out of all proportion to what it has been since. In 1812, for instance, $1,000 was raised for that purpose, while only $785 was raised for the schools and $800 for the church. In 1813 the poor cost $1,665, or as much as both the schools ($800) and the church ($850) combined. A reform was then instituted, and in 1819 the schools cost $1,000, while the church cost $850, and the poor had been reduced to $770. In 1824 their cost had been still further reduced to $628, while that of the schools had risen to $1,150; but the poor yet occasioned one quarter part of the whole tax levy. Meanwhile the highway tax did not appear in the estimates at all, for it was still, as in 1766, paid in kind, or, as the vote of April, 1825, read, "For each Day's work one Dollar, for each yoke of oxen one dollar per Day, for each Horse and Cart one dollar per Day, for each plow fifty cents per Day, and for each ox-Cart twenty-five cents per day." In 1829 the total assessment was $3,668. Of this, $1,563 was for the support of the schools, the master at the centre grammar school receiving $500, for which sum regularly paid he had, it has already been seen, agreed four years previously "to give up all other business and devote his whole time to the school." The school committee was further allowed $5 for " ink and brooms," which were all the "incidentals" then recognized, and $60 for fuel. The district schools were allowed from $30 to $120 each. For their services as selectmen, assessors and overseers of the poor, Messrs. Souther, Wood and Taylor received respectively $70.28, $30.14 and $25.68. For the repair of highways $600 was deemed sufficient. One thousand dollars, or nearly a fourth part of the whole, was appropriated to the support of the poor.

Such were the simplicity and economy of a town which now counted a population of 2,200 souls, and which was at last rapidly growing in wealth, for its assessed valuation in 1830 exceeded $800,000. The burden of taxation, when compared either with population or wealth, was scarcely a sixth part of what it afterwards became, and the amount appropriated for the education of each child in the public schools, which half a century later was sixteen dollars a year, was then but three. Without entering into any comparison of the schools or the roads of 1830 with those of 1880, it may confidently be asserted that the years between 1810 and 1830 were in Quincy the golden period of the old Massachusetts town government. Never before had it been so strong, so pure and so systematic as then ; never had it done its work so well. It was, in fact, an absolutely model government " of the people, by the people, for the people."

That this was so was due in part to the condition of the town itself, and partly to the influence of one man. In 1810 the population of Quincy was still thoroughly homogeneous ; and it had not ceased to be so in 1830. It was the original Massachusetts stock ; the people were the children of the soil. Still following the old, simple vocations, they were either tillers of the soil, or the citizens and tradespeople who did the work and supplied the wants of those who tilled the soil. They composed a single religious society, worshipping in one meeting-house. Each knew the other; they were almost members of the same family ; nor had the political family become too numerous. It numbered about 1,300 in 1810, and about 2,200 in 1830. As respects worldly condition those composing it were not far separated. No one was rich, and most of those who took any part in town affairs were well to do. There was no alien element; that is, no one lived in the town and had interests outside of it. The town partook also of the spirit of that era of good feeling which followed the war of 1812. The old Federalists were then absorbed in the party which supported the administration of Monroe, until at last during the six years 1825–30 the opposition in Quincy never threw more than nine votes on election day, and in 1828–9 it was limited to a single vote. The largest vote the town ever threw before 1831 was 217 in 1824, when Governor Eustis was chosen. It then gave a heavy majority to the defeated Federalist candidate ; a parting salute, as it were, fired over the grave of that political party. Then followed the presidential election of 1824, and every vote cast (140) was for the Adams electoral ticket. Nor did the Jackson Democracy obtain any foothold in the town during the next four years; for in November, 1828, the Adams electoral ticket, defeated in the country at large, had 140 votes in Quincy out of a total of 143.

These circumstances were all favorable to a good administration of affairs. The people were well to do; but they looked closely to their taxes, and they had a traditional horror of waste. Corruption in public office was practically unknown. The scale of town expenses was so limited that no item was too small to escape notice. The sum of five dollars unnecessarily spent, or spent for an unaccustomed purpose, might lead to a town-meeting discussion. Prior to 1810 all business had been done in a loose, unsystematic way. The annual appropriations were made by *vivâ voce* vote; the treasurer received the money which the constable collected; and the selectmen drew it out and paid it over to the minister, the schoolmaster, and those who cared for the town's poor. No report or estimates were made; no papers were placed on file. Everything was done on a general understanding. A cruder, less organized system could not be imagined. All that could be said was that it was natural, and, like most natural things, it worked well under the circumstances. As the town increased, some one was needed to organize such a degree of system as the new conditions demanded. That some one appeared in Thomas Greenleaf, — the natural leader and administrator of a Massachusetts town during the period which immediately preceded and followed the war of 1812, while the colonial gentry still controlled Massachusetts through the old Federal organization. As a public man generated by the New England town system, Mr. Greenleaf was as typical in the first thirty years of the nineteenth century as John Quincy was in the eighteenth century, or as Edmund Quincy was in the seventeenth. The only difference was that the period of immobility in which they lived was closed by him, — "the ages of monotony" extending through two full centuries, of which it has been well said they "had their use, for they trained men for ages when they need not be monotonous." [1]

Boston born, Mr. Greenleaf was graduated at Harvard in 1790; and coming to Quincy to live in 1803, he remained there until his death in 1854. He speedily began to take an active interest in town affairs, and he showed how useful in a local way a man of character, fair parts and good business capacity can always be. Mr. Greenleaf was a man of property, and, it has already been seen, a strong Federalist. In 1808, and for thirteen consecutive years thereafter, he was chosen to represent the town in the General Court. He was then the leading man in Quincy, and so continued until towards 1840, when the growth of the democratic element superseded him. In his day he organized the town's business, and he did it admirably. Everything was systematized. The change began about 1812, when the charge of the town poor had grown to be a scandal. Under Mr. Greenleaf's close business management the cost of maintaining the poor was reduced by more than one half, and his reports on the subject, entered in full in the records, are as interesting to-day in presence of that still unsolved problem of pauperism as they were when written, more than seventy years ago.

[1] Quoted by J. A. Doyle from Bagehot's *Physics and Politics* as the motto for the *English in America, The Puritan Colonies*.

Having reduced the care of the poor to a system, Mr. Greenleaf turned his attention to other matters. Insensibly, but steadily, the method of conducting the town business in all its branches was brought into order. In March the annual town-meeting took place. Over this Mr. Greenleaf, as matter of course, presided as moderator. The full list of town officers was chosen, and the various articles in the warrant were referred to special committees. The meeting then adjourned. In April another meeting was held, and the committees on the almshouse, the schools, the town lands and the town finances presented their reports, which were in writing, and entered into every detail. They were all spread on the record. Another adjournment was then had, and in May the appropriations were voted. Everything was thus made public and of record; and everything was open to criticism and debate. As a system, under the conditions then existing, it did not admit of improvement, and the so-called democratic methods which later succeeded it were a mere degradation of government.

It is needless to say that under this régime the town prospered. The debt incurred during the war of 1812 was paid off, as was also a new debt incurred for rebuilding the town-hall and school-house burned to the ground in 1816; and through good financial management this result was brought about with no increase of taxation. Apart from the support of the church, the total town levy of 1818 was less than $2.00 to an inhabitant. Thus as the end of the provincial period drew near, there was in Quincy a condition of general good feeling and prosperity such as the town had not before known. It showed itself in various ways. John Adams was then closing his long life. The wife who had watched the smoke of Bunker's Hill from the heights on the Plymouth road beyond the old Braintree farmhouse had died in 1818, and the son who then stood, a little boy, by her side, was at the head of the national cabinet and soon to be chosen president. The meeting-house of 1732 still stood on the training-field; but it was old and out of repair. The townspeople began to talk of a new edifice more in keeping with their increased numbers and wealth. Under these circumstances, John Adams, in June, 1822, moved, as he expressed it, "by the veneration he felt for the residence of his ancestors and the place of his nativity, and the habitual affection he bore to the inhabitants with whom he had so happily lived for more than eighty-six years," — thus moved, he conveyed to the people of the town a tract of quarry-land, from which the material for the building they wished might in part be derived. A special town-meeting was called in July to take action on this matter, and a committee was appointed to wait on the ex-President and express to him the gratitude with which his townsmen received his gift. They were instructed to say that, highly as the inhabitants of Quincy estimated the advantages that would result from the gift itself, they valued it more as coming from one who by his patriotism had shed honor on his native place, and "to whom, under the smiles of Providence, we are so largely indebted for our independence and prosperity as a nation." So gratified was the old man by this cordial expression of kind feeling that he at once added to his former gift not only a deed of further lands, but the whole of his private library, consisting of some three thousand volumes. Again the town met and spread upon its records further and even warmer expressions of gratitude and veneration.

Immediate steps were taken towards erecting the new meeting-house, but not until April, 1826, were arrangements so far perfected that a building committee was appointed. Thomas Greenleaf was its chairman. During that summer, and before work of construction was begun, John Adams died. He was over ninety, and his life thus covered one half of the whole settlement of the town, lacking only two years. The old order of things, like the old meeting-house symbolical of it, was about to pass away. A new generation, with other customs and modes of thought, was fast coming to the front, and it was fit and proper that the transition should be strongly marked. It was strongly marked. On the 4th of July, 1826, the town celebrated with special rejoicings the fiftieth anniversary of independence. It was celebrated, as its sturdiest supporter had fifty years before predicted it would be, as " a day of deliverance, with pomp and parade, with shows, games, sports, guns, bells, bonfires, and illuminations." On that fair, glad day — in the midst of peace and prosperity and political good feeling, with the sound of joyous bells and booming guns ringing in his ears, with his own toast of " Independence forever" still lingering on the lips of his townsmen — the spirit of the old patriot passed away. But he had lived to see with his own eyes that " ravishing light and glory " the distant rays of which had reached him in 1776, and he had found that the end was indeed " more than worth all the means."

Warned of the approaching event, President John Quincy Adams had left Washington on the morning of the 4th of July, and at Baltimore he received word of his father's death. He reached Quincy on the morning of the 13th, the funeral having taken place on the 7th, in the presence of a great concourse of people. The following Sunday, when the church-bell rang, he went to the old North Precinct meeting-house, and a few hours later he thus recorded his feelings: —

"I have at no time felt more deeply affected by [my father's death] than on entering the meeting-house and taking in his pew the seat which he used to occupy, having directly before me the pew at the left of the pulpit which was his father's, and where the earliest devotions of my childhood were performed. The memory of my father and mother, of their tender and affectionate care, of the times of peril in which we then lived, and of the hopes and fears which left their impressions upon my mind, came over me, till involuntary tears started from my eyes. I looked around the house with inquiring thoughts. Where were those I was then wont to meet in this house? The aged of that time, the pastor by whom I had been baptized, the deacons who sat before the communion table, have all long since departed. Those then in the meridian of life have all followed them. Five or six persons, then children like myself, under the period of youth, were all I could discern, with gray hairs and furrowed cheeks, two or three of them with families of a succeeding generation around them."

## CHAPTER XIX.

### THE ERA OF CHANGE.

THE original migration from Old to New England ceased before 1640. No steady westward movement of population across the Atlantic again set in until the beginning of the nineteenth century, nor, even when it did set in, did it gain any great volume until after the year 1830. It was accordingly remarked by Palfrey in his History of New England that probably there was no county in England where in 1825 the strain of English blood was so free from all foreign admixture as it was among the people of Cape Cod. Up to the year 1800 the same thing might have been said of Quincy. The original settlers bore all of them English names. There were scarcely any exceptions to this rule, and such exceptions as there were — some eight or ten in two hundred and forty — indicated a French and, possibly, a Norman origin. All of these names are recorded before 1728. A few Scotchmen, the prisoners of Dunbar, may have been landed in Boston in 1651, and sent out to the ironworks;[1] but, if such was the case, they did not leave a single "Mac" behind them in Braintree. In 1752 there was a small infusion of German blood, — "poor, suffering Palatines." But these people mostly went away ten years later to join more prosperous commu-

[1] See an interesting passage on this subject in Robbins' 200th Milton Anniversary Address, 20–1.

nities of their own race at the eastward, and a few only remained to perpetuate the German face under Anglicized names. There were a certain number of negroes in the town, — sixty-six, according to the census of 1765, — the descendants of slaves owned by the Quincys, Vassals, Apthorps and Borlands; and their names — Pompey, Cæsar and Scipio; Samson and Fidelia; Psyche, Dutchess and Flora — read strangely in the old records of marriages and deaths. In a few years more these had wholly disappeared, and the vacant space made by the removal of the old stairway in the meeting-house was presumably without occupants. When, in 1792, the North Precinct of Braintree was set off as Quincy, the names appended to the petitions were all English names, — names, nearly every one of which had appeared in the town-book for a century. Old, familiar English patronymics all. An Irishman or an Irish name was as strange and as much a matter of wonderment as a Frenchman or a German, and more than an African or Indian.

Nor had there as yet been anything to cause the influx of a new population. Even down to 1825 the industries of the town had not multiplied. It was still the old farming community already described, — a community made up of those who tilled the soil, and those who supplied the tillers' wants. More than a century and a half before an iron foundry had been established in "the Woods," but it had soon collapsed, for "it was found that every pound of iron made cost more than two pounds imported from Europe;" and only beds of cinders and slag, and old bits of petrified foundation on the banks of Furnace Brook marked where the experiment had failed.

Even the tradition of it had died away, and as late as 1699 John Marshall wrote in his diary that " the woods swarmed much with bears — many were killed, and more escaped " — while for years afterwards the region thereabout was the haunt of the deer. Again, shortly after 1750, the poor refugees who settled at Germantown had sought to gain a living by making glass. But such glass as they made was of the coarsest description, for which even then there was small demand; and this attempt soon shared the fate of the iron-works. The little capital ventured in it was lost.

But these were premature attempts at the introduction of strange industries. It was not so with shipbuilding, or with the stone deposits of the town. The dwellers along Quincy bay, in common with all other seaboard Yankees, took naturally and kindly to salt water, and the ship-yards throve at Braintree from an early day until that change of policy took place which caused the United States to withdraw as a competitor for the carrying trade. This was not until after 1860. Meanwhile up to 1825 the stone deposits of the town remained undisturbed; but that year the site of a quarry was secured for the Bunker Hill Monument Association, and then the change took place. The fame of Quincy granite was now to spread far and wide. The existence and durable character of the stone had, it is true, long been known; but up to this time it had been worked only on the surface. The coarse, rough, glacier-tumbled boulders which lay scattered over the north and south commons had alone been used. In Boston, King's Chapel was built of this material between 1749 and 1752, and later the famous old Hancock mansion on Beacon Hill. At that time they had so little conception of the extent of this syenite formation, that in Braintree much alarm was felt lest the use of the stone for buildings in other towns would exhaust the supply. For years the subject was discussed at each town-meeting, and new measures of ever-increasing stringency — protective measures — were devised to avert the threatened dearth. Accordingly, in 1753, immediately after King's Chapel was finished, a vote was passed forbidding the further removal of boulders from the commons until otherwise ordered; for, if the drain went on, unchecked, there would not be enough stone in Braintree for the town's own use! The difficulty seems to have been that, with the tools then in use, they were unable to work into the rock. The King's Chapel stone, it is said, was broken into a degree of shape by letting large iron balls fall upon the heated blocks. At last, upon one memorable Sunday in 1803, there appeared at Newcomb's Tavern, in the centre of the North Precinct, three men, who called for a dinner with which properly to celebrate a feat they had just successfully performed. The fear of the tithingman not restraining them, they had that day split a large stone by the use of iron wedges. Their names were Josiah Bemis, George Stearns and Michael Wild. It was indeed a notable event, for the crust of the syenite hills was broken.

Quarries were then opened, but at first only slowly and in a small way. The men did not yet know how to work the rock, nor had they the necessary tools and appliances. Such stone as was taken out was roughly dressed for use as door-steps, foundations and gable walls. There were two problems still unsolved: one related to handling and dressing the rock; the other to its carriage. Both of these problems Solomon Willard and Gridley Bryant solved. Neither of these two remarkable men was Quincy born. Willard came of Maine stock transplanted to Petersham, in Worcester County; and Bryant was of that Scituate family which seventy-five years before had furnished Braintree its active-minded minister. While Willard laid open the quarry and devised the drills, the derricks and the shops, Bryant was building a railway.

This famous structure marked an epoch not only in the history of Quincy, but in that of the United States; and in every school history, it is mentioned as the most noticeable event during the administration of the younger Adams. Its projector, Gridley Bryant, has given his account of how he came to construct it, and of the obstacles he had to overcome. His story of private apathy and legislative obstruction reads like a repetition of the similar experience of George Stephenson at nearly the same time in England; and, while his project was looked upon as "visionary and chimerical" on the exchange, at the State-house it was solemnly argued that corporations in abundance already existed, and that it was wrong to take people's land under eminent domain for purposes of more than questionable utility. Finally the success of the enterprise was altogether due to the munificence and public spirit of one of the most eminent and energetic of Boston merchants at a period when Boston still boasted of a race of merchants foremost in foreign trade, — Col. Thomas Handasyd Perkins. He supplied all the funds needed to build the railway, over which, on the 7th of October, 1826, Bryant passed the first train of cars.[1]

This railway was operated, always by horse-power,

[1] *Mem. Hist. of Boston*, iv. 116-20.

for about forty years. At last, it having then been for a time in disuse, its franchise was purchased by the Old Colony Railroad Company. The ancient structure was completely demolished and a modern railroad was built on the right of way. This was formally opened for traffic on October 9, 1871, forty-five years and two days after the original opening in 1826. There is a certain historical fitness in the fact that, through the incorporation of the Granite railway into the Old Colony railroad, the line which connects Plymouth with Boston has become the original railroad line in America.

After 1825, under the strong impetus given to it by the building of the railway and the growing shaft on Bunker Hill, the granite business of Quincy developed rapidly; and, as the years went on, it revolutionized the town. Its influence was everywhere felt, — in habits, and modes of life and thought, and in politics. One by one the old traditions gave way. Business was no longer done as formerly. Firms grew up possessing large means and employing many laborers, and a steady tide both of wealth and population set in. As compared with the statistics of similar growth which has gone on during the same time at the great commercial centres of the country, the figures representing the growth of the Quincy granite business are not large. Boston and St. Louis, New York, Chicago and San Francisco have accustomed the minds and eyes of modern Americans to industrial strides on a wholly different scale. Those cities deal in workmen by the thousand and in products by the million. Against such exhibits no New England town can have anything to show which would cause surprise, their figures amounting at most to the modest statistics of a prosperous trade. It is so with Quincy granite. In the hard, slow work of producing it no large fortunes were made, no crowded communities grew up. On the eastern slope of the Blue Hill range, where in 1825 the Milton and Quincy woods still stood, is a village containing a population larger than was the population of Quincy in 1830. The creaking of the derrick, the blows of the sledge, and the click of the hammer are everywhere heard from the week-day morning to its night; and from year's end to year's end the blocks of split and chiselled syenite pass out in a steady stream. Yet in the great aggregates of modern life it all represents but the labor of a few hundred men, and the well-earned return on the not large capital of a dozen enterprising firms. But in this, as in other local industrial respects to be presently referred to, it will be found to be merely a question of scale; and the results of new and extended business enterprises on previous and existing social, economical and political systems and conditions which through the last sixty years have been working themselves out in the country as a whole on the largest imaginable scale, to the astonishment and perplexity of those concerned in it as well as of an observing world, — all these results can, it will be found, be seen and studied in little, in the experience of the individual town. Similar causes have produced the same results; and the transformations, puzzling from their magnitude, which have taken place on the larger stage of the whole, can best be explained, as well as witnessed, in the comparatively simple changes of the single unit.

The period of immobility and sameness had come to an end, and the quickening was felt not only every-

## THE OLD TANNERY.

where, but in all sorts of ways; so stone-working was not the only new industry which about 1830 began to make its influence felt in Quincy. For more than a century and a quarter there had then been one tannery in the town, and at a later day there were several. The earlier tanneries were strange, primitive establishments. The vats were oblong boxes sunk in the ground close to the edge of the town brook at the point where it crossed the main street. They were without either covers or outlets. The beam-house was an open shed, within which old, worn-out horses circled round while the bark was crushed at the rate of half a cord or so a day by alternate wooden and stone wheels, moving in a circular trough fifteen feet in diameter. In the early years of the last century the prices were as primitive as the methods; for, while green hides sold for threepence and dry hides for sixpence a pound, the tanned article brought but twelvepence.[1] Then and long afterwards the dress, especially of the working classes, was largely composed of leather, out of which as a material leggings and breeches, coats and shirts were made, as well as shoes and gloves. Working in leather was therefore one of the common vocations in all New England towns, and those who worked in it were referred to in the records as cordwainers, than which no calling was more frequently specified; while sealers of leather were officers elected at each annual town-meeting.

Consequently, as markets and means of communication developed, it was natural that the Quincy people should drift into shoemaking. They did so as matter of course, and as early as 1795 the business had taken root; the pioneer firm in it making in that

[1] Pattee, *Old Braintree and Quincy*, 604–5 n.

year nine hundred and fifty-one pairs of shoes, paying for such as were hand-sewed two dollars a dozen pair. In 1822, a large southern trade was opened, and thirty years later it seemed for a time not improbable that Quincy might vie with Brockton, Lynn or Marlborough as a great centre of this industry; but the War of the Rebellion dealt a heavy blow to Quincy's southern trade, and the rapid development elsewhere of machine-made work left its old-fashioned methods far behind.

Nevertheless, the presence in the town of this industry, together with that of stone-cutting, greatly influenced its character, causing it to reflect with singular precision the larger change going on in the country as a whole. The population was radically transformed. A new race, of different blood and religion, had come in. The native New Englander seemed to pass out of the fields into the shops, and men of foreign blood took his place. In 1830 the Congregational meeting-house, — though then called "the Stone Temple,". — and the Episcopal church were still the only buildings in the town in which religious services were held. Mass had once or twice been observed in dwelling-houses. In 1831 a Universalist society was organized, and in 1832 the society built for itself a house, the pastor of the day asserting, it is said, among other things, that "the old parish worshipped a man," a mural tablet in memory of John Adams, surmounted by his bust, having been placed in the new church building.[1] In 1834 another such house was built by an Evangelical Congregational society; and a third by the Methodist Episcopal in 1838. From the time Sir Christopher Gardiner, leaving his wooded hum-

[1] Cornell, *Recollections*, 68.

mock on the banks of the Neponset, fled into the forest in March, 1631, down to the beginning of the nineteenth century, there is reason to suppose that no communicant of the Church of Rome had a permanent abode in Braintree or Quincy; and, writing in 1765, John Adams used the expression, already once quoted, that a certain most unusual thing was "as rare an appearance [in New England] as a Jacobite or a Roman Catholic, that is, as rare as a comet or an earthquake."[1] Even as late as 1838 the Roman Catholics could boast of no consecrated edifice in Quincy. The opening of the granite quarries brought the Roman Catholics in, and the story connected with the first celebration of the Mass in the ancient Puritan town runs thus: —

"Late in the year 1826 a gentleman called to see President J. Q. Adams, who was then at home. He introduced himself as a Roman Catholic clergyman, and gave his name as Rev. Father Pendergast. He told the President that he came to visit the Catholics of this vicinity and administer the sacraments to them, and being a stranger he made bold to ask Mr. Adams for information as to how he could find the Catholics. The President received him very kindly, and, after some conversation, called in John Kirk [an Irishman in his employ for many years] and introduced Father Pendergast. The news soon spread through the village that 'the Priest had come.' Confessions were heard that night, and early next morning the first Mass was celebrated."[2]

A few years afterwards there were many of the faith in Quincy: but they were immigrants and they were poor; the narrow but traditional prejudice against them and their faith, also, was strong, and

[1] *Works*, iii. 456.    [2] *Quincy Monitor*, May, 1886.

slow to be outgrown. Even as late as 1855 there were those in the town, and among them was a member of the board of selectmen for that year, who angrily demanded that the elaborate granite gateway of a new cemetery should be taken down because it had a cross carved upon it;[1] and the consecration of the ground was opposed as a Papist custom inconsistent with the idea of a Massachusetts burying-place. It was thirteen years after Father Pendergast is said to have made his call on Mr. Adams before an occasional Mass was celebrated in the small West Quincy school-house; and then and long after, under the combined Native American and anti-Catholic feeling, Massachusetts was in a dangerous mood. The Ursuline convent school in Charlestown had not long before been destroyed by a mob; and now in West Quincy those of the district who held other religious views expelled the Catholics from the school-house. Fortunately, better counsels and a kinder feeling prevailed, and after a short time the services were renewed; nor were they again disturbed. In 1842 there were about one hundred Catholics in Quincy; in 1888 there were more worshippers in the three Catholic churches than in all the other eight religious edifices of the town combined.

[1] Pattee, *Old Braintree and Quincy*, 151.

## CHAPTER XX.

### THE QUINCY SCHOOL SYSTEM.

IF the multiplication of sects and churches after 1830 was considerable, that of schools was still more so. In the matter of education the state of things had, indeed, then become such that it was obvious a change of system must be made. The old centre grammar school could no longer be made to suffice. Its condition and methods have already been described, and in 1827 the school committee, of which Thomas Greenleaf was then chairman, reported the whole number of children in all the schools as four hundred and sixty-one. Of these, twenty-five only — nineteen boys and six girls — were over fourteen years of age, so early even at that late period did the schooling stop. In order to relieve the centre of an excessive attendance, two winter schools under masters — called in the reports "men's schools," to distinguish them from the old dames' schools for children — had been opened, but this measure failed to bring the wished-for relief. The increase of scholars was such that seven score children of all ages were throughout the winter crowded into the single school-room at the centre, there to be taught by one master, who was paid five hundred dollars a year, aided by one female assistant, who was paid one hundred and twenty dollars. Under these circumstances the committee of 1827 suggested, not "for immediate adoption, but for deliberate consideration," the idea of building a second school-house, which, it stated, would "afford an immediate and effectual relief for many years." Accordingly, after two years of "deliberate consideration," the town, in 1829, voted to build three new school-houses, at widely separated points, and the scale and economy of school-house construction in vogue may be inferred from the fact that in 1830 two of these then newly constructed buildings, standing within nine miles of Boston, cost respectively $523 and $422. But even this addition to its facilities failed to satisfy the town. A pernicious idea had gained footing that it was desirable " to bring the school to every man's door; " and instead of concentrating children so that they might be divided according to age and taught by several teachers in graded schools, the mistaken policy of neighborhood schools of all ages under one teacher was adopted. Accordingly, the next year, after a sharp struggle in which the town divided by a vote of 84 to 78, it was decided to build two more school-houses. The neighborhood school system was thus definitely fixed upon.

That this should have been so was in some respects unfortunate, but it was probably necessary. It was a mistake naturally incident to government through town-meeting, and merely one more proof that those meetings are not inspired. Having fortunately no infinite wisdom to guide and dwarf them, they go stolidly on, working their way in human and commonplace fashion through almost infinite waste and failure to a certain degree of success. The process is slow and expensive. Accordingly, the policy as respects its schools fixed on by Quincy in the town-meeting of March 8, 1831, remained its policy for over forty years. From an educational point of view it was al-

## OLD-FASHIONED SCHOOLING. 935

together wrong. The school was near the child's home, but at the school the child learned the least possible. The grading of scholars was out of the question, and incompetent teachers wasted their time trying to impart a little knowledge to many children of various ages. It was like carrying on war through the same town-meeting machinery; and a more wasteful system could hardly have been devised. From the money point of view it did not cost much, for in 1827 the annual appropriation was $3 for each scholar, and the neighborhood system only increased it in 1831 to $3.67. In 1840 it had fallen to $2.89, and it was only $3.81 in 1850. Not until 1868 did the annual cost per scholar increase to over $10. The town had then so grown that what at first was a neighborhood system had become a system sufficiently centralized.

Yet even then, though the public schools had for years been more or less graded, and a somewhat better instruction was possible, the system in vogue had little to commend it; and again the unit reflected the condition of the aggregate. The teaching was almost wholly confined to verbal memorizing, and that singular mental exercise known as parsing, or the mechanical application of certain rules of grammar to words and sentences. These rules never had any meaning to the scholars, nor did the knowing how to parse in any way affect the scholar's mode of speaking or writing his mother-tongue. It was the same with arithmetic. It was taught by rule. This was that old-fashioned schooling, so called, which is still commonly supposed to have been simple, but, in some unexplained way, peculiarly thorough. Accordingly there are not a few who lose no opportunity to refer to it with respectful regret. In point of fact, in no true sense of the word was it either simple or thorough. By force of constant iteration, emphasized by occasional whippings, the child did indeed have certain rules and formulas so impressed on the memory that they never afterwards faded from it; but so did the horse, the dog and the parrot. One and the same method of instruction was applied to all, human and brute. It was purely a matter of memorizing and imitation; the observing and reasoning faculties, it was supposed, — if, indeed, any thought was given to them, — would develop themselves. Since the days of the "Learned Schoolmaster," Benjamin Tompson, school methods in Quincy had become more elaborate and far more expensive; the child was taught more, such as it was, because it went to school more hours, and there were more teachers and better text-books: but, so far as intelligence of method and system was concerned, there had been little change and no considerable improvement. Nor were the results anything to be proud of. The average graduate of the grammar school in 1870 could not read with ease, nor could he write an ordinary letter in a legible hand and with words correctly spelled.

Nor in these respects were the schools of Quincy worse than those of its sister towns. This was at one time confidently asserted; and the friends of every system which breaks down under investigation always assert that such system was notoriously defective at the precise point where the investigation took place. In the case of the Quincy schools it was nothing of the sort. They were, prior to 1870, quite as good as the average of Massachusetts town schools; and this appeared very clearly as the result of careful inquiries made by agents of the State Board of Education in

1879. It was then found that in a very large proportion of the towns in Norfolk County the educational methods in use were the same that had been immemorially in use. They were queerly primitive. Children were still taught to spell orally and in classes, and the writing was limited to what was done in the copy-books. Accordingly, when told to write a letter of a few lines, many pupils showed at once that they had never been taught even the mechanical part of a written exercise, while certain of the teachers actually would not permit their schools to be subjected to so unheard-of a test. Their scholars were taught to parse, and say the multiplication table; writing letters was no part of school work! Out of eleven hundred scholars in two hundred and twelve schools who used in composition the adverb "too," no less than eight hundred and fifty-nine spelled the word incorrectly. The three words "whose," "which" and "scholar" were given out for written spelling, and while there were fifty-eight different wrong spellings of "which," there were one hundred and eight of "whose" and two hundred and twenty-one of "scholar." For thoroughness and magnitude these examinations were probably never surpassed. They included the schools of twenty-four towns, returning five thousand scholars. The tests, of the simplest and most ordinary description, were confined to showing the results actually obtained in reading, writing and ciphering. There was no escape from the conclusions reached, for the published fac-similes of the examination papers spoke for themselves.[1]

In 1873 doubts as to the value of the results ob-

---

[1] See Report of Examination of Scholars in Norfolk County, in the Forty-third Annual Report (1880) of the Massachusetts Board of Education.

tained through the methods then long in use had for some time been forcing themselves on the minds of those composing the Quincy school committee. They referred in their reports to the condition of "immobility" which seemed to prevail. There were now twenty-seven schools in the town, in which thirty-two teachers were at work on twelve hundred scholars. The annual cost of teaching each scholar exceeded fourteen dollars. Thus since 1830 the number of those taught had increased much less than threefold, while the cost of teaching them had increased over fifteen fold. Under these circumstances it was obvious that a great waste of public money was steadily going on. The cost of the article purchased had been immensely increased, without any corresponding improvement in its quality. It was perfectly true the schools had been humanized. Boys were no longer compelled by way of punishment to clasp each other's hands across the top of an overheated stove until holes were burned in their clothes; nor, supplied with raw-hides, were they made to whip each other, while the master stood over them and himself whipped that one who seemed to slacken in his blows.[1] Scenes like these, worthy of Dotheboys Hall, were reminiscences of the past. But there was no reason to suppose that the children when they left school read more fluently, or wrote more legibly, or computed with more facility than had their fathers and mothers before them. Under these circumstances the committee came to the conclusion that if the town was not spending an undue amount on its schools, yet certainly not more than fifty per cent. of what it did spend was spent effectively. The whole thing needed to be reformed; but the

[1] *Quincy Patriot*, February 21, 1874.

members of the committee did not feel themselves qualified to reform it. They therefore stated the case to the town, and asked for authority to employ a specialist as a superintendent.

In the spring of 1875 the desired authority was given. The result was that reform in school methods which, known as the "Quincy system," within the next few years excited far and wide an almost unprecedented interest and discussion. The essence of the system was simple, nor was it in any respect new. It was a protest against the old mechanical methods. There was to be something in the schools besides memorizing and the application of formulas. The child was no longer to be taught on the same principles that dogs and parrots were taught. The reasoning and observing faculties were to be appealed to. The object always to be kept in view was a practical one. A race of men and women were to be produced who might indeed not be able readily to commit things to memory or to repeat rules out of a grammar; they would not be disciplined in the ancient way, but they would be accustomed to observe and think for themselves, and at least to read and write English with ease and decently.[1]

This reform was the work of the superintendent then employed, a native of New Hampshire, F. W. Parker, who, attaining the rank of colonel in the Union army during the Rebellion, after its close had studied elementary instruction as a science in Ger-

---

[1] The leading features of the so-called Quincy system were set forth at the time in a paper entitled The New Departure in the Common Schools of Quincy, which was printed in pamphlet form, and passed rapidly through six editions, exciting much public discussion.

many, and now put the results of his studies in practice in the Quincy schools. What he did attracted almost at once the notice of educators. He was, of course, severely criticised by the adherents of the old system, who vigorously asserted that what was good in his methods was not new, and that what was new was not good. The assertion that the results produced by the old system were not satisfactory was angrily denounced as a slur on the well-earned fame of Massachusetts. Even if such things were true, it was said, they ought not to be published to the world, for they gave comfort to the enemies of the common school. The educational journals referred to the arguments of Mr. Parker's friends as "monumental displays of ignorance," and it required the unanswerable facts of the Norfolk County investigation to satisfy them that the earlier condition of affairs in the Quincy schools was both correctly stated and not exceptional. All this noisy discussion did but spread far and wide the fame of Mr. Parker's efforts, and strangers soon began to come to Quincy to see what the thing amounted to. Then they came to study it. Finally, the town schools became an educational curiosity for the display to the world of the new system. Visitors trooped to Quincy by hundreds, and at times they crowded the school-rooms to such a degree that they became a serious hindrance to instruction.

Nor were the means of acquiring a higher education in Quincy now limited to its schools. The way to self-culture had been thrown wide open to every one who wished to tread it, for a free access to books was no longer the exclusive privilege of the rich or the educated. In 1871 the sum of $2,500 was at the annual town-meeting voted towards the establishment of a free public library, provided an equal sum could be raised by private subscription. At that time the town practically had no collection of books in it which was open to all. Accordingly, as it had been in the beginning so it remained down to the year 1846, when, for those who could afford to buy, the railroad made the bookstores of the city accessible: but, so far as the bulk of inhabitants were concerned, they neither had any books within their reach, nor did they know how to use them. The purpose of John Adams in giving his library to the town had wholly failed of accomplishment. When he did it he had his own youth in mind; for, brought up in the Braintree of former days a country lad wholly cut off from the means of a larger education, he had been compelled to break out his own way to success, and his wish in old age was to remove the obstacles which had impeded him from the path of future generations of his townsmen. Out of narrow means he accordingly endowed an academy, and he gave to it his own library, the collection of a lifetime. His motives were generous; but he could not foresee the changes of the future. Many of the books thus given were rare and valuable; but students were few, and they found what they wanted more easily elsewhere. For popular use the collection was almost ludicrously inappropriate. The scholar and the public man would feel at home in it, but to the average frequenter of the modern public library it was much what a rare edition of Shakespeare or of Milton is to one as yet untaught to read.

Such was the situation in 1871 when the move in behalf of a modern public library was made. The conditional $2,500 required to be obtained by private subscription to secure the town endowment was soon raised, and in the autumn of 1871 there was opened in Quincy one of those institutions, undreamed of in former times, which may without exaggeration be called the universities of the poor. The crying need which existed for something of the kind at once became apparent. The public library was thronged with young people, and during the next twelve months nearly forty-five thousand volumes were borrowed. Accordingly, it at once assumed a foremost place among the educational influences of the town.

The gift of a public library building to Quincy nine years later was one of those incidents, both interesting and in this case peculiar, which have of late years shown in New England how much private munificence can in its results be relied upon to excel all forms of public bounty. Designed by the most original and brilliant architect[1] of his day, the Crane Memorial Hall commemorates in a typical way one who was himself singularly typical of New England and of Quincy. Born of old Braintree stock, Thomas Crane had gone to the centre grammar school, and worshipped in the old North Precinct meeting-house until he became a man. He had then in the year 1827 gone away, as so many others went then and later, seeking his fortune. A stone-cutter by trade, he settled in New York city, and there married and had children. A plain, straightforward, energetic man, he gradually amassed a fortune, and at last died in New York, April 1, 1875, in his seventy-second year. Though he often came back to Quincy as a visitor, he never was an inhabitant of the town from the time he left it

[1] Henry Hobson Richardson; born 1838; graduated at Harvard, 1859; died 1886.

in 1827. The members of his family had few associations with it. Yet when the husband and father died, their thoughts turned to his old Massachusetts home as the place where he would most have desired to have his memorial stand. It seemed proper also that it should stand there; for, of all the many young men who early and late had gone out from the town, Thomas Crane had been the most successful. Dealing all his life in the granite which underlaid his native place, his success had been due to the possession of those qualities which made New England. He was honest; he was temperate; he was religious; he was energetic and enterprising and patient. His life was wholly unassuming, and when he died not many in Quincy remembered that such an one had ever lived there. His name is now and will long be a household word in the place where he passed his youth, and from which he went forth; nor could a better example of native strength and homely virtues be held up before its children for imitation.

## CHAPTER XXI.

### THE ALIEN INFUSION.

THERE is a degree of individuality in the business history of Quincy since the year 1830, and consequently a certain interest attaches to it, owing to the fact that it centred mainly in the syenite which underlaid the soil. The town dealt in its native stone. The religious development had also a certain character of its own. It was liberal. Indeed, the utter absence of Calvinism, or strong orthodoxy, in the tenets of those inhabiting the North Precinct and Quincy, is so marked, and so unusual for a Massachusetts community, that it cannot escape notice. The Unitarian movement under Channing's lead, it has already been seen, excited no surprise among those who recalled the teachings of Lemuel Briant. On the contrary, the tendency in Quincy then was towards Universalism. Thomas Crane, for instance, feeling a strong religious craving which the teachings of Mr. Whitney did not satisfy, found what he needed, not in the Braintree church, where Dr. Storrs still held up the rigid belief of the fathers, but in the broader Christianity of " Father " Hosea Ballou. The young stone-cutter would walk twenty miles of a Sunday to listen to his favorite preacher. No orthodox church ever struck root in Quincy. In matters of education the individuality of the town was less marked. The schools were much like the schools elsewhere, and the sudden development of the "Quincy system" came from without, and was largely a matter of chance. None the less, it was something that such a movement was possible. It showed a mental receptiveness, a faculty of accepting new ideas and responding to them, which was in keeping with the whole religious and political record of the community which John Wheelwright had first taught. The soil was kindly to the reformer, and his labors brought forth speedy fruits. Politically, also, the later history of Quincy was not without its individuality and significance. The old and new elements were always at work in it. Sometimes the one would attain a mastery, and its influence would forthwith appear unmistakably in town-meeting, and stamp itself on the records; then the other would by degrees assert itself, and the ancient order of things would, to a certain extent, be restored. The old political habits and traditions could not be destroyed; and yet the rapid infusion of foreign elements would through long periods of time seem to obliterate them. Absorption and education went on continually; the new affected the old, and the old gradually influenced the new. Again, the process which upon the large scale was working itself out all over the continent, in Quincy can be studied in detail. Here was one of the individual units of which the other was the aggregate.

After the formation of the United States government, all through the administrations of Jefferson and Madison, including the war of 1812, it has been seen that Quincy politically was a strong Federalist town. Down even to the year 1824 it stood firmly out. In 1823, Dr. Eustis was elected governor over Harrison Gray Otis, the candidate of the old Federalists; but Quincy none the less gave Mr. Otis a majority of 66 in a total vote of 204. Nor did it change under defeat; for the next year it gave 63 majority against Governor Eustis, though his election in the State was a foregone conclusion. Then came the presidential campaign of 1825, and the Federal party disappeared forever. In Quincy all were Adams men, and they so remained until long after the election of four years later. But now the Jackson democracy began to make its presence felt, though its growth was very slow. In November, 1830, ex-President J. Q. Adams was brought forward as a candidate for Congress in the Plymouth district. In Quincy Mr. Adams received 76 votes to 10 cast for the Jackson candidate. At the next state election Marcus Morton, the Democratic candidate for Governor, had 14 votes, while Governor Lincoln received 211. Then gradually a change came. A new element had found its way into the town. The old agricultural interest was no longer the only interest. In 1837 more than five hundred hands were employed in the quarries. The greater portion of these were not Quincy born; many of them were foreigners, especially Irish, and Catholics; more yet were Americans, from New Hampshire. These last were a sturdy, rough, floating population, with little knowledge of town traditions, and less respect for them; and with a strong general disposition to vote the Democratic ticket. They did not live in Quincy, but came down from the north in the spring to get a summer's work; and, at the season of their coming, stage-coach after stage-coach from Boston would be loaded down with them and their luggage. In March they voted for Isaac Hill, or his Democratic nominee, in New Hampshire; and in November they voted for Marcus Morton in Quincy. They were a foreign voting element; but there was also a new domestic voting element which had now to be taken into account. The shoemaking population had greatly increased. This was of a wholly different type from the stone-working population. The day of great shoe-factories and machine-made work was yet distant, and the men and women who made shoes as a trade worked mainly at their homes; but, as an occupation, shoemaking lacked the manliness and robust, out-door vigor of stone-cutting. The shoemaker worked day in and day out in the little ill-ventilated cobbler's room attached to the dwelling, — a room which in winter was heated by a stove and smelled of burnt leather. He stuck to his last; and, in doing so, he talked a great deal of politics and of political issues, thoroughly canvassing all men in public life, from President Jackson down to Mr. Greenleaf, the traditional moderator at town-meeting. The shoemaker was, as a rule, not a Federalist; but he did not vote the Democratic ticket in the same way the quarry-man voted it. His was not that rough and somewhat turbulent independence. Intellectually, he was of a finer, keener type; physically, he did not sustain the comparison well. He was apt to be round-shouldered and hollow-chested, thin and long-limbed. He lacked the muscle of the stone-cutter. In politics he was inclined to admire what he called "smartness" rather than grasp; and, though he would not vote for a convicted knave, he felt a good deal of lurking kindness for the successful rascal, and an absolute contempt for the well-intentioned dolt. He loved political intrigue and combination, and could be depended upon by the wire-puller;

though he soon saw through the merely loud-voiced demagogue.

Such were the political elements which between 1830 and 1840 began to mingle and contend for mastery in the Quincy town-meeting. First were those of the old, native stock, living by agriculture,— slow, conservative and generally disposed to show much deference to the opinions of the gentry. Next came the quarry-men, composed of noisy, muscular, hard-living native Americans, with small reverence. Then the foreign-born Catholics, who instinctively sided against all settled political traditions. Lastly, the shoemakers, mainly Americans, but disinclined to the old ways and the old leaders; and disposed to manage things by intrigue and combination, without much regard to precedent. It is almost needless to say that in the presence of such elements as these the downfall of the local gentry influence was a mere question of time. The spirit of democracy was afloat in the land, and the movement which had carried Jackson into the Presidency on the larger theatre, on the smaller was destined soon to drive Thomas Greenleaf out of the management of town affairs. The growth year by year of the vote cast for Marcus Morton marks the advance of the tide. In 1829 he received one ballot only; and in 1832 he had but 20. In 1835 he had got up to 42, and the next year to 148. Two years later the revolution in public opinion was complete, and Marcus Morton polled 260 votes to 172 for Edward Everett, then governor and seeking a reëlection. The size of the vote showed also the rapid increase of the population under the new business development. In 1830 only 138 ballots were cast in the state election; in 1840 the number had increased more than fivefold, aggregating 700. This, it is true, was a presidential election, and a very exciting one, — the famous hard-cider and log-cabin campaign. But the presidential election of 1828 was also an exciting one, in which a Quincy man was a candidate. Yet in 1828 only 123 votes were cast, or scarcely a sixth part of those cast in 1840.

In the town, as in the nation, the process of absorption and amalgamation was now to be gone through with. The inrush of foreign elements had been too rapid. It tended to unsettle everything. Nor did it soon stop. Up to this time the agriculturists — the farm-hands — had been mainly Americans. The Irish now began to take the place of these men in the fields; while the new generation of Americans either found employment in shops and mechanical pursuits, or became shoemakers. The more adventurous and enterprising went to the cities, or sought their fortunes in the West. But the result of it all was a complete change in the character of the town. It was a change also for the worse. The old order of things was doubtless slow, conservative, traditional; but it was economical, simple and business-like. The new order of things was in all respects the reverse. The leaders in it prided themselves on their enterprise, their lack of reverence for tradition, their confidence in themselves; but they were noisy, unmethodical, in reality incompetent, and much too often intemperate.

Accordingly, neither the business record nor the moral record of the town was now creditable. There was, as respects the first, no absolute corruption; the method of doing business was simply loose. The town debt was an illustration. It was a small affair, amounting to only a few thousand dollars, when, in 1837, Congress passed an act for the distribution of the surplus national revenue. Under the operation of this act no less a sum than $5,148 fell to the share of Quincy, and was regularly appropriated to the payment of the town debt. It should have sufficed to extinguish it; yet the very next year the debt was larger than ever. The surplus was muddled away. The expenses exceeded the appropriations; the deficiencies were not provided for; the treasury was falling into a system of yearly arrears. So also on the moral side. In 1835, and again in 1836, a movement was made in the direction of temperance reform, through the insertion of an article in the warrant of each year to see if the town would instruct the selectmen not to license places for the sale "of Rum, Brandy, Gin, or other Spirituous liquors." After a sharp struggle, the proposition was rejected in 1835 by a majority of two only in a total vote of 158. At the election of that year 138 votes were thrown for Governor Everett to 42 for Marcus Morton. The next year Morton's vote increased to 148, and the proposal not to license was defeated by 38 majority; nor was it again renewed. The growth of sentiment, on the contrary, was distinctly in the other direction. Three years later, in 1839, Morton received 326 votes to 231 cast for Everett; the Jackson Democracy was in full ascendency. And now the seventeenth article in the warrant for the annual meeting was "to know if the Town will allow a temperate use of ardent spirits to the Paupers when they work on the road or farm," and by a vote of 96 to 86 it was so ordered. The same year the mysterious disappearance of the contents of a cask of rum stored at the almshouse was made the subject of a jocose paragraph in a formal report made to the town by one of its committees.

But the slow phase of transition through which Quincy was now passing is marked more distinctly in the support it accorded to John Quincy Adams than in any other one thing. It is hardly necessary to repeat that the phase referred to was not peculiar to Quincy. It was a popular movement which originated in the West, and spread all over the country. Andrew Jackson was its political exponent. His methods were its methods. The nation, therefore, was its field; but its spirit and peculiarities can be most closely studied in the town. It is needless to say, also, that J. Q. Adams was no less obnoxious to the new spirit than the new spirit was to him. He had met it before in the country at large, and been forced to succumb to it. He was now to meet it in his own town. Unlike his father, Mr. Adams had never been closely identified with his birthplace. Indeed, from that February day, in 1778, when, a boy of ten going with his father to Europe, he got into Commodore Tucker's barge on Mount Wollaston beach to be rowed out to the frigate Boston at anchor in the offing, to the time when, in 1829, he came home a defeated candidate for reëlection to the Presidency, — a period of half a century, — he was almost a complete stranger in Quincy. Still, he loved the old town, and was fond of telling how during the siege of Boston he used to go up on Penn's Hill every evening to see the shells thrown by besieged and besiegers, and how he never afterwards drove over that hill without watching the squirrels and wrens running and flying about, whose ancestors' nests he had taken many a time when a boy.[1] So, in spite

[1] *Memoir of Mrs. Quincy*, 209.

of the half century of absence and a natural coldness of manner, the townsmen of old English descent saw in him one of themselves. Accordingly, in 1824 the town gave the Adams electoral ticket a unanimous vote; and in the campaign of four years later his victorious opponent received only three ballots in Quincy. Between 1830 and 1836, Mr. Adams was four times elected to Congress from the Plymouth district, of which Quincy was then a part. At each election he had almost the entire vote of the town.[1] In 1833 he was the candidate of the Anti-Masonic party for governor, and in Quincy he had 149 votes to 97 for the two other candidates. In 1836 the change began, and two years later Morton, the Democratic candidate for governor, had 88 majority over Everett in a vote of 432. Notwithstanding this, Mr. Adams still held the town, receiving 183 votes to 76 cast for three other candidates. Two years later, in the Harrison campaign, Quincy was closely contested. Mr. Adams, owing to his anti-slavery course in Congress, was peculiarly obnoxious to the Democrats. The Harrison ticket had a plurality of 5 votes in the town out of a total of 700, but Marcus Morton for governor ran 48 votes ahead of John Davis. Mr. Adams, though receiving 20 more votes than Governor Davis, the head of the ticket on which he ran, yet fell 3 behind his own opponent, William M. Jackson, who had 349 votes. In 1842 there was a general collapse of the Whig party. John Tyler was President, and the Democracy was altogether in the ascendant. In Quincy, Morton had a plurality of 31

---

[1] The exact votes at each election were as follows: — November 1, 1830: Adams, 76; Baylies, 2; Thompson, 10. April 1, 1833: Adams, 164; Lincoln, 39; Doan, 11. November 10, 1834: Adams, 125; Brewer, 1. November 14, 1836: Adams, 175; Lincoln, 9; Burrell, 1.

and Mr. Adams, though handsomely leading his ticket, was again beaten, Ezra Wilkinson receiving 289 votes, or 4 more than he. Philosophizing over this result in his diary, he remarked that " the people are a wayward master." In 1844 took place the exciting struggle which preceded the Mexican war, and Polk was elected over Clay. In his district Mr. Adams had two opponents, and as the election drew near he looked forward " with scarcely doubting anticipation" to his own defeat. In Quincy the vote was close, but the Democrats maintained their ascendency, though " consisting," as Mr. Adams wrote, " of transient stone-cutters from New Hampshire." George Bancroft, the Democratic candidate, received 8 votes more than Governor Briggs; but this time Mr. Adams had the satisfaction of running over 40 votes ahead of the Whig presidential ticket, receiving 345 votes to 312 cast for Isaac Hull Wright, his Democratic opponent. The election of 1846 was the last in which Mr. Adams was concerned. That was a year of Whig triumph, and even in Quincy the Whig candidate had a large majority. As for Mr. Adams, he seemed to have outlived the opposition to him, and his parting majority from Quincy was a gratifying one. It spoke of earlier times. He received 232 votes to 213 cast for five different opponents.

Like the others, this last vote in Quincy was significant. To a certain degree only was it personal. The town was entering upon a new and distinct phase of transition which already began to show itself in the election returns. In November, 1845, the Old Colony railroad was opened to travel, and from that time Quincy became a suburb of Boston. Not, of course, that the change made itself felt at once. The people went on in their accustomed ways; but none the less, from the beginning of 1846 the country village (for it still was a country village then) and the city were in quick and easy connection. The rest was a mere question of time; and, indeed, it was twenty-five years before the transition was complete. The successful organization of a suburban land company in the northern part of the town in 1870 marked the event. Boston again, just two hundred and forty-five years later, had enlargement at Mount Wollaston, and Quincy became a species of sleeping apartment conveniently near to the great city counting-room.

In 1875 the population was returned at 9,155, or a little more than fourfold that (2,201) of 1830, and the order of change from the agricultural village to the suburban town can be briefly recapitulated. Upon the original yeoman and farm-hand basis the quarry-men had first come in from outside; while at the same time the young townsmen had gone out of the fields into the shop, abandoning the plough and the scythe for the desk and the awl. Then came the Irish laborer, working in the quarries, on the roads and as farm-hands, bringing with him the church of Rome, and combining with the stone-cutter to vote the Democratic ticket. Last of all appeared the dweller near the city, having store, office or counting-room in Boston, and regarding Quincy simply as a place convenient, at which his family lived and he slept. This last class to a very great degree absorbed the descendants of the original settlers, and the whole mass gradually resolved itself into the modern town community. But certainly the change from Parson Tompson and Teacher Flynt, and Judge Quincy and Deacon Bass to the modern stone-cutter, clerk and merchant was noticeable. Nor as an historical study, though the stage was small, were the characters of the several periods devoid of interest.

The final change in the character of the town thus began with 1846. Less than two years later John Quincy Adams died. The annexation of Texas had then been effected, and the war with Mexico was over. A new political question had forced its way to the front, and slavery was the impending issue. Quincy was never a pro-slavery town. The quarry-men and the Irish voted the Democratic ticket; but the old native element had always sympathized with Mr. Adams during his long struggle in Congress, and among his townsmen his teachings had not been lost. Many of them were Democrats; but they were the old Jackson Democrats, who had grown up opposed to the local Federalist and gentry rule of men of the Thomas Greenleaf type, and, once they were satisfied that Democracy meant the spread of African slavery, their revolt was a foregone conclusion. But they were slow in coming to that conviction; for these men were closely identified with the leather interests, and the Quincy boot-makers dealt largely with the South. The break came in 1848. The conscience Whigs of Massachusetts then refused to vote for General Taylor, and the Barnburners of New York refused to vote for Lewis Cass. The two factions met at Buffalo in August of that year, and nominated a separate ticket with Martin Van Buren at its head. The political effect of this in Quincy was singular, and showed how deep the Congressional action of J. Q. Adams had sunk into the minds of the people there, though the majority of them had twice voted against him. In November, 1848, the Democratic party practically disappeared in the town. The Whig party, which had always supported and elected ex-President Adams, for the time being retained its strength. It cast 246 votes for General Taylor, having cast 314 for Mr. Clay four years before. But the Democratic strength fell from 324 to 212, while the new liberty party rose from 68 to 170. Horace Mann, Mr. Adams' successor in Congress, received a majority of 458, in a total vote of 558. A week later came the state election, and the Democratic vote fell to 34, while the Free-Soil vote ran up to 250, just failing of a plurality.

The work of political disintegration had now fairly begun. The Whig organization was crumbling away, while the Democratic, except in its foreign vote, was honeycombed with anti-slavery sentiment. The Free-Soilers, as they were called, held the balance of power. So things went on until 1854. Then the general collapse came, and in Quincy it was complete. As usual, the result of political disintegration was at first in no way what those who had been engaged in bringing it about either anticipated or desired. For more than a dozen years they had been working to break up the old parties, neither of which could in the least be depended on when any question of slavery was at issue. Both were afraid of it, and the Democracy were at heart false upon it. To break up the old organizations, and form a new one on an anti-slavery basis was the darling wish of the agitators. Prominent among these was Charles Francis Adams, who, all his earlier life a resident in Boston and one of its representatives in the Legislature, had upon his father's death become a citizen of Quincy. Mr. Adams in 1848 broke away from the Whig party, and was a candidate for the Vice-Presidency on the ticket with Van Buren. He was now laboring to build up the Free-Soil party, and in 1853 he had in Quincy been made the victim of a wretched political intrigue among the foreign Democratic voters of the town.

A convention was then to be held to revise the constitution of the State. Quincy was entitled to two representatives, and it was understood in the town that the Democrats and Free-Soilers would unite, each party naming one delegate. The Free-Soilers were true to their part of the agreement, and on the first ballot a Democrat was chosen. Mr. Adams was the candidate of the Free-Soilers; but the Democratic party of Quincy, as elsewhere, was largely made up of Irish, and here again was developed in local town experience one of those race characteristics which on the larger scale and the broader theatre constitute problems of history. The Irish as a class never, then or afterwards, liked Mr. Adams, and politically looked askance at him. Just as the native Yankee element, sprung from the old English stock, did like John Quincy Adams because in him, in spite of an outward coldness and restraint of manner, they recognized one of themselves, so the Irish did not like his son, because, Celts themselves, they instinctively saw in him those characteristics of English and Saxon origin which a few years later contributed in so marked a degree to the success of the representative of the country at the Court of St. James during the trying diplomatic episodes of the War of the Rebellion. Quick of impulse, sympathetic, ignorant and credulous, the Irish race have as few elements in common with the native New Englanders as one race of men well can have with another. Belonging to different branches of the same family, the two have for centuries grown up amid surroundings wholly unlike; and when the Irishman comes in contact with a public man in whom the characteristics of New England are ingrained, the small politician and village intriguer finds a rich field in which to work, ready to his hand. It was so in Quincy in 1853. Stories, ludicrously false but implicitly believed, were quietly circulated among the Irish as to the course Mr. Adams had pursued years before in the Massachusetts legislature in regard to compensation for the destruction of the convent school on Mount Benedict, and when the day came enough of them were induced to withhold their votes from him to bring about his defeat. It was simply a case of bad faith and village intrigue; but, for the Irish of Quincy, it was locally as unwise and ill-considered an act as they could well have been guilty of. As usual, they had been worked upon to their own injury; nor had they long to wait for the fruits of their folly.

The incident occurred in March, 1853, and excited deep feeling in the town; for already, in the disintegration of parties, the deep-seated popular antipathy to foreigners, and especially to the Irish, was making itself felt: and the curious feature in it locally was that Mr. Adams, by far the most prominent political character in Quincy, was one of the few native Americans in the town who did not share in that antipathy. None the less, the latent hostility, amounting to race hatred, was there, and the occasion only was needed to bring it into violent action. In November, 1853, the proposed revision of the state constitution, the work of the convention chosen in the previous March, was rejected, and twelve months later the town was swept from its moorings by the Native American uprising of the year 1854. As by magic, the old party lines disappeared. In Quincy the Know-Nothing (as it was called) candidate for governor, a man not before heard of in politics, received 549 votes to 140 divided among three other candidates. The foreign element stood helpless. The old party leaders were not so much sent to the rear, as they were left out of sight and mind in the senseless rush. The slavery issue was forgotten in the presence of race prejudice. It was, as the result showed, but one phase of political disintegration; the old collapsed as the new crystallized: but, for the moment, it seemed to the anti-slavery workers as if their labors had resulted in chaos; they had endeavored to inspire the popular mind with the spirit of liberty, and instead they had evoked a demon of hate.

Nowhere did this spirit of intolerance rage more strongly than in Quincy. It required four whole years to allay it; and in 1857, when the Know-Nothing candidate for governor was overwhelmingly defeated in the State at large, in Quincy he had more than one hundred plurality. Quarry-man and shoemaker united against the Irish. At last, in 1858, the anti-slavery issue asserted its supremacy, and the Republican party came solidly to the front. Even then Quincy, reflecting its unassimilated constituency, worked but slowly back to its moorings; and accordingly, in the great Lincoln campaign of 1860, when the Republican ticket received a majority of 44,000 in the State, in Quincy it had only a plurality. Again in 1862, the year of deepest discouragement during the war, Quincy was one of those towns in which Governor Andrew fell behind, his Whig and Democratic opponent receiving 87 more votes than he. Yet in the State Andrew had over 28,000 majority. Like the constituencies of certain of the western states, that of Quincy consisted largely of different foreign elements, which, while they clearly predominated over the old, homogeneous, native element, yet, from race antipathy, would not combine with each other; and hence came confusion. But, as is usual under such circumstances, time worked a remedy; only, in this case, the arena of action being small, the remedy came quickly; and, in the crucial election of 1864, Quincy at last squarely ranged itself on the loyal side, the Lincoln ticket receiving a majority of 234 in a total vote of less than a thousand. Indeed, all the other elements were then united against the Irish vote and that large faction, composed of the croakers, the fault-finding and the otherwise-minded, which never fails to make its presence felt under the wearisome pressure of war.

## CHAPTER XXII.

### THE REBELLION.

FIRST and last Quincy did its full share in the work of educating New England and the North up to the point of facing and overcoming the Rebellion. It also was not wanting later. Yet, as in the War of Independence so now, the largest contribution of the town was neither in men nor in money, though as respects both the calls were honored. As John Adams was the great contribution of Braintree North Precinct to the Revolution, so his grandson, Charles Francis Adams, was the great contribution of Quincy in the Rebellion. When the war broke out Mr. Adams represented the Quincy district in Congress. He had been elected in 1858, on the final subsidence of the Native American deluge, and in 1860 he was reëlected on the Lincoln ticket.[1] In March, 1861, his first Congressional term being just completed, he was nominated by Mr. Lincoln as minister to Great Britain. In May he left the country, and he remained abroad until the summer of 1868. His services in London are part of the Quincy war record, but they do not belong to local history.

[1] In neither of these elections did Mr. Adams receive a majority vote in Quincy. In both he received more votes than any one else on the ticket with him; but while, in the election of 1858, he had a plurality of 59 votes, in that of 1860 his opponent, Leverett Saltonstall, had 17 more votes than he, 465 to 448, with 7 scattering.

In other respects the record of Quincy in the Rebellion was in no way remarkable. The town did its share. It freely contributed money and supplies, and it sent out men. But of the men it sent out, whether to the army or the navy, there were none who rose to distinction. At the close of the Rebellion as before it, Deacon Joseph Palmer, the Revolutionary brigadier-general, was still Quincy's ranking officer. During the war, that is, between the years 1861 and 1865, the population of the town was about 6,750, while its valuation was returned at a little less than four millions of dollars. It could number probably 2,200 men capable of bearing arms. First and last it sent into the field almost one entire regiment, or 954 men, 757 of whom enlisted for the full term of three years. Of the whole number, 39 were killed in battle and 18 died in rebel prisons. In all 105, or one in every nine who went out, lost their lives. Still others were maimed. But a Quincy lad, a member of one of the families the name of which is most often found in the more recent records of the town, fell in the very first action of the war. On the 10th of June, 1861, occurred the affair at Big Bethel, Va., and young Theodore Winthrop was killed. For days after the country rang with his name; nor is it yet forgotten. At the same time Francis L. Souther, of Quincy, was mortally wounded. A mere boy, he was a member of the Hancock Light Guard, as the Quincy company was called, and had gone with it when the Fourth Regiment of Massachusetts militia was rushed off to Fortress Monroe. His companions presently sent his body home, and it was buried in his native town. Afterwards many others were killed or died, and war's mortality became a thing of course; but it was the sudden tidings of young Souther's death, coming in those early days of June, 1861, which first caused the people of Quincy to realize that their young men had gone out to actual battle.

The money cost of the Rebellion to the towns of Massachusetts, apart from what their inhabitants then or later contributed in national taxes, was not large. In the case of Quincy it amounted to less than $50,-000, including the subscriptions of citizens to bounty funds. In 1861 the town owed $35,000; in 1865 it owed $57,000. The whole increase of debt due to the war was not equal to one per cent. of the valuation. Neither was the rate of taxation between 1861 and 1865 peculiarly high, or the increase of it rapid. Indeed, the era of extravagance and heavy expenditure followed the Rebellion rather than marked its progress. Nor was the excessive taxation subsequently imposed the result of an effort to clear off burdens due to the war. On the contrary, the debt yearly grew larger, so that while between 1861 and 1865, the war period, the rate of taxation increased but one third, and the debt but $35,000, in the four years of peace which followed the rate of taxation increased eighty per cent., while the debt was $16,000 larger in 1869 than it had been in 1865. Compared with that of the Revolution, the war burden of the Rebellion, whether in men or in money, was for Quincy light and easy to be borne. In the Revolution there was no general government or system of national taxation to fall back upon. The states had to meet the requisitions directly; and the states made their calls upon the towns. Accordingly, it has been already seen that Braintree then sent into the field, first and last, two men out of every three capable of bearing arms, while a fourth part of the whole wealth accumulated through a century and a half was consumed in the struggle. During the Rebellion not two men in five did military duty, nor was the accumulated wealth diminished at all. On the contrary, even allowing for an altered standard of value, in 1865 the town was unquestionably richer than it was in 1860.

## CHAPTER XXIII.

### TOWN-MEETINGS AGAIN.

THE close of the Rebellion left Quincy a town of nearly 7,000 population, and from that time forward the increase both in numbers and in wealth was rapid. The last vestiges of village life now passed away, and the suburban town assumed shape. This change could not take place without bringing up new problems for solution; and again the experience of the individual town reflected that of the common country, for first and most important of these new problems was that relating to municipal government. It was one thing to manage the affairs of a small village community through the machinery of town-meetings; it was quite another to manage those of a place numbering a population of 12,000. In 1830 the annual appropriation for necessary town expenses was $4,500. It has been seen how this sum was voted by a small body of men, all knowing each other well, having a community of interest and acting under a usage which had the force of law. Forty-five years later, in 1876, the annual appropriation was $116,000, and the articles in the warrant had swollen from half a dozen in number to nearly forty. The character of the town-meeting also had changed. In place of the few score rustics following the accustomed lead of the parson and squire, and asserting themselves only when they thought that their traditions or equality were ignored, — in place

of this small, easily-managed body, there was met a
heterogeneous mass of men numbering hundreds, jealous, unacquainted, and often in part bent on carrying
out some secret arrangement in which private interest
overrode all sense of public welfare. To maintain in
these meetings that degree of order which is necessary
for transacting business in a methodical way was not
easy, and the multifarious affairs of a year were to be
attended to in a single day. Town officers were to be
elected; the appropriations were to be considered and
voted; the policy of the town on all disputed points
was to be decided. These points also included everything, — education, roads, health, temperance; for, as
the result of growth, the functions of municipal government expanded and branched out until simplicity
had become a tradition. The poll-lists contained the
names of more than two thousand voters. For these
to come together as one legislative body, and pass
upon numerous and difficult questions in a few hours,
would at first seem so impossible that the suggestion
of such a scheme of municipal government as a new
idea of his own would cause any political thinker to
be looked upon as a foolish theorist. The thing was
practical simply because it was habitually done. But
to adapt the old village system to the new town conditions was the problem which Quincy, in common with
many other Massachusetts towns still clinging to the
ancient ways, found forced upon it. Nor is the town-meeting in its actual working fully understood. Since
De Tocqueville brought it into wide-world notice, this
New England institution has been often described
and infinitely lauded: but it may well be doubted
whether one in ten of those who have philosophized
over town-meetings ever attended one, much more

## A SYSTEM OVER-TAXED.

ever took part in one. Yet, without having done so, it is as difficult to understand the practical working of the system as it is to describe war without ever having served in an army or seen a battle. The ideal town-meeting is one thing; the actual town-meeting is apt to be a very different thing. To the theorist in history who should attend one, it would, not improbably, be the rude dispelling of a fanciful delusion. He would come away from it rather amazed that civilized government was possible through such a system than understanding how New England had been built up on it.

That the town-meeting, as a practical method of conducting municipal affairs, should break down under the stress to which a dense city population must subject it, is a matter of course. It did so in Athens and in Rome before it did so in Boston; for Demosthenes and Cicero as well as James Otis and Josiah Quincy were town-meeting orators. Just in the degree in which civic population increases, therefore, the town-meeting becomes unwieldy and unreliable; until at last it has to be laid aside as something which the community has outgrown. It becomes a relic, though always an interesting one, of a simpler and possibly better past. Moreover, the indications that the system is breaking down are always the same. The meetings become numerous, noisy and unable to dispose of business. Disputed questions cannot be decided; demagogues obtain control; the more intelligent cease to attend. In all these respects, the experience of Quincy affords interesting matter for study.

Between the years 1840 and 1870 the town-meeting there fell to its lowest point of usefulness, as prior to 1840 it might have been seen in its most perfect form;

but during the later Jacksonian period Thomas Greenleaf, and the class of men of which he was a type, lost their hold, and were supplanted by others. They, together with their old-fashioned dress and formal manners, were looked upon as antiquated and out of date. Their simple, straightforward, business-like way of managing the affairs of the town was not in accordance with the democratic, young-America ideas then in vogue. It was a somewhat dreary period in national history, — the period of emergence from colonial conditions before the country yet felt sure of its own position, — the up-start period, during which, while noisily and vulgarly asserting itself, the United States as a whole was more self-conscious than ever before, and continually anxious to know what was thought of it abroad. Owing to the facts connected with the development of the town which have in this narrative so repeatedly been referred to, all these phases of the national drama were curiously reproduced on the small Quincy stage. Not only did Thomas Greenleaf and the other veterans of the colonial time and federal politics lag superfluous on the stage, but they were made to feel that they lagged. If they were not actually hustled off the boards, they were dismissed quite unceremoniously and with scant respect. Other men brought other methods; and, while these men and the new methods unconsciously paved the way to better things in the end, they were in themselves in no respect an improvement on what went before. On the contrary, for a time the deterioration as respects both men and methods was as marked and discouraging as it was in manners; and it must have required either profound insight into causes and effects, or great saving faith in the future to enable any one in those days to speak hopefully of the outcome. So far as Quincy and its town-meeting government were concerned, when at last this change fairly took place the business of the town had for years been done in the orderly and intelligent way already described; everything of importance at the annual meeting being referred to committees for consideration, and these committees subsequently making reports upon which the town acted at its adjourned meetings. No method of government could have worked better, for the townsmen were accustomed to it; and this it was which De Tocqueville lauded so highly. But there was another and far from uncommon phase of the system which might at any time have been studied in Quincy during the score of years between 1850 and 1870. Had De Tocqueville then visited the place on a town-meeting day, he would have gone into a large hall the floor of which, sprinkled with sawdust and foul with tobacco-juice, was thronged with men of various types, coming in or going out, standing in groups or moving incessantly to and fro, while among them unruly boys circulated rapidly, often engaged with shouts and screams in some game of undisturbed tag, to them as interesting as it was noisy. There were no rows of seats in the room, and but one bench, which ran along its sides. All the men wore their hats, and many of them had pipes or cigars in their mouths; while the air reeked with odors, tobacco-smoke being among the least objectionable. Not a few of those present had plainly been drinking. On a platform at the further end of the hall was a desk, behind which were the moderator and the clerk. The town business for the whole year was being disposed of and the appropriations voted. Amid a continuous sound of voices and moving feet the moderator would bring up in succession the articles in the warrant. The custom of referring them to committees had fallen into disuse, and been abandoned in 1852, as un-democratic and not in accordance with what men are accustomed to designate as the spirit of the times. After 1852, accordingly, everything in the Quincy annual warrant was disposed of in a single day and on the spot. It was supposed to be a more prompt, more energetic, — a more popular way of dealing with business. The disposition which might be made of any subject was consequently very much matter of chance. Certain questions the town, or individuals in the meeting, might be on the watch for. These had been discussed outside, and were or were not to pass unchallenged; but orderly debate was impossible. Now and again some one would uncover and address the moderator. For an instant there would be silence. If the speaker then knew what he wanted to say and how to say it, he would be listened to, always provided he spoke briefly and to the point. If he told a humorous story or made a broad joke he would be uproariously applauded; for the comic performer and funny man is a dangerous opponent in town-meeting. If, on the other hand, the would-be debater was long, or dull, or pointless, his voice was soon lost in the hubbub of those moving and talking about him. For the moderator to preserve order and quiet was simply impossible. The audience was numerous, and almost no one was seated. Tired and restless, those composing it were also excited and noisy. Many of them wanted what they called "fun," and there was a great deal of horse-play going on. The Dutch auction in the choice of tax-collector was in this respect the episode of the occasion. The office was put up to the lowest bidder. Some one would offer to make the collections for five per cent. of the levy, and then would follow bid upon bid, each lower than the other; until at last, amid shouts of laughter and applause, the prize would be struck off at three mills or less on the dollar. Finally the warrant would be disposed of, the appropriations voted, and the meeting adjourned. Then at last the moderator and the clerk would get together, and from their notes and memories manufacture a record. A few days later the town would for the first time know what it had done at its annual meeting.

Such a meeting as that described would also be looked upon as usual and orderly; one in which the business had been transacted in a regular way. All meetings were not so, for occasionally there would be an organized faction bent on putting through some job. When the affairs of any community are managed in this way, it scarcely needs to be said that they soon fall into confusion. Want of method may be democratic, but it is not business-like. Quincy proved no exception to the rule. In 1870 government by town-meeting was there plainly breaking down. A general laxity in ways of doing public business had crept into all the departments. The school committee, the surveyors of highways, the overseers of the poor, the engineers of the fire department, were in the custom of asking for such appropriations as they thought sufficient. If in the hurly-burly of town-meeting these were voted, it was well and good. Those who had the disbursements to make would then keep within the sum allotted them — provided they were under no special temptation to exceed it. If the whole amount asked for was not voted, it would be spent all the same; and the town found itself liable for the bills its agents had contracted. There was no great amount of jobbery and scarcely any corruption, except in the small and more contemptible way; but the soil was being rapidly prepared for both jobbery and corruption. The growth of a municipal "ring," the members of which would live on the town just as parasites live on a dog, was a mere question of time. The laborer who worked on the roads, the pauper who lived at home while the town paid his rent, the tradesman who supplied the pensioned poor, all began to feel a direct interest in the growth of bad government. As yet the evil had made no great headway, but the sense of official responsibility and obedience to instructions was already relaxed. Officers were disposed to do what seemed in their own eyes "about right," regardless of rule; and the town good-naturedly condoned offences. The result was that the finances fell into confusion. Every year a liberal appropriation would be made to reduce the town debt, but each year saw that debt grow larger. It rose in this way from $8,000 in 1844 to $112,000 in 1874, and a committee then reported that it represented an outlay incurred neither for educational or war or other special purposes. It was a pure deficiency debt. The money time and again raised to pay it off had been regularly diverted and applied to those ordinary purposes, the amount spent on account of which almost invariably exceeded the sums appropriated by the town.

Such were the facts. It remained to find a remedy. This remedy was found, not in a representative city government, for the time for that had not yet come, but in a return to the old and correct town-meeting methods; and in this matter the experience of Quincy might be of value to sister towns, for many of them have already found themselves, and others yet will find themselves, in the same position. The younger John Quincy Adams had then for years been chosen by common consent as the moderator of all town-meetings at which he was present. Mortified at the way in which business was done and at his own inability to preserve order, he announced a reform. In 1870, when the town came together at the annual meeting, after the polls for the choice of officers were closed the hall was ordered to be cleared and seats brought in. Then, after the vote was declared, the articles in the warrant were taken up; but not until every voter was uncovered and seated, and pipes and cigars extinguished. .Order was thus established, and in so establishing it history was but repeating itself; for, as long before as 1782, when on the 5th of March the town-meeting of old Braintree assembled " by Adjournment from yesterday," it was voted "that Every member of the Town Present at this meeting take a seat when order'd to it by the moderator." So, in 1870, as doubtless it was in 1782, when every one was seated and order was established, deliberation became possible. This was a great step gained; but more was necessary. The warrant had now grown to thirty and even forty articles, all of which were acted upon in the single evening of a day which had been occupied with voting. The townsmen were tired, excited, noisy and in no mood to do business. Accordingly, in 1874 a new step was taken, and the town went fairly back to that old system which had been abandoned more than twenty years before. When at the annual meeting officers were elected, it was also voted to refer all the business articles in the warrant to a large committee, which was to subdivide itself, investigate everything, and at an adjourned meeting report its conclusions in the form of votes properly drawn up. These the town would then consider.

The result of this return to business-like methods was remarkable. The town-meeting at once showed itself equal to the occasion. After 1874, for fourteen years, and until other elements of growth, population, increase of business and change of political elements naturally developed themselves, every question was again fairly considered and acted upon intelligently, with full opportunity for debate; the appropriations were carefully made, and all officers required to keep expenditures within them; a responsible government was established. Then, as if by magic, the finances assumed shape. The debt, which for nearly half a century had defied every effort to extinguish it, now fell in nine years from $112,000 to $19,000, and then shortly disappeared. Deficiencies were met by special appropriations; exceptional outlays were distributed over a series of years; rigid accountability was established. This was done through an intelligent development of the ancient village system; and it is probably safe to assert that never in the two centuries and a half of town history had that system worked so well, or to such general satisfaction, as during those years when Quincy had grown in wealth and population to city limits.

## CHAPTER XXIV.

### A LONG BATTLE WON.

NOR did the reform in town methods stop here. It extended itself into other fields. The work done at this time in the schools has already been described; but, while Mr. Parker was busy in one way there, another man was busy in a very different way elsewhere. In the days of John Adams it has been seen that Braintree did not enjoy a reputation for temperance. His labors in that field of reform, and the poor results derived from them, have been referred to. As time passed on things hardly seem to have improved, and about the year 1820 it has been said the Rev. Mr. Norton, of Weymouth, took occasion of an exchange of pulpits to remind his brother Whitney's Quincy flock of the unsavory reputation in this respect of the town in which they lived; and it is further asserted that "rum-drinking was so common in those days that the discourse made but little impression, except to be ridiculed." [1] Later, the large foreign element which the working of the quarries brought into town tended to make matters distinctly worse. The Washingtonian movement made some headway before 1840; but, even then, when a temperance convention was to be held in Quincy, the use of the stone temple was refused it. John Quincy Adams, being invited to deliver an address before that convention, accepted;

[1] Wilson, 250*th Anniversary*, 119.

and, to their dismay, the parish authorities found that they had shut the ex-President out of his own place of worship. It was too late to retract, and Mr. Adams' address on temperance was delivered elsewhere. It was now that the town voted (117 to 81) " to discontinue the use of ardent spirits at the almshouse ; " but still, and for several years to come, the post-office was in the bar-room of the principal tavern, and thither, among drinking men, daily went women and little girls and boys to have letters and papers handed to them across a counter which reeked of rum. Then came the period of anti-slavery education, and the minds and thoughts of all were otherwise absorbed. At last, when the Rebellion was suppressed, it is not too much to say that, through its peculiarities of position, population and labor, Quincy was a stronghold of the liquor interest. Indeed, peace was scarcely established, and the wave of sectional feeling had not yet begun to subside, before the town was again Democratic. In 1867 it gave J. Q. Adams, as candidate for governor, 650 votes to 348 which it cast for the Republican ticket. For a town to be Democratic on state issues and Republican on national issues — and such was the position of Quincy — meant then but one thing. It meant intemperance. The foreign vote combined with the Democratic vote, and, having the ascendency, decreed that unrestrained sale of spirits against which John Adams, more than a century before had so manfully contended.

Where a crying evil exists, some man is sure soon or late to rise up and protest against it. In Quincy that man appeared in the person of one descended from original North Precinct stock, for the name of Faxon is met with on many pages of the town records, and can be found on not a few head-stones in the old burying-ground. Henry H. Faxon, a man of considerable individuality as well as of numerous peculiarities, became interested in the cause of temperance, — or perhaps, it would be more correct to say in the cause of total abstinence; for in the virtue of temperance, whether in drink or speech, he had but a limited faith. Somewhat imperfectly educated, Mr. Faxon could not truthfully be described as conspicuous for dignity of bearing; and as a public speaker his deliverances were more noted for directness and frequency than for eloquence or correctness of speech. He was known to address the audience forty times by actual count at a single annual town-meeting, and hardly once in those forty times did his remarks fail to elicit laughter, cheers or hisses. That he was deficient in judgment it is hardly necessary to say. Yet, though often exciting unnecessary opposition and ridicule by his methods and the way with which in place and out of place he advocated the reform he had come to have at heart, he clung to it with a tenacity sure to produce results. Many at first doubted his sincerity; but he convinced them that he was in earnest by the freedom with which he contributed his labor, his time and his money. His attacks on individuals were so open, public and fearless that from the mouth of any one else they would have been sure to lead to blows. Once they did so in his case; and he was often threatened. Much of his security lay probably in the fact that he was neither vindictive nor malignant. Indeed, he was good-natured in his enmities. He did not lose his temper, and become ugly and bitter under defeat; nor did he follow up wrongs or slights in any spirit of revenge. He had apparently none of that brooding desire to "get even," as it is expressed, with a successful opponent, which is always the characteristic of small, secretive and sour-tempered men. Under these circumstances, while in town-meeting, and not without cause, his opponents laughed and jeered at him, and not infrequently hustled him, yet he laughed and jeered in return, and took the hustling in no ill part. "Henry," as he was familiarly called, was entirely at home in town-meetings. So Yankee met Yankee; but the work went on. It was a long, hard fight. Not only was the sentiment of reform to be aroused, but a strong business and political combination had to be broken down. The town had become in a certain way a liquor-selling centre, and, as usual, the thing had worked its way into local politics. The reputation of the place suffered. John Adams noted down in 1760 that to be "as litigious as Braintree" had become a common expression; so now it was said that other towns were "as intemperate as Quincy." It was spoken of as "a hard place," and the stone-cutting population was held accountable for the bad condition of affairs. The evils of the thing also were keenly felt in many households. Mothers and fathers saw their young sons falling into drunken ways. But it had always been so, and the political combination which favored the continuance of the system was strong. The Democratic leaders controlled the Irish vote; and the liquor interest had a complete understanding with the Democratic leaders. The Irish vote was thus once more juggled into perpetuating a system under which those whom it represented suffered more than any others in the community.

So things went on year after year. But as wealth and population increased it grew plain that it was not a question of temperance only. The cause of good and honest municipal government was also involved. The condition of affairs in this respect already described was rapidly growing from bad to worse. No reform in town-meeting methods would suffice unless the dominant combination was broken down. Then Mr. Faxon found new and potent allies, and suddenly the town was revolutionized. In March, 1881, a Democratic and liquor-licensing board of selectmen was, as usual, chosen. That same year, largely through the efforts of Mr. Faxon, the law of the State was changed so that the question whether " licenses be granted for the sale of intoxicating liquors in this town" was presented squarely to the voters. The result was astonishing. In 1882 there were 1,057 who voted " No " to 475 who voted " Yes." When the thing was presented in this plain way the issue was understood, and the Irish vote broke from Democratic control. At the same time the friends of good government and temperance came together. The town-meeting had been reformed, and now the bar-room was closed. But the length of the struggle against the last is worthy of record. It largely exceeded a century; for in 1760 John Adams described himself, to use his own words, as discharging his venom "against the multitude, poverty, ill government, and ill effects of licensed houses, and the timorous temper, as well as criminal design, of the selectmen " who licensed them ; but not until 1882, one hundred and twenty-two years later, did his local successor in that crusade close, at least for the time being, the last of those houses in Quincy.

## CHAPTER XXV.

"THE KING IS DEAD! LONG LIVE THE KING!"

IN his History of the English People, John Richard Green traces the origin of town-meeting government to a remote period and a distant region. Whether as an historical proposition what he asserts can be accepted as wholly sound may be open to question;[1] but his genetic theory of the familiar Massachusetts political organization of to-day is hardly less plausible than it is attractive, for he goes directly back to the fifth century after the birth of Christ, and "the district which is now called Sleswick, a district in the heart of the peninsula that parts the Baltic from the Northern seas. . . . Of the temper and life of the folk in this older England we know little. But . . . in their villages lay ready formed the social and political life which is round us to-day. . . . The life, the sovereignty of the settlement, resided solely in the body of the freemen, whose holdings lay round the moot-hill or the sacred tree where the community met from time to time to deal out its own justice and to make its own laws. . . . It is with reverence such as is stirred by the sight of the head-waters of some mighty river that one looks back to these village moots of Friesland or Sleswick. It was here that England learned to be a 'mother of Parliament.' It was in these tiny knots of farmers that the men from whom

[1] *Supra*, 814-15.

Englishmen were to spring learned the worth of public opinion. . . . The 'talk' of the village moot . . . is the groundwork of English history."

But, no matter how ancient or whence derived, town-meeting government must always remain a primitive form of government, adapted only to the needs of a comparatively simple community, homogeneous, and neither too numerous nor with wealth unequally distributed. Its chief excellence lies in the fact that it is the most perfect government of the people by the people which has ever been devised; and its simplicity is its most striking characteristic. In New England this form of government has now had an unbroken continuance of two centuries and a half, and two hundred and fifty years are no small portion of recorded history; there are few human institutions, much less mere governmental machines, to which so long an existence is given. But, besides that decadence which seems to be a necessary incident to mere lapse of time, the New England government by town-meeting has limitations in other respects, often experienced and to which reference has more than once been made. Though, as this narrative has shown, admitting of very considerable development, and far more elastic and adaptable to circumstances than would naturally have been supposed, this, like other forms of government, does not admit of boundless development, nor has it an infinite elasticity. The requirements of a Massachusetts village community during the colonial period were few and comparatively simple, — the church, the schools, the highways and the poor completed the list. But not only were the requirements of the original communities few and their annual outlay small, but the communities themselves were made up of human material of like character, living under conditions not very dissimilar. Those composing it were, in fact, members almost of a common family.

When this is duly considered, the matter for surprise is, not that the town-meeting governments of Massachusetts have during the nineteenth century showed a tendency to break down, but that they have stood the strain to which they were subjected so well and lasted so long. It is now sixty years since the colonial system in Massachusetts finally passed away. It died with the original constitution of 1780; and it was within the limits of Quincy that the building of Gridley Bryant's railway in 1826 struck the key-note of change for the coming time. That the original municipal system improvised in 1630 should have yet survived and worked satisfactory results through the long period of sixty years after that key-note was plainly sounded, affords conclusive evidence of its vitality as well as its excellence.

During those sixty years the differentiation in modern town life has taken place. The simple has become complex. The church has indeed been separated from the state; but in place of the one function of which the state as represented in the municipality was thus relieved, the town government has assumed an almost infinitude of others. The schools have been multiplied no less than the branches of instruction, until even the more rudimentary forms of education have become the province of specialists. The highways are crushed under the weight of a traffic, which, in the case of Quincy, reduces the firmest known pavement to powder, and exhausts the ingenuity of the engineer. The care of the sick, the poor and the insane has been magnified into a science and reduced to a system. These were the ancient and traditional functions of the town, and all of them have through the natural process of development passed in the larger centres of population beyond the handling capacity of the ordinary official, and of necessity devolved upon a class of men specially trained to deal with them. Meanwhile other and new needs have made themselves felt: — the public peace must be provided for; scientific provision must be made against fire; streets need to be lighted; questions of public health are to be considered; the introduction of water necessitates drainage; the old burying-ground develops into the modern cemetery; the public school is supplemented by the public library; and the training-field and ancient common, having passed away, are now replaced by the public garden and the park. The performance of the duties necessarily pertaining to all these things, calling as they do for almost infinite special knowledge and a complicated financial machinery, was imposed little by little on the old town governments. It is as if an ancient country cart — well designed, honestly made of excellent material, altogether good in its day and for the work then needed of it — should by degrees be called upon to do that for which a modern railroad train is required. As a matter of course the cart must break down under a strain to which it was never designed to be subjected.

As it was with Boston in 1822, and has been with many other municipalities since, so was it with the town government of Quincy in 1887. Never had it been better administered, never had it performed its work in a way more satisfactory, never had the reputation of the town stood so high among its sister towns, as it then had for fifteen years; but, nevertheless, those in position to watch most closely the working of the machine could not but be sensible that it was rapidly being subjected to a strain it could not permanently bear, and that its continued satisfactory results were a mere matter of chance, — they depended on the absence of any considerable disturbing element. This could hardly be expected to continue; and when a serious cause of disturbance did occur, the machine, it was evident, would not prove equal to the demands made upon it.

The decree of fate was indeed written in the figures of the census. The population of 2,200, with which the town passed out of the colonial period in 1830, had at the close of the Rebellion in 1865 risen to 6,700; and this enumeration had again twenty years later grown to over 12,000. The whole success of town government depends upon the active interest taken by those entitled to participate in it. A small attendance as the town meetings recur indicates a lack of interest in public affairs; and yet, after population passes a certain point, a large attendance necessarily makes a town-meeting unwieldy, and incapacitates it for the transaction of business. A full meeting of voters is then apt, in the presence of some exciting issue or popular craze, to degenerate into an unruly mob. In the case of Quincy there were in 1885 more than 2,500 names on the voting list, while over 2,000 ballots were actually cast at the election which preceded the annual March meeting of that year. No hall in the town contained space-room in which to seat such a number of people; nor were such numbers consistent with the idea of a deliberative body.

Those composing the body were also no longer in any way homogeneous. The large infusions of alien

## THE ALIEN ELEMENT.

material which from time to time had taken place in the Quincy constituency have been referred to, and the disturbance they caused in the practical working of town-meeting government described. Had the increase of population during the sixty years which followed the close of the colonial period (1830–1890) continued at the same ratio as the increase during the first thirty years of the century (1800–1830) the aggregate in 1890 would have been less than eight thousand; in reality it was over sixteen thousand. The question of nativity then presented itself. Of the sixteen thousand only a little more than one in each three was even born in the town, and yet fewer came of the old town stock; while a clear majority of the whole were either of foreign birth or the children of immigrants. The process of change also was still rapidly going on, for, while in 1875 twenty-six in each hundred inhabitants were foreign born, in 1885 this number had increased to over thirty. Even of those of American birth one out of each three, having been born elsewhere, had moved into the town.[1]

Thus, so far as mere numbers went, the old original stock had well-nigh disappeared; and, though such of it as was left still made itself potently felt, a new force might at any time assert itself — as new forces had asserted themselves before — which would in a moment set aside the traditions of the town and revo-

[1] *Census of Massachusetts*, 1885, vol. i. Part I., lxxv. 75, 542, 596. With a total population of 12,145, Quincy in 1885 had 4,372 town-born inhabitants, in which number were, of course, included the town-born offspring of the foreign-born. Of the foreign-born 1,565 were Irish and 573 Scotch. Of the Americans born in other States of the Union 647 came from Maine and 269 from New Hampshire. There were 6,382 inhabitants both of the parents of whom were foreign-born; while those of pure American parentage numbered only 4,632.

lutionize its methods. All depended on the popular will of a large and growing business community expressed through the forms of an annual election, and subsequent general town-meetings. The time had been when almost every man in those town-meetings knew by face and name and reputation every other man in them, while the bulk of those who attended were tillers of the soil. In the census of 1885 thirty-seven inhabitants only reported themselves as farmers and one hundred and twenty-four as farm laborers, while the stone-workers and quarry-men were fourteen hundred in number. The agriculturist had practically disappeared, while at the town-meeting, in place of the eighteenth century freeholders, — the colonial yeomanry, — there now assembled a great mass of men who, engaged in multifarious occupations, not only neither knew of, nor cared for, the ancient ways and old-time traditions, but many of whom regarded those traditions and ways with an impatience and contempt they were under no pains to conceal as part of the rubbish of an antiquated past. They wanted a new town, organized on modern ideas, — wide-awake, as the expression goes, and in touch with what men are pleased commonly to designate as the spirit of the times.

The business the town-meeting was called upon to dispose of had grown also with the growth of the constituency and of taxation; the growth of the latter, indeed, had, in Quincy as in most other Massachusetts towns, been phenomenal and well calculated to excite attention, if not alarm. When contrasted with those of the earlier time, and especially of the last century, the figures indicating the self-imposed burden of the later period are curiously significant. For reasons already pointed out,[1] the returns of the assessor are, for the purposes of this comparison, worse than useless, — they are deceptive. From them, as data, not even an approximation can be reached. But, while the worldly possessions of the inhabitant of Quincy in 1890 as compared with the possessions of his predecessors of a century before could not even be guessed at with any approach to exactness, it was a fact clearly established that the burden of taxation each inhabitant had to bear was increased twenty fold. In 1790 it was a little less than sixty cents; in 1890 it was a little less than twelve dollars.

Such had been the growth of taxation, and mainly within thirty years. The increase of the town business as measured by the articles in the annual warrant had been hardly less. In 1830 the warrant contained but thirteen articles, and, excluding mere formal positions, only twelve town officers were chosen, among the twelve being a school committee of eight and the constable; the total amount appropriated did not exceed $3,700. In 1865 the warrant had grown to eighteen articles, the number of officials to be elected was seventeen, and the annual appropriation was $30,000. This was all within reasonable limits, and the growth indicated nothing calculated to subject town government to an undue strain. In 1885 it was no longer so; the warrant had grown to forty-eight articles, the ballot for town officials contained fifty names, and $120,000 was appropriated. There was, moreover, no recognized executive, — no systematic responsibility for results. In the old days the selectmen had attended to everything; but as town functions increased and special knowledge was required, little by

---

[1] *Supra,* 691.

little the selectmen had been stripped of authority until at last the business of the town — and of necessity too — had passed into the control of boards and commissions; — each of these bodies held authority direct from the people of the town, and was responsible to them alone.

The only thing that could be said in favor of a system of government so obviously outgrown was that practically it worked well. The results produced were sufficiently good; and, in fact, would compare favorably with those produced under any other system of municipal government which human wit had yet devised: and to say this was to be able to say much. Yet this could still be said; nor could it be denied.

But, none the less, the change, naturally to be anticipated and long expected, took place in the spring of 1887. What are commonly known as the labor organizations were at that time actively at work, not only in Quincy but throughout the State and country; and, during the previous winter, arrangements had been made for widespread strikes to take place on the first of May, the object of which was of course to secure to those who worked with their hands an increase of pay, combined with shorter hours of labor. It was well known that these questions had been much discussed in the unions of West Quincy, the region in which the quarries chiefly lay and a community by itself; and it was understood some sort of an organized demonstration would be made at the annual town-meeting. It of course does not need to be added that demonstrations of this character, organized privately and outside, are the greatest elements of danger to which popular government, and especially town-meeting government, can be subjected. It was so in the days of Athens and of Rome, and it will continue to be so as long as human nature and human institutions remain as they are. Cleon and Clodius are recurring characters.

The warrant for the annual town-meeting for 1887, when issued in February of that year, was found to contain, among other articles calculated to excite notice, the following:—

"ART. 54. To see if the town will instruct the Selectmen, Overseers of the Poor, Road Commissioners, and Managers of the Mount Wollaston Cemetery not to employ any person as a laborer in their respective departments unless he be a resident of the town.

"ART. 55. To see if the town will vote that not less than two dollars per day shall be paid to the employees of the town for the ensuing year.

"ART. 56. To see if the town will vote that nine hours shall constitute a day's work for all employees of the town."

When these articles were read in the warrant, it was well understood that the old order of things, and the management of town affairs which had become traditional, were challenged and on trial. Nevertheless, at the first day of the meeting, when the voting took place and the general committee to consider the articles in the warrant was appointed, business went on in the usual way. John Quincy Adams was chosen moderator; the committee on the warrant was made up wholly irrespective of party, and contained the usual names of men well known in the town; and the vote against the licensing of liquor shops was even more decisive than it had been the year before,—or very nearly three to one. Nothing so far indicated any unusual popular movement. Three weeks later the adjourned meeting was to be held, at which the committee on the warrant would make its reports, and the town was to act upon them.

When that day came it was apparent to all that the end of government by town-meeting in Quincy had come also. The meeting was held as usual at one o'clock, and at that hour the old town-hall, though not yet full, showed unmistakable indications that a new power was about to make itself felt in the transaction of the day's business; for a solid phalanx of men — young, energetic and very earnest, but of a different type of face and bearing from the old attendant of the meetings — crowded the benches on the moderator's right; — they were evidently men who worked with their hands, largely Americans of Irish descent, and they took pride in calling themselves Knights of Labor, for so the order to which they belonged was named. They were there with a plan and for a purpose; which, as it subsequently appeared, had been carefully matured in a course of meetings held by their secret order in St. Mary's Hall in West Quincy. These meetings had, indeed, been quietly going on during the regular and open sittings of the committee on the warrant, whose action step by step was thus supervised.

Presently the hall, which would seat only some 700 persons, became so crowded that many had to stand in the aisles, while many more turned away unable to pass the doors; though not one voter out of four on the poll lists was present, it was obvious the town-house could not contain all who sought to attend. A large portion of those entitled to take part in the transacting of business were in this way debarred from so doing, — practically disfranchised; and, had this not been so, by their presence they would merely have contributed to make the meeting, when it came to a decision of contested issues, more unmanageable than it already was.

At first things proceeded in the regular way, though all were conscious of a certain unusual atmosphere, — a species of electric tension; but the customary votes were passed providing for the order of business, and the earlier recommendations of the committee on the warrant were adopted. At last an issue was presented, and a trial of strength took place. It came on a recommendation of the committee on the warrant instructing the selectmen to appoint certain police officers to enforce the laws against the sale of intoxicating liquors, and making appropriation therefor. The committee, in accordance with the precedents established in previous years, further reported for adoption a form of vote in which the selectmen were requested to appoint Henry H. Faxon a special officer for the enforcement of the laws referred to.

While the town at the annual meeting three weeks before, had, as already stated, voted by an overwhelming majority against the licensing of bar-rooms, it had at the same time, acting on party lines, elected a board of selectmen, a majority of the members of which were Democrats, and, as such, known to be against the enforcement of this vote; and it soon became evident that those composing the effective voting force in the adjourned town-meeting were in sympathy with the majority of the board of selectmen rather than with the mass of the voters of the town. An industrial organization — a trades union — was present, whose forces were combined and marshalled as a unit to put certain measures through, regardless of logic, expense or legality, and without listening to reason.

So those composing this organization now proceeded to carry out the purpose for which they had come. After a spirited debate, the vote recommended by the committee was defeated by a large majority, and its defeat greeted with noisy applause. The question who dominated over the meeting was then settled once for all; and, for the remainder of the day, as measure after measure came up, the defeat of the party which, for fifteen years, had conducted the business of the town became more and more pronounced, until their demoralization and rout were complete, and, indeed, ludicrous. The final test was on the articles of the warrant, which have been recited, relating to the employment of town laborers. The committee had recommended the indefinite postponement of these articles; but all of them were now carried by triumphant majorities, and it was frankly avowed, in the course of debate, that those present and in control of the meeting were not only able to have their own way, but, regardless of law or sense, intended to do so. It was an effective working combination of the Knights of Labor, the payers of a poll-tax and those who had voted against the closing of the bar-rooms. And yet, at this meeting, although not above one out of four of the legal voters of the town was present, the largest number voting on any one question upon which the meeting was polled was but 505, while the Knights of Labor and their allies numbered, as nearly as could be computed, but about 250. In other words, under the existing conditions and system of government, two hundred and fifty men, voting in an organized form, were able to place such results as they saw fit on the record book of the town.

It is, of course, needless to say that, so far as the

votes in relation to the employment of town laborers went, they were neither more nor less than an open and unblushing robbery of treasury and tax-payer; a robbery in degree only less than if the majority had reversed the figures and decreed nine dollars a day for two hours' work. In the whole hall there was not a single man who in the management of his own affairs would for a moment have thought of doing that which the majority now decreed town officials should do in the management of public affairs; and the reign of common sense would instantly have reasserted itself could the question then have been presented in a reverse form through a kindred proposition to the effect that, in borrowing money for the use of the town, such borrowing should be confined to citizens or inhabitants of Quincy, and that the lenders should receive therefor not less than eight per cent. interest instead of six per cent., if six per cent. chanced to be the current rate; or, if it had been proposed that all supplies purchased for public use, including tools and articles for the workhouse, should be purchased only of those in Quincy who dealt in such articles, and that the sellers should uniformly receive for them at least twenty per cent. over and above the current market rates. Such propositions, if advanced, would have been received with derision, and incontinently voted down without a voice in their favor. On the other hand, it was even then well known, and afterwards became apparent, that, with the current rate of wages at $1.50 per day, a town which insisted upon paying its employees $2.00 would be overrun with applicants. This proved to be the case; and within ten days after the town-meeting the commissioners in charge of the highways had applications from four times the number of men they needed, all of whom were anxious to work ten hours a day for the wages fixed by the town. Under these circumstances, acting with creditable independence, the board declined to recognize the vote of the town-meeting, and for that year laborers were paid $2.00 a day for ten hours' work. More than they asked was not forced upon them. But at the next annual meeting, the same organization being still in control, this action of the officials was reversed; and not only did the town formally request its officers to squander the public money by paying for a given commodity more than it was worth in the market, — thus itself inciting those in charge of its affairs to jobbery and embezzlement, — but certain of the foreign-born manual laborers of Quincy were also made by vote of town-meeting a favored class. And in this last respect the action taken was not without interest as illustrating the complete way in which the wheel turns under a pure system of popular government. Probably nine out of ten of those thus favored were men born in Ireland, many of whom had not been in America long enough to be naturalized. It was but a few years since the town by overwhelming majorities had voted in favor of greatly restricting the political rights of the foreign-born; and now, by a majority so large that the vote was not contested, it insisted on paying men of that class larger wages than they demanded for fewer hours of work than they stood ready to give.

Yet, in itself, even for Quincy, the action of the adjourned town-meeting of March 28, 1887, under other circumstances would have meant little. The town had before in its existence repeatedly passed through such episodes. It was merely one of those movements — irregular as well as spasmodic, — necessarily incident to the imperfections of any form of human government. A disturbing element had been introduced; and difficulty followed. That the difficulty was more than temporary there was on the surface no good reason to suppose. Exactly such a difficulty had arisen after the disturbances of the Revolutionary period, at the time of Shays' insurrection, when Azariah Faxon's extraordinary manifesto was entered on the town book. Indeed, the attempt of 1887 to affect the working of the great law of supply and demand, through town-meeting action, might well have closed with Faxon's announcement, borrowed from the records of just a century before, that the names of those responsible for such action — at once childish and demagogic — "will shine Brighter in the American annals than if they were to Cary the Terror of their Armes as far as Gibraltar." [1] But, passing on in the history of the town, another exactly similar disturbance to that of 1888 occurred in 1837, when work on the newly opened quarries brought into the place great numbers of voters, introducing a new element into the management of its affairs, so that, it will be remembered, John Quincy Adams then wrote that the Democrats maintained their ascendency, "though consisting of transient stone-cutters from New Hampshire;" [2] just as fifty-six years before, his father, at the time of Shays' insurrection, had described how the people, in the course of annual elections, had "discarded from their confidence almost all the old, stanch, firm patriots, and had called to the helm pilots much more selfish and much less skilful." [3] And again another similar disturbance occurred in

[1] *Supra*, 896–7.  [2] *Supra*, 853.  [3] *Supra*, 898.

1854, when the Native American or Know-Nothing epidemic raged in the manner which has been described.[1] In all these cases, the town, for the moment, was torn from its moorings; but it merely required some degree of patience and the passage of a moderate amount of time to restore it to order, system and good sense. The difficulty now was that the fundamental conditions were changed. Not only was the constituency no longer homogeneous, — that difficulty time would cure, — but in size it had become unmanageable; — and time would in that respect only tend to make matters worse. It was the consciousness of this fact which oppressed J. Q. Adams, as at the close of the meeting he wearily left that moderator's chair which he had occupied by common consent through the sessions of almost a score of years. Meeting at the foot of the platform, Mr. Porter, who had acted as chairman of the defeated committee on the warrant, and who a year later became the first mayor of the city, — meeting Mr. Porter as they together left the hall, Mr. Adams sadly remarked that his work in connection with town affairs was ended. Quincy was merely repeating the experience of Boston seventy years before, an experience which many other places had gone through since, and which many more are destined to go through hereafter. The old order of things had come to a close. Nevertheless, the immediate process through which it came to its close was not without interest, nor, as a lesson, without its use.

Already, at a public meeting of the citizens of Quincy held as long before as the 14th of December, 1885, the question of a city charter had been discussed, and the ancient traditions seemed again to assert them-

[1] *Supra*, 959.

selves; for the movement now went on in the same formal and methodic manner which had more than a century back characterized the similar action when the constitution of 1780 was submitted for approval.[1] Once more it was a question of organic law. A strong party still adhered to the ancient ways and the town-meeting form of government; but those composing it were forced to admit that things could no longer go on as they were then going, and the only alternative to a city government was a division of the town. The argument against a division of the town was not easy to meet; for such a division failed to remove the difficulties of the situation. Those difficulties arose even more from the increased requirements, than from the mere numerical growth, of the population. Police and water supply and drainage were territorial questions; and they involved also financial methods and a systematic administration of large affairs and complicated details inconsistent with the simplicity of town-meeting government. A division of the town, therefore, would prove a mere temporary alleviation; if, indeed, it would even be that.

After long and earnest debate a committee of fifteen was appointed to whom was entrusted the difficult task of framing a charter which should meet the objections of those opposed to a city form of government and afford some adequate protection against the acknowledged dangers incident thereto, as seen in the experience of other places; for, throughout the debate, it had been argued that this could be done. The committee of fifteen put the details of the work committed to it in the hands of a sub-committee consisting of Messrs. Josiah Quincy, the sixth of the name, and

[1] *Supra*, 890.

Sigourney Butler, both young lawyers; and for over
a year the matter was under the careful advisement
of these two. In January, 1887, two months before
the fateful annual meeting of that year took place,
another meeting of citizens had been called to which
the committee of fifteen presented a report. Subsequently, after lengthy discussions at various meetings, the form of charter recommended was in the
main adopted, and the committee instructed to submit
it to the legislature.

At the time, this charter was regarded with no inconsiderable degree of curiosity, and its subsequent
working has been watched with interest. As the first
mayor elected under its provisions stated in his inaugural address, no New England city then had, nor
has any since received, a similar charter. It constituted, in fact, as it was intended it should, an attempt
at a new departure in the matter of municipal government. As such the principles upon which it was
framed are worthy of consideration.

Following the analogy of the constitution of the
State and of the United States, the Massachusetts
municipalities have always been organized with executive, legislative and judicial departments; but the
fact has more and more been lost sight of that municipal governments are business rather than political
organizations. It is no part of the proper function of
those handling municipal affairs to consider philosophical principles of state-craft. They are, on the contrary, persons selected by the constituencies to do the
work entrusted to them, because the constituent
masses have grown so large that they can no longer
meet in one body to do that work themselves. The
function of the municipal officers is, therefore, to ad-

minister the affairs of a local community in an intelligent and business-like way. Nevertheless, in Massachusetts the municipal governments have always been traditionally framed with the cumbrous machinery of the larger political bodies. They have, as matter of course, had their Boards of Aldermen, representing the Senate, and their Common Councils, representing the more popular branch of the Legislature. Yet in the election of these two bodies to manage the current affairs of a business corporation, the existence of a divided interest in the community has never been recognized; any more than the fact that the essential feature of a correct municipal administration is the economical expenditure of the money collected from the tax-payers. As no political rights are involved, those being sufficiently provided for in the constitution and laws of the State, one of the two municipal legislative bodies should, on any correct theory, represent property as distinguished from individuals, — tax-payers as distinguished from the beneficiaries of the money raised by taxation. But, owing to the fact that political principles are allowed to dominate in making provision for the conduct of corporate business, this distinction has never been made. Again, the functions of the several departments of the ordinary city government have, in the course of time, become irretrievably confused. Responsibility has ceased to exist; for the legislative has by degrees encroached on the executive until, in the greater number of cities, the mayor is reduced to a mere cipher, while certain irresponsible combinations in the legislative chambers and the city-hall, generally known as "rings," really control the administration of affairs. Almost of necessity, the executive functions have more and more fallen into the hands of commissions and boards, as the special requirements for streets, sewers, lighting, police, etc., grew in importance. These boards, if not irresponsible, are certainly as a rule not responsible to the chief executive.

Public attention had for years been forcibly called to these gathering difficulties by the occurrence of scandals of ever increasing notoriety, more and more discussed in the press; and the nature of these scandals, as well as the drift of the discussion, it has already been said those who drew up the Quincy charter bore freshly in mind. Accordingly, their charter was framed in consultation with those both within and without the State who had made a special study of the subject. It was long, consisting, in the form in which it was finally passed, of no less than seven distinct titles, containing fifty-six articles beside subdivisions. The seven titles related to the Constituency, the Legislative Department, the School Committee, the Executive Department, and the Administration offices, or Boards, with a final title in which various general matters were provided for. The fundamental principle of the whole instrument was the distinct line of demarcation consistently preserved throughout between legislative and executive functions and responsibility.

The Quincy city charter was based on correct political theories in so far, at least, as it was not a creation, but an outgrowth. In this respect, the principle at the foundation of all successful constitutional government was in it carefully regarded, — the fundamental principle that " everything which has power to win the obedience and respect of men must have its roots deep in the past, and that the more slowly every institution has grown, so much the more enduring it is likely to prove." [1] The system under which the town business had for fifteen years been successfully handled — that of the reference by the town-meeting of the annual warrant as a whole to a general committee appointed by the moderator — had been productive of good results. It was not this part of the machinery which had failed in its working: the failure had been in the primary body, — that is, in the town-meeting; and the failure had been caused simply by the natural growth of that body. Changing, therefore, the system to which the community had become accustomed in the least possible degree, it was proposed through the charter simply to do away with the town-meeting as a legislative body, leaving the rest of the machinery as unchanged as possible. The scheme was to substitute a responsible single executive, in the person of the Mayor, for the old board of three selectmen; and then to make the customary committee on the warrant, under the name of a Council, an elective and permanent body, dispensing with the town-meeting which hitherto had been accustomed to pass, legislatively, upon the committee's action.

Building upon this foundation, it then became necessary merely to distribute the power and functions of the proposed government. This the framers of the charter did by following the maxim, — "Deliberation is the work of many; Execution is the work of one." The absolute power of appointing and removing all executive officers was, under the charter, conferred upon the Mayor, wholly irrespective of the legislative department, except in so far as conferring such full appointing power was, as in the case of

[1] Bryce, *The American Commonwealth*, i. 26.

schools, etc., in conflict with the general policy of the Commonwealth. But wherever these exceptions occurred, the municipal officers or boards elected under the general law of the State had the same absolute power of appointment and removal of the subordinates in their departments as the Mayor had in his. The Mayor of Quincy was avowedly intended to be clothed with a more arbitrary power within his department than had ever been confided in the United States to the executive head of an organization deemed political. He only was elected by the people; all other administrative officials, except in the one case stated, were appointed by him and responsible to him.

To compensate for the large power thus given to the Executive, equally large responsibilities were imposed upon him. The Mayor might attend, and he and all the administrative officers were, if so called upon, required to be present at every regular meeting of the Council, in order to give such information as might be asked for as to the business of their respective offices. They had no votes; but they were subject to being interrogated, and they had a right to speak upon all matters pertaining to their departments. And this right of executive officers to participate immediately in the deliberations of the legislative department, combined with the obligation to meet inquiry, was looked upon as one of the essential features of the scheme, remedying a serious defect which experience had developed in the practical working of all American constitutions, — a defect to which attention had frequently been called, but for which a remedy was now for the first time, it was believed, sought to be applied. In addition to this privilege of influencing the discussions of the Council, and the liability of being subject to its inquiries on all matters pertaining to their several departments, the administrative officers were required to place upon public record the reasons for every removal from office made by them. The term of service of the Mayor, as well as of all others in the city government not removable by him, was left at one year, the customary term in the cities of the Commonwealth; as those who framed the charter saw no objection to requiring the chief executive, as well as those composing the legislative body, annually to present themselves to the people for approval of their course, such approval to be evinced by a reëlection.

The only members of the city government, beside the Mayor, to be elected by the constituency, were the members of the Council and the members of the School Committee. Instead of dividing the legislative department into two branches, the Council comprised the sole body; for the framers of the charter reasoned that the arguments urged in favor of two legislative branches in the larger and purely political organizations did not seem to be of weight in the case of cities, while that division did tend to confusion and division of responsibility. The Quincy city council was in fact intended to be more in the nature of the board of directors of a corporation than of a state legislature or the Congress of the United States. Of the Council, five members were elected on one ticket at large, and the remaining eighteen were to be elected three from each of the six districts, or wards, into which the city was to be divided.

Such was the framework of the charter under the provisions of which the old town of Quincy became a city, in January, 1889. It seemed right and appropriate that the instrument under which the change took place should have been drawn by one who, bearing the same name as the town, was descended from its first land-owner, and even then was living upon the soil which had been granted to his ancestor when, in 1634, Boston received enlargement at the Mount. Prepared in full sympathy with the current political theories of the day, it still remains to be seen whether the Quincy charter will, or will not, constitute a new and successful departure in municipal government. The period during which it has been in operation has not as yet been sufficiently long to afford a basis upon which to pass judgment on this point: but whether, as a new departure, it proves in the result a success or a failure, it was undeniably an honest, an intelligent and a well-considered attempt at the solution of a problem which, now that slavery is disposed of, is at once the most important and the most perplexing before the American people. The tendency of population to concentrate itself at given points is no less unmistakable than its increase; and hitherto the failure of the democratic system in cities has been quite as marked as its success in towns.[1] Of late the attempt has been, through an ingenious and carefully studied readjustment of the parts of government and their relations to each other, to devise a machine, — a species of patent back-action, self-regulating constitution, — which once set in motion, will work of itself; and, so working, is warranted infallibly to produce all, and even more, of those results which under the old system were the fruits of public spirit and of active and interested individual coöperation. On the other hand, the enlargement and complication of functions of municipal government, and the conse-

[1] Bryce, *The American Commonwealth*, i. 593–619.

quent increase of municipal expenditure, have made it more and more difficult for the average citizen, properly as well as necessarily absorbed in his own affairs, to obtain that knowledge of ward and city business without which he cannot expect to influence it. What was many years ago remarked of English tendencies is measurably true of the tendencies now to be observed in the United States: — "To do their own governing for themselves has been, in former times, the guiding spirit of our fathers. To gratify their selfish ease by giving up all this to somebody else to do for them, is, unfortunately, the spirit and tendency of our day;"[1] but, while this has a familiar and plausible sound, the real difficulty is that the old, simple government, set in motion and supervised by the citizen without undue neglect of his necessary business, is no longer adequate to the work. Municipal affairs have become, like public life, a profession; and, while the experiment has doubtless got to be tried, contributing something to the final result, there is certainly no great reason to hope that a good and satisfactory system of municipal government can be brought about through any mechanical charter process, no matter how carefully studied or how well contrived. If subjected to that test, the Quincy charter, it is needless to say, is doomed to failure. Nevertheless, in devising it the town once more rose to the occasion, and grappled in a fearless and individual way with the question which to-day chiefly occupies practical publicists. Once more, and for the last time, the complicated movement of the great whole was reflected on the mirror of the unit.

But recurring to the course of events in Quincy, the

[1] Toulmin Smith, *The Parish*, 118.

action of the annual town-meeting held in March, 1888, emphasized in the minds of all the conclusions reached at the close of the annual meeting of the year previous; for the industrial organizations now again asserted their power, and showed themselves for the time being in complete control. With a view to removing the complaint that many citizens who desired could not obtain admission, the meeting was held, not in the old town-hall, but in a large wooden barrack, called the Coliseum, built not far from it some time before for purposes of public entertainment. It was vast in space, a room in which it was not easy to make one's self heard, and the number of persons who, either from interest or curiosity, appeared there, was such that the management of the business of the meeting was difficult; and yet, even at this meeting, the most fully attended the town had ever known, the largest number of votes recorded upon any division was less than 650, or not one quarter part of those whose names were recorded upon the voting lists.

The annual election, of which the meeting was an adjournment, had resulted in what is politically known as "a clean sweep." It was, in fact, just such a political upturning as had occurred nearly forty years before in the Native American or Know-Nothing days; the only difference being that it was now in the interest of what was known as labor, instead of as then in hostility to foreigners.

Throughout, the meeting was marked by the same peculiarities, both as respects those who composed it and its modes of action, as the meeting of the year previous. Measures were again passed regardless of their cost or their legality, and those who passed them defiantly refused to listen to reason. Especially was this the case with the articles relating to employment of labor. Under the operation of a rude previous question, now for the first time imposed in a Quincy town-meeting, these articles were forced to an early vote and passed by large majorities. The various boards by whom all town laborers were employed were instructed, under the form of a request, not to employ any person as a laborer in their respective departments unless he had been a resident of the town for at least one year previous to such an appointment. Then followed another vote that the town desired to pay " not less than $2.00 per day to its employees during the ensuing year; " and opposition to this vote, on the ground of its manifest illegality, was summarily met by the reply that the majority preferred the town should become insolvent rather than not have it pay the sum named. To pay the wage-earner in excess of the market price of labor was a principle; and Quincy ought to go on record in favor of it. The vote was then passed; followed quickly by another instructing the various town boards, again under the form of a request, to consider that " nine hours shall constitute a day's work for laborers employed in their respective departments during the ensuing year." Having then, in the course of one session covering nine and one half hours, passed all the appropriations included in a warrant of seventy-three articles, amounting in the aggregate to $177,000, the meeting adjourned; the last annual town-meeting ever held in Quincy.

Early in the following May, the proposed city charter, as it came from the hands of the committee, was passed by the legislature without debate, and immediately signed by the Governor. Becoming a law upon the 17th of May, it was, if adopted by the town, to take effect on the first Tuesday of the ensuing December; and the selectmen, in response to a petition to that effect, promptly called a special town-meeting for June 11th to take action upon it. At this meeting the new form of government was adopted by ballot, the number of votes cast being 812 in favor to 454 against, — a majority of 358 in a total poll of 1,266. In the town there were over 2,400 legal voters: and it thus appeared that but one half of those entitled to express an opinion on a question not lacking in importance, took the trouble so to do; but by many of those who failed to cast a ballot, whether for or against, the result was looked upon not only as a foregone conclusion, but as a necessity, as unavoidable as it was to be regretted. It was useless to vote against it; they would not vote for it. When the poll figures were declared from the platform of the town-hall, the announcement was received with every manifestation of delight, and soon the bells rang loudly out, amid the sound of horns and guns and the explosion of fireworks. The tower of the old stone church opposite sent forth a peal as if some great victory had been achieved. "The King is dead! Long live the King!" And yet there were those, nor were they few in number, upon whose ears the clang of the bells and the shouts of rejoicing grated harshly. An old political system, indisputably great, was gone, — a system, the admiration of philosophers, which had carried the people in safety through periods of sore trial, and brought them up into what they had become. More than once it had been the ark of New England's salvation. In the case of Quincy, the change might be necessary, — probably it was necessary, — but was it to be rejoiced at? — The past was secure; — would the future better it? — In any event, those who thought in this way would have preferred to see the ancient system — so endeared to them by custom and time — laid away as a parent that was gone, — silently, tenderly, reverently.

# INDEX.

Aberdecest, sachem of Wessagusset, 1622, Weston's agents exchange gifts with, 60; escapes after Wessagusset killing, 94; kills captives, 98; desires peace, *ib.*; fear of Standish, 103;

Aborigines, *see* Indians.

Absentee land-ownership, effort to prevent, in Mass. Bay, 646-50; protective measures at Braintree against, 649-50, *et seq.*

Acadia, Lord Monckton's removal of people of, 641.

Adams, Abigail, wife of President John, descendant of Joanna Hoar, 705; daughter of Rev. Wm. and Elizabeth [Quincy] Smith, 711, 904; sister of Mrs. Richard Cranch, *ib.*; citations from letters of:

1774, alarm of church people at Braintree, 632; prayers for the king, 633, 852; removal of powder from Braintree, 851; Braintree men called for military duty, 854; conspiracy of Boston negroes, *ib.*;

1775, school closed at Braintree, 856; apprehensions from British, *ib.*; enemy at Weymouth, 857; feeds and shelters soldiers, *ib.*; battle of Bunker's Hill, 858-9; interruption and resumption of church services, 860; colonial militia quartered at Braintree, *ib.*; election of representative to General Court, *ib.*; dysentery epidemic 801, 862-3; illness of her family, 863; removes to Weymouth, *ib.*; death of her mother, *ib.*;

1776, occupation of Dorchester Heights, 865; enlistment difficulties, 871; privateering, the rage of Braintree young men, 879; spirit of jobbery, 881;

1777, Christ Church closed, 853; General Palmer's failure in Rhode Island, 886;

1778, officers of French fleet at Boston, 788; prices current during Revolution, 790;

1780, money, prices, enlistments, taxes, 892;

1784, joins her husband in London, 888, 889;

1799, cider for the President, 686-7;

1818, death of, 919.

Adams Academy, Quincy, 941.

Adams, Charles Francis, 1848, breaks with Whig party, 956; 1853, nominated for Vice-Presidency, *ib.*; victim of Irish intrigue, 957-8; Quincy's contribution to national defence in the Civil War, 961; its representative in Congress, elected 1858 and 1860, *ib.*; U. S. Minister to Great Britain, 1861-8; *ib.*

Adams, Ebenezer, disciplined by Braintree church, 1753, 640, 762; made deacon, 640, 835.

Adams, Elihu, under arms, 1775, 857; his death, *ib.*, 863.

Adams, Hannah, remarks humble origin of Adams family, 711; John Adams' reply, 712.

Adams, Henry, first brewer of Braintree, 686.

Adams, Herbert B., dogs in churches, 744-5, *note.*

Adams, Hugh, 1707, ordained minister of Braintree South Church, 613.

Adams, John [1st], Deacon, Braintree North Precinct Church, *b.* 1692, *d.* 1761, son of Joseph and Hannah [Bass], 714; father of President John, 715; typical of New England farmer class, 713; character and career, 715; services to church and town, 715-16; 1728, elected constable, 825; 1742, refuses captain's commission under Gooch, 708, 715, 835; 1758, selectman, 838; death, 1761, *ib.*, 846, 857.

Adams, John [2d], *b.* 1735, 617; graduated at Harvard, 1755, 714; genealogy, 714; reflections concerning his father, 716; his wife, granddaughter of John Quincy, 711.

1758, entertained by Gridley and Pratt on admission to the bar, 788;

1759, opinion of Rev. A. Wibird, 642; a visitor at Josiah Quincy's house, Braintree, 703; habits of fellow visitors, *ib.*;

1761, efforts in cause of temperance, 789-90; chosen Surveyor of Highways, Braintree, 675, 824, 838; his services, 675;

1762, provides for sale of Braintree commons, 664-5;

1765, causes protest against Stamp Act at Braintree, 838; prepares instructions to town representative at General Court, 839; Stamp Act favored by Braintree Episcopalians, 632, 840; in support of memorial for opening law courts, 839; opposed to election of pro-stamp-act men, 840; 841-2; visit to John Quincy, Christmas, 708, 840;
1766, drive to Salem, 677, again in 1776, 678; defeated at election, 743, 746; account of election, 843; relations with Major Miller, 844; planting of liberty tree, 844, 845; repeal of Stamp Act, *ib.*;
1767, elected Selectman, 846;
1768, established in practice of law at Boston, 846; excused from town service, *ib.*; thanks voted him, *ib.*;
1771, account of Judge Cushing riding the circuit, 678;
1774, defence of Captain Preston, 704; delegate to Continental Congress, 850; his family return to Braintree, *ib.*;
1775, drafts anti-slave trade covenant, 855; desires to be a soldier, 858; at Braintree during epidemic, 863; on prayers for king, 852; rumored departure for England, 865; on coast-defences in Congress, 867; fortifications for Boston harbor, *ib.*; estimate of his property, 872;
1778, embarks in Quincy Bay for voyage to France, 886, 951;
1779, returns from France, 887; Braintree's delegate to Constitution Convention, 887; of committee to draft Constitution, *ib.*, 889; returns to Europe, 887;
1781, at the Hague, 879;
1787, Vassall house bought by, 681; his death there, *ib.*;
1788, returns from London mission, 888, 898; remarks prosperity of Braintree, 695, 898;
1792, his property at Quincy, 691-2;
1795, establishes Quincy post-office, 803, 812-14; supports Madison's administration, 909; rebukes "Tom" Greenleaf, *ib.*;
1822, gift of quarry for granite to build meeting-house, 918-19; gift of his library to Quincy, 804, 919, 941; Academy founded by, 941;
1826, death, 681, 920; calls Lemuel Briant, a Unitarian, 643-4; a cider-drinker, 686-7; pride of descent from New England farmers, 711-12; on jobbery in care of Braintree poor, 729; his receipt for making a New England in Virginia, 732, 764, 783; "a church-going animal," 732, 751; recollections of boyhood in meeting-house, 737; detestation of taverns, 783, 788; his account of political discussion at Shrewsbury tavern, 1774, 783-4; belief in American independence gained from talk in taverns, 785; his drunken farm-hand, 786; his Sunday reading in youth, 805; last years of his life at Quincy, 805-7; dislike of winter, 682, 805-6; habits of life, 806; his one o'clock dinner, *ib.*; subjects of talk with a young lady, 806; his bust in Universalist meeting-house, 930; infrequency of Roman Catholics in New England, 931; Quincy's contribution to national defence in Revolution, 961; 975, 978, 979.

Adams, John Quincy [1st], *b.* 1767, *d.* 1848, descendant of Joanna Hoar, 705; named for his great-grandfather, 711; 1774, without school at Braintree, 856; becomes post-rider, *ib.*; reminiscences of events, Penn's Hill, May 21, 1775, 857-8; with mother, watches signs of Bunker's Hill battle, 858; his recollections of, 859; goes with his father to Europe, 1778, 886-7, 951; in conveyance of title of graveyard to Quincy, 1809, 906; U. S. Minister to Russia, 1809, 909; Secretary of State, 1822, 919; Quincy's vote for presidential electors of 1824, 916; 1826, on his father's death, visits Quincy, 920-1; improved conditions of town, 695; Sunday service at old meeting-house, 921; Quincy's vote, presidential election 1828, 916, 949; elected to Congress, 1830, 946; on democratic stone-cutters, 1837, 995; address at temperance convention, Quincy, 1840, 975, 976; death, 1848, 926, 955; his relations to Quincy, 951; Quincy's support of, 952-3; his career in Congress, *ib.*, 956.

Adams, John Quincy [2d], moderator, Quincy town-meetings, 973; his reforms in, *ib.*; moderator, 1887, Quincy town-meeting, 989; termination of his service as moderator, 996.

Adams, Joseph, marries, 1688, Hannah Bass, 714; grandparents of President John, *ib.*

Adams, Peter, 835.

Adams, Peter Boylston, brother of John, in 1766 Braintree election, 843; chairman of Braintree state Constitution committee, 1780, 890.

Adams, Samuel, on committee to draft Constitution for Mass., 1779, 889.

Adams, ——, Braintree, schoolmaster, 1710, 823.

Addison, Joseph, 772.

African slavery, 955.

Agamenticus, now York, Maine, 1640, Thomas Gorges at, 310-11; his seat of government, 311; names it Gorgeana, *ib.*; 1643, abandons it, 312; 1634, Blackstone called to church at, 323; declines, 324; Maverick proprietor of land at, 330; Gorges charter of 1641, attested by Morton, 343; Morton at, 350.

Agricola, John, his adherents called Antinomians by Luther, 432.

## INDEX. 1013

Alaska, 274.
Alcock, George, deacon of Dorchester church, death, 1630, 237.
Alden, John, and wife Priscilla [Mullins], of Plymouth, Mayflower emigrant, parents of Ruth, wife of John Bass, 714.
Alden, Ruth, daughter of John and Priscilla, marries, 1657, John Bass, 714.
Alderman, ——, of Bear Cove, lost in wilderness, 1634, 338, 364, 582.
Alderton, Point, see Allerton.
Alewives, fish in Monatiquot River, 1736, cause of contention at Braintree, 831–4.
Alexander, Sir William, his map of New England, 139, 210.
Alford, England, home of William Hutchinson, 368, 393, 539.
Algonquin tribe destroyed by pestilence, 1616–17, 4.
Alien law, passed by General Court, 1637, its object, 458, 461; bitter controversy over, at Boston, 463; unhappy effects of execution of, 463–4, 648.
Aliens in Quincy, 946, et seq.
"Aligarto," alligator, 357.
Allen, ——, 678.
Allen, Ethan, 764.
Allen, John, minister at Dedham, 1640, 595.
Allen, Jonathan, of Braintree, 834.
Allerton, Isaac, deputy-governor of Plymouth, his name given to point in Boston Bay, 20; 1623, of Committee on Indian conspiracy, 75; 1629, agent at London to obtain patent for Kennebec and charter for Plymouth, 223; letter to Bradford, ib., aided by Gorges, 224; brings Morton back to Plymouth, 224; again in England, ib.; concerning court influence, 274; aids Tompson and Knowles at New York, 598.
Allerton, Point, Boston Bay, 14, note; origin of name, 20; fortification proposed, 1776, 867, 911.
Alligator, brought by Gibbons from West Indies, 357.
Almshouse built at Braintree Middle Precinct, 1786, 728; at Braintree, 900; 1785; at Quincy in 1815, 905.
American Jezebel, Mrs. Hutchinson, so called by clergy, 437, 538, 573.
America, land grants in, seventeenth century, 651.
Ames, ——, account of a husking, 1767, 791.
Amherst, General Jeffrey, capture of Ticonderoga, 1759, 837.
Anabaptists, of Munster, 248, note; a term of reproach in time of Luther, 432, 565, 567, 568.
André, John, execution of, 1780, 891.
Andrew, John A., election of 1862, 959.
Androscoggin, Thomas Purchase a settler at, 258.
Andros, Edmund, Governor, imprisoned,
701; his overthrow in New England, 1689, 818.
Ann, Cape, touched by the ship Sparrow, 1622, 52.
Anti-masonic political party, 952.
Antinomian, origin and definition of term, 432–4; name improperly applied to Anne Hutchinson and party, 435; eradication of heresies of, object of 1637 synod, 470; an extension of Calvinistic tenet of predestination, 457; hesitation of General Court to consider, 474; the party in majority at Boston, 1637, 571; fate of party, after exile of Mrs. Hutchinson, 546-58, 559.
—— Controversy, 363; its significance, 367; a political as well as religious issue, 435; comparison of position of Vane and Winthrop in, 465; Cotton Mather's view of, 493; historical aspect of, 559–78; Flynt an adherent of Wheelwright in, 603, 648, 700. See Hutchinson, Anne, Wheelwright.
Anti-slavery question, 955, 956.
Applegate, Elizabeth, punished for swearing, 672.
Applegate, Thomas, his ferry across Monatiquot, 1635, 672; accidentally drowns nine persons, 973; prosecuted but discharged, ib.
Apthorp family, slaves owned by, 923; of Braintree Episcopal church, 632.
Aquidneck island, now Newport, Wm. Hutchinson's residence after 1638, 536, 537; Mrs. Hutchinson removes from, 537, 597.
Arbella, Lady, wife of Isaac Johnson, 234.
Architecture, at Braintree, 680–4.
Ariosto, 390.
Armenianism, Briant of Braintree accused of, 638, 639.
Arms confiscated at Boston, 1637, 511–12.
Armstrong, Archie, jester to Charles I., 300.
Army of Revolution, Braintree's contributions to, 870–8, 884–6; value of service of men enlisted for long terms, 847.
Arnold, Benedict, treason of, 1780, 891, 892.
Articles of Confederation of United States, 1778, 889–90.
Arundel, Thomas, 1st baron, of the 1620 Plymouth Company, 122; his character and influence at court, 124; at meetings of Council for New England, 131; his share of territory in New England drawn at Greenwich, 1623, 139.
Asa, Salem and Uzzia, cited by Winthrop in his justification, 512.
Aspinwall, William, elected to General Court, 1637, 475; expelled for adhering to Wheelwright, 479; replaced by John Oliver, 480.
Ashton, England, Sir F. Gorges' country seat, 313; see Long Ashton.

# 1014  INDEX.

Aspinet, Indian, restores John Billington, 32.
Assacomet, captured by Hunt, 24, *note*.
Assistants of Mass. Bay, Court of, *see* Court of Assistants.
Astor, John Jacob, 196.
Athenæum library, Boston, in 1830, 804.
Athens, Greece, 967, 989.
Attleborough, R. I., William Blackstone's son driven from, 327.
Auchinleck, James Boswell, Laird of, remark to Samuel Johnson, 126.
Augusta, Maine, 54.
Aulnay, La Tour d', *see* La Tour.

Bacon, Sir Francis, of the Crown counsel, trial of Essex, 113; ingratitude to Essex, 114; 1621, impeached by Parliment, 126, 390.
Badlam, Colonel, commands militia, Shays' rebellion, 898.
Bagnall, Walter, 1625, at Mount Wollaston, 343; mentioned by Morton, 351; at Richmond Island, 351, 352; trades with Indians, *ib.*; 1631, murdered, 260, 352, 353, 354.
Bainbridge, William, Commodore U. S. N., 912.
Balch, John, of Salem, 201.
Baldwin family, descended from Joanna Hoar, 705.
Ballou, " Father " Hosea, 944.
Balston, William, refractory Boston sergeant, 568.
Baltic, folk-moots of villages on the, 980.
Baltimore, Maryland, 920.
Bancroft, George, 890; as democratic candidate for governor, 1844, 953.
Bancroft, Richard, Archbishop of Canterbury, 142.
Banks of Newfoundland, Weston's fishing and trading ventures to, 45.
Banks, Sir John, Atty. General, files *quo warranto* against Mass. Bay Co., 291, 296, 301.
Barbadoes, Rev. Thomas Eager removes to, 625.
Barclay, George, with Charnock, plots assassination of William III., 1696, 625.
Barclay, William, Church of England minister at Braintree, 1702, 622, 623.
Barnburners, political party, 1848, 955.
Barnstable, Mass., 31, 64.
Bartholomew, William, in discussion over Anne Hutchinson's speech, 505.
Bartlett, Thomas, ordered by General Court to be whipped, 337.
Basing House, Hugh Peters at capture of, 375.
Bass, David, pew in Braintree meeting-house, 1725, 736.
Bass, Hannah, daughter of John and Ruth [Alden] Bass, marries, 1688, Joseph Adams of Braintree, 714.
Bass, Hezekiah, bass-viol player, Quincy meeting-house, 741, 907.

Bass, John, Vestryman, Christ Church, Braintree, 622.
Bass, John, son of Samuel, 1657, marries Ruth Alden, 714; his daughter Hannah marries, 1688, Joseph Adams, *ib.*
Bass, Jonathan, leader of Church-party, Braintree election, 1766, 843; his absence at tavern from town-meeting loses his candidate, 743, 844, 856.
Bass, Josiah, a privateer, in Plymouth jail, 1781, 879.
Bass, Josiah, leader of Braintree choir, 1812, 741.
Bass, Samuel, *b.* 1601, *d.* 1694, typical of farmer class in New England, 713, 716; comes from England, 1632, 714; settles first at Roxbury, *ib.*; removes, 1640, to Braintree, services in church and colony, *ib.*, 757, 835; his offspring, 609; appointed to fix site of bridge across Neponset, 1655, 671, 954.
Bass, Samuel, of Committee for sale of Braintree commons, 665.
Bass, Samuel, Jr., of Braintree, 835.
Bass, Thomas, bell-ringer, Braintree, 820, 823.
Bass-viol in Braintree choir, 741; Quincy meeting-house, 1804, 906–7.
Bath, Earl of, of the Plymouth Company, 122.
Bath-rooms, unknown in Quincy prior to 1830, 807.
Baxter, James P., cited concerning execution of regicides, 376, *note*.
Baxter, Joseph, affair with bounty-jumper, 1781, 876.
Baxter, Richard, his Nature of the Human Soul, John Adams' Sunday reading, 805.
Bayley, John, of Roxbury, 726.
Beacon Hill, Boston, called Sentry Hill prior to April, 1635, 288, 322; signals on, for revolt of 1689 against Andros, 818.
Beal, Caleb, overseer of boys, Hingham meeting-house, 738, *note*.
Beale, Benjamin, of anti-privateer committee, Quincy, 1793, 906.
Bear Cove, former name of Hingham, 338; residence of Alderman, 364.
Bears in Braintree woods, 1699, 924.
Beauchamp, John, with Weston sends out ship Sparrow to coast of Maine, 1622, 51.
Beaver skins, Plymouth colonists learn of, 35; currency in Massachusetts, 219.
Beer, commonly drunk in colonial times, 785.
Belcher, John, Braintree supports widow of, 724, 819.
Belcher, Jonathan, Governor, 616.
Belcher, Joseph, 1677, disciplined by Braintree church, 756–7.
Belcher, Moses, of Braintree, 825.
Bell, Charles H., his work on Wheelwright cited, 435, *note*.
Bellingham, Richard, 377.

## INDEX. 1015

Bellomont, Earl of, reception at Boston, 1699, as Governor of Mass. Bay, 718–19; his death, 1701, 719.
Bell-ringing, Quincy, 906–7.
Bemis, Josiah, one of three who first split granite with iron wedges, 925.
Benton, Thomas H., 662.
Bernard, Sir Francis, Governor Mass. Bay, 708; refuses information on project of quartering British troops at Boston, 847.
Beverages in colonial New England, 785, *et seq.*
Bible, source of New England law, 348, 382 *et seq.*; Puritan interpretation of, 383–7; in every colonial house, 805.
Big Bethel, Va., fight at, 1861, 962.
Billington, John, boy stolen by Indians, 31; his surrender, 32.
Billington, John, the first hanged in Massachusetts, 187.
Bilsby, England, Wheelwright's first parish, 369, 459, 482, 565.
Bishop, George, cited, as to persecution of Quakers at Boston, 1659, 408–10, *note.*
Bismarck, Strafford compared with, 273.
Black, Moses, one of Quincy's antiprivateer committee, 1793, 906.
Blackstone, William, Church of England clergyman, in New England, 142, 143; his lost records of Robert Gorges, expedition, 1623, 143-4, *note;* removal from Wessagusset, 190, 198, 233; 1625, establishes himself at Shawmut, 160-1, 167; sole occupant of site of Boston, 1630, 238; his hut on Sentry Hill, 322; a Church of England man, 171, *note;* assessed for expenses of arrest of Morton, *ib.;* leads Winthrop to site Boston, 238, 252; in 1634, 269; friendly relations with Winthrop, 322; allotted fifty acres in Boston, *ib.;* new neighbors uncongenial, sells his land, 323; removes to Narragansett Bay, 324; revisits Boston, *ib.;* his marriage, 324–5; his death, 325; his character and life, 325–8; destruction of his manuscripts and books, 326; relations with the Indians, 327; children, 327, 340, 342; Lechmere's remark concerning, 366, *note;* not submissive to church authority of Boston, 382, 454.
Blackstone, John, son of William, warned to leave Attleborough, 327.
Black-strap, a drink of New England farm-hands, 790.
Black William, Indian, sells Nahant to T. Dexter, 260; hanged for murder of Bagnall, 260, 353.
Bliss, Wm. R., cited as to dog-whipper in colonial meeting-house, 745, *note.*
Block Island, 466.
Blue Hills, Mass., seen by Standish, 1621, 19, 363, 582; granite formation of, 928.

Blue Laws of Connecticut, 83.
Blunt, Sir Christopher, trial of, 109, *note.*
Boccaccio, on the Florence plague, 2; 390.
Bolingbroke, his works in houses of colonial gentry, 805.
Bolton, Duke of, appoints Ebenezer Miller of Braintree his chaplain, 628–9.
Bondish, John, 754.
Bondish, Temperance, disciplined by Braintree church, 1683, 754, 755, 757.
Book of Common Prayer, Church of England, Morton's use of, 171, *note;* masters of vessels required to read service from, during voyage, 1634; 270-1; an offence to Judge Sewall, 627.
Book of Sports by King James, 336.
Books in colonial New England, 804–6.
Borland family, of Episcopal church at Braintree, 632; slaves owned by, 923.
Borland, John, chosen constable at Braintree, 1756, 1757, 825.
Boston, England, 368, 393.
Boston Bay, 1614, explored by John Smith, 5; Indians capture French ship in, 7; their plantations on islands of, 9; 1616–17, centre of plague, 11; 1621, first visited by Standish, 13 *et seq.*, 34; 1622, second visit of Plymouth people, 36, 37, 38; 1622, visited by Captain Squeb, 232; settlement attempted by Weston on, 43; his men from Sparrow explore, 52; source of his knowledge of, 58, 130-1, *note;* company sent out in the Swan to, 59; arrival in, 60; settlement at Wessagusset, 61; expedition for provisions from, 62-5; settlement abandoned, 97; 1622, grant to R. Gorges, territory on northeast side of, 136; 1623, territory allotted to Lord Gorges, 139; arrival of Wollaston in, 162; Morton's description of, 164–5; features of, 166–8; Morton on, 173; 1625 - 27, two settlements on, 183; 1625, settlers on north side of, 190; 1626, Thompson on island in,192; 1627, number of persons dwelling on, 193; 200, 201; 1628, Standish expedition, for arrest of Morton, to, 203; 1628, territory granted to Endicott on, 210–11; John Gorges inherits title to northeast side of, 212; transfer of same to Oldham, 212–13, 227; tobacco grown on shores of, 219; 1630, arrival of Winthrop in, 228, 321, 330; its aspect in June, 229; Winthrop begins settlement on, 234; 1631, remains of Pokanokets on, 255; allotted again to Lord Gorges, 283, 363; British foraging parties, 1775, 856–7; British troop ships in, after evacuation, 866–7; cleared of same, 868; United States man-of-war Constitution in, 1812, 910–11; the Chesapeake in, 911; frozen

over, winter of 1779-80, 888; 1637, character of settlements on, 581.

Boston, frigate, carries John Adams to Europe, 1778, 886; 951.

Boston, Mass., site, possibly within Weston's grant, 131, *note;* 1623, assigned to Lord Gorges, 139; 1630, occupied first by Blackstone, 238, 322; character of site, 238; settlement established by Winthrop, *ib.;* his house removed to, 239; its names, Shawmut, 167; Trimount, 236, 238; called Boston, 236; Wessagusset people at, 321; 1634, condition and population, 269, 322-3; 1634, need of enlargement, 364; enlarged at Mt. Wollaston, 365, 583, 651, 668, 1004; Morton and Ratcliff report to Privy Council on its religious and political affairs, 278-9; 1635, false alarm of arrival of Governor Gorges, 288; memorial, March, 1637, to General Court, 444, 477; opprobrium of Winthrop, 463; seat of government removed to Cambridge, 447-8; its delegates to General Court, 455; anger over Vane's defeat, 460-1; sergeants refuse to escort Winthrop, 461, 462, prosecuted, 509-10; excited by alien law, 463; indignation caused by expulsion from General Court of three deputies, 479; electors submit to Cotton's direction, *ib.;* three new deputies elected, 480; arms taken from persons suspected of ill will towards government, 511; 1637, good order succeeds disposition to revolt, 535; described by Josselyn, 1638, 331-2; alarm caused by order to return charter, 305; Morton, 1644, visits, is arrested, fined, and imprisoned, 344-50; 1645, Gibbons, captain of train band, 356-7; his residence, 358; 1646, La Tour d'Aulnay visits, 358; Scotch emigrants of 1651, 922; persecution of Quakers, 408-10, *note;* hanging of Quakers on Common, 1659, 550; and of Mary Dyer, 551; 1689, uprising against Andros, 818; reception of governor, Earl of Bellomont, 1699, 718-19; Stamp-Act Memorial, 1764, 708; Stamp-Act Riots, 1765, *ib.;* question of indemnity to sufferers from, 845; 1765, memorial for opening law-courts, 839; 1768, agitation caused by rumor of scheme for quartering British troops at, 847; convention called, *ib.;* massacre, 1770, 704; tea thrown into harbor, 1773, 850; Port Bill, 1774, 847; takes effect, 850; negro conspiracy, 1774, 854; epidemic of chronic dysentery, 1775, 801; 862; siege of, 1776, 951; British evacuation of, 1776, 864, 866; John Adams' plan for defence of harbor, 1776, 867; frigate Boston at, 1778, 886; mother of Braintree, 814; supplied by Braintree with provisions and fuel, 1710, 771; Quincy its suburb after 1845; 953; 954; farms within its boundaries, 1637-40, 646; foreign and domestic trade of, 698; criminal class, 797; John Adams' house in, 872; 1768, John Adams practising law at, 846; difficulty of access to Cambridge, 1637, 453-4; no road to Plymouth, 1637, 581; road in 1655, 671; roads running from, 1639, 666-79; road to Braintree and Quincy, 1641-1803, 673; stage-coach line to Providence, 1767, 677; town-meeting government, 814-15; of slow development, 816; 967; its high character, 983; great fire, 1872, 150.

Boston, Church, site of first meeting-house, 238; its elders, as peacemakers, visit church at Weymouth, 1638, 341; John Wilson, first pastor, 370; John Cotton, teacher, *ib.;* 1636, Wheelwright admitted to membership, *ib.;* advocated as a teacher, 411-12, 413; project fails, 415; Vane admitted, 376; Mrs. Hutchinson admitted, 397; she causes dissensions, 407 - 17, 425; 1637, 430; Vane kept in Massachusetts by, 422; Wilson criticised, 328; censured, 428-9; disturbances, 401; 432; Fast-day observances, 1637, 437; protest of members against jurisdiction of conscience cases by General Court, 444; remonstrance against action of court concerning Wheelwright, 446; 478; dissensions not subsided, May, 1637, 451; summons Anne Hutchinson for discipline and excommunication, 515; story of prosecution, 516-32; sends mission to warn her companions in Rhode Island, 537; excommunicates Underhill, 553-4; receives him again into communion, 557; church members of, refuse military service in the Pequot campaign, 461; church at North End, 607; First Church record of excommunication of Anne Hutchinson, 532; meeting-house, 1643, overseers appointed for galleries, 736.

——, Common, 1741, 323; executions on, 550-1; preaching of Whitefield, 749.

——, Neck, way of access to Cambridge, 454.

——, Athenæum library, 1830, 804.

——, Hancock house built of Quincy granite, 924-5.

——, King's Chapel, 621; built of Quincy granite, 924.

——, Public Latin School, support derived from sale of lands to Braintree, 651.

——, South Church, 739.

Boston, East, formerly Noddle's Island, 192; settlers at, 321.

Boston, South, 910.

Boston and Providence stage-coach line established, 1767, 677.

## INDEX. 1017

Boston Gazette, 1765, Stamp Act instructions, printed in, 839.
Boswell, James, Laird of Auchinleck, remark to Samuel Johnson, 126.
Bound-servants, "redemptioners" in colonial times, 722.
Bounty-jumper of the Revolution, 876.
Bowdoin, James, of committee to draft Massachusetts constitution, 1779, 889; vote of Braintree for governor, 891; calls out militia, Shays' rebellion, 1787, 897; his unpopularity after the same, 898; defeated of reëlection 1788, *ib.*
Boys, meeting-house galleries appropriated to, 736-8; Boston overseers of, 736; also at Hingham, 738, *note.*
Brackett, James, of Braintree, Liberty Tree planted near his tavern, 1766, 844; 845.
Brackett, Richard, of Braintree, 834; 835.
Brackett's Corners, Braintree, 897.
Braddock, General Edward, defeated by Indians, 1755, 641, 704, 835.
Bradford, William, Governor of Plymouth, concerning pestilence, 1616-17, 1633-4, 1, 2, 3, 4, 11; lawless traders on New England coast, 1614; 5, 6; 20; cited as to kidnapping of Squanto, 23, *note;* Dermer attacked by Indians, 1620, 28; 1621, Squanto's aid to Plymouth people, 29; return of ambassadors from Massasoit, 31; first harvest at Plymouth, 34; opinion of Squanto, 36; 38; 1622, Squanto's attempts at imposition, 40; reproves him, *ib.;* desire to protect him from Massasoit, 41; decides to surrender him, *ib.;* saves him, 42; Squanto's death, 44; 47; 1621, Weston's rebuke, 49; his reply, 49-50; 1622, warned of Weston's designs, 56, 57; 53; 58; appeal for food from Wessagusset, 62; expedition for food in the Swan, 63; takes command of Swan, *ib.;* voyage around Cape Cod, 63-5; abandons vessel and returns afoot to Plymouth, 65; 1623, appealed to again by Wessagusset, 66-7; protests against extortion of food from Indians, 67-8; provides corn, 68; corn bought of Manomet, 69; announces Indian conspiracy to magistrates, 75; one of committee for defence, *ib.;* offer of refuge to Wessagusset people, 96; observations on fate of settlement, 97; message to Aberdecest, 98, 105; unlicensed fishermen, 1622, 136; 1623, R. Gorges announces his arrival as governor to, 144; 145; pacificator for Weston with Gorges, 148-9, 151; on return of Gorges to England, 1624, 153; remark on Wollaston, 162; called enemy of Morton, 171, *note;* remark about Morton, 172; his source of knowledge of Wollaston, 174, *note;* opinion of Morton's May-day verses, 179, 182; Christmas, 1621, at Plymouth, 180-1; account of Lyford's arrival, 1624, 184; intercepts letters to Lyford and Oldham, 185-6; both arraigned for conspiracy and exiled, 187-8; Oldham returns 1625, again exiled, 189; as to Nantasket, 190, 230, 231; price of beaver skins, 196; 1628, Morton's fur-trade, 197; Morton's men, 198; 1628, indignation over trade in fire-arms and spirits with Indians, 199; Morton admonished, 201; 1629, Morton "fooled" Oldham, 221; his letters to Gorges about Morton, 222; Allerton's letter on patent to, 223; account of Ralph Smith, 230-1; on report of murder by Morton, 246; on Gardiner's companion, 252; account of Gardiner's capture, 255; 265, *note;* letter from Winthrop, 1633, on Massachusetts charter, 267; Winslow's examination at London, 1635, 281-2; 1644, permits Morton to stay at Plymouth, 345; Merry Mount a resort of scum of country, 354; concerning metheglin, 356; his social station in England, 364; reflections on immorality of Plymouth, 799.
Bradstreet, Simon, 1630, 241; informed of failure of impressments, 1690, at Braintree, 830.
Braintree,
1639, establishment of church, 586; Boston's claim on, adjusted, 588-9; land allotments prior to incorporation, 585-6;
1640, incorporation of town, 587, 787; its first delegates to General Court, 589; site of settlement, 590;
1641, sale of land restricted to inhabitants, 647;
1644, land granted to John Winthrop, Jr., for iron works, 646;
1645, share of burden in Indian wars, 827; service in Indian war, 828;
1647, protective measures against absentee land-ownership, 649-50; advantage of resident land-ownership, 652; population, 766;
1648, route of coast road through, 672; town-commons, difficulties caused by, 655-65;
1675, Indian raid in King Philip's war, 828-9; military committee disallows bill of R. Thayer, 829, and *note;*
1688, records of government of, begin, 817; effect in, of English revolution, 818; complete establishment of machinery of government, 819;
1689, sympathizes in overthrow of Andros, 817-8;
1690, furnishes thirteen men, French war, 830; fate of six, *ib.;*
1692, claimed under Indian title by R. Thayer, 654-5;
1693, paucity of town records prior to, 817;

1694, its first appropriation for charity, 724;
1695, conflict over division of the town, 611-3, 821-2;
1699, wealth of, 768, *note;* population, 768, *note;* aid given to Harvard College, 767-8;
1700, acquires, by purchase, lands claimed by Boston, 650-1; Mrs. Edmund Quincy's funeral, 678-9;
1702, small-pox epidemic, 719;
1704, its support of pastor Fiske, 610; impressments for colonial forces, 719;
1709, for Canada expedition, 720;
1710, supplies provision and fire-wood to Boston, 771;
1717, sends John Quincy delegate to General Court, 707; continues him its representative, until 1741, *ib.;*
1731, meeting-house, entertainment provided at raising of, 787;
1736, contention with Vinton over fish in Monatiquot River, 831-4;
1741, Paul Dudley delegate to General Court, 708; not accepted, John Quincy reëlected, 708;
1750, eight public houses in, 788;
1756-9, during period of French War, 835; its quota of men for colonial army, *ib.;* 837;
1757, election of selectmen, 834-5; men from, at Fort William Henry on its capitulation, 836; company under Peter Thayer goes out on alarm after Montcalm's victory, 836; 837;
1761, restriction on sale of liquor, 789;
1765, Middle Precinct meeting-house, Stamp Act meeting in, 838; under lead of John Adams, holds public meeting on Stamp Act, 838-9; adopts his instructions to representative of town, 839; Episcopalian pro-Stamp Act interest, 840-3;
1766, election, the first popular struggle of Revolution in, 843; no celebration of Stamp Act repeal at, 845; elects E. Thayer representative, *ib.;* votes on indemnity to sufferers from Boston riots, *ib.;*
1767, elects Norton Quincy and John Adams selectmen, 846; excuses Adams from town service, votes him thanks, *ib.;*
1768, suggestion of question of improvement of public welfare, 847; sends Josiah Quincy and E. Thayer to Boston convention, 848; its instructions, drawn by J. Adams, *ib.;* other such papers in its records, 1765-76, 849;
1770, town officers, salaries paid prior to, 820;
1773, young Palmer of, aids in tea riot, Boston harbor, 850;
1774, John Adams removes family from Boston to, 850; its delegates to county convention, *ib.;* its committee of safety, *ib.;* town powder removed from North Precinct meeting-house, 850-2, 854; its protest against rumored persecution of Episcopalians, 852; Mrs. Adams' report of continuance of prayers for the king at Christ Church, 852; men called to train for military duty, 854; military preparations, 855;
1775, resolves to discontinue slave-trade, 855; alarm from British foraging party, 856-7; church services interrupted and resumed, 860; sends Joseph Palmer representative to General Court, *ib.;* scarcity of food, 862; sickness, *ib.;* mortality, *ib.;*
1775-1782, its supplies for army, 880; compelled to borrow money, 881; financial crookedness in, *ib.;* contributions to army of Revolution, 870-8, 884-6; its debts, 884; cost of Revolution to, 885;
1776, agitation of, over rumors of events of war, and Congress, 865; measures for guarding shores of bay, 866; by Lieut.-Col. Tupper, 867; provisions for safety of town funds, 866; peace in, after departure of British troops, 868; Declaration of Independence entered in town records, 870; difficulty in supplying quota of men for Canada expedition, *ib.;* its population during Revolution, *ib.;* its available wealth, 871; enlistments for army in, 873; rage of its young men for privateering, 879; its men captured by British, *ib.;*
1777, Tories, nine named as inimical to popular cause, 853; property of some confiscated, 854;
1777-81, difficulty in obtaining recruits, 875; indemnity voted to pay fines of militia officers for not drafting men, 875, 892; its poorest men go to army, *ib.;* town-meeting inducements to obtain recruits, 876-7; estimate of men supplied from, 878; 879 *et seq.;*
1777, John Adams' return to, 886; comes home from France, 1779, 887; from England, 1788, 888;
1778, approves, with amendments, Articles of Confederation, 890;
1780, sends R. Cranch to General Court, 889; a form of town government considered, *ib.*, 891; disapproves of constitution for Massachusetts, 890; votes for candidates for governor, 891;
1783, meeting to consider Mass. Sunday law, 894; its report, *ib.;*
1786, its paper on tax question, 896;
1786-7, share of defence, Shays' rebellion; overseers of poor, 728;
1788, prosperity of, 898;
1792, North Precinct, becomes town of Quincy, 642, 903;
free from difficulties with Indian neighbors, 827; woods, the haunt of bears

# INDEX. 1019

and deer, 924; land titles, and town commons, 646-65; highways, 666-79; town roads and highways, developed, 674-9; militia, not an effective force, 765; its condition subsequent to 1780, 891 *et seq.*; subsequent to 1785, 899; taxes in, *ib.;* pauper question, 900; almshouse built, 1785, *ib.*, 1815, 905; reorganization of schools, 900-2; town division question agitated, 1790, 902; 1639-1830, population and wealth, 689-98; support of paupers, 723-4; treatment of insane, *ib.;* no almshouse till 1786, 728; vicious, poor and insane, 722-31; office of constable avoided, 824-5; difficulties of tax collecting, 823; 882; office of collector avoided, 824; intemperance in, 787, 975; taverns pictured, 792; frequenters of, *ib.*, 793; indications of high state of morality in, 796; quiet of, in last century, 803; people little accustomed to reading, 805; industries of, prior to 1825, 923 *et seq.;* iron-works, Scotch workmen at, 922; fate of enterprise, 923; ship-building a thriving business at, 924; granite quarries, development, 924-8; slaves owned at, 923; customary names of, *ib.*; mentions in town records of, *ib.;* dwellings and modes of life, 17th century, 680-4; social life, 699-721; nationality of colonial settlers in, 922; birthplace of John Adams and John Hancock, 617; John Adams, Braintree's contribution to Revolution, 961; sends Samuel Bass a delegate twelve times to General Court, 1641-64, 714; John Marshall, a treasurer of, 716, 717; its records of Edmund Quincy and William Coddington, 546; Josiah Quincy's life at, 703; Rev. John Wilson, first landowner of territory, 583; Middle Precinct church, dissensions over psalm-singing, 740; Middle Precinct church a powder magazine, 743. *See* Mount Wollaston, Passonagessit and Quincy.

——, burying ground, contains graves of William Tompson, 602; of Joanna Hoar, President and Bridget Hoar, 704; its condition prior to 1809, 905; title to conveyed to town of Quincy, 906.

——, church, establishment of, 1639, 586; ordination of William Tompson, 595; ministers of, 1639-59, William Tompson, 595-602; 1659-68, Henry Flynt, 602-4; 1672-1708, Moses Fiske, 608-15; 1709-26, 617; North Precinct, ministers of, 1709-26, Joseph Marsh, 616-17; 1726-44, John Hancock, 618-35; 1745-53, Lemuel Briant, 635-41; First church of, 570; its history, 590-645; trouble in filling Henry Flynt's place, 606-7; Moses Fiske made minister, 1672, 607; struggle over project of a new meeting-house, 1695, 611-12; division of parish, 612-14; 616; 1695, struggle for division of, begun, 611; dispute carried to General Court, 613; separation accomplished, 1708, 616; 1706, South Precinct meeting-house raised, 612; 1707, Hugh Adams ordained minister, 613; First or North Precinct, ministers of, 1755-92, Anthony Wibird, 641-2; becomes church of town of Quincy, 642; silver communion cup, given by Samuel Bass, 714; choir singing in, 741; hymns authorized to be sung in, *ib.;* musical instruments in, *ib.;* requirement of relation of "experience," 753; attempt to dispense with, 753-4; definite organization of, 747; its relation to political organization, prior to 1793, *ib.;* a paramount influence, prior to 1693, 747; practical separation from political organization, 1693-1792, *ib.;* a reunion, 1792-1824, 748; again separated under new state constitution, *ib.;* discipline of faulty members, 754; confessions required from, *ib.;* cases of, 754-61; discontinued, 762-3; records of discipline, 796.

——, meeting-house, the first, 417, 591, 594; its meeting-houses, 593-96; 1726, bad condition of, 619; abandoned, 620; new one dedicated, 1732, 619; no pews in, 734; men and women seated separately, *ib.;* change of this system, *ib.;* privilege given to construct pews, 1698, 735; consequence of, 735-7; galleries appropriated to boys, 736; privileges in, determined by money, 737; that erected, 1732, pews in, 737; psalmody in, 739; Major Quincy, 1723, Psalm-tuner, 739; not kept in repair, 742; its secular uses, *ib.;* dogs forbidden admittance, 1729, 744; space allotted to negroes, 923; renews covenant, 1739, 620; charges for support of church, 646; Samuel Bass, first deacon of, 713; John Adams [1st], deacon of, 714, 715; records, 750; discontinued, 1741, a social centre, *ib.*

——, Christ Episcopal church of, beginnings, 621; first edifice, 1728, 621; aided by English society, 622; its history, 1689-1802, 621-35; members taxed for support of town's minister, 623-7, 629-30; prayers for king, 1776, 852; closed, 1777, 853; population, 1647, 766; 1799, 767; 1699, 768, *note;* 1890, *ib.*

——, schools, provision for, 723, 724; 765; free Latin school established, 1645, *ib.;* one of 1635, 766; 1719, noted for, *ib.;* support of, 767-8; first school-house, 769; 774; charges for tuition, 769-70; provision for poor children, 770; fire-wood for school-master, 769-70; B. Tompson, master,

## 1020                              INDEX.

1678–1704, 769–72; development of, 774 *et seq.;* 1715, two new schoolhouses voted, 774; text-books, 778–80; instruction, 780; punishment, *ib.;* results, *ib.;* contrast of old and new, 782; dismisses schoolmaster, 1775, 855; without grammar school, 856.
Braintree, town-meeting at, 812; system inherited from Boston, 814; a slow development, 816; after 1673, biennial, *ib.;* officers chosen by, 1693, 819; those of 1694, *ib.;* other business transacted, 819-20; compensation for services of officers, 820; its usual business, *ib.;* occasional conflicts in, 821; story of, 1710–11, 822-3; March, 1766, election of officers, division on Stamp Act, 843-4; considers petition to General Court for creation of a new town, 1791, 902.
Brattle, Thomas, Daniel Quincy married at his house, 1682, 706.
Brattle, Mrs., her death, 706.
Brereton, Sir William, grant of land in New England to, 212.
Brewster, William, 20.
Brewsters, islands Boston Bay, origin of name, 20.
Briant, Lemuel, succeeds Hancock, as minister of Braintree church, 1745, 635; support of, 635-6; sermon on moral virtue, 637; accused of Arminianism, 638; 639; his treatment of adversaries, *ib.;* his church divided, 640; asks dismissal from pastorate, 1753, 641; death, 641; his liberal theological views, 643; considered a Unitarian by John Adams, 643-4; 926; 944.
Bridges, 1644, over Monatiquot, 673; 1654, over Neponset, *ib.*
Bridgewater, Mass., 255; Mr. Cary of, 857; 858; 829; frontier post established on road from Braintree to, 829.
Brierly, ——, comes with colonists from England, 459, 584; refused residence in Mass. Bay, 584-5.
Brigden, Thomas, Charlestown bellringer and dog-whipper, 745, *note.*
Briggs, George N., Governor of Mass., 953.
Bright's disease, frequent in colonial times, 800–1; called dropsy, 801.
Brimsmead, Rev. William, of Marlborough, death of, 719.
British soldiers, scheme for quartering, at Boston, 1768, 847; foraging parties, Boston Bay, 1775, 856-7; evacuation of Boston, 1776, 864, 866; troop-ships, in Boston Bay after evacuation, March, 1776, 867; proceed to Halifax, 868; capture Charleston, May, 1780, 891.
Bristol, England, Thomas Weston dies at, 1645, 154; captured by Prince Rupert, 313; royalist attack, 1643, *ib.;* retaken by Fairfax, 314.
Broadway, New York, Maverick's house in 365.

Brockton, Mass., shoemaking centre, 930.
Brooke, Lord, a proprietor in Connecticut, 374.
Brownists, religious party, 248, *note.*
Brunswick, Maine, 258.
Bryant, Gridley, constructor of Quincy granite railway, 926; 982.
Bryce, James, cited, 1001, 1004.
Bucaneering in the West Indies, 358.
Buckingham, George Villiers, first Duke of, emulates the popularity of Essex, 115; of the Plymouth Company under charter of 1620, 122; influence with the King for the Plymouth Company, 124; sustains the 1620 charter, 125; his share of New England, drawn at Greenwich, 1623, 139; 273; 275; his influence for Gorges at court 1622, 275; 317.
Buckle, ——, at church trial of Anne Hutchinson, 522, *note.*
Buffalo, New York, Free Soil party convention, 1848, 955.
Bulkley, Peter, 476.
Bullard, Samuel, 726.
Bunhill Fields, London cemetery, Edmund Quincy 4th, buried in, 1738, 702.
Bunker's Hill, battle, June 17, 1775, 642; character of fighters at, 765; signs of, seen by Mrs. Adams from Penn's Hill, 858-9; 919.
Bunker's Hill Monument, built of Quincy granite, 924; 927.
Bunyan, John, 702.
Burdet, Rev. George, in control of Maine province, 1640, 310; his character, *ib.;* Thomas Gorges' difficulties with, 312; association with Underhill, 554–6.
Burgoyne, General John, 874.
Burial ground, Quincy, condition prior to 1809, 905-6; title conveyed to the town, 906.
Burke, Edmund, 662; 805; 809.
Burnet, Gilbert, description of Hugh Peters, 375.
Burnet, William, Governor of Massachusetts Bay, 616.
Burrell, ——, 905.
Bursley, John, remains at Wessagusset after 1624, 161; a leading man of Wessagusset, 338; 342.
Burton, Henry, punished by Star Chamber, 248, *note.*
Butler, Samuel, Wessagusset hanging in Hudibras, 81-2.
Butler, Sigourney, one of authors of Quincy city charter of 1888, 998.
Buzzard's Bay, drawn by Dr. Gooch, at Greenwich, 1623, 139; 209.

California, migration from New England to, 793.
Calvin, his writings favorite reading in early New England, 391; his system,

## INDEX. 1021

434; predestination tenet accepted by Vane and Cotton, 457.
Calvinism, absence of, at Quincy, 944.
Cambridge, Mass., Winthrop removes his house from, 1630, 239; Dudley's property at, 365; described by him, 1631, 484; seat of government removed to, 1637, 448, 483; difficulty of access from Boston, 453–4; 1637, annual charter election, May, 1637, at, 452–5, 460; Synod of 1637 at, 470–4; action in Antinomian controversy, 571; 1637, practically remote from Boston, 483; 484; character of settlement, 1637, 483; 484; church at, 484; Synod of 1648, snake episode, 500; 1729, regulation forbidding dogs in meeting-house, 745, *note*; 1755, provincial army at, 765; 1774, meeting at, after removal of powder from Charlestown, 850; 1775, Provincial Congress, 849; 1779, state constitution convention of, 887; 889; 677; 706.
Camden, S. C., battle of, 891.
Campbell, Chief Justice, cited as to authority of royal proclamations, 203.
Canacum, sachem of Manomet, visited by Standish, winter of 1622-3, 69; his treatment of Standish, 71; his treatment of Massasoit, 73; dies of starvation, 103.
Canada, 122; conquered by England, 641; military expedition to, 1690, 758, 760; military expedition to, 1709, 720; difficulty of enlisting soldiers for, 1776, 870; 875.
Canary Islands, trade between New England and, 698.
Canonicus, chief of Narragansetts, challenges Squanto, 35; 359.
Cape Ann, Dermer in danger of wreck, 1619, off, 26; touched by the ship Sparrow, 1622, 52; region about drawn by Earl of Warwick at Greenwich, 1623, 139; allotted to Mason in partition of 1635, 283; 346.
Cape Breton, northern limit of territory granted to Plymouth Company, 1606, 118.
Cape Cod, Dermer visits, 1619, 26; 49; 62; 131, *note;* pure strain of English blood of settlers on, 922.
Cape Porpoise, Maine, 316; Wheelwright settles near, 1641, 539.
Capen, Josiah, of Braintree, 835.
Carlisle, Earl of, concerned in 1635 partition of New England, 283.
Carlyle, Thomas, cited, 83.
Carver, John, 48; 49; his station in England, 364.
Cary, ——, visits J. Q. Adams at Quincy, and recalls events of May 21, 1775, at Braintree, 857–8.
Caryl, Joseph, writings of, favorite reading in New England, 391.
Casco Bay territory drawn at Greenwich 1623, by Earl of Holderness, 139; northern limit of Gorges province in Maine, 1637, 301; 351.
Casco tribe of Indians, party of, murder Bagnall, 352–3.
Cass, Lewis, in election of 1848, 955.
Casting of the Stools, *see* Jenny Geddes.
Castle Island, Boston Bay, fortification of, 284; 287; 464; John Marshall employed on, 717.
Catholics at Quincy, 946, 948.
Caunbitant, *see* Corbitant, 36.
Cavalier and Puritan forces in England, 107.
Ceawlin, Saxon king, survival of customs of his time in New England, 655.
Cervantes, 390.
Chaleur Bay, northern limit of Plymouth Company's territory 1620, 122.
Champlain, Lake, first called Lake Irocoise or Iroquois, 120.
Channing, William Ellery, Unitarian movement of, 643, 944.
Charing Cross, London, Hugh Peters' execution at, 376.
Charity, Weston's vessel, 54; brings part of Weston's company, 1622, to New England, 58; sails April 22, 59; bound also to Virginia, 59; in charge of Andrew Weston, *ib.;* returns from Virginia, 61; returns to England, 62; brings news of Indian massacre in Virginia, 1622, 74; 163.
Charles I., of England, 202, 223; attitude of Puritans toward, 248, *note;* the beginning of his struggle, 1634, 270; reasons for granting Mass. Bay charter, 271 *et seq.;* his character, 273; 274; ignorance of New England question, 275; 300; 306; influence of Mass. Bay Company at court of, 266–7; approves report of Privy Council committee on charter, 267; his straightened finances, 1635, 290; 292; 293; 294; attempt at absolute government, 299; Laud's conference with, concerning liturgy at Edinburgh, 300; defeated at Kelso, 1639, 307; Gorges' plan of attack on Bristol sent to, 313; 318; 347; sends Sir Harry Vane to New England, 374; Hugh Peters' influence at the trial of, 375; his projects for England, 561; probable effect of his success in New England, 570; 701.
Charles II., of England sustains grant made to Endicott, 213; issues charter for same, 213; 214; appoints Maverick a royal commissioner for America, 334; commission denounced and ignored 334–5; influences of his court adverse to New England, 654.
Charles River, 159; 161; its mouth within the Robert Gorges' territory, 136; 210; 232; the Spragues settle on on the north side of, 217; 233; 269; 363; 365; 484.

# 1022　INDEX.

Charleston, S. C., captured by British, 1780, 891.

Charlestown, Mass., first refuge of Mass. Bay Colony, 1630, 363; its site visited by Standish, 1621, 16; called Mishawum, 161; first settlers, 1629, 218; their apprehensions of newcomers, 220; intended the seat of Mass. Bay government, 218; expedition from the Mary & John to, 1629, 232-3; Winthrop's party landed at, 1630, 234; provisions made for, *ib.;* people of, in severe straits, *ib.;* sufferings at, 235; bad sanitary condition, *ib.;* mortality at, 237; party reduced, 238; first meeting of magistrates, 240; 258; defences ordered for, 1634, 287; increased by people from Wessagusset, 321; Walford compelled to remove from, 336; quarrel of Dudley and Winthrop, 1633, 377; destroyed in battle of Bunker Hill, 859; Ursuline convent destroyed, 932; its dog-whipper and bell-ringer, 745, *note;* in the route to Cambridge from Boston, 453; powder taken from by Gage, 1774, 850.

Charnock, Robert, associate of Barclay in plot against William III., 625.

Charter of Mass. Bay of 1629, reasons of King for granting it, 271 *et seq.;* attacked by Gorges, 1632, 263 *et seq.;* sustained by Privy Council, 266-7; attack renewed by Gorges, 1634, 271 *et seq.;* its surrender demanded by Privy Council, 270; 279; not obeyed, *ib.;* order ignored by General Court, 1635, 289; 296; its legal abrogation, 292; Lords Commissioner, 1638, issue second order for surrender, 304; General Court refuses to obey, 305; lost sight of, 307; abrogated, 1686, 817; provincial, 1691 granted, *ib.*

Charter to Plymouth Company of 1606, 117-18, of 1620, its concessions of territory, 121-3; jurisdiction conferred by, 123-4; becomes the Great Charter of New England, 123; assailed by Virginia Company, 124; opposition overcome, 124-5; Allerton's efforts at London to obtain new one, 1629, 223.

Charter, City of Quincy, its authors, 998, principles of, 998-1000, terms of, 1000-3.

Charter election, *see* Election.

Chastity in New England, 795-9.

Chatham Harbor, Cape Cod, 43; refuge of the Swan, 1622, 63.

Chauncey, Rev. Charles, pastor of First Church, Boston, 639; habit of driving in Boston, 678.

Cheeseborough, William, one of Braintree's first delegates to General Court, 589.

Chelsea, Mass., site visited by Standish, 1621, 16; called Winnisimmet, 161, 330; 192.

Cheney, John, of Braintree, 830.

Chesapeake, U. S. man-of-war, in Boston Bay, 911.

Chevyot Hills, name given to range about Milton, by Captain John Smith, 167.

Chicago, Illinois, 927.

Chickatabot, sachem, driven by pestilence from his plantation, 11; 15; his dwelling at Passonagessit, 167; his mother buried there, *ib.;* sells Nantasket, 183; 363; his descendants confirm Mount Wollaston land-title, 653.

"Child of the Covenant," definition of, 751-2.

Childs, Dr. Robert, difficulty in New England, 333; sustained by Maverick, 334; 349, 574.

Choir singing, 739-41.

Christ Church, Braintree and Quincy, 1689-1802, account of, 621-35; its library, 622, 804; 844; closed, 1777, 853.

Christmas, 181; Mass. Bay law forbidding the celebration of, 181, *note;* at Plymouth, 1621, 180-1; observance discouraged, 623.

Church, Benjamin, officer in Indian wars, 764.

Church in Mass. Bay, an oligarchy, 1636, 382-92; controls legislature, 513; church and state, 590; a social centre, 750-1; its system, 732-46; its members only, freemen in Massachusetts until 1693, 747; requirements for membership, 752; necessary of parents, for baptism of children, 751; form of admission to 752; ordeal of relation of "experience," 753; discipline of erring members, 747-63, 795-6; confessions to church, required of offenders, 754; confessions discontinued, 762.

Church of England, project to extend, in New England, 142; Book of Common Prayer, 171, *note;* Laud's rule in, 297; he regulates its ceremonials, *ib.;* reformation in England, causes transfer of authority from one to many heads, 382; its establishments in New England, 621; inspired with evangelicalism by Wesley, 733; rule in Virginia exercised to drive away Tompson and Knowles, 599.

Church of Rome, at Quincy, 931.

Cicero, proficiency in, of Braintree school-boys, 1647, 766; 967.

Cider, consumption, colonial times, 785-6.

Clapp, Roger, expedition from the Mary & John, to Charlestown, 1629, 232-3.

Clarendon, on popularity of Essex, 116; court influence of Lord Lenox, 124; Maverick's letter to, concerning the burning of Morton's house, *ib., note;* 246; on disregard of Scotland at English Court, 294; Attorney General

INDEX. 1023

Noy, and Sir John Finch, 295 ; opinion of Sir Harry Vane, 373.
Clark, John, of Braintree, 835.
Clark's tavern, Portsmouth, Tutor Flynt's mishap, 1754, near, 787.
Clay, Henry, defeated by Polk, 1844, 953 ; 956.
Cleanliness, habits of, colonial New England, 806 ; in British Isles, 807.
Cleeve, George, commission to New England, 1637 ; 301 ; 302 ; authorized to explore for Lake Erocoise, 1637, 301 ; resuscitates Plough Patent, 314 ; sells patent to Rigby, *ib.*; returns to America, 315 ; 344.
Cleon, Athenian demagogue, 989.
Clergy of New England, 392 ; intermarriage in families, 608-9 ; consider question of submission to a royal governor, 1635, 811-12 ; united in troubles of 1637, 535 ; sermons on Stamp-Act, 1765, 840-1 ; use of liquor by, 792.
Cleverly, Joseph, of Braintree, 851 ; judged inimical to popular cause, 1777, 853 ; officiates at Christ Church in absence of minister, 634 ; J. Adams' opinion of, 1758, 841-2 ; favors Stamp-Act, 842 ; politic attitude, election, 1766, 843.
Cleverly family, of Episcopal church at Braintree, 632.
Clodius, Roman demagogue, 989.
Clothes, 17th and 18th centuries, 684-5.
Coast defences, 1776, 867.
Cod, Cape, 62.
Coddington, William, Assistant of Mass. Bay colony, death of wife, 1630, 237 ; 256, *note;* acquires land at Wessagusset, 1634, 583 ; one of the two proprietors at Mt. Wollaston, 1634, 365 ; succeeds Morton, as owner of Mt. Wollaston, 546 ; the property bought by William Tyng, 1639, 707 ; his name perpetuated in connection with school lands, Quincy, 546, and *note;* 767 ; treasurer of Mass. Bay, 396 ; 415 ; not in sympathy with minister Wilson, 426 ; his election to General Court, 1637, set aside, 455 ; sits in church with the deacons instead of with the magistrates, 462 ; reëlected to Court of Nov. 1637, 475 ; 479 ; not expelled, 480 ; attempts defence of Anne Hutchinson, 505 ; 506 ; effect of his interposition, 507 ; one of two who voted in her favor, 508 ; as her partisan exposed to annoyance, 547 ; 1638, removes to Providence, *ib.*; father of Rhode Island, 365 ; his brick house at Boston, 547 ; 1640, conciliatory letter to Winthrop, reports Morton in Rhode Island, 1644, 346 ; 1678, his death, 548 ; 568, 593, 700 ; 905.
Coffee, not in common use, colonial times, 785.
Coggeshall, John, elected to General Court, Nov. 1637, 475 ; expelled for adhering to Wheelwright, 479 ; replaced by William Colburn, 480 ; at trial of Anne Hutchinson, 495 ; as witness, browbeaten by Peters 496 ; 498, 564, 568.
Cohasset, Mass., 910.
Coke, Sir Edward, Crown counsel, trial of Essex, 112, 113 ; on powers conferred to Plymouth Company, charter, 1620, 124 ; antagonism to Gorges, 126-7 ; his vindictive character, 127 ; as speaker of the House of Commons, sits during the examination of Gorges, 1621, 127 ; personal interest in case, 128-9 ; on legal authority of royal proclamation, 202.
Colburn, William, elected to replace Coggeshall in General Court, 1637, 480 ; votes in favor of Anne Hutchinson, 508.
Coles, Robert, fined for dram drinking, 356.
Colony of Mass. Bay, becomes a province under charter of William and Mary, 747.
Comber, Thomas, his Help to Devotion, in Christ church library, Quincy, 804.
Commission Royal of 1664, its reception in Boston, 334-5.
Commodore, British man-of-war, in Boston Bay, May 1776, 868.
Common, Boston, *see* Boston Common.
Common-lands, custom of, 656 ; at Braintree, difficulties caused by, 655-65.
Common prayer, *see* Book of Common Prayer.
Communion, Braintree church, Episcopalians admitted to, 629, 630, *note.*
Community of women, 522, *note.*
Comus, Milton's poem, 390.
Conant, Roger, of Salem, 201.
Concord, Mass., 136 ; 364 ; Dudley's property near, 365 ; battle, 827, 828, 852, 855, 856, 878, 879.
Confederation of United States, 1778, Articles of, 889-90.
Confiscation of arms at Boston, 1637, 511-12.
Congleton, England, church dog-whipper of, 744, *note.*
Congress, Continental, Braintree's instructions on recommendations of 1775, 849 ; John Adams a delegate to, 1774, 850 ; sends him minister to France, 1778, 886 ; prayers for the King forbidden, 852 ; its right to declare peace or war objected to at Braintree, 890.
Congregational Society of Quincy, new church organization, 1824.
Connecticut, the Plymouth people establish a trading station in, 160 ; patented to Lord Brooke and Lord Say and Seale, 374.
Connecticut River, 898 ; British flotilla, in, during war of 1812, 910.

Conscience Whigs in Mass., 955.
Constable office avoided at Braintree, 824-5; elections to, a town joke, 825; penalty of fine for refusing office, *ib.*
Constitution, U. S. man-of-war, in Boston Bay, 910.
Constitution of Mass., 1779, convention 887, 889, 890.
Convention, Boston, 1768, to consider British soldiers in Mass., 847.
Copeland, Ephraim, of Braintree, 830.
Cook, John, regicide, executed with Peters, 376, *note.*
Corbitant, sachem, allies himself with the Narragansetts, 32; endeavors to compass Squanto's death, 32-3; quarrels with Squanto and Hobamack, 33-4; unsuccessful expedition to capture, 34; rumor of Squanto as his spy, 36; alarm at Plymouth of attack from, 1622, 38; 39.
Cornhill, Boston, 358.
Cornwallis, defeats Gates at Camden, 1780, 891.
Cotton, Rev. John, cited, 300; teacher of Boston Church, 332, 370; result of his election sermon, 1634, 371; 377; of reconciliation committee between Dudley and Winthrop, 379; on compelling conformity to interpretations of Bible, 386; his writings, 390; cause of Anne Hutchinson coming to New England, 393; his sermons, particularly considered at her weekly meetings, 398; 409, *note;* her favorite minister, 393, 411; in the investigation of Covenants of Grace and Works question, 413; his theological tenets, 418; 425; 457; attempt to detach him from Mrs. Hutchinson, 422; submits to theological inquiry, 423; takes issue with Wilson, 1636, 425; not in sympathy with him, 426; distinguished by Anne Hutchinson, as under the Covenant of Grace, 427, 492-3, 494, 495; at her examination Dec. 1636, 426-8; at meeting of church to rebuke Wilson, 429; engages in a controversy with Winthrop, 1637, 430; required to reply to written questions, *ib.;* his relations with Anne Hutchinson, 1637, *ib.;* the cause of contention between her and Wilson, 436; his adherence desired by both parties in Antinomian controversy, *ib.;* contrasted with Wheelwright, *ib.;* preaches fast-day sermon, Jan. 1637, 437; invites Wheelwright "to exercise," *ib.;* 456; disposed to abandon the colony because of alien law, 463; desire of Puritan elders, 1637, to reconcile him with Wilson, 468; the effect on his position in Boston church by Vane's return to England, 469; announces Wilson's concessions, 469; his theological views considered by synod of 1637, 472-4: sustained by synod, 474; prevents Boston electors from resenting expulsion of deputies from General Court, 479; regarded friendly to Wheelwright party, Nov. 1637, 480; attends trial of Anne Hutchinson, 486; his position in the trial, 492; 496; called on for testimony, 497; effect of his testimony, 498; 501, 503; 1637, involved in arguments concerning miracles, 504; criticised by Dudley, 505; 506; 507; advises taking arms from disaffected, 512; abandons Mrs. Hutchinson, 514; pronounces admonition to her sons for defending her 521; in discussion on community of women 522, *note;* takes custody of her at close of first day's trial, 523; 524, 525, 526, 527; reiterates a charge that she had lied, 530; consents to her excommunication, *ib.;* the leader of the minority in Boston, 534; effect on good public order of his submission to the authorities, *ib.;* is not unhappy in Mrs. Hutchinson's misfortunes, 535, *note;* respecting invitation to Wheelwright to take refuge in Rhode Island, 539; Underhill writes an abusive letter to, from Maine, 555; 563, 564, *note;* attends ordination of Tompson at Braintree, 1640, 595; admired by Henry Flynt, 603; accompanied to this country by Edmund Quincy, 700; his Spiritual Milk for American Babes, a school text-book, 778-9.
Council for New England, style of Plymouth Company under charter of 1620, 122; David Thompson agent of, 1622, 58; organized under Gorges patent, 131; its meetings and place of same, *ib.;* want of interest of noble members of, *ib.;* adopts rules for protection of the fisheries, 132; 133, *note;* inadequate response to call of Robert Gorges, 1622, 137; its patent of land to Weston, 58; their rules violated by him, 145; 149; Thompson's complaints against him, 146; on its last legs, 1624, 152-3; informed of Morton's offences, 1628, 208; territory granted to Endicott by, 209; difficulties with Mass. Company, 222; unequal to exigencies of 1634, 276; scheme for extending its powers, *ib.;* its poverty, 1635, 290; surrenders patent, 1635, 283-4; 295; petitions of Associates for patents in severalty 283, 292; 298; Morton in service of, 1637, 301.
Council of the North, a tribunal of England, 1634, 270.
Court of Assistants of Mass. Bay, first meeting of, 240; fines Endicott for beating Thomas Dexter, 261; punishment decreed for Ratcliff, 261; cases of punishments ordered by, 262, *note;* deliberates on the order to return charter, 259; decides to procrastinate,

INDEX.                                                                 1025

*ib.*; tries Morton, 346; imprisons and fines him, 348; Shepherd, Coles and Gibbons fined for drinking, 356.
Court of High Commission, English tribunal under Charles I., 270.
Court of King's Bench, decision on legal authority of royal proclamation, 202; *quo warranto* writ against Mass. Bay Company filed in, 1635, 291, 295, 298, 301, 302, 303, 304.
Court of St. James, John Adams, U. S. Minister to, 888; C. F. Adams, U. S. Minister to, 957.
Covenants of Grace and Works, Anne Hutchinson's theory of, 402; 492-3; discussed at her examination, 1636, 426-8; her discovery of, 500; defined, 402-6; subject of clerical investigation, 413 *et seq.;* preached by Wheelwright, fast-day, 1637, 438 and at Mt. Wollaston, 475; 472; Greensmith fined for naming Ministers of Works, 442; Grace party strong, Boston church, 447; discussed by 1637 Synod, 471; Nov. General Court undertakes to purge community of, 479; 491; 494; 539; Winthrop sees anarchical tendency of, 568. See Antimonian Controversy.
Covenant of Quincy church, 749.
Covenant, Scotch, signed, 1638, 304; 306.
Coventry, Lord, 304.
Cradock, Matthew, Governor, listens to Oldham's propositions, 214; instructs Endicott to maintain possession of territory in New England, 216; encouragement of fur-trade, 219; 259; in defence of Mass. Bay charter, 1632, 265; called upon for charter, 270; 275; his influence in Privy Council overcome, 278; transmits order for return of charter, 1634, 279; 282, 284, 286, 291, 304, 347.
Cranch, Richard, of Quincy's anti-privateer committee, 1793, 906; first postmaster of Quincy, 1795, 804, 904; suggests the name for town of Quincy, 711, 904; 856; represents Braintree in General Court, 1780, 889; his wife a sister of Mrs. John Adams, 904; father of Justice William, *ib.*
Cranch, Judge William, at Salem, 1766, 677; son of Richard, 904; reporter of U. S. Supreme Court, *ib.*
Crane, Thomas, library building given to Quincy in memory of, 942; his career and character, 942-3; 944.
Cromwell, Oliver, 318; 347; his relations with Wheelwright, 369; with Sir Harry Vane, 373; 375; his funeral, 375; 450, 594, 710.
Cromwell, Richard, dispersion of Long Parliament, 860.
Crosby, Joseph, his pew in Braintree meeting-house, 1712, 735; his report in fish contention, 832.

Crown Point expedition, 1756, 835; capture of, 837.
Cummaquid, Indian, 33.
Cumberland, R. I., death of William Blackstone at, 144, *note.*
Curfew, at Quincy, 1810-1880, 907.
Cushing, Judge William, riding the circuit, 1771, 678.
Cushman, Robert, 1622, on deterioration of Mass. Indians, 10; with Weston charters the Mayflower, 47; his relations with Weston, 47, 48, 50; letter to Bradford about him, 57; visits Plymouth in the ship Fortune, 50, 130; urges compliance with Weston's demands, 50; on territory granted to Robert Gorges, 131, *note.*
Dagon, Mount, Endicott's name for Merry Mount, 211.
Damariscove Islands, visited by ship Sparrow, 1622, 51; 53, 54.
Danforth, Samuel, minister of Roxbury, 601.
Danish names of Lincolnshire towns, 369.
Dante, 390.
Davenport, John, 527; his lecture before Boston church, 1637, 469; at 1637 synod, 470; at the church trial of Anne Hutchinson, 519; on community of women, 522, *note;* labors to convince Mrs. Hutchinson of errors, 523; credited by her with enlightenment, 526; 527; as a revivalist, 620.
Davis, John, in election of 1836, 952.
Deacon, office of distinction in New England, 713.
Deane, Charles, on conflict of 1632 over Massachusetts Bay charter, 267, *note.*
Decatur, Stephen, Captain, U. S. N., 1812, breakfasts with Josiah Quincy, 911; 912.
Declaration of Independence, 1776, 642; Braintree's instructions on, 849; read at, 852; entered on records of, 870.
De Costa, F. B., on Morton as a Church of England martyr, 171, *note.*
Dedham, John Allen, minister, 1640, 595; church at, 607; 718; 726; its meeting-house dog-whipper, 745, *note;* husking at, 1767, 791; 828.
Deer in Braintree woods, 924.
Definitive treaty of peace, United States and Great Britain, signed, 1783, 893.
Defoe, Daniel, on the London plague, 2.
Delft Haven, sailing of the Pilgrims from, 47.
Democratic party, Quincy, 945 *et seq.;* influence in 1887 town-meeting, 991 *et seq.*
Demosthenes, 967.
Derbyshire, England, 603.
Dermer, Thomas, 1615, explores coast of New England and Newfoundland, 25; takes Squanto to England, *ib.*; on Indian pestilence, 1619-20, 3; redeems kidnapped Indians, 1619, 7; visits

# 1026  INDEX.

New England, 25-8; redeems French captive from Indians, 26; passes winter at Jamestown, Va., 27; 1620, again in New England, *ib.*; conflict with Indians, Martha's Vineyard, 27-8; death, in Virginia, 28; 43.

Devereux, Robert, Earl of Essex, *see* Essex.

Devereux, W. B., his History of Earls of Essex cited, 115.

D'Ewes, Sir Symonds, Autobiography cited, 291.

De Tocqueville, *see* Tocqueville.

Dexter, H. M., editor of Mourt's Relations, 24, *note*.

Dexter, Thomas, his affair with Philip Ratcliff, 260; assaults Samuel Hutchinson, *ib.*; is beaten by Endicott, *ib.*; his case against Endicott, 337.

Dimblebee, William, Braintree pauper, 724; 819-20.

Diphtheria, a scourge in 1735 and 1751, 801.

Disease in colonial Massachusetts, 800-1; 801, *note*.

Diversions, in colonial New England, 808-9.

Dogs in Braintree meeting-house, 744; in other meeting-houses, 744-5, and *note*.

Dog-whipper, in old English churches, 744-5, *note*.

Domestic habits, colonial New England, 807.

Don Quixote, 390.

Dorchester, Lord, intervenes in obtaining charter for Endicott, 213; his influence in obtaining Mass. Bay charter, 274.

Dorchester Company, removes Lyford and others from Nantasket, 1625-6, 190.

Dorchester Fields, 233.

Dorchester Heights, 15; 233; 865-6; 902.

Dorchester, Mass., French coins found at, 1631, 8-9; within territory granted to Robert Gorges, 131, *note*; its Indian name, Mattapan, 233; 238; defence ordered for, 1634, 287; 338; wild region about, 1630, 364, 365; road to Weymouth made, 1648, 594; to Stoughton's mill, 1634, 669; bridge across Neponset, 1652, 670; on the road, Boston to Plymouth, 669, 671; 717; 726; service in Indian war, 1645, 828; occupation of Heights by colonial forces, March 4, 1776, 865-6; 902.

——, church established, 1630, 586; Richard Mather, minister, 1640, 595; collection taken for Tompson, 1665, 602; Josiah Flynt, minister, 607; discipline of Mary Modesly, 1681, 754-5, *note*.

Dorothy Q., *see* Quincy, Dorothy.

Dover, New Hampshire, 201, 556.

Downing, Emanuel, Winthrop's brother-in-law, aids defenders of Mass. Bay charter, 266; 275.

Doyle, John A., concerning Winthrop, 378, *note*.

Drafts for army, unwillingness in New England to submit to, 875, 892.

Drake, Sir Francis, explorations on the Pacific coast, 122.

Dreadnaught, British ship, Gorges in command, expedition against Spain, 1597; 106.

Drink in New England, colonial times 686-7, 785 *et seq.*

Drunkenness in colonial New England, 786 *et seq.*; 800.

Dryden, John, reputed cousin of Anne Hutchinson, 392; 772.

Dublin University, Laud as Chancellor of, 297.

Dudley, Joseph, Massachusetts Bay agent at London, 1692, 654; as Governor, letter concerning Thomas Eager of Braintree, 624; favors Veazie in church tax question, 626.

Dudley, Lieut. Samuel, in the capture of Gardiner, 256.

Dudley, Governor Thomas, 241; writes of Morton to Countess of Lincoln, 169, 246, 256, *note*, 484; supersedes Winthrop as governor, 279; project for fortifying Castle Island, 1634, 284; calls meeting of Assistants to consider Endicott's mutilation of royal banner, 295; a partner in Maverick's commercial ventures, 330; major-general of Massachusetts Bay forces, 359; his farm lands, 365; elected governor, 1634, 371; succeeded by Haynes, 1635, *ib.*; his differences with Winthrop, 1636, 377; Doyle's opinion of, 378, *note*; a reader of theological disquisitions, 390; the site of his dwelling at Cambridge, 484; elected deputy-governor, May, 1637, 455; life member of council, *ib.*; at trial of Anne Hutchinson, 487, 495, 502, 503; interrogates Cotton, 498; interrupts him, 504; his attitude towards, 514; in discussion over Anne Hutchinson's speech, 505; 507; joins in attack after her confession, 528; 572; 573; 595.

Dudley, Madam, at funeral of Edmund Quincy, 1698, 701.

Dudley, Paul, 1741, Braintree's delegate to General Court, 708; election negatived by Governor Shirley, *ib.*

Dummer, William, 568; causes settlement of church tax question, 629.

Dunbar, Scotland, prisoners from battle of, emigrants to New England, 1651, 922.

Dutch of New York, encroachments on Plymouth colony, 280; pretensions to New England, 306, 319.

Duxbury, Mass., 88; Morton shoots over marshes of, 345.

# INDEX. 1027

Dwellings, at Braintree, seventeenth century, 680-4.

Dyer, Mary, a milliner at London, 548; follower of Mrs. Hutchinson, 532, 548; removes to Rhode Island, 549; becomes a Quaker, *ib.*; 1659, seeks persecution at Boston, *ib.*; is persecuted, 408, *note*, 409-10, *note*; arrested and banished, 549; returns again to Boston, *ib.*; imprisoned and sentenced to death, *ib.*; accompanies William Robinson and Marmaduke Stephenson to the scaffold, 550; compelled by force to leave Boston, *ib.*; returns to Boston, and hanged, 551; believed to have received divine punishment, 389.

Dyer, William, husband of Mary, 548.

Dysentery, chronic, epidemic of 1775, 801, 862.

Eager, Thomas, minister of Christ Church, Braintree, 1713-14, 623; his protest against taxing Episcopalians for support of town minister, 624; his character, 624-5.

East Boston, formerly Noddle's Island, 192; settlers at, 321.

Eastham, Mass., 31, 64, 65.

Edgar, of England, law forbidding dogs and swine in churches, 745, *note*.

Edict of Nantes, 248, *note*.

Edinburgh, St. Giles' Church, rejection of Laud's liturgy, 300, 302.

Education in New England, 765-82.

Edward VI. of England, 248, *note*.

Edwards, Jonathan, his influence in New England, 798; his religious revival at Northampton, 1735, 749.

Egerton, Thomas, lord chancellor, attempts to prevent the Essex treason, 108; confined at Essex House, *ib.*; liberated by Gorges, 109-11.

Election, annual charter, 1637; sergeants refuse escort to Winthrop, 461.

Elections held in meeting-houses, 743.

Eliot, John, reference to Hugh Peters, 375; 430; attends trial of Anne Hutchinson, 486; his evidence, 492; 507; takes oath, *ib.*; 525; 607; takes part in persecuting her after her confession, 526; charges her with lies, 529.

Elizabeth, of England, 45; sends Gorges to relief of Huguenots, 1591, 106; her relations with Essex, 107; sends Popham and Egerton to prevent his insurrectionary project, 108; her estimation of the plot, 110; 116; 248, *note*; 313; 316; her grants of land in America, 651.

Ellis, George E., cited as to synods, 468; as to Winthrop's conduct of trial of Anne Hutchinson, 488, *note*.

Emigrants to colonial New England, nationality of, 922.

Emigration from Old to New England, limit of, 689, 922.

Endicott, John, 155; arrives, 1628, at Salem, 209; extent of his territory, *ib.*; his application for land through Earl of Warwick, 210; hews down Morton's May-pole, 211; calls settlement Mount Dagon, *ib.*; his grant contested by Gorges, 213; sustained by the King, *ib.*; permits settlement at Mishawum, 217; encourages it, 218; his fur-trade policy, 219; encourages tobacco growing, 220; 224; calls a general court at Salem to consider difficulties with the older colonists, 225; statement of Morton as to his intolerance, *ib.*; called by Morton, Captain Littleworth, 228; his effort to arrest Morton, *ib.*; stayed by famine and sickness at Salem, 1629-30, *ib.*; refuses to receive Rev. Ralph Smith as a settler at Salem, 230; attends the trial of Morton, 1630, 241; his action respecting Morton discussed, 245; 249, 250; the severity of a judgment mitigated, 257; 259; beats Thomas Dexter, 260; his excuse, *ib.*; fined therefor, 261; 337; his affair with Ratcliff, 261; in the cases of persons punished by Court of Assistants, 262, *note*; out of harm's way, 279; mutilates royal banner, 1634, 287; 295; officiates at marriage of William Blackstone, 324; watches to arrest Morton, 1644, 346; 347, 354; major-general of Massachusetts Bay forces, 359; Doyle's opinion of, 378, *note*; his reading confined to theological disquisitions, 390; puts motion for removal of General Court to Cambridge, 450; chosen member of council for life, 455; 479; sits with Winthrop at trial of Anne Hutchinson, 487; 494; 503; his attitude towards Cotton, at trial, 514; 549; 551; mouthpiece of Hugh Peters, 572; his company called Separatists, 568; contempt for Coggeshall, 495.

England, prosperity under Charles I., 299; importance of peace to, *ib.*; civil war, 1688, 313; miserable state of church cause of fast-day in New England, 1637, 437; 817; government unfriendly to Puritan enterprise, 559; intellectual condition of, seventeenth century, 566; war with France, 641; 642; conquest of Canada, 641; war with Spain, 1718, 703; influence of its institutions upon those of New England, 815; its commercial forms followed, *ib.*; limit of emigration to colonial New England from, 922; Parliament, origin traced to Baltic settlements, 980.

English, adventurers, typified by Weston, 45; sports and games in New England, 179-81.

Enlistments for Revolutionary army, difficulties, 870; 873, 875-9, 892.

Epenow, Indian captured, 24, *note*; induces Gorges in 1614 to send an expe-

dition to New England, 26 ; goes with Hobson to Martha's Vineyard to find gold, 1614, 119 ; his character, 26–7 ; escapes at Martha's Vineyard, 27 ; meets Dermer, 1619, *ib.;* in attack upon Dermer at Martha's Vineyard, 1620, 27–8.
Epidemic among Indians, 1616–7, 1–4, 9–12.
Episcopacy in New England, 321 *et seq.;* 631 ; 634–5 ; of short duration at Weymouth, 342.
Episcopal Church, Braintree, opposed to the division of town, 822 ; its pro-Stamp Act interest, 840–3 ; in Braintree election, 1766, 843–4 ; a tory hotbed, 850 ; 851 ; 852 ; at Quincy, 930.
Erocoise, Lake, *i. e.* Iroquois, described in New English Canaan, 301 ; 314, 344.
Essex, Earl of, sent by Elizabeth to relief of Huguenots, 1591, 106 ; commands party sent out against Spain, 1597, *ib.;* his conspiracy, 107 ; his character, *ib.;* his relations with Elizabeth, *ib.;* his failure in Ireland, 1600, *ib.;* his treason conference, February, 1601, 108 ; his extrication planned by Gorges, *ib.;* captured at Essex House, 110 ; his trial, 111 – 12 ; effect of Gorges' testimony, *ib.;* his colloquy with him, *ib.;* the tribute of Gorges to, 114 ; his popularity, 115 ; the protector of the Puritans, 116 ; 117 ; the effect of Gorges' supposed disloyalty, among the Puritans of 1621, 126 ; 275 ; 313 ; 316 ; 317.
Essex House, meeting of conspirators at, 108, 109, 110.
Essex, a Salem privateer, 879.
Estaing, Count d', at Boston, 1758, 788.
Etter, Peter, of Braintree, 843.
Europe, seventeenth century thought in, 565 *et seq.*
Eustis, William, elected governor of Massachusetts, 1824, 915; vote for at Quincy, *ib.;* 945.
Evangelical Congregational religious society, Quincy, builds church, 1834, 930.
Evarts family, descendants of Joanna Hoar, 705.
Evarts, William Maxwell, 705.
Everett, Edward, votes at Quincy for, as governor, 948, 950.
Excommunication of Anne Hutchinson, from Boston church, 515–32.
Exeter, Dean of, of the Plymouth Company under charter of 1620, 122.
Exeter, England, Morton committed to jail in, 1630, 250 ; church dog-whipper, 744, *note.*
Exeter, New Hampshire, English emigrants, 1637, supposed to have settled at, 460 ; 1637, Wheelwright takes up residence at, 482 ; 539.
"Experience," religious, required of candidates for church - membership, 753.
Ezion-Geber, Arabia, burial place of W. P. Lunt, 641.
Faber, Joseph, cooper, Piscataqua settlement, 555.
Fairfield, Connecticut, John Hancock and Dorothy Quincy married at, 1775, 681.
Fairfax, Thomas, Lord, captures Bristol, 314 ; protects Sir F. Gorges, *ib.;* 317.
Falkland, Lord, slain at battle of Newbury, 313.
Farmers of New England, importance of, in shaping the state, 712 ; habits of saving, *ib.;* on equality with gentry and clergy, 713 ; send sons to college, *ib.*
Farm School Island, first occupied by David Thompson, 191.
Farm-hands, supplied with drink rations, 790.
Fast - day, 1637, Boston, sermon, by Wheelwright, 437–40 ; effect of, 441–50 ; 489 ; Mount Wollaston, 593 ; 1659, to restore habits of simple life, 802.
Faxon, Azariah, manifesto of Sept. 1786, 995.
Faxon, Henry H., of Quincy, advocate of total abstinence, 977–9 ; 979 ; 991.
Faxon family, in Braintree town records, 976.
Federalist party, Quincy devoted to, 909 ; 915, 945.
Fen hamlets, England, names of Danish origin, 369.
Ferrol, English expedition to, 1597, 106.
Ferries across Neponset river, 669, 672.
Feudal system, projected for America, 651.
ffinch, ——, master of French vessel, killed by Indians in Boston Bay, 8.
Fiat money, 1780, 883.
Fiddle in Braintree choir, 741.
Field, Ebenezer, of Braintree, 1766, 843.
Field, Job, a privateer, in Plymouth jail, 1781, 879.
Fields, William, of Braintree, 1728, declines office of constable, 825.
Fifth monarchy, 565.
Finances of the Revolution, 883–5.
Finch, Sir John, promotes ship-money tax scheme, 295.
Firearms, trade in, forbidden by King, 1622, 195 ; supplied to Indians by Morton, *ib.;* the evil effect of, 199 ; number in possession of Indians, 1627, 200 ; trade in, carried on by Morton, 244.
First Colony, afterwards called London Company, incorporated 1606, 118.
Fish in Monatiquot River, 1736, cause of contention at Braintree, 831–4.
Fisher, Fort, *see* Fort Fisher.
Fisheries, restrictions on Banks of Newfoundland, in 1620, Plymouth Com-

## INDEX.    1029

pany charter, 123; North Atlantic coast, protection of, 1622, 132; 133, *note.*
Fiske, Anna, daughter of Rev. Thomas Shepard, widow of Daniel Quincy, second wife of Moses, 615.
Fiske, Moses, made minister of Braintree church, 1672, 607; his family connections and children, 609; 612; 613; 614; his second wife, 615, 707; 623; his salary, 642; 693; his pew in meeting-house, 1700, 735; 748; his records of church discipline, 754-8; 760; 821; 822.
Fitcher, ——, succeeds Rasdell in command of Wollaston's settlement, 168; Morton supersedes him, 1626, 174; not mentioned by Morton, 174, *note;* takes refuge at Wessagusset, 175.
Fleet prison, Winslow's confinement in, 1635, 282, 344.
Flint, Henry, *see* Flynt, Henry.
Flora, May-day revels a survival of the worship of, 182.
Florence, Italy, plague, 1.
Flushing, Long Island, Underhill's residence at, 558, *note.*
Flynt, Dorothy, "Dorothy Q." the wife of Edmund Quincy, 4th, 605; her descendants, 702.
Flynt, Henry, first teacher Braintree church, 586; ordained, 1640, 596; made minister of same, 1659, 603; duration of ministry, 748; account of his life, 603; on probation because of adherence to Wheelwright, *ib.;* his wife, Margery Hoar, 604; 705; his descendants, 605; 643; 647; his last will, 603.
Flynt, Henry [2d], son of Josiah, grandson of Rev. Henry, tutor at Harvard, 605; his character, 606; his journey to Portsmouth, 1755, 677, 787.
Flynt, Josiah, son of Rev. Henry, father of "Dorothy Q.," 605; candidate, for ministry at Braintree, 606; accepts call at Dorchester, 607; his name given to grandson, 702.
Folk-mote, theory of derivation of town-meeting from, 814; 815.
Food, in colonial New England, 685-6; 806, 807.
Fort Duquesne, 835.
Fort Fisher, North Carolina, captured by General Terry, 705.
Fort William Henry, capitulation of, 1757, 836, 875.
Fortress Monroe, Va., 962.
Fortune, ship sent to New England by Weston, July, 1621, 48; her arrival, Nov., 35; returns to England with cargo of skins, 35; 48; brings Cushman and Trevore, 1622, 130.
Fourth of July, celebration, Quincy, 1826, 920; day of John Adams' death, *ib.*
Fourth Regiment, Mass. Militia, 962.

Fox, George, voyage from Newport to New York, 1672, 598.
Fox, Thomas, punished by Court of Assistants, 262, *note.*
Foxcroft, Rev. ——, of Boston First Church, Briant's allusion to, 639; his reply, *ib.*
France, 270; 476; colonial wars with, 912; war with England, 641; 642; war with Great Britain, 1793, 906; intellectual condition of, seventeenth century, 566; 567.
Franklin, Benjamin, prediction as to increase of population in America, 689; friend of Josiah Quincy, 1st, 704.
Frederick II. of Prussia, 874.
Freeman, Edward A., on dog law of Edgar, 745, *note.*
Freemen in Mass., church-members only, until 1693, 747.
Free-soil party, convention, 1848, Buffalo, 955; vote of, at Quincy, 956; its influence, *ib.;* its strength at Quincy, 957.
French emigrants to colonial Massachusetts, 922.
French, encroachments of, on Plymouth colony, 1634, 280; a pretext made by Mass. Bay for not returning charter, 306.
——, fleet at Boston, 1778, 788.
——, traders in Boston Bay, 6; attacked by Indians, 7-8; vessel captures one of Gorges' under Captain John Smith, 1615, 119.
——, war, 1690, Braintree's contribution of men to, 830; burden of, on New England, 827; 835-7; of 1744, 767.
French, Samuel, of Braintree, 623.
Friendship, vessel, men fined for drinking on, 356.
Friesland, village moots of, 980.
Fuller, Dr. Samuel, takes care of the sick of Weston's company, 61; on condition of settlers at Charlestown, 1630, 236; 344; death from small-pox, 1634, 3.
Fur trade, conserved to Plymouth Company, in charter of 1620, 123-4; Morton engages in, 194; the profits of, 196; importance to the Mass. Company, 216; policy to make it a government monopoly, 219.
Furnace Brook, Braintree, site of iron-works, 923.
Furniture in New England, 684.

Gage, General Thomas, takes powder from Charlestown, 1774, 850; alarm caused by his foraging parties, 856-7; restores Nantasket lighthouse, destroyed by militia, 1775, 861; return to England, 864.
Gager, ——, one of Winthrop's party, death of, 1630, 236.

Galleries in New England meeting-houses, 736.
Games and sports frowned upon in New England, 179–81.
Gardiner, Sir Christopher, the story of, 250–8; assumed to be Gorges' agent, 252; his female companion, *ib.*; his reasons for coming to America, 253; his marriage relations, *ib.*; General Court orders his return to England, 254; escapes from officers sent to arrest him, *ib.*; finds place of concealment in the forest, *ib.*; his hiding-place revealed by Indians, 255; captured, *ib.*; taken to Boston, 256; his letters opened by Winthrop, 257; in favor at Boston, 257; 259; Winthrop's policy towards, 258; goes to Maine, *ib.*; obtains mitigation of Ratcliff's punishment, 261; witness for Gorges in attack on Mass. Bay charter, 1632, 263 *et seq.*; disappears from history, 268; 275; 283; 321; cited in charges against Morton, 346; 582; 930.
Gardiner, Lady, wife of Sir Christopher, 253.
Gardiner, Stephen, Bishop of Winchester, 251.
Gates, Horatio, on "dreaming deacons" in army, 886; defeated at Camden, 1780, 891.
Gay, Ebenezer, minister of Hingham, sermon on submission to Stamp Act, 840.
Gaza, 211.
Geddes, Jenny, story of stool-throwing at St. Giles', 300.
General Court of Plymouth, Oldham and Lyford tried for conspiracy, 1624, 187, 188.
General Court, *see* Mass. Bay, General Court.
Gennison, Ancient, appointed receiver of Thomas Walford's effects, 337.
George I. of England, war with Spain, 1718, 703.
George, vessel of Mass. Co., bringing settlers, arrives at Salem, 1629, 217.
George's Island, Boston Bay, 1776, 867.
German emigrants to Massachusetts, 1752, 922; descendants of, *ib.*; 923.
Germantown, Braintree, alarm from British foraging party, 1775, 857; colonial militia stationed at, 860; 861; glass works at, 924.
Germany, the miserable state of its churches a cause of fast-day in New England, 1637, 437; seventeenth century intellectual condition of, 566; theory of derivation of town-meeting from "Tun" of, 814; 815.
Gerry, Elbridge, 910.
Gibbons, Ambrose, of Piscataqua, 354.
Gibbons, Capt. Edward, 333, *note*; 343; his story in New England, 354; one of the Mt. Wollaston Company, *ib.*; his conversion, 355–60; his conduct at Salem, 356; fined for disorderly behavior, *ib.*; marries, *ib.*; captain of Boston train-band, 357; suspected of piracy, *ib.*; his wonderful deliverance, 358; involved in La Tour's schemes in Acadia, 1645, *ib;* entertains him at Boston, *ib.*; his residence, *ib.*; in command of Suffolk regiment, *ib.*; his later military services, 359; Mather's account of his character, 360; visit to Aquidneck to warn Mrs. Hutchinson's companions, 537; Underhill his guest, 1640; 558; major-general of Massachusetts, 1645, in Indian war, 828.
Gift, the ship, 243.
Glasgow, Scotch General Assembly, 1638, convened at, 306; University of, makes Cotton Mather, D. D., 630.
Glass works at Germantown, Braintree, 924.
Gloucester, England, Charles Hoar, sheriff of, 704; 706.
Gloucester, Mass., Lyford settles on site of, 190; 346, 912.
Gooch, Dr. Barnaby, treasurer of Council for New England, 1622; his share of New England, drawn at Greenwich, 139.
Gooch, Joseph, by intrigues takes command of Suffolk regiment from John Quincy, 1742, 708; 715; offer of captaincy to John Adams, 1st, declined, 708, 715.
Gookin, Elizabeth, widow of John Eliot, Jr., marries Edmund Quincy, 3d, 701.
Gookins, Daniel, removes from Virginia to New England, 599.
Gorgeana, a city founded, 1642, by Sir F. Gorges in Maine, judicial procedure, 311.
Gorges family, their troubles with Maine patent, 316; they sell the same, *ib.*
Gorges, Lord Edward, council meeting, 1635, at his house, for redivision of New England, 283; territory allotted to, 283; 651, 652.
Gorges, Elizabeth, wife of Sir Ferdinando, 315.
Gorges, Sir Ferdinando, his history and character, 105–6; 316–20; at the siege of Sluys, 1587, 106; at siege of Paris, 1589, *ib.*; sent to aid of Huguenots, 1591, *ib.*; at siege of Rochelle, 317; refuses to give up the Neptune to Richelieu, *ib.*; at siege of Rouen, 106; military governor of Plymouth, England, *ib.*; sent with Essex in expedition against Spain, 1597, *ib.*; a friend and partisan of Essex, 107; concerned in the Essex treason, 1601, *ib.*; his unsuccessful scheme to extricate Essex, 107–10; his examination and testimony at trial, 111–14; his tribute to Essex, 115; believed by Puritans to have betrayed him, 116; released from prison by James I., 117; and restored

# INDEX. 1031

to his position of Governor of Plymouth, *ib.*; occupied with schemes concerning America, *ib.*; takes under his protection Indians carried to England by Weymouth, *ib.*; cited as to Squanto's capture and captivity, 23-4, *notes*, 45; relations with Popham, 117; with him obtains royal patents for colonization in America, 1606-7; 117-18; attaches himself to the Plymouth Company, 118; his first exploring party captured by Spanish, 1606, *ib.*; in the control of company, *ib.*; his remarks on his position, 119; continues his trading and exploring ventures to America, 1608-20, *ib.*; sends vessel to Martha's Vineyard, 1614, *ib.*; 1615, sends out vessel under command of Captain John Smith, *ib.*; want of success of his ventures, 119-20; his knowledge of New England, 120; its erroneous character, *ib.*; 1620, obtains charter superseding that of Plymouth Company, 121; his associates under charter, 122; his sagacity in selection of them, 124; the territory granted by new charter, *ib.*; charter assailed by Virginia Company, *ib.*; is sustained, 125; the advantage of the Puritan establishment to, *ib.*; his difficulty in persuading settlers to go to New England, *ib.*; issues a patent to the Plymouth colonists, *ib.*; ignorant of the Puritan expedition, 126; his difficulties with the English Parliament of 1621, *ib.*; summoned to answer charges of the Virginia Company, 127; Sir Edward Coke's dislike of, 126-7; his examination before the House of Commons of 1621, 127-8; his answers in the case, 128; the contention quieted, 129; his scheme given a death-blow, *ib.*; informed by Trevore as to Boston Bay, 130, *note*; 1622, organizes Council for New England, 131; complaint against Weston, *ib.*; on protection of fisheries, 132; proposes to govern in New England, 133; recalls Robert Gorges, 1622, 134; his knowledge of New England, *ib.*; 136-7, *note*; his son Robert, governor of New England, 137; holds meeting at Greenwich, June, 1623, to allot territory in New England, 138-9; his share drawn at meeting, 139; his establishment for his son in New England, 141; attached to Church of England, 142; a high churchman, 222; his plans for a church in New England, 142; his expectations from the 1623 colony, 143; his anger on account of Thomas Weston, 145; censured by Council for New England, *ib.*; his colony not supported, 1623-4, 152; advises return of his son, *ib.*; 191; Morton's offences explained to, by Plymouth magistrates, 1628, 208; 210; contests the grant made to Endicott, 213; his struggle to preserve his territory through Oldham, 214; his inconsistency as to trade in firearms, 221; his policy in aiding Morton, 222-3; his patent endangered by Massachusetts Company, 222; aids Allerton to obtain patent to lands on the Kennebec, 224; 249; Morton supposed to be an emissary of, *ib.*; a tool of, in England, 250; their relations after 1630, 250; Sir Christopher Gardiner supposed to have been his agent in New England, 252; his letters to Gardiner, opened by Winthrop, 257; a letter to Morton, among them, 258; aided in his attack on charter by Morton, Gardiner, etc., 1632, 263-4; attack fails, 266-7; retains Ratcliff to serve in attacks on charter, 268; relations with Morton subsequent to 1632, 268; 343; influence on Laud, 271; 1634, renews attack on charter, 271 *et seq.*; influences James I. through Buckingham, 1622, 275; through Laud, 1634, 276; persistent to his ruin in efforts in New England, *ib.*; determination to maintain his claim unimpaired, *ib.*; his scheme of 1634, *ib.*; obtains royal patent for Commission to govern New England, 277; plans for going to New England as governor-general, 280; 281; at examination of Winslow by Lords Commissioners, 282; territory allotted to in partition of 1635, 283; hopes revive, 282; makes new division of territory on New England seacoast, 283; announced as governor-general in New England, *ib.*; Maverick suspected because of his relations with, 288; false alarm of his arrival in Boston, April, 1635, 288; cause of failure of 1635 expedition, 289-93; dubious prospect of his scheme, 1637, 296; attached to Laud's party, *ib.*; his schemes affected by remoteness of his government, 296-7; 300; sends by Cleeve, 1637, patent of government for Maine, 301; his attitude towards office of governor-general, *ib.*; his probable policy, 302-3; his letter to Winthrop, Sept. 1637, 303; 305; 307; defeated in assault on charter, 308; system for government of Maine, 309; obtains, 1639, patent for Maine, 309, extent of same, *ib.*; founds a city called Gorgeana, 311; his projects come to an end, 313; plans royalist attack on Bristol, *ib.*; his house occupied by royalist forces, 1643, *ib.*; taken prisoner by Fairfax, 314; submits to Parliament, *ib.*; his title to Maine questioned, *ib.*; Parliament sustains Rigby's claim to part of it, 315; subsequent history of the patent, 316; story of his colonists, 321; 342;

grants land at Agamenticus to Maverick, 330; 331; royalist during civil war, 344; 347; Bagnall's claim on Richmond Island, 352; 373, 539, 583, 616; his death, 1647, 315.

Gorges, Ferdinando, grandson of Sir Ferdinando, sells property in Maine, 316.

Gorges, Henry, father of Thomas, cousin of Sir Ferdinando, 310.

Gorges, John, son of Sir Ferdinando, grants of land to Oldham, 212; grant to, 215; 217; his land colonized by Endicott's people, 220.

Gorges, Robert, son of Sir Ferdinando, his colonization enterprise in New England, 105; unlike Thomas Weston, *ib.*, 154; the probable extent of his territory, 131, *note;* his ambition in his father's plantation, 133; enters the service of Venice, *ib.;* recalled by his father, *ib.;* appointed governor, 153; the establishment proposed for his government, 135; patent for land issued to, December, 1622, 136; extent of territory, 136; his efforts in collecting colony, 137; 138; with his colonists sails for New England, 141; arrives in Boston Bay, September, *ib.;* commissioned lieutenant, *ib.;* his council, *ib.;* his jurisdiction, 141-2; his father's hopes in the colony, 143; character of colonists, *ib.;* 144, *note;* takes possession of the buildings at Wessagusset, 144; announces his arrival and his authority as governor, *ib.;* starts for coast of Maine, in search of Weston, 144-5; in stress of weather takes shelter at Plymouth, 148; finds Weston there, *ib.;* his threats to arrest him, *ib.;* mollified by Bradford, 148-9; discharges him, 149; returns to Wessagusset, 149-50; his seamen set fire to buildings at Plymouth, 150; his ship goes to Virginia, *ib.;* he seizes the Swan, *ib.;* spends winter of 1623-4 at Wessagusset, 151; Weston in arrest at, *ib.;* spring of 1624 goes to Piscataqua, 152, 192; returns to England, 153; supposed to have died soon after his return, 153, 154; his settlement abandoned, 153-4; Puritan settlers troubled by his claim in New England, 155; his character, *ib.;* the results of his attempt in Boston Bay, 155; the fate of his settlement, 156; 161, 163, 168, 184, 212; the Massachusetts Company seek to set aside his grant, 216; his plantation on the Piscataqua, increased, 236; 240; 258; his expedition of 1623, 289; 329; story of his Boston Bay colonists, 321; his settlement a permanent one, 342; 616.

Gorges, Thomas, cousin of Sir Ferdinando, sent in 1640, governor of Maine, 309-10; visits Agamenticus, 311; difficulties with Burdett, his discipline at Agamenticus, retirement from government, 311-12.

Gorges, William, nephew of Sir Ferdinando, appointed governor of New Somersetshire, 1635, 308; extent of his jurisdiction, *ib.;* returns to England, 309.

Gorton, Samuel, Quaker, 409, *note.*

Gouch, Ruth, disciplined at Agamenticus by Gorges, 312.

Government by town-meeting, 810-26.

Gracchus, Caius Sempronius, 452.

Grace, Covenant of, discussed, 403-6.

Granite quarries, Quincy, their development, 924-8.

Granite railway, of Quincy, built, 1826, 591; projected and constructed by Gridley Bryant, 926.

Grants of land by the Council for New England, 212; list of, 213; *note;* Endicott's contested by Gorges, but sustained, 213.

Graves, Thomas, with the Spragues, founds Charlestown, 1629, 218; 234.

Graveyard, Quincy, its condition prior to 1809, 905-6; title to, conveyed to town, 906.

Gray, John, an original purchaser at Nantasket, 183.

Gray, Thomas, an original purchaser at Nantasket, 183.

Gray, Thomas, his Elegy quoted, 716.

Great Awakening, religious revival in New England, 1739, 749; 763.

Great Britain, Navigation Acts, 697; war with France declared, 1756, 835; of 1793, Quincy's action in, 906; John Adams minister to, 888; treaty of peace with United States, 1783, 893; war with United States, 1812-14, 909-12; men-of-war on New England coast, 910; C. F. Adams, United States minister to, 1861-8, 961. *See* England.

Great Watt, Indian name for Bagnall, 352.

Green, John Richard, on origin of town-meeting government, 980.

Greene, General Nathanael, 764.

Greene, Richard, employed by Weston 55; 163; at Plymouth, 1622, 59; his relations with the Indians, 60; in charge of plantation at Wessagusset, 62; asks food for Wessagusset people, 1622, *ib.;* death of, *ib.*

Greene, Robert, dramatist, on dogs in churches, 745, *note.*

Greene, William, endeavors to inform Plymouth of Weston's 1622 expedition, 56; 57.

Greenleaf, Thomas, of Quincy, rebuked by John Adams, 909; a representative Federalist, *ib.;* leadership at Quincy, his life and services to the town, 917-18, 920; 933; moderator Quincy town-meetings, 947; in Quincy politics, 948, 955; 967.

# INDEX. 1033

Greensmith, Stephen, fined for opinion as to ministers under Covenant of Works, 442.
Greenwich, England, allotment of territory in New England, June 29, 1623, 138-9, 140, 141, 209, 283, 651.
Gridley, Jeremiah, entertains S. Quincy and John Adams on their admission to bar, 1758, 788; retained to support memorial for opening law-courts, 1765, 839.
Gridley, Richard, a follower of Anne Hutchinson, 400.
Grievances, Parliament of 1621, 126.
Grotius, Hugo, his works, in Christ Church library, Quincy, 804.
Grove, Mary, the companion of Sir Christopher Gardiner, 252; arrested, 254; data concerning her, 256-7, notes; married to Thomas Purchase, 258; her death, ib.
Guerriere, British ship captured by Constitution, 1812, 911.
Gunpowder kept in meeting-houses, 743; removed from Charlestown by Gage, 1774, 850; from North Precinct meeting-house by people, 850-1, 854.
Guns supplied to Indians by Morton, 195.
Gurnet, Point, 38, 52.
Guy Fawkes' day at Plymouth, 1623, 150.

Habits of life, past and present, 802-3, 806-9.
Haddington, Thomas Hamilton, Earl of, in Plymouth Company, charter of 1620, 122.
Hague, Holland, John Adams at the, 879.
Halberd bearers, refuse attendance on Winthrop 1637, 461; prosecuted, 509-10.
Half Moon Island, Boston Bay, 681.
Halifax, British soldiers transferred from, to Boston, 1768, 847.
Hallam, Henry, tribute to Hudibras, 81; on the Histrio-Mastix of Prynne, 262; on lumber in libraries, 366-7.
Hamilton, James, 2d marquess, of the Plymouth Company, 122; influence at court for charter, 124; his share in New England, partition of 1635, 233.
Hampden, John, in the ship-money case, 296, 306; purchases land on Narragansett Bay, 299; 317, 450, 710.
Hancock, John, minister at Lexington, then of Braintree, 616; ordained, 1726, 618, 619; his support, 618; called "Bishop," ib.; father of Governor John, ib.; cited as to Braintree meeting-house, 592-3; his centennial sermon, 1739, 620; influence in settlement of church-tax question, 1727, 629; new meeting-house during his pastorate, 737; 748; his death, 1744, 749; 763; his church records, 750;

church discipline of his pastorate, 796.
Hancock, John, son of Rev. John, born, 617, 618; marriage with Dorothy Quincy, 1775, 680-1; 784; rumored departure of, for England, 1776, 865; vote of Braintree for, as governor, 891; 893, 898; approves act creating town of Quincy, 1792, 903; his name suggested for new town, 904.
Hancock Light Guard, Quincy, in War of Rebellion, 962.
Hancock, lot, Braintree, Josiah Quincy's dwelling on, 703.
Hancock mansion, Boston, built of Quincy granite, 924.
Handmaid, ship, Morton sent to England in, 1630, 243; 244, note.
Hanging at Wessagusset, Morton's account of, 79-81; allusion to, in Hudibras, 81-2.
Hanson, Captain, companions of R. Gorges in New England, 151; sent to Plymouth to arrest Weston and seize the Swan, ib.
Hard-cider political campaign, 1840, 949.
Harlakenden, Roger, at trial of Anne Hutchinson, 495-7.
Harlow, Captain Edward, Epenow kidnapped by, 24-5, note; 26.
Harrison, Thomas, regicide, his head fastened to the hurdle of John Cook, 376, note.
Harrison, William Henry, in election of 1838, 952.
Hartford, Conn., 467.
Harvard College, instituted for supplying ministers, 733; old rule for order of students' names in catalogue, 733; 739; Stoughton Hall, 668; Braintree a benefactor of, 767; its library, 804; its third president, Hoar, 704; 716; Samuel Willard, vice president, 1732, 720; President Quincy, 856, 910; John Quincy graduate of, 615; Ebenezer Miller, 1722, 621; Benjamin Tompson, Braintree schoolmaster, 769, 771; Thomas Greenleaf, 917.
Harvest, 1621, at Plymouth, 34.
Hawkins, Jane, follower of Anne Hutchinson, 400, and note.
Haynes, John, Governor of Massachusetts Bay, 1635, 371; 377; at reconciliation meeting of Dudley and Winthrop, 1636; 379; superseded by Vane, 1636, 380.
Hayward, Joshua, of Lord's Day committee, Braintree meeting, 1783, 894.
Hazelrig, Sir Arthur, member of Commission for Plantations under Parliamentary government, 315.
Health and disease in colonial Massachusetts, 800-1.
Heaton, Nat., Dedham dog-whipper, 745, note.
Hebrew Bible, the basis of Puritan law and government, 382 et seq.

## 1034　INDEX.

Hell Gate, East River, N. Y., Dermer in danger of wreck in, 1619, 27; proximity of Anne Hutchinson's residence to, 537.
"Hell-huddle," common name for pauper settlements, 722.
Henry VIII., of England, 248, *note;* his grants of lands, 651.
Henry IV., of France at siege of Paris, 1589, takes Gorges wounded from the breach, 106; edict of Nantes, 248, *note.*
Heresies in the Boston Church, consequent on the Anne Hutchinson dissension, 1637, 430.
Hessian soldiers at Saratoga, 874.
Highways of Braintree, 666-79.
Higginson, Rev. Francis, cited, 173.
High commission of England, 278; the General Court likened to, 444.
Hill, Isaac, New Hampshire politician, 946.
Hilton, Edward, of Dover, New Hampshire, Winthrop's letter to, concerning Underhill, 554.
Hiltons, of Dover, 201.
Hingham, Mass., formerly Bear Cove, 338; 364, 582; church of, established, 1635, 586; Peter Hobart, minister, 1640, 595; Lemuel Briant dies at, 1754, 641; coast road from Newbury to, 666; Rev. John Norton, third pastor of, 707; 717; meeting-house seats appropriated to negro servants and Indians, 738, *note;* to English boys, *ib.;* overseers appointed, *ib.;* minister's sermon on submission to Stamp Act, 840; provisions for defence, war of 1812, 912.
Hinsdale, Mrs., under ordeal of relating religious "experience," 753.
Hoar, Charles, sheriff of Gloucester, England, 704.
Hoar, Joanna, widow of Charles, comes to New England, 704; dies, 1661, buried at Braintree, her offspring, 705.
Hoar, Joanna, daughter of Charles and Joanna, first wife of Edmund Quincy, 3d, 701; her history, 704-6; her descendants, 705; 706.
Hoar, Leonard, third president of Harvard, 704; his wife and mother buried with him at Braintree, *ib.;* Marshall mends monument to, 718.
Hoar, Margery, wife of Henry Flynt, buried in Quincy, 604; her progeny, 605.
Hobamack, Indian, friend to the Plymouth colonists, 33; Corbitant quarrels with, *ib.;* land allotted to, at Plymouth, *ib.;* regarded a rival by Squanto, 37; who plots to undermine him, 37-40; he excites suspicion of Squanto's loyalty, 37; accompanies Winslow on visit to Massasoit, March, 1623, 72; informed by Massasoit of plot to destroy Wessagusset, 73; accompanies Standish on expedition to Wessagusset, 90; his part in fight with Aberdecest, 94.
Hobart, Daniel, of Braintree, 907.
Hobart, Peter, of Hingham, 595.
Hobson, Captain, commands vessel sent to Martha's Vineyard in 1614, 119.
Holbrook, Samuel, moderator of Braintree meeting, 1783, for consideration of Lord's Day, 894.
Holderness, Earl of, Casco Bay, his share of New England at Greenwich partition, 1623, 139.
Holland, John, of Dorchester, his ferry across Neponset, 1635, 669-70.
Holland, the Pilgrims in, 45, 75.
Holmes, Obadiah, cited as to Wilson's treatment of Quakers, 408, *note.*
Holmes, Oliver Wendell, poem, "Dorothy Q.," 605.
Holmes family, descendants of "Dorothy Q.," 605.
Hook, Walter Farquhar, on religious intolerance of Puritans, 248, *note.*
Hooker, Rev. Thomas, 377; one of committee for reconciliation between Dudley and Winthrop, 1636, 379; 466; pastor of church at Cambridge, 484.
Hopkins, Ann, considered crazy by Winthrop, 399.
Hopkins, Stephen, joint ambassador to Massasoit from Plymouth colony, 1621, 30.
Hospitals, Quincy, 1792, 906.
Hough, Atherton, a resident of Mount Wollaston, 415; not in sympathy with minister Wilson, 426; elected to General Court by freemen of Boston, 1637, 455; election set aside, *ib.;* re-elected, 456; 475; made responsible for Wheelwright's keep while remaining in Mass., 481; 568; acquires territory at Wessagusset, 1634, 583; his name preserved in Hough's Neck, Quincy Bay, 625.
Hough's Neck. William Veazie's farm at, 625; corruption of name, *ib., note.*
Houses, at Braintree, seventeenth century, 680-4.
House of Commons, England, Revenue Bill of 1767, 846.
Howe, Lord, killed at Ticonderoga, 1758, 836.
Howes, Edward, letter to J. Winthrop, Jr., cited, 259, *note.*
Hudibras, Hallam's tribute to, 81; story of the Wessagusset hanging in, 81-2.
Hudson river, Mrs. Hutchinson's residence at mouth of, 538.
Hue's Cross, renamed Hue's Folly, 339.
Huguenots at Rochelle, English expedition for relief of, 1591, 106; 317.
Hull, Isaac, Captain, U. S. N., breakfasts with Josiah Quincy, 1812, 911; 912.
Hull, John, at marriage of Daniel Quincy, 706.

## INDEX. 1035

Hull, Mrs., at Daniel Quincy's wedding, 706.
Hull, Rev. Joseph, minister at Weymouth, 1635, 340; 368.
Hull, Mass., the Plymouth people establish a trading station at, 160; settlement at, 1622, 183; population of, 1627, 193; 229; passengers from the Mary & John landed at, 232; military station at, 1776, 874.
Hume, David, on authority of royal proclamations, 202; 203; on writings of Sir Harry Vane, 373.
Humphrey, John, an early settler of Swampscott, 265, *note;* scandal in N. E., caused by his daughters, *ib.;* in defence of Mass. Bay charter, 265; 278, 282, 286, 347.
Humphrey, Lady Susan, 266, *note.*
Hunt, John, of Braintree, 832; 835.
Hunt, Mrs. Ruth, at Mrs. Edmund Quincy's funeral, 700, 679.
Hunt, Captain Thomas, 1614, kidnapper of Indians, 7; capture of Squanto, 23; 24, 25, 31-2.
Hunt's Hill, Mass., site of Wessagusset, 61, *note.*
Husking at Dedham, 1767, 791.
Hutchinson, Anne, controversy excited by, 1637, 331; comes to New England, 1634, 370; 371; her house the intellectual centre of Boston, 381; her intelligence and wit, described by Weld, *ib.;* disturbs the peace of Boston, *ib.;* her revolt against the oligarchy, *ib.;* one of her adherents frozen to death, 388-9; said to have been a cousin to John Dryden, 392; her home in England, 393; her personal appearance, *ib.;* her religious emotions, *ib.;* her course towards the New England clergy, 395; her early career at Boston, 397; her residence, *ib.;* her weekly female meetings, 397, 398; her visions, 399; the growth of her influence in Boston, 397-400; her follower Jane Hawkins, 400, and *note;* shows publicly contempt for Boston preachers, 401; her discrimination between the Covenant of Grace and of Works, 402; dislike of Rev. John Wilson, 407; her quarrel with him, 1636, 410 *et seq.;* Cotton and Wheelwright her favorite preachers, 411; supported by Vane, *ib.;* intimates Wilson to be under Covenant of Works, 412; her party his opponents, 412; advanced religious tenets, 413; her revolt against Wilson, 418; her friends try to prevent Vane's resignation of governorship, 422; in December, 1636, summoned before magistrates and clergy, 426; account of conference, 426-8; her relations with Cotton and Vane, 1637, 430; name Antinomian misapplied to, 435; the religious phase of struggle, between her and Wilson, 436; loved in Boston, hated in churches outside, *ib.;* not fully sympathized with by Wheelwright, *ib.;* her effect on his reputation, *ib.;* derisive names given her, 437; Wheelwright's 1637 fast-day sermon preconcerted with her, 438; her opponents in control of churches, 442; difficulties with Wilson not adjusted, May, 1637, 451; her adherents in minority in General Court, 1637, 456; her brother-in-law comes to Boston, 1637, 459; her weekly meetings voted disorderly by Synod of 1637, 474; disregards the decision of Synod of 1637, 475; her exile determined on by magistrates, 476; 479, 481; arraigned by General Court, 483; great interest in her trial, 486; her condition and demeanor at trial, 487; her offence stated by Winthrop, 489; her defence, *ib.;* her altercation with Winthrop, 490; charged with discriminating between Cotton and other ministers, 491; development of character of trial, 492; demands testimony under oath, 494; called on to produce testimony, 496; her first witness browbeaten, *ib.;* her unfortunate speech to the court, 499-501; hopes delivery by special providence, 502; her case injured by her conduct of it, 497; charged by Dudley as possessed of the devil, 505; banished by General Court, 508; duration of her trial, 509; permitted to remain at Roxbury until spring of 1638, *ib.;* 511; beset at Roxbury by ministers, 512; banished for traducing ministers, 513; her life at Roxbury, 1637-8, *ib.;* abandoned by Cotton, 514; found to be the root of all dissensions, 515; indicted by the church, *ib.;* permitted to leave Roxbury to appear before the church, 516; proceedings begun March, 1638, *ib.;* cause of excitement, *ib.;* the importance of an excommunication, 517; appears before church, 518; her denunciation of Wilson, *ib.;* her attempt at vindication, *ib.;* effect of Davenport's remarks upon her, 519; deprived of advocacy of her son and son-in-law, 520; posed with a charge of inclining to doctrine of community of women, 522, *note;* persuaded by Cotton and Davenport, confesses her errors to the church, 523; a humiliation to Wilson to be ignored by her, 524; attacked by Shepard, 525; her confession not sufficient, recantation required, 527; victim of inquisition, 528; 529; charged with lying, 529; 530; excommunicated, 531; 532; the public feeling at Boston in her favor and against Winthrop, 533-4; the story of her subsequent history. 533-9; 1637, her faction dispersed, 535; her physical trials, *ib.*, and note; remains

1036   INDEX.

in her own house after excommunication, 536; 1638, warrant issued for her removal from Mass. Bay, *ib.*; goes to Aquidneck, R. I., 536–7; pursued by intolerant authorities of Boston church, 537; 1642, her husband dies, *ib.*; removes to Manhattan Island, *ib.*; slain by Indians, 538; her misfortunes and death complacently regarded by Boston church, *ib.*; her daughter redeemed from Indian captivity, *ib.*; her fate contrasted with Wheelwright's, 539; 540, 542, 546, 547, 548, 552, 556, 559, 563; her career in New England, typical of the times, 566; 567, 568, 569, 570, 571, 572, 573, 574, 576.

Hutchinson, Edward of Alford, his daughter Mary marries John Wheelwright, 370.

Hutchinson, Mrs. Edward, mother of William, and Mrs. Wheelwright, shares exile with Wheelwright, and dies in Maine, 539.

Hutchinson, Edward, refractory Boston sergeant, fined by General Court, 510; fine remitted on condition of his leaving colony, *ib.*

Hutchinson, Mary, daughter of Edward, the wife of John Wheelwright, 370.

Hutchinson, Samuel, assaulted by Thomas Dexter, 260.

Hutchinson, Samuel, brother of William, comes to Boston, 459; ordered to remove from Mass. Bay under the alien law, 460; 463.

Hutchinson, Governor Thomas, cited as to Gorges' projects for New England, 319; as to Blackstone's removal from Boston, 323; as to the basis of New England law, 348, *note*; 568; as to dispersion of colonial army, 1756, 856; comments on Boston's call for convention, 1768, 847; on increase of population in America, 689; leaves America, 1774, 850.

Hutchinson, William, with his wife Anne, comes to New England, 370; brother-in-law of Wheelwright, 381; his character, *ib.*; allotted lands at Mount Wollaston, by General Court, 1636-7, 366, and *note*; seen by his wife in a vision, in the governor's chair, 399; 415, 459, 508; death of, 1642, 537.

Hyde, Nicholas, a warrant for Morton, issued by, 246.

Immorality, colonial times, 783–99.
Impressments, 1690, fail at Quincy, 830; unwillingness in Massachusetts to submit to, 875, 892.
Independents, religious party, 248, *note*.
Indians, kidnapped by traders on New England coast, 5–7; pestilence among, 1616-7, 1-4, 9-12; described prior to pestilence, 9; inhabit islands in Boston Bay, *ib.*; make friends with Weston's party of 1622, 60; fear of colonists overcome, *ib.*; complain of illusage from same, 61; on Cape Cod, supply crew of Swan with food, 63; attacked by pestilence, 1622, 64; robbed by Wessagusset people, *ib.*; 65, 66; conspiracy to destroy Wessagusset settlement, 73, 85-6; probable effect of the success, on Plymouth, *ib.*; treatment of Weston's people, time of 1623 famine, 77; 78; their sufferings from . Weston's people, *ib.*; they surmise the purpose of Standish's visit to Wessagusset, 91; their plot prevented by him, 92–5; his captives confined in the Plymouth fort, 98; the historical treatment of, by the whites, 100; the propriety of Standish's conduct toward them, 101; a widespread conspiracy fails, 101–2; 811; their warfare contrasted with that of civilized nations, 102; their fear of Standish, 103; wholly demoralized after Wessagusset affair, 104; at mouth of Merrimack strip Thomas Weston, 146; desire spirits and firearms, 194–5; engage in fur trade with Morton, 194 *et seq.*; ally themselves with him, 195; act as his guides and huntsmen, *ib.*; effect of Morton's dealings on, 197; dangers of trade in spirits and guns with, 199; bewailed by Bradford, *ib.*; number of weapons supplied to, 200; Morton's dealings with, 245; reveal hiding-place of Gardiner, 255; their friendly relations with Blackstone, 327; remnants of Massachusetts tribe in 1630, 363; survivors, 1637, 581; five carried off by the devil, 389; massacre of Mrs. Hutchinson and family by, August, 1642, 538; land titles in New England derived from, 653; provision in Hingham meeting-house, for seating, 738, *note*; wars of, in Massachusetts, 827–30; their trail along the coast of Boston Bay, 581; Casco tribe, party of, murder Bagnall, 352-3; Black Will, one of Lynn tribe, hanged for murder of Bagnall, 353; massacre in Virginia, March 22, 1622, 74.

Industries at Braintree, prior to 1825, 923 *et seq.*
Inhabitant, colonial definition of word, 647.
Insane, old-time treatment of, 724 *et seq.*
Institutions of New England, origin of, traced to primitive systems of Europe, 814, 815.
Instruction, Quincy schools, 935–7.
Intemperance in colonial New England, 783–99; among clergy, 792.
Intolerance in religious matters at Salem, 1630, 230–1.
Ireland, troubles in, of more importance than New England affairs to Charles

INDEX. 1037

I., 275; 1637, Wentworth and Laud in affairs of, 297; Strongbow's land system, 652; scheme for quartering soldiers from, at Boston, 1768, 847.
Irish names little known in colonial Braintree, 923; in population of Quincy, 946, 948, 954, 957, 958, 959, 960; dislike of Charles Francis Adams, defeat his election by intrigue, 958.
Irocoise, *i. e.*, Iroquois Lake, name formerly given Lake Champlain, 120.
Iron wedges, proved serviceable for splitting granite, Quincy, 1803, 925.
Iron-works, provision for encouraging, at Braintree, 1644, 646; established by John Winthrop, Jr., 673; site of, in contention with Vinton, 831-4; Scotch workmen at, 922; fate of enterprise, 923.
Iroquois, Lake, name formerly given Lake Champlain, 120.
Isle of Rhé expedition, 1626, commanded by Buckingham, 115.

Jackson, Andrew, his party without foothold at Quincy, 916; 946, 947, 950, 951, 955, 968.
Jackson, William M., opposes J. Q. Adams' election, 1838, 952.
Jackson family, descendants of "Dorothy Q.," 605.
Jacobite in Braintree, 1696, 625;
Jamaica rum, sold in New England, 786, 790.
James I. of England, submission of Indian sachems to, 16; 45; restores the associates of Essex to favor, 116-17; 1606, grants patents to the London and Plymouth Companies, 117-18; 1620, grants a new patent to the Plymouth Company, 121-4; contention over subsidies with the House of Commons, 1621, 129; adjourns and dissolves Parliament, *ib.*; attends Greenwich meeting for partition of New England, 138; represents Duke of Buckingham, 139; 141; proclamation of 1622, forbidding trade in fire-arms in New England, 195; Morton denies authority of proclamation, 202; its authority discussed, 202-3; Gorges' influence on, 275; his Book of Sports, 336; affair with the Scotch ministers, 424; grants to Virginia Companies, 651.
James II. of England, 701.
Jamestown, Virginia, Dermer passes winter of 1619 at, 27; Indian massacre of March 22, 1622, 74.
Jefferson, Thomas, 945.
Jeffreys, Lord George, Judge, executes Lady Alice Lisle, 705.
Jeffreys, William, one of R. Gorges' colonists, remains at Wessagusset, after 1624, 161; 252; communicates to Winthrop letter from Morton, 1634, 285; 295; the letter cited in charges of Court of Assistants, 1644,

347; a leading man of Wessagusset, 338; 342.
Jenner, Rev. Thomas, at Weymouth, 341.
Jennison, William, declines to vote at trial of Anne Hutchinson, 508.
Jewett, Rev. ——, minister at Rowley, 1755, 677.
Jezebel, the American, name given Anne Hutchinson by Massachusetts clergy, 437, 538, 573.
John, of England, 700.
John of Leyden, 395.
John, Sagamore, son of Nanepashemet, 217.
John and Francis, ship of the Council for New England, 232.
Jonathan, ship, David Thompson comes to Maine in, 146.
Johnson, Lady Arbella, wife of Isaac, one of Winthrop's party, 1630, 234; her death, 1630, 237; 241, 265.
Johnson, Captain Edward, of Woburn, cited as to David Thompson, 192; Gibbons' military qualities, 359-60; as to the farms of Bostonians, 646.
Johnson, Isaac, of Winthrop's party, 1630, 234; death of, 1630, 237; at Morton's examination by magistrates, 241.
Johnson, Samuel, Auchinleck's remark to, 126; verses on Robert Levet, cited, 714.
Johnson, Sergeant, overseer of galleries in Boston meeting-house, 1643, 736.
Jonson, Ben, 390.
Josselyn, John, visits America, 1638, 331; his account of entertainment by Maverick on Noddle's Island, *ib.*; 332; return to England, *ib.*
Josselyn, Sir Thomas, father of John, 331.
Judith, Point, Narragansett Bay, named for Judith Quincy, 700.
Jurisdiction conferred on Plymouth Company by the 1620 charter, 123-4; of Robert Gorges, in his colony, 141-2.
Juxon, Bishop William, made Lord Treasurer of England by Laud, 297; 304.

Keayne, Captain Robert, his quarrel with Goodwife Sherman, 456; 511.
Kelso, Scotland, battle at, 1639, 307.
Kennebec, river, Plymouth people establish a trading station at, 54; 160; 1629, they seek a patent for, 223; the Popham colony on, 1607-8, 118; southern limit of Gorges' province in Maine, 1637, 301; 309; Morton's fur trade on the, 351; 353.
Kieft, William, governor of New Amsterdam, 1642, 598.
King, prayers for, Christ Church, Braintree, 1776, 852.
King George, ship of war, Braintree men serve on, 1758; 836.

# 1038  INDEX.

King's Bench Court, decides question of legal authority of royal proclamation, 202; *quo warranto* filed in, 1635, against Mass. Bay Company, 291; result of proceedings, 292; 296, 298, 302, 303.
King's Chapel, Boston, 621; built of Quincy granite, 1749, 924, method of preparing stone for, 925.
King Philip's war, 827.
Kingman, Henry, his ferry across the Monatiquot, 1636, 672; his tavern, *ib.*, 673.
Kinsley, Stephen, one of Braintree's first delegates to General Court, 589.
Kirk, John, employed by J. Q. Adams, 931.
Knight, Walter, one of three original proprietors of Nantasket, 183.
Knights of Labor, interference in Quincy town-meeting, 1887, 990 *et seq.*
Knipperdolling, Bernhard, Anabaptist fanatic, 395.
Knowles, John, of Watertown goes a missionary to Virginia, 597.
Know-Nothing political party, support of, at Quincy, 958–9; 996, 1006.
Knox, General Henry, 764.
Knox, John, discussion with Mary Stuart, 383.

Laconia, name of region about Lake Iroquois, or Champlain, 120.
Lake of the Woods, 122.
Lancashire, England, William Tompson resigns living in, 596.
Land allotment system of Mass. Bay colony, 585–6.
Land titles derived from Indians, 653.
Lander, John, disciplined at Agamenticus by Gorges, 312.
Langbourne, Major, receipt given him by John Adams for creating a New England in Virginia, 732, 764, 783.
La Sensible, French frigate, John Adams returns from France in, 1779, 887.
Latin School, Boston, support derived from sale of lands to Braintree, 651.
La Tour d'Aulnay, his operations in Acadia, 358; visits Boston, *ib.*
Laud, William, Archbishop of Canterbury, 247, 248, *note*, 250; responsible for Star Chamber punishment of Prynne, 262; made Archbishop, 1633, 271; his war against Puritanism, *ib.*; his influence in Star Chamber, *ib.*; influenced by Gorges, *ib.*; 276, 278; 1634, attends to affairs in New England, 273; in Gorges' scheme of 1634, for government of New England, 277; his anger caused by Ratcliff's account of religious affairs at Boston, 279; 281; examination of Winslow, 1635, 282, 286; 290, 291, 292; his supremacy in 1637, 296; the extent of his powers and activities, 297; Wentworth's letter to, on tax for army, 299; effect of his interference in Scotch Church, 299 *et seq.*; rejection of his liturgy in Edinburgh, 300; presides, 1638, meeting of Lords Commissioners, 304; 306; Scotch troubles divert his attention from New England, 307; 313; prisoner in Tower, 315; 318, 347, 373; insulted at his trial by Hugh Peters, 375; his practices repeated by Puritans in New England, 446; 470; his methods and Winthrop's compared, 489; arguments for defence of, 561; persecutes Puritans in England, 563; 570.
Law courts, Mass. Bay, memorial for opening, 1765, 810.
Law of New England, founded on the Bible, 348.
Lawrence, James, U. S. N., commander of the Chesapeake, his departure from Boston harbor to engage the Shannon, 911.
Lawyers, discontent with, in Massachusetts, alleged a cause of rebellion, 1786, 897.
Leather manufacture, Quincy, 928.
Lechford, Thomas, remark concerning Blackstone and Williams, 366, *note*; his Plain Dealing cited as to marriage and funeral customs at Boston, 396.
Legal tender act of Massachusetts, 1780, 892; repealed, 1781, *ib.*
Legaree, Daniel, 824.
Legge, John, ordered whipped by General Court, 1631, 337.
Leighton, Alexander, punished by Star Chamber, 262, *note.*
Lenox, William Cavendish, Duke of, associated with Gorges in Plymouth Company, charter of 1620, 122; his influence at court in favor of charter, 124; at meetings of the Council for New England, 1622, 131; one of eight to receive land by partition of 1635, 283.
Lenthal, Rev. Robert, a rival of Rev. Hull's, 1637, in ministry of church at Weymouth, 341; disciplined by General Court, *ib.*
Leo X., Pope, 563.
Letetrs, rates of postage on, 1795, 804.
Levett, Christopher, with R. Gorges, at Piscataqua, 1624, 152; 192.
Leverett, Thomas, elder of Boston church, at examination of Anne Hutchinson, 426–8; testifies for Anne Hutchinson, 496; at church trial of Mrs. Hutchinson, 524.
Lexington, battle, character of fighters at, 765; 852, 855, 856, 858, 879.
Ley, James, Lord, comes to New England, 1637, 301; entertained by Maverick, 331; 462.
Leyden, John of, 395.
Leyden, the Dutch home of the Pilgrims, 46, 47, 50.

Liberty tree, Braintree, 1766, 844–5.
Libraries, lumber in, 366–7; in Massachusetts, 804.
Library, Quincy, Christ Church, 1701; gift of Society for Propagation of the Gospel, 622, 804; free public library established, 1871, 940–1.
Lilbourne, John, punished by Star Chamber, 262, *note.*
Lincoln, Abraham, presidential campaign of, 1860, 959; 1864, 960; 961.
Lincoln, Benjamin, General, 764; unpopularity after Shays' rebellion, 898.
Lincoln, Bridget, Countess of, Dudley's letter to, concerning Morton, 169; 246, 484, 256, *note.*
Lincoln, Levi, Governor of Mass., 946.
Lincoln, Thomas, 3d Earl of, father of Lady Arbella Johnson, 234; of the wife of John Humphrey, 265; 286.
Lincolnshire, England, its contribution of men to New England, 368; 539.
Lindsay, Bishop, in St. Giles', Edinburgh, Stoniefield day, 1637, 300.
Lion, the ship, 256, *note.*
Lisle, Lady Alice, mother of Bridget, wife of President Hoar, 704–5; executed by Jeffreys, 1685, *ib.;* commemorated in picture, *ib.*
Lisle, Bridget, daughter of John and Lady Alice, wife of Leonard Hoar, buried at Braintree, 704.
Lisle, John, father of Bridget, 704.
Lisle, Belgium, Gorges prisoner at, 106.
Literary culture in New England, 390.
Little Harbor, Maine, house built by David Thompson at, 192.
Little James, pinnace, mutiny on, 154.
Littleworth, Captain, Morton's name for Endicott, 228; 347.
Liturgy, prepared by Laud for Scotch Church, rejected, 300, 302.
Livingstone, David, 327.
Locke, John, his works in houses of the colonial gentry, 805.
Log-cabin political campaign, 1840, 949.
London, plague, 1; Essex insurrection of 1601, 108–11; its sanitary condition, 1630, 235.
London Company, incorporated by royal patent, 1606, 118.
Long Ashton, Sir F. Gorges' country seat, occupied by royalist forces, 313, captured by Prince Rupert, *ib.;* retaken by Fairfax, 314; Gorges dies at, 1647, 315.
Longevity in colonial Massachusetts, 800–1.
Longfellow, H. W., The Courtship of Miles Standish, its accuracy discussed, 94–5.
Long Island, Boston Bay, 464; descent on, by colonial militia, July 9, 1775, 861; 867.
Long Island, N. Y., battle, 874.
Long Island Sound, explored by Dermer, 1619, 27; 828.

Long Parliament, 115, 373, 563, 701; dispersed, 860.
Long Wharf, Boston, 453.
Lord-bishops and lord-brethren, Blackstone's remark, 382.
Lords Commissioners of Plantations, Winslow's business with, 1634, 280; examination of Winslow by, 282; project, 1635, for recovery of New England from Puritans, 284; establishment of, announced to Mass. Bay, 1634, 286; review of origin and policy of the board, 295–6; Laud's control of, 298; provisional government for New England ordered by, 1637, 301; issue a second command for the Mass. Bay charter, April, 1638, 304; at Boston, 305; superseded by Parliament, 315.
Lord's Day, Braintree meeting to consider law defining Sunday, 894.
Louis XIV. of France, 248, *note,* 270, 476, 561.
Louis XV. of France, 616.
Louis XVI. of France, 318.
Lovell's Grove, Weymouth, Mass., 61, *note.*
Lovell's Island, Boston Bay, fortification proposed, 1776, 867.
Lowell family, descendants of "Dorothy Q.," 605.
Loyola, Ignatius, and Hugh Peters compared, 565.
Lucas, Henry, minister of Christ Church, Braintree, 627; removes to Newbury, *ib.*
Luddam, ——, a guide, 339.
Luddam's Ford, 339.
Ludden, Benjamin, of Braintree, 832.
Ludgate, London, the limit of Essex insurrection, 108, 109, 110.
Ludlow, Robert, overseer of Castle Island fortification, 284.
Lunt, Rev. William Parsons, minister of Quincy Church, cited as to investigation of Lemuel Briant, 639; his death in Arabia, 1857, 641.
Luther, Martin, term Antinomian coined by, 432; 434, 563.
Lyford, John, 183; comes to New England, 1623, 184; an Episcopal clergyman, *ib.;* his reception at Plymouth, 185; with Oldham, becomes centre of discontents, *ib.;* letters to England opened by Bradford, *ib.;* proposes the reformation of Plymouth church, 186; charged with conspiracy, 187; ordered to leave Plymouth, 188; his letter intercepted, *ib.;* his private life not exemplary, 189; exiled to Wessagusset, 190; established at Nantasket, *ib.;* removes to Cape Ann, *ib.;* settles on the site of Gloucester, *ib.;* removes to Virginia, where he dies, 190; 215, 232, 257.
Lygonia claim to Maine, *see* Plough Patent, 314.

# 1040 INDEX.

Lynde family, in possession of Thompson's Island, 1666, 342.
Lynn, Mass., 677; Samuel Whiting minister of, 773; a shoemaking centre, 930.
Lyon, Henry, punished by Court of Assistants, 262, *note*.
Lyon, the ship, 339.

Macaulay, T. B., concerning Barclay and Charnock plot, 625; story of Lady Alice Lisle, 705; 725.
Madison, James, his administration supported by John Adams, 909; 945.
Magistrates of Massachusetts Bay, first meeting of, at Charlestown, 1630, 240; the members of, 241; their character, *ib.*; banish Thomas Morton, 242; visit Plymouth and Wessagusset, 1632, 338; not amenable to church for official acts, 513.
Magna Charta, signed by Saer de Quincy, 700.
Magnalia Christi Americana. *See* Cotton Mather.
Maine, visited by Dermer, 1619; 25–6; by the ship Sparrow, 1622, 51; winter, 1622–3, by Saunders, in Swan, to get food for Wessagusset, 68; Popham's colony in, 1607–8, 118; Thomas Weston flees to, in disguise, 146; some of R. Gorges' colonists go to, 154; trade in fire-arms on coast of, 195; the northern limit of Gorges' projected colony, 1634, 276; allotted to Sir F. Gorges, partition of 1635, 283; limits of Gorges' province, in, 301; 308; patented to Gorges, 1639, 309; title questioned, 1643, 314; Rigby's claim sustained by Parliament, 315; subsequent history of Gorges' part, 316; Morton visits, 1644, 345; Rigby's territory in, *ib.*; Wheelwright, 1641, takes refuge in, 539; Massachusetts expeditions to, Revolution, 884.
Manawet Indian kidnapped by Hunt, 24, *note*.
Manhattan Island, Mrs. Hutchinson removes to, 537.
Manida, a kidnapped Indian, 24, *note*.
Mann, Horace, succeeds J. Q. Adams in Congress, 956.
Manomet, now Monument, Mass., 52; Standish goes to, for wood, winter of 1622–3, 69; Indians of, in conspiracy to destroy Wessagusset, 73.
Mansell, Sir Robert, draws Mt. Desert at Greenwich, 1623, 139.
Marblehead, Mass., protest against Stamp Act, 1765, 839; 912.
Ma-re Mount, name given by Morton to his settlement, 175; 344.
Marlborough, Earl of, father of Lord Ley, 301.
Marlborough, Mass., a shoemaking centre, 930.
Marriage, Boston forms of, as reported by Ratcliff to Privy Council, 279; civil, performed by Winslow, 282; 1636, 396, and *note*.
Marsh, Lieut. Alexander, of Braintree, 756.
Marsh, Joseph, made minister of First Precinct of Braintree, 1709, 616–17; his support, *ib.*; marriage, death, *ib.*; 626; 748.
Marshall, John, of Braintree, his pricelist of food and drink, 686; diary cited, 687; his occupations, *ib.*; typical of skilled workman class, 716; his career, and services to town, 717; extracts from his diary, 717–20; religious reflections, 717; militia expenses, 718; reception of Governor, Earl of Bellomont, 1699, 718–19; occurrences of 1701, 719; small-pox epidemic, 1702, *ib.*; impressments for army, 1704, 1709, 719, 720; comments of S. Willard on death of, 720–1; notice of bears in Braintree woods, 1699, 924; the haunt of deer, also, *ib.*
Marston Moor, 347.
Martha's Vineyard, visited by Dermer, 1619, 26, 27; his troubles and conflicts with the Indians at, 27, 28; expedition to find gold, sent to, 1614, 119.
Mary, Queen of England, 248, *note*, 251.
Mary Stuart, of Scotland, discussion with John Knox, 383; 424.
Mary and John, ship of Mass. Co., arrives at Hull, 1630, 228; brings new settlers to Salem colony, 228–9; some, still at Nantasket, June, 1630, 233–4.
Mason, Captain John, governor of Maine, 25; his Piscataqua plantation, increased from Winthrop's party, 1630, 236; with Gorges attacks the Mass. Bay charter, 1632, 263; 280; at Winslow's examination, 282; his share in redistribution of territory, 1635, 283; Winthrop's comments on the failure of his schemes of 1635, 289; 290; death of, and its effect on Gorges' schemes, 1635, 292; attached to Laud's party, 296.
Mason, Captain John, of Connecticut, serves as lieutenant under E. Gibbons in war with Narragansetts, 1645, 359.
Massachusetts Bay, Weston's purpose to establish plantation on, 58; the early name of Boston Bay, 234. *See* Boston Bay.
Massachusetts Bay Colony, 1630–1691, a business corporation, 815; established under Winthrop, 1630, 209 *et seq.*; involved in the Antinomian controversy, 407; lasting effect of Hutchinson persecution, 559; government denounced in England, 263; its growth and success, 269; allotted to Lord Gorges, 1635, 283; its insignificance at Court of Charles I., 294; takes New Hampshire under its jurisdiction, 1641, 539; project for obtaining Rhode Is-

## INDEX. 1041

land, 537; war with Narragansett Indians, 1645, 359; the royal commission of 1664 refused in, 334-5; purchase of territory under Sir F. Gorges' patent, 316; population of, 1634, 340, *note;* 1655, 671; its remoteness from England an advantage, 296, 297, 298; denounced to Laud, by Burdet, 310; arbitrary power and use of it, of magistrates, 348; highways of, 666-79; a business corporation, 815.

——, Charter of 1629, attacked by Gorges, 1632, 263 *et seq.;* Privy Council pay no heed to his petition, 266-7; called for by Privy Council, 1634, 270; reasons which caused the granting of, 271 *et seq.;* Gorges' renewed attack, *ib.;* Morton announces its abrogation, 1634, 277; Privy Council demands its return, 279; preparations for its defence, 286-7; its legal abrogation, 1635, 292; General Court, 1635, ignore order for its return, 289; 296; 1638, Lords Commissioners issue second command for its return, 304; General Court declines to obey, 305; Scotch troubles prevent attention to, 307; vacated, 1686, 817.

——, Province, 1691-1776, Charter of William and Mary, 701; 817; transforms the colony to a province, 747; separation of church and state, *ib.;* theocracy extinguished by 1691 charter, 819; religious tolerance secured, to all but papists, *ib.;* Earl of Bellomont comes as governor, 1699, 719; impressments of 1704 and 1709 for militia, 719, 720; militia and army expenses, *ib.;* boundary dispute with New Hampshire, 1737, 702; Boston's memorial for reopening Law Courts, 1765, 839-40; scheme for quartering British soldiers in, 1768, 847; restraining habits of people, 793-4; moral standards, 794; smallness of criminal class in, 797; health and disease in colonial times, 800-1; royal governor question, 1635, 811-12; town records of, 813; its position during colonial wars, 827; burden of Indian Wars, *ib.;* response to Pitt's appeal, for forces, 836; quiet in, after repeal of Stamp Act, 846.

——, during Revolution, 1775, scarcity of money, and rise of prices, 864; rid of British troops, 1776, 868; struggles after evacuation of Boston, 869; rise of prices, difficulty of enlistments, spoils of contractors, *ib.;* money, 880 *et seq.;* contributions to militia, 884; Legal Tender Act, 1780, 892; repealed, 1781, *ib.*

——, State, Constitution of 1780, 887, 889, 890, 891; tax question, 1786, 895-6; Shays' Rebellion, 1786, 893, 895, 896, 897; cost of, 898; 899; attitude towards war of 1812, 910; apprehensions of danger on seaboard, *ib.;* provisions for defence in coast towns, 912; town-meeting government, tendency to break down, 982; militia, 818, 855, 861, 865, 874, 875, 878, 881, 892, 897, 898; Fourth Regiment, War of Rebellion, 962.

——, General Court, originally of the nature of a stockholders' corporation council, 815-16; enlarges Boston at Mount Wollaston, 1634, 365, 583; its committee allots lands to Coddington and Quincy, there, *ib.;* its pretext for refusing to return charter, 280; its action on creation of Lords Commissioners for Colonial Government, 1634, 286; declines to return charter, 1638, 305; reply to Lords Commissioners of, 306; denounces the royal commission of 1664, 335; assigns fifty acres in Boston to Blackstone, 322; its discipline for non-churchgoers and other offenders, 336, 337; Bursley a member of, 338; changes name Wessagusset to Weymouth, 1635, 339-40; 1637, disciplines Rev. Lenthal of Weymouth, 341; takes cognizance of the Anne Hutchinson difficulty, 413 *et seq.;* meeting of, to arrange for departure of Vane, 420; considers Antinomian controversy at March, 1637, meeting, 441; two parties on Antinomian question, 442; case of Greensmith, *ib.;* Wheelwright summoned on charges because of fast-day sermon, 443; protest of Boston church-members against its jurisdiction, cases of conscience, 444; petition returned as presumptuous, *ib.;* examination of Wheelwright, 444-6; judgment of Wheelwright, 445; refuses to record Vane's protest against judgment, 446; petitioned in favor of Wheelwright, *ib.;* postponement of sentence, *ib.;* its seat removed to Cambridge, 447-8; 451; Wheelwright decision not sustained by people, at May, 1637, election, 452; composition of Court elected, 456; its procedure, *ib.;* division into two chambers, 1642, *ib.;* 1637, passes an alien law, 458; party feeling in, 1637, 460; its hesitation to consider the Antinomian question, May, 1673, 474; dissolution of, Sept. 1637, new election ordered, 475; result of new election, *ib.;* composition and meeting of new Court, *ib.;* Wheelwright business taken up, 479; his adherents expelled, *ib.;* 480-1; banishes him, 481; form of sentence, *ib.;* appeal to the King denied, *ib.;* arraigns Anne Hutchinson, Nov. 1637, 483; its sessions held in Cambridge meeting-house, 485; disregard of legal procedure in trial of Anne Hutchinson, 487; 488; story of the trial, 488-508; banishes her, 508; its revenge

1042　　　　　　　　INDEX.

on refractory sergeants, 509; prosecutes signers of Boston remonstrance, 510; banishes suspected persons, 511-12; reasons, *ib.*; subservient to the church, 513; gives leave to Boston church-members to attend church proceedings against Anne Hutchinson, 517; its temper during the trial, 527-8; the Boston delegates of 1637, elected to sustain Mrs. Hutchinson, 533; Boston quieted by banishment of refractory persons, 534; redeems from Indian captivity, daughter of Anne Hutchinson, 538; warns settlers of Piscataqua against Underhill, 554; historical aspect of Antinomian persecution discussed, 559-78; Flynt makes submission to, 603; 1648, grants title to John Thompson of Thompson's Island, 342; its grants of land, subject to Indian rights, 653; its action in Braintree commons question, 658, 659; 661; its action as to roads, 666, 668, 670, 671, 673; erects monument to Judge Edmund Quincy, 702; John Quincy, Braintree delegate to, 1717-41; 707; Samuel Bass appointed one of commission to build bridge over Neponset, 1655, 714; sends five delegates to Continental Congress, 1774, 850; fines imposed on remiss recruiting officers, 875; 1779, becomes a Constitution convention, 890; defines legal limits of Sunday, 893; petitioned for creation of Quincy town, 902; city charter for Quincy passed by, 1889, 1007.

——, Schools, Law of 1647, establishing, 766; town-schools, report on, 1879, 936-7.

——, Settlers of superior character, 364; men of substance, *ib.*; of purest English blood, 655; 922; limit of colonial emigration from England to, 922.

Massachusetts, Company, controversy with Gorges over his rights in New England, 214-17; negotiations of Oldham with, 214-16; composed of Puritans, 222; difficulties with the Council for New England, *ib.*; considers Morton's case, 223; fears caused by Oldham, 225; instructions to Endicott, looking to the expulsion of older settlers, 226; 283; *quo warranto* filed against, 1635, in King's Bench Court, 291; result of proceedings, 292; 296, 298, 302, 303.

Massachusetts, Fields, 14, *note*; 167, 252, 363, 699.

Massasoit, Indian Chief, 28; visits Plymouth Colony, 29; 30; Hopkins and Winslow, as ambassadors, visit him, 30-1; attack upon, threatened by the Narragansetts, 1621, 32; plans at Plymouth for his protection, 34; relations of Hobamack with, 37; Squanto's scheme to destroy influence of, 37-40; reported as about to attack colony, 38; he becomes enemy of Squanto, 40; visits Plymouth to contradict the report, 1622, 41; demands Squanto's death, *ib.*; compliance obviated, 42; sends messengers for Squanto, *ib.*; they return without him, *ib.*; his illness, spring of 1623, 72; cured by Winslow, *ib.*; reveals plot against Wessagusset, 73; service rendered Plymouth by, 1623, 75; his grandchild made a slave in West Indies, 104, and *note*.

Mather, Cotton, cited as to pestilence among Indians, 12; Blackstone's occupancy of Boston, 322-3; the wonderful deliverance of Edward Gibbons, 358; Magnalia and Theopolis Americana, favorite reading in early New England, 391; 409, *note*; as to synod of 1637, 470; the Antinomian controversy, 493; 577; verses on Tompson, 598, 602; on Gookins, 599; account of Tompson's mental infirmity, 600-1; mention of Henry Flynt, 603; 609; made D. D. by Glasgow university, 630; record of winter weather, 1720, 682-3; on degeneration of psalm-singing, 739; B. Tompson's complimentary verses to, 773; on a winter hearth-fire, 1697; 806; advice on personal cleanliness to candidates for ministry, 807; 830.

Mather, Increase, attack on rum drinking, 786.

Mather, Richard, minister at Dorchester, 1640, 595.

Mattakeese meeting-house, 679.

Mattapan, Indian name of Dorchester, 167; 233.

Maurice, Prince of Nassau, Underhill's service under, 551.

Maverick, Amias, the wife of Samuel, 161, 329, 335.

Maverick, Samuel, birth and marriage, 329; comes to New England, 1624, 161, 329; account of his life in New England, 328-35; settles at Winnisimmet, now Chelsea, *ib.*; his house in 1659, the oldest in Massachusetts, *ib.*; builds fort on Noddle's Island, 192; 193, 198; cited as to the burning of Morton's house at Merry Mount, 244, *note*; 351, *note*; his letter to Clarendon concerning Morton, 246, 330; 252; description of Winslow, 281; compelled to remove from Noddle's Island to Boston, 1635, 288; letter to Winthrop cited, 333, *note*; entertains Winthrop, 1630, 330; delay in admitting him freeman of Boston, *ib.*; engages in commerce, *ib.*; visits Virginia, *ib.*; 331; suspected of relations with Gorges inimical to colony and put under restraint, *ib.*; entertains Vane and Lord Ley, *ib.*; 462; entertains Josselyn, 331; a Church of England

INDEX. 1043

man, 332; his relations with Winthrop, 333; supporter of Robert Childs, *ib.*; persecuted and imprisoned, 334; removes from New England, *ib.*; returns from England, 1664, as royal commissioner, meets with contempt at Boston, 334-5; his services in office at New York, 335; his death, *ib.*; 340, 342, 349, 356; Braintree's industries, 770-1.

May, Thomas, his History of the Long Parliament cited, 115-6.

May Day revels at Merry Mount, 1627, 176-82; of Pagan origin, 181; its celebration in England in the year 1585, 182.

Mayflower, the ship, 28; chartered by Cushman and Weston for the Pilgrims, 47; carries the Pilgrims and returns to England, 48; perils off Cape Cod, 1620, 63; 125; John Alden and Priscilla Mullins, emigrants to Plymouth in, 714.

Maypole, Merry Mount, 354, 355.

Medford, 16, 19; some of Winthrop's party settle at, 1630, 238; Winthrop's farm at, 364; 678.

Meeting-house in New England, 732-46; distinction of persons in, 738; not regarded a sacred place, 742; its secular uses, *ib.*; that of Braintree Middle Precinct used for elections, 743; rules for decency in, *ib.*; on occasions a powder magazine, *ib.*

Melville, Andrew, rebukes James I., 424.

Memorial from Boston Church to General Court, 1637, 444; the signers punished, 509-10.

Merchant Adventurers of London, concerned in the settlement of the Pilgrims in New England, 46; 53; buy Weston's interest in their company, 1622, 54; 56, 57.

Merrimack river, Thomas Weston and his party cast ashore at mouth of, 1623, 146; 210, 482, 666.

Merry Mount, 171, *note;* condition of the colonists at, 1626, 174; the scheme of Morton to obtain command of, 174, and *note;* named, 175; population of, 1627, 193; fur trade at, 196-7; dangers apprehended by Bradford from, 198; character of settlement, *ib.*; Morton captured at, June, 1628, 206-7; he returns to, 209; its name changed to Mount Dagon, by Endicott, 211; Morton's house destroyed, 243; 363, 345, 351, 352, 354, 355, 356, 582, 828.

Merry, Walter, 1643, overseer of galleries, Boston meeting-house, 736.

Metheglin, a drink, described by Bradford, 356.

Methodist Episcopal Church, Quincy, meeting-house, built, 1838, 930.

Mexico, war with United States, 953; 955.

Middleborough, Mass., 33, 255.

Middle Precinct, Braintree, schools in, 1790, 901.

Middlesex County, Mass., within the territory granted to R. Gorges, 136.

Militia, Mass. Bay, 1689, Waitstill Winthrop, Major General of, 818; in revolution, 855; 861, 865, 874, 875, 878, 881, 892, 897, 898.

Mill, John, of Braintree, 1704; 623.

Mill, Stoughton's, the first run by water power in Mass., 669.

Miller, Ebenezer, 1727, rector of Christ Church, Braintree and Quincy, 621, 628-31; made D. D. by Oxford, 1747, 630.

Miller, Major Ebenezer, an Episcopalian Tory, 841; pro-stamp-act candidate for selectman, 1766, defeated, 843-4; elected fence-viewer and surveyor of highways, 846; 851; judged inimical to popular cause, 1777, 853; ill of pestilence, 1775, 863; 871; elected selectman, 1792, 904.

Miller, Samuel, of Milton, father of Rev. Ebenezer, 627.

Miller family, of Episcopal church at Braintree, 632.

Milton, John, his sonnet to Sir Harry Vane, 373; Hugh Peters walks with, at Cromwell's funeral, 375; cited, 385; 390, 476, 571-2, 702, 710; his works in houses of colonial gentry, 805; 806, 941.

Milton, Mass., 717, 902, 928.

Milton Falls, 1654, bridge across Neponset at, 673.

Milton Hill, site of first water-power mill in Mass., 669; 671.

Minute-men of Braintree, 1775, 857.

Miracles, Puritan opinions concerning, 503.

Mishawum, site of Charlestown, 161; within the territory granted to Oldham, 217; the brothers Sprague settled at, 271; they name place Charlestown, 218; 233.

Missouri, bridge at St. Louis, across, 668.

Mitchell, Mrs. Zerviah Gould, descendant of Massasoit, 104, *note.*

Modesly, Mary, disciplined by Dorchester church, 1681, 754-5, *note.*

Monatiquot, stream, supposed to be same as Phillips Creek, 61; 159, 166, 205; 363; 582, 583; ferry established across, 1635, 672; 1644, stone bridge across, 673; contention over fish in, 1736, 831-4.

Monckton, Lord, removal of Acadians by, 641.

Morell, Rev. William, minister of congregation south of Neponset, 368.

Money in Mass., scarcity of, 1775, 864; 1780, 880; 882, 883 *et seq.*; 892.

Monhegan, Dermer's visit at, 1619, 26; Saunders of Wessagusset goes to, on

# 1044    INDEX.

expedition for provisions, 69; 76; 146.
Monmouth, battle, 874.
Monomoy Point, Cape Cod, 63.
Monroe, James, President, his administration, effect on Quincy politics, 915.
Montaigne, Michel de, 390.
Montcalm, capitulation of Fort William Henry to, 1757, 836.
Moon Island, Boston Bay, descent on, by colonial militia, July, 1775, 861; 1776, 867.
Morals in colonial New England, 783-99.
Morell, William, Church of England clergyman, comes with Robert Gorges to New England, 142; 143, 144, *note*; in charge of Wessagusset, 153; continued a year there, 154; returns to England, 156; his career in New England, *ib.*; his Latin poem, 157-8; 327, 159, 162; minister, 368.
Mortality at Plymouth and Wessagusset in famine of 1623, 77.
at Charlestown, 1630, 235-7.
at Salem, 1629-30, 228, 234, 240, 241.
Morton, Marcus, Governor of Mass., vote for at Quincy, 946, 947; 948, 950, 952.
Morton, Nathaniel, accusation of Thomas Morton as murderer, 169.
Morton, Thomas, probably one of Andrew Weston's party, 1622, 56, 57; 59, 163, 164, *note;* his return to England, 1622, 62; comes with Captain Wollaston to New England, 1624, 163; his love of nature, 164; 172; citations from New England Canaan concerning New England, 164; its charm for him, 165; settles at Passonagessit, 166; builds a house, 167; his influence in settlement, 1626, 168; opposed to the abandonment of the enterprise, *ib.;* his character and history, 169; accused of murder in England, *ib.;* regarded a profane man at Plymouth, *ib.;* 175; described by Governor Dudley in a letter to the Countess of Lincoln, 169; a Church of England man, 170, *note;* regarded a martyr, 170-1, *note;* his revels and debaucheries at Merry Mount, 170, *note;* a sportsman, 171, 172, 175; a gentleman of Clifford's Inn, 171; his moral character, 172; value of his New English Canaan, *ib.;* his former life in London, *ib.;* plots to obtain command of Passonagessit, 1626, 174; no mention of Wollaston in New English Canaan, *ib., note;* expels Fitcher from Merry Mount, 175; his objects in America, names settlement Ma-re, or Merry Mount, *ib.;* May-day revels 1627, 176-82; his poem, 177, his song for dance, 178-9; 183; his account of Wessagusset hanging, 79-81; cited as to fear of Standish by the Indians, 103; describes John Oldham, 184; 215; his account of the Lyford and Oldham episode, 189-90; 1628, causes of his disfavor at Plymouth, 194-200; engages in the fur trade, 194; 196; supplies Indians with spirits and guns, 194; 196; they frequent his settlement, 195; a danger to Plymouth, 200; admonished by the colonial magistrates, 201; his reply, *ib.;* again warned, 202; his indifference, *ib.;* Standish sent to arrest, 203; taken in custody at Wessagusset, *ib.;* he escapes from the guard, 204; returns to Merry Mount, 205; captured, 206; carried to Plymouth, 207; sent to England, *ib.;* 208; prosecuted in England on charges from Plymouth, 221; escapes punishment, *ib.;* 223; represents himself a church martyr, 222; protected by Gorges, *ib.;* whose favor he gains, 223; his case considered by the Mass. Company, *ib.;* 1629, returns with Allerton to Plymouth, *ib.,* 224; resumes residence at Merry Mount, 209, 224; under Endicott's jurisdiction, 211; an uncongenial neighbor to the Salem people, 225; attempts to make a party of the jealous older colonists against the new, *ib.;* an intriguer for Gorges, *ib.;* his opposition to, Endicott's policy, 225-6; plan to arrest him for violation of trade regulations, 227; his escape, 227-8; famine and sickness at Salem and Charlestown takes attention from him, 240; 1630, ordered to appear before magistrates, 241; his examination and banishment, 241-2; put in the stocks at Charlestown, 243; sent to England in the ship Handmaid, *ib.;* his house at Merry Mount burned, *ib.;* his account of burning, 244, *note,* 321; a warrant from England for his arrest, 246; his arrests in 1628 and 1630, discussed, 244-50; his influence at Whitehall, 250; committed to jail in Exeter on arrival in England, *ib.;* 257, *note;* a letter to, from Gorges, opened by Winthrop, 258; states the case of Philip Ratcliff, 259; account of affair of Endicott and Ratcliff, 261; a witness for Gorges in his attack upon the Mass. Bay charter, 1632, 263 *et seq.;* 263, 268, 275; reports the success of Gorges' scheme for colonial government, 277; the establishment of royal commission to govern New England, 1634, 278, *note;* complains of Winslow to Lords Commissioners, 282; appointed Solicitor for Deeds, 1635, 284; his letter to Jeffreys communicated to Winthrop, 1634, 285; 295; the announcements of his letter confirmed, 286; causes *quo warranto* to be filed in King's Bench Court, 1635, against Mass. Bay Co., 291; result of proceedings, 292; 297, 300; in the pay of George Cleeve, 301, 344; disclaimed

INDEX. 1045

by Gorges, 1637, 303; 307; countersigns charter of city Gorgeana, 311; publication of New English Canaan, 303, 343; his relations to Gorges, 343-44; attached to Parliamentary side in civil war, 344; reappears at Plymouth, *ib.*; avoids Boston magistrates, *ib.*; stays at Plymouth, winter of 1643-44; goes to Maine, 1644, and to Rhode Island, 346; summoned before Court of Assistants of Mass. Bay, September, 1644, *ib.*; the charges brought against him, 346-8; imprisoned and fined, 348; sent to England after year's imprisonment, 350; discomfort in prison, 351; experiences on coast of Maine, 1627, *ib.*; his story subsequent to 1641, 343-51; 354; bad name given to Merry Mount region by his occupation, 364; succeeded by William Coddington, in ownership of Mt. Wollaston, 546; 582; Edward Gibbons his companion at Mt. Wollaston, 828.
Mount Auburn street, Cambridge, 484.
Mount Dagon, Merry Mount so called by Endicott, 211.
Mount Desert, drawn at Greenwich, 1623, by Sir Robert Mansell, 139; visited 1622, by Captain Squeb, 232.
Mount Wollaston, Passonagessit, Chickatabot's plantation at, 11; named for Captain Wollaston, 162; 167; affairs of the colony at, summer of 1626, 174, and *note*; name changed by Morton to Merry Mount or Ma-re Mount, 175; position relative to Wessagusset and Thompson's Island, 193; within the territory granted to Endicott, 211; 224, 240, 243, 244, 250, 321, 353; General Court orders its annexation to Boston, 1634, 365, 583, 651, 668, 669; bay front in 1634, assigned to Coddington and Quincy, 365; ownership of property passes from Morton to Coddington, 546; grant of land to Edmund Quincy at, *ib.*; Coddington sells, 1639, to William Tyng, 707; inherited by Mrs. Thomas Shepard, 1661, *ib.*; bequeathed to John Quincy, her grandson, 1709, *ib.*; his house at, 681; 701; Edmund Quincy's allotment, 365, 669, 700; lands allotted to William Hutchinson and John Wheelwright, 1636-7, 366, and *note*; other allotments, 1636-40, 584; 585-6; settlers at, 1637, 459; 475; 585; farms set apart for Bostonians, 646; land-title confirmed by Chickatabut's descendants, 653; chapel of ease established 415, 593, Wheelwright appointed minister, 416-17, 436; his fast-day sermon, 437; preaches Covenant of Grace at, 475; his expulsion, 565, 581; first stage of Mrs. Hutchinson's journey into exile, 536; site of her house there, 536, *note*; church established,

1639, 586; to be purged of Antinomian heresies, 595; ferry communication with Wessagusset, 1635, 672; 828; John Adams' Christmas visit to John Quincy at, 1765, 840; petition for town incorporation, granted, 1640, 587; adjustment of claim of Boston, 588-9; observations of British ships from, 1776, 868; 886, 887; John Adams' embarkation for England at, 1778, 951; 1004. *See* Braintree, Merry Mount.
Mourt, George, cited as to Standish's excursion to Boston bay, 1621, 14, *note*; respecting Corbitant, 33.
Munster, Anabaptists of, 565, 567, 568.
Music in churches, 739-41; string and wind instruments in Braintree church, 741; choir of Quincy meeting-house, 906-7.
Muster-field, *see* Training-field.
Mystic river, visited by Standish, 1621, 16, 19, 159, 161, 218, 233, 238, 363.

Nahant, within territory granted, 1622, to Robert Gorges, 136; its purchase by Thomas Dexter, 260.
Names in colonial Massachusetts, indicative of pure English origin, 922; some French, *ib.*; of slaves at Braintree, 923.
Nanepashemet, Indian Sachem, 16; Standish visits his former home, 17; 217.
Nantasket, visited by Gov. Winthrop, 1630; settlement at, 1622, 183; purchase of, from Chickatabut, *ib.*; Lyford and Oldham take up residence there after expulsion from Plymouth, 190; 193, 229; in 1629, 231; the temporary residence of Rev. Ralph Smith, 230-1; engagement of colonial militia with British at, 1775, 861; lighthouse destroyed, 1775, *ib.*; reëstablished, and again destroyed, *ib.*
Nantasket Roads, 867; 886, frozen, winter of 1779-80, 888.
Nantes, Edict of, 248, *note*.
Narragansett Bay, home of Massasoit, 1621, 30; southern limit of territory allotted to Lord Gorges, 1635, 283; Blackstone removes to, 324, 345, 597; 537; Point Judith, named for Judith Quincy, 700.
Narragansett Indians, not affected by pestilence, 1616-7, 4; threatened attack on Massasoit 1621, 32; attack from, feared at Plymouth, 1622, 38, 75; dangers to be feared from, 1623, 102; war with the New England colonies, 359, 828.
Naseby, battle of, 154, 313.
Natick, Mass., property of Saltonstall at, 365.
Native American political party, 958, 961, 996, 1006.
Naumkeag, Indian name of Salem, 211.

# 1046 INDEX.

Nauset tribe, Indians captured by Captain Hunt, 23; 33.
Navigation acts of Great Britain, 697.
Neal, Abigail, insane woman of Braintree, 725; 726.
Neal, Benjamin, of Braintree, 832; 833.
Neal, Henry, his offspring, 609.
Negro conspiracy, Boston, 1774, 854.
Negroes, in Braintree, colonial times, 923; provision made at meetinghouses for seating, 738 and note.
Neponset river, 14, note; mouth of, 15; 159, 167; home of Sir C. Gardiner, 252; the southern boundary of European settlement of Mass. Bay colony, 1630, 363; 365, 417; in 1637, 582, 583; 581, 585, 586, early projects for crossing, ferries and bridges, 668–73; 1654, bridged at Milton Falls, 673; 714, 902, 931.
Neptune, English ship, at siege of Rochelle, 317.
Neutrality, Quincy town-meeting regulations to preserve international, 1793, 906.
New Amsterdam, New York, project of Pilgrims for settling in, 46; 597; William Kieft, governor of, 1642, 598.
New Braintree, Worcester County, Mass., created from Braintree town commons, 660.
Newbury, New Hampshire, 628, coast road from, to Hingham, Mass., 666.
Newcomb's tavern, Braintree North Precinct, 925.
New England, developed on the basis of the 1620 charter to Plymouth Company, 123; allotments of territory at Greenwich, June 29, 1623, 138–9; royal laws and proclamation for, against trade in firearms, 195; Gorges' scheme for new colonial organization in, 1634, 276–7; his dreams for, 317; the significance of Antinomian controversy in, 367; Puritans of, adopt the Bible as the basis of law and government, 382 et seq.; clergy of, 392; intermarriage in families of, 608–9; immigration in, 1637, 458; Puritan settlement a business enterprise, 560; land titles derived from Indians, 653; Saxon customs in, 655–6; gentry of, 699; 710; influence of farmers in development of, 712–13; artisans or mechanics, 716; dependent classes, 722–31; insanity in, 724; meeting-house in, 732–46; town customs derived from old England, 745, note; 1735–41, religious revival, 749; the church a social centre, 750–1; not the mother of great soldiers, 764; influence of training-field in, ib.; influence of schools, 765; John Adams' opinion as to cause of success of, 732; 764, 783; the slavery influence in, 783 et seq.; migration to California and the West, from, 793; causes modifying intemperance in, 793–4; chastity in, 795–9; church discipline of, 795–9; conditions of life, colonial times, 802–3; diversions in colonial times, 808–9; town-meeting government, 810–26; burden of Indian wars upon, 827; stress in, during Revolution, 868 et seq.; before the problem of the war of Revolution, 874, before that of the Indian and French wars, 875; limit of colonial emigration to, 922; limited industrial development of towns, 927; infrequency of Roman Catholics in, 931.
New England Primer, 778–9.
New England's lamentations for Old England's errors, 564.
New English Canaan, by Morton, account of Wessagusset hanging in, 79–81; account of Lake Erocoise in, 301; publication of, 303; 343; no copy at Plymouth, 344; 351.
Newetowne, see Newtown.
Newfoundland, Squanto sent to, 1615, with Dermer, 25; 45; Gorges sends trading vessels to, 119; restrictions on Banks of, in Plymouth Company's charter of 1620, 123.
New Hampshire, Captain John Mason, the patentee of, 263; 283; Burdett removes to, from Salem, 310; Wheelwright takes refuge from persecution in, 482; 581; dread of banishment to, salutary for good order of Boston, 534; Mrs. Hutchinson abandons project of settling in, 536; Underhill removes to, 554; 1641, admitted to jurisdiction of Mass. Bay, 539; boundary dispute with Mass. Bay, 702; foreigners come to Quincy from, 946.
New Haven, 345; end of Pequot war at, 466; residence of Isaac Allerton, 598.
New Jersey, the southern limit of colonial organization under Gorges' scheme of 1634, 276; Washington's army encamped in, winter of 1779–80, 888.
New London, 466.
Newman, Rev. Samuel, a rival of Rev. Hull's, 1638, in church at Weymouth, 341.
New Mexico, 534.
Newport, R. I., formerly called Aquidneck, 536; in seventeenth century, point of embarkation for New York, 597; Trinity Church, 621.
New Somersetshire, name of Sir F. Gorges' province in Maine, 301; William Gorges appointed governor of, 308.
Newspapers, daily, not received at Quincy, prior to 1830, 804.
Newtown, or Newetowne, early name of Cambridge, 448, 453, 483; described by Dudley in letter to Countess of Lincoln, 484.
New York, project of the Pilgrims for settling in, 46; Morton would have been unmolested in, 225; Sir C. Gardiner's

## INDEX. 1047

project of a refuge in, 255; Maverick's official services in, 335; route to, from New England, 597; 677; Tompson and Knowles at, 1642, 598; Rev. Edward Winslow buried in St. George's Church at, 633; prayers for King at, 1776, 852; 927.
Niantic tribe of Indians, war with, 1653, 828.
Nicholson, Edward, marshal of Boston, at hanging of Quakers, 550.
Niles, Samuel, minister of Braintree Middle Precinct Church, attacks Lemuel Briant in a sermon, 1749, 638; of committee on Braintree commons, 1762, 665; 740; Stamp Act Committee meets at his house, 839.
Ninigret, sachem of Niantic, war of 1653 with, 828.
Noddle's Island, fort built upon, by Samuel Maverick, 192; Maverick compelled to remove from, 1635, to Boston, 288; 331; Josselyn's account of his entertainment at, 331-2; deeded by Maverick to his son, 334; Vane and Lord Ley visit Maverick at, 331; 462.
Norfolk County, Mass., town schools of, 937.
Norfolk, Virginia, route to, from New England, 597.
Norman, John, fined by General Court, 337.
Northampton, Mass., religious revival, 1735, 749; militia employed in Shays' rebellion disbanded at, 898.
North Precinct of Braintree, 590; schools in, 1790, 901; incorporated as the town of Quincy, 1792, 903; meeting-house, 921.
North Quincy, part of allotment to Wm. Hutchinson, 366, *note*.
North River, Mass., 88.
Norton, Elizabeth, marries John Quincy, 1715, 707.
Norton, Rev. John, third pastor of Hingham, 409, *note;* his daughter marries John Quincy, 1715, 707.
Norton, Mrs. Mary, gift to Braintree meeting-house, 737; her seat in, *ib.*, 738.
Norton, Rev. ——, minister of Weymouth, 975.
Nowell, Elder Increase, of Winthrop's colony, 23; examines Mrs. Hutchinson, 502; in discussion over her speech, 504.
Nowell, Samuel, at marriage of Daniel Quincy, 706.
Noy, William, Attorney General, England, files *quo warranto* against Mass. Bay Company, 1635, 291; engaged in ship money project, 295; death, *ib.*
Obbatinewat, sagamore, 15; visited by Standish, 1621, 16-18; 19.
Ohio River, Washington's expedition to, 1754, 641.

Old Colony Railway, opened, 1845, 923; granite railway franchise bought by, 927; the original line in America, *ib.*
Old Corner Bookstore, Boston, on site of Anne Hutchinson's house, 397, *note*.
Oldham, John, comes to New England, 1623, 183; "a mad Jack," 184; causes trouble at Plymouth, *ib.;* with Lyford becomes centre of Plymouth discontents, 185; his letters opened by Bradford, *ib.;* his disturbances at Plymouth, 186; brought before the General Court for conspiracy, 187; his defence, *ib.;* ordered to leave Plymouth, 188; of character superior to Lyford, *ib.;* reappearance at Plymouth, 189; rebukes Plymouth people, *ib.;* is imprisoned, *ib.;* stays at Nantasket, 190; takes Morton to England, 207-8, 212; 209; territory conveyed to, by John Gorges, 212; seeks employment from Mass. Company, 214; his character, 215; his difficulties with company, *ib.*; his grant contested, *ib.;* outgeneralled by Mass. Company, 216-17; settlement made on his land by brothers Sprague, 217; his efforts to regain his title, 220; returns to New England and settles at Watertown, 221; fooled by Morton, *ib.;* his efforts in the prosecution of Morton, *ib.;* cause of his relaxing same, 223; his influence feared by Company, 225; 232; gives information of Morton, 249.
Old South Meeting House, Boston, 238.
Oliver, Captain James, in persecution of Quakers, 1659, 408-9, *note*.
Oliver, John, elected to General Court, 1637, 480; refused a seat by the Court, *ib.;* electors refuse to send a substitute, *ib.*
Oliver, Thomas, suggests Anne Hutchinson's sons be admonished, 520.
Opinionists, Mrs. Hutchinson's party called, 422; fifty-eight in all, 511.
Orleans shoals, 43.
Otis, Harrison Gray, Federalist candidate for governor, Mass., 1823, 945-6.
Otis, James, appointed to support memorial for opening law-courts, 1765, 1839-40; town-meeting orator, 967.
Ovid, Art of Love, read by John Adams to Mrs. Savil, 805.
Owen, Ebenezer, of Braintree, 1699, "his distracted daughter," 726.
Owen, Ebenezer, of Braintree, 1690, goes on Quebec expedition, 758; dies of small-pox, *ib.*, 830; his widow causes scandal, 759.
Owen, Josiah, of Braintree, 726; 1692, disciplined by church, 759.
Owen, Mary, insane woman of Braintree, 726.
Owen, Nathaniel, Braintree constable, 1713, 626; 627; substitute in militia

1048                    INDEX.

for J. Marshall, impressment of 1709, 720; in Braintree records, 727.
Oxford University, Laud's supervision of, 1637, 297; William Tompson a graduate of, 596; makes Ebenezer Miller D. D., 630.
Oyster Bay, Long Island, Underhill dies at, 1672, 558.

Pacific Ocean, limit of territory granted Plymouth Council, 122.
Palfrey, J. G., cited as to religious intolerance in New England, 248, *note;* concerning Mary Grove, 256, 257, *notes;* sentence of Ratcliff, 262, *note;* cause of granting Mass. Bay charter, 272; population of Mass. Bay, 1634, 340, *note;* his partiality for Winthrop, 378, *note;* Wheelwright's fast-day sermon, 440, *note;* temper of General Court during Anne Hutchinson's trial, 527; 528; English colonial emigrants, 922.
Palfrey, Peter, of Salem, 201.
Palmer, ——, of Braintree aids in throwing tea into Boston harbor, 850.
Palmer, Deacon, General Joseph, 1744, declines office of constable, 825; delegate from Braintree to General Court at Cambridge, 1775, 849, 860; to the county convention, 1776, 850; 871; contributions to town recruiting fund, 1780, 877; military service, 885-6; failure of Rhode Island expedition, 886; Braintree's delegate to Constitution convention, 1780, 891; head of committee on town government, 1780, 889, 891; 962.
Paomet, Indian tribe, 72; in conspiracy to destroy Wessagusset, 73.
Paper currency, depreciation in Massachusetts, 1775, 864.
Papists, no provision for toleration of, Massachusetts charter, 1691, 819.
Paradise Lost, 809.
Paris, siege of, 1589, Gorges at, 106.
Parker, F. W., superintendent Quincy schools, 939-40; 975.
Parker, Theodore, 643.
Parkman, Francis, cited, 901.
Parliament of 1621, called the Grievances Parliament, 126; attacks Gorges' patent, 127-9; contention with the King, 129; adjourned and then dissolved, *ib.;* 130; 272; under Charles I., 297; its Commission for Plantations, 315; the Long, dissolved by Cromwell, 373; 860; origin traced to Baltic settlements, 980; its right to tax colonies, 842-3; repeal of Stamp Act, 846; Revenue Bills introduced, 1767, 846-7.
——, House of, its picture of Lady Alice Lisle, 705.
Parma, Duke of, Sluys besieged by, 106.
Parmenter, John, of Braintree, 830.
Parmenter, Joseph, 1730, clerk, North Precinct, Braintree, 742; 744; disciplined by church, 761.
Partridge, ——, of Duxbury, 873.
Passacus, Indian, war with, 1645, 828.
Passonagessit, afterwards Mt. Wollaston, Chickatabot's plantation at, 11; site of Wollaston settlement, 166; character of, 166-8; delineated on maps by Captain John Smith, 167; the region round about, 166-8; condition of the colony, summer of 1626, 174; name changed to Ma-re Mount, or Merry Mount, by Morton, 175; 194; 285; fate of Wollaston's colony at, 343.
Patuxet, *i. e.* Plymouth, pestilence at, 9; 23, 28; Indian from, kidnapped by Gorges, 24, *note.*
Pauper class, Braintree, 722-4; 727-31; 900; 917; 918.
Peace, treaty of, 1783, United States and Great Britain, 893.
Pearce, Gen. E. W., 104, *note.*
Pecksuot, Indian, as to attack on French trader in Boston Bay, 7-8; taunts Standish, 92; killed by Standish, 92-3.
Peddock's Island, Boston Bay, 7.
Peirce, William, master of ship, 185.
Pemaquid, 24.
Pembroke, William, third Earl of the Plymouth Company, 122; his character and influence in behalf of charter, 124; at meetings of the Council for New England, 131.
Pendergast, Rev. ——, Roman Catholic clergyman, visits J. Q. Adams, 1826, 931, celebrates first Mass at Quincy, *ib.:* 932.
Penn's Hill farm, Braintree, birthplace of John Adams, 617; his home, 805; first residence after marriage, 845; scene at, May 21, 1775, 857, 858; Mrs. Adams and son, John Quincy, watch signs of Bunker's Hill battle from, 858-9; her observations from, during affair of Dorchester Heights, 866; of the fleet of British troops' ships in Boston Bay, 867; 868, 886, 888, 919; 951.
Penniman, James, disciplined by Braintree church, 760-1.
Penniman, John, in Braintree records, 727.
Penniman, John, of Swansea, 823.
Penniman, Samuel, in Braintree records, 727, 756, 772.
Penniman, Stephen, 903.
Penniman, Thomas, Braintree delegate to county convention, 1774, 850.
Penniman, William, of Braintree, 835; appointed to obtain evidence against Tories, 1777, 853.
Penobscot, 24, *note,* 308, 912; expedition to, 1778, 874.
——, Indians, captured by Weymouth, protected by Gorges, 1605; 23-4, *note,* 117; Gorges trades with, 119.

INDEX. 1049

Pepperell, General Sir William, at Louisburg, 764.
Pepys, Samuel, cited, 762.
Pequot Indians not affected by pestilence of 1616-7, 4; strength of, 1634, *ib.;* dangers feared from, 1623, 102; troubles with, one cause of fast-day, 1637, 437; fear of trouble with, 1637; 451.
——, war, men furnished by Weymouth in, 340; Wilson attends military campaign, 463; Boston church-members refuse to serve in, 461; termination of, 466; 480; Stoughton's return from, 470; Underhill serves in, 551; 571.
Perkins, Thomas Handasyd, funds for building Quincy granite railway supplied by, 926.
Pestilence among Mass. Indians, 1616-7, 1-4, 9-12; among Connecticut Indians, 1634, 2-3; at Charlestown, 1630, 235-7; at Salem, 1630, 240, 241; at Braintree, 1775, 862.
Peters, Hugh, 347, 371, 372; comes to New England with Sir Harry Vane, 1635, 374; his character, *ib.;* appointed to Salem church, vice Roger Williams, 375,; his career as minister, *ib.;* sent to England, 1641, as agent of the colony, *ib.;* serves in parliamentary army, *ib.;* his services as soldier and preacher, *ib.;* abuse of Laud, *ib.;* at the trial of Charles I., *ib.;* walks with Milton at funeral of Cromwell, *ib.;* trial and execution as a regicide, 376; rebukes Vane, 423; their subsequent friendly relations in England, 425, *note;* at examination of Mrs. Hutchinson, 426-8; introduces Laud's practices in General Court, 446; 456; at synod of 1637, 470; 476; at trial of Mrs. Hutchinson, 486; gives evidence, 492; cause of his bitterness, 493; his testimony, 494; browbeats Coggeshall, 496; 497; examines Cotton, 498; testimony under oath, 507; his conduct towards Cotton at trial, 514; joins in attack on Mrs. Hutchinson, after her confession, 528, 529; compared with Loyola, 565; Endicott his mouthpiece, 572; 577.
Petersham, Worcester County, Mass., 926.
Petfree, ——, captain of French man-of-war, befriends Gibbons, 357.
Pew system permitted in Braintree meeting-house, 1698, 735.
Philadelphia, the southern limit of Plymouth Company territory, 1620, 122; John Adams goes a delegate to Congress at, 1774, 850; he returns from, 855; letter from, 1775, 858; 859; goes to, 863; 865; returns from, 1777, 886; cider sent from Quincy to President Adams at, 686.

Philip II. of Spain, 248, *note;* model of Charles I., 270, 476, 561.
Philip, Indian king, 326; war with, 659, 827, 828-9.
Phillips, George, minister at Watertown, death of, 1630, 237; 417; not under Covenant of Grace, 427; at Mrs. Hutchinson's trial, 486; Mather's notice of, *ib.*, *note.*
Phips, Sir William, Governor, 760; in Quebec expedition, 1690, 830.
Pickering, Edward, attempts to inform Plymouth of Weston's expedition, 1622, 56; 57.
Pierce, William, the master of ship Lyon, 339.
Pilgrims of Plymouth, Weston's influence in their settlement in North America, 45-51; their amended agreement with him for aid and supplies, 1621, 50; their first shipment to him in the Fortune, *ib.;* abandoned by him, 51; learn the way to Damariscove Islands, and establish a station on the Kennebec, 54; at Provincetown, 1620, 125; their reception of Thomas Weston, 147. *See* Plymouth.
Piscataqua River, settlement, Thomas Weston sheltered at, 146; David Thompson builds house at, 192, 329; increased by people from Winthrop's party, 1636, 236; Sir C. Gardiner's plans of refuge at, 255; 309, 316, 353, 354, 357; Wheelwright removes to, 482; settlers warned against Underhill, 554; Underhill made governor of, 555; deposed, 556; called Dover, *ib.*
Pitt, William, Lord Chatham, 1756, 835, 836.
Plague, *see* Pestilence.
Plough patent, or Lygonia claim to Maine, 314; sold by Cleeve to Sir Alexander Rigby, 314; his claim sustained by Parliament, 315; 344.
Plymouth, England, Sir Ferdinando Gorges, governor of, 106; reappointed, 1601, 117; Oldham's return to, 212; Braintree privateers, confined in, 1781, 879.
Plymouth Company, England, incorporated 1606, by royal patent, to Popham and Gorges, 118; extent of territory granted to, *ib.;* exploring parties sent to America by, 1606 and 1607, *ib.;* reorganized by Gorges under new charter, 1620; 121, territory granted to, 122; jurisdiction conferred by 1620 charter, 123; assailed by the Virginia Company, 1621, 126-7; reorganized under name of Council for New England, 1622, 131.
Plymouth, New England, small-pox epidemic at, 1634, 3; excursion from, in Boston Bay, under Standish, 13-18; Patuxet its Indian name, 23; visited by Dermer, 1619, 26; land allotted to Hobamack, 33; first harvest, 34-5;

# 1050  INDEX.

alarm of conspiracy planned by Squanto, 38; people from the ship Sparrow visit, 1622, 51; 52; Weston's selfish purposes, 55; his projected expedition reported from London, 56; 57; magistrates remonstrate with Weston's settlers, 61; Greene dies at, 1622, 62; severity of winter, 1622-3, 63; scarcity of provisions, 65; Council protests against Saunders' extortions of food from Indians, 67; alarmed by revelation of plot to destroy Wessagusset, 74, 811; constructs a fort for defence, 74; insecurity in dangers from Indians, 75; measures taken for defence, 1623, 75-6; mortality at, 1623, 77; Phineas Pratt's expedition to, 1623, 86; 88-9; fort of 1623, an Indian its first prisoner, 98; Governor of, one of Robert Gorges' Council in New England, 141; Thomas Weston comes destitute to, 1623, 147; provided with means for trade at, *ib.;* visited by R. Gorges, 148, contention over Weston, 148-9; settlement nearly destroyed by fire, November 5, 1623, 150; peril of the colony, *ib.;* Weston, released from arrest, appears at, 154; Morell returns to England from, 156; assistance rendered Gorges' people at Wessagusset, *ib.;* not a good trading station, 159; establishment of trading stations at Hull, on the Kennebec and in Connecticut, 160; Morton at, 174, *note;* considered a profane man, 169; first Christmas day at, 1621, 180-1; scandalized by Morton's May-day revels, 181, 182; distance from Merry Mount, 194; colonists abstain from trade in firearms with Indians, 195; their alarm caused by Morton's trade, 197; number of people at, 1628, 198; measures taken for common safety in dangers feared from Morton, 201; magistrates admonish him, *ib.;* Morton returns to, with Allerton, 224; 240; its prosperity inferior to that of Mass. Bay, 269; its people called Separatists, 322; visited by the magistrates of Mass. Bay, 338; visited by Thomas Morton, 344; no copy of New English Canaan there, *ib.;* Morton permitted to remain at, 345; Allerton its agent at London, 1629, to secure a new patent, 223; character of the people of, 364; refuge refused Mrs. Hutchinson, 536; no road from Boston, 1637, 581; the road of 1639, 666-7; road of 1655, 671; residence of Isaac Allerton, 598; 666; its size in 1655, 671; Judge Sewall's journey from, 1712, 679; John and Priscilla Alden of, 714; 927.

Pocahontas, 104.

Point Allerton, 14, *note;* named for Isaac Allerton, 20; proposed fortification of, 1776, 867; 911.

Point Judith, Narragansett Bay, named for Judith Quincy, 700.

Point Shirley, formerly Pullen Point, Gibbons' residence at, 358.

Pokanoket Indians, their region, 23; 24, *note;* 28; Sir C. Gardiner takes refuge with, 255.

Pole's Synopsis, a favorite book in early New England, 391.

Politics, discussion of, in New England taverns, 783-4; in Quincy, 945 *et seq.*

Polk, James K., elected president, 1844, 953.

Pollocks Rip, Cape Cod, 63.

Pope, Alexander, 772; 806.

Popham, George, President of Maine Colony, dies, 118.

Popham, Sir John, Chief Justice of England, his effort to prevent Essex insurrection, 108; confined in Essex House, 109; acts as spy on the conspirators, 109-10; released by Gorges, 111; sits a judge at Essex trial, 109, *note;* with Gorges obtains royal patents for America, 117-18; he sends out exploring party, 1607, 118; his name given to Maine Colony, *ib.;* death in 1607, *ib.*

Popham Colony, coast of Maine established, 1607, 118; it breaks up, 1608, *ib.*

Population of settlements on Boston Bay, 1627, 193; of Braintree, Revolution times, 870-1. *See* Braintree, Quincy, Weymouth.

Port Bill for Boston, 847.

Porter, Benjamin, of Braintree, 834.

Porter, Charles H., at Quincy town-meeting, 1887, 996; first mayor of Quincy, *ib.;* his comment on Quincy city charter, 998.

Porter, Rev. John, of Bridgewater, joins attack on Briant, 638.

Portsmouth, N. H., territory about, drawn by Duke of Buckingham, at Greenwich meeting, 1623, 139; 199, Walford removes from Charlestown to, 336; 536; Henry Flynt's journey to, 1755, 677; 787.

Portugal, trade between New England and, 698.

Postal facilities, lack of, at Quincy, prior to 1795, 803.

Potomac river, the southern limit of territory granted, 1606, to Plymouth Company, 118.

Powder, *see* Gunpowder.

Pratt, Phineas, his journey from Wessagusset to Plymouth, 86-9, 581, 582; remains at Plymouth, 90; 98; his statement as to project for Weston's plantation, 130, *note;* cited as to the persons who accompanied Robert Gorges to New England, 1623, 144, *note;* 146.

Pray, John, player of fiddle in Braintree church, 1812, 741.

## INDEX. 1051

Prayer-book of Church of England, *see* Book of Common Prayer.
Prayers for the King, Christ Church, Braintree, 1776, 633, 852; at New York, *ib.*
Predestination tenet accepted by Vane and Cotton, 457.
Presumpscot Falls, 353.
Price, Ezekiel, on clearance of Boston Bay of British ships, 1776, 868.
Prices current of Revolution time, 790; rise of, 1775, 864–5; 869; in 1780, 880; 892.
Primer, New England, 778–9.
Prince, John, overseer of boys, Hingham meeting-house, 738, *note.*
Printing press, none in Boston, 1637, 456.
Privateers of Revolution, out of Braintree, 879; service of, *ib.*; 1793, Quincy town-meeting regulations to prevent, 906.
Privy Council, England, sustains the 1620 Plymouth Company charter, 125; appealed to, for redress by persons punished in Mass. Bay, 1632, 263; appealed to by Gorges for abrogation of the Mass. Bay charter, 1632, 264; refuses to comply, 266–7; 268; jurisdiction of, in colonial cases, 270, its interference in affairs of Mass. Bay, 1634, 270; 275; its establishment of royal commission for New England of 1634, 278; orders return of Mass. Bay charter, 279; petitioned by Thayer to confirm his title to Braintree, 1692, 654.
Proclamation of James I. prohibiting trade in fire-arms with Indians, 1622, 195; its authority as law discussed, 202; 222.
Providence, R. I., 466; stage coach communication with Boston, 1767, 677; route from, to New York, *ib.*; 828.
Province of Mass. Bay, created by charter of William and Mary, 747.
Provincetown, 63; Mayflower at, 1620, 125.
Prynne, William, 248, *note*; his punishment for the Histrio-Mastix, 262, and *note*; compared with that ordered for Ratcliff, 262.
Psalmody in church service, 739–41; that of Quincy church discussed in town-meeting, 907.
Puddington, Ivory, disciplined at Agamenticus, 312.
Puffer, James, of Braintree, 720.
Puget Sound, 122.
Pullen Point, now Point Shirley, 358.
Punishments, Mass. town-schools, 938.
Purchase, Thomas, marries Mary Grove, 258.
Purgatory, a common name for pauper settlements, 722.
Puritans, forces in England, 107; Essex their hero, 107, 116; Gorges not allied with, 142; their removal from England, influences the granting Mass. Bay charter, 272, 274; Laud's antagonism to, 1637, 297; persecuted by him, 563; adopt their interpretation of the Bible as the basis of law and government, 382 *et seq.*; satirized in Hudibras, 81–3; contempt for, in England after Restoration, 83; probable effect upon, of project for extension of the Church of England, 1623, 142; the Mass. Company composed of, 222; intolerance in religious matters in Mass. Bay, 1630, 230–1; custom of days of fasting and prayer, 237; their religious intolerance discussed, 247–9; a persecuting race, 574.
Putnam, General Israel, 764.
Pym, John, member of Parliamentary Commission for plantations, 315; 450.
Pynchon, William, Assistant of Winthrop's colony, death of, 1630, 237; 241.

Quakers, persecuted at Boston, 1659, 408 and *note*; 409–10, *note*, 542, 549–51; Mary Dyer joins Society of, 549; persecuted by Endicott, 572.
Quarles, Francis, letter to John Cotton, 332.
Quebec, Colonial expedition of 1690 to, 758, 760, 830; captured by Wolfe, 1759, 836.
Quarrymen in Quincy politics, 947.
Quincy, Ann, daughter of Daniel and Anna Quincy, 706.
Quincy, Anna, widow of Daniel, marries Moses Fiske, 615, 678, 707.
Quincy, Daniel, son of Edmund 3d, and Joanna Hoar, 701; father of John, *ib.*; his ancestry, 704; 706; marries Anna Shepard, 1682, 706; 707; Sewall's account of marriage, *ib.*; his children, *ib.*; death, 1690, *ib.*; his career, 707; his widow marries Moses Fiske, 615; 678.
Quincy, Dorothy, "Dorothy Q.," daughter of Edmund 4th and Dorothy Flynt, her descendants, 605.
Quincy, Dorothy [2d], wife of John Hancock, 605; her marriage, 1775, 680.
Quincy, Edmund [1st], of Achurch, Northamptonshire, England, 700.
Quincy, Edmund [2d], born, 1601, died, 1637, and wife Judith, English Puritans, 700; first of family to come to New England, *ib.*; assessor at Boston, 1634, 323; proprietor of Mount Wollaston, 365, 546, 700, 704; further acquisition of land, 1634, 583; 917.
Quincy, Colonel Edmund [3d], born, 1627, died, 1698, son of Edmund and Judith, husband [1] of Joanna Hoar, [2] Elizabeth [Gookin] Eliot; father of Daniel and Edmund, his career, 700–1; builder of mansion at Braintree, 1685, 605, 619, *note*, 680, 700; opposes erection of new meeting-

house, 1695, 611; 1692, author of address to King, 654; 655; his two carpets, 684; 756, 760; of Committee of Safety, 1689, 818; 821, 822; reports failure of impressment, at Braintree, 1690, 830; his death and burial, 1698, 701; his widow's funeral, 1700, 678-9.

Quincy, Judge Edmund [4th], son of Edmund 3d, and Elizabeth [Gookin] Eliot, b. 1681, d. 1738, 701; marries Dorothy Flynt, 605; 616; 702; argument for taxing Episcopalians for support of town minister, 1704, 623; his public services, 702; death at London, *ib.;* buried in Bunhill Fields, *ib.;* monument erected by General Court, *ib.;* his sons, Edmund and Josiah, *ib.;* 954.

Quincy, Edmund [5th], son of Edmund 4th, and Dorothy Flynt, 702; typical of New England gentry, 713.

Quincy, Edmund, son of Josiah 3d, his life of Josiah Quincy cited, 910-12.

Quincy, Elizabeth, daughter of John, wife of Wm. Smith, mother of Abigail, Mrs. John Adams, gives a grandson her father's name, 711; her death, 863.

Quincy, John, son of Daniel and Anna, born, 1689, 615, 617; 663, 706; Mount Wollaston farm, a legacy from his grandmother Shepard, 707; graduate of Harvard, 1708, *ib.;* marriage with Elizabeth Norton, 1715, *ib.;* builds house at Mount Wollaston, 681, 707; his public services, 707-9; loss of colonelcy of Suffolk regiment, 1742, 715; his character, 709-10; his name given to town of Quincy, 711, 904; perpetuated by his great grandson, John Quincy Adams, *ib.;* typical of his time 709, and of New England gentry, 713; of the Hampden, Washington class, 710; his grave unknown, *ib.;* 762; of Braintree school committee, 1730, 901; and 1739, 776; offended by election of his son as constable, 1756, 825-6; his last appearance at town-meeting, 1758, 838; John Adams drinks tea with, Christmas, 1765; 708, 840; Mrs. Richard Cranch his granddaughter, 904; 917.

Quincy, Mrs. John, 1765, mentioned by John Adams, 708.

Quincy, Josiah [1st], son of Edmund 4th, and Dorothy Flynt, named for his grandfather Flynt, 605, 702; acquires wealth by capture of Spanish treasure ship, 703; his quiet life, at Braintree, *ib.;* friend of Franklin, 704; serves as Commissioner of Mass. French War, *ib.;* his son Josiah, Jr., *ib.;* of Committee on town commons, 1753, 663; 1761, gives fifty dollars for Braintree roads, 674; use made of it, 675; Colonel of Suffolk Regiment, 703; chosen to tune the psalm in meeting-house, 1723, 739; 740; elected constable, 825, fined for refusing office, *ib.;* 834; anti-stamp-act candidate for selectman, 1766, 843; a delegate to Boston convention, 849; 856; on military camps about Braintree, 1775, 864; 1775, watches ship carrying Gage to England, *ib.;* reports to Washington observations of British fleet in Boston Bay, March, 866-7; 871; 1780, his unfortunate money transactions with town, 881; town-meeting orator, 967.

Quincy, Josiah, Jr., 1744-75, son of Josiah 1st, public career, 704; defends Captain Preston, *ib.;* patriot agent at London, 1774, *ib.;* his death, 1775; *ib.;* his widow at Braintree, 1775, 856.

Quincy, Josiah [3d], 1772-1864, son of Josiah, Jr., 704; his wife's account of Quincy church, 741; his home at Quincy, 856; President of Harvard College, *ib.,* 910; recollections of departure of Mrs. Adams for England, 1784, 888; his opinion as to the severity of early magistrates, 248, *note;* in conveyance of title of graveyard to town of Quincy, 1809, 906; life of, cited, as to ship Constitution in Boston Bay, 910-12.

Quincy, Josiah, Jr. [4th], son of Josiah 3d, Figures of the Past cited, 909.

Quincy, Josiah [6th], one of authors of Quincy city charter, 1888, 997.

Quincy, Judith, wife of Edmund 2d, 700.

Quincy, Judith, daughter of Edmund 2d, and Judith, her descendant marries a Sewall, 700; Point Judith, Narragansett Bay, named for her, *ib.*

Quincy, Norton, son of John, 711; declines office of constable, 1756, 825; accepts, 1757, 826; presides over Braintree Stamp Act meeting, 1765, 839; 1767, elected selectman, 846; head of Braintree Committee of Safety, 1774, 850; observations of British ships, 1776, 868; 886, 887; taxes paid at Quincy, 692.

Quincy, Saer de, a signer of Magna Charta, 700.

Quincy, Samuel, entertained at tavern on admission to the bar, 1758, 788; as a Tory, driven to exile, 854.

Quincy family, its origin, 699; establishment in New England, 700; 605; not of Episcopal church, 632; 698 types of colonial gentry, 716; slaves owned by, 923; Mrs. Edmund Quincy's funeral, 1700, 678; Sewall's visit at, 1712, 679; 680, 701; view from mansion on the bay, 910.

Quincy Bay defined on Smith's map, 5; Chickatabot's plantation in, 11; 22; military operations in, 1775, 861-2; John Adams sails from, to Europe, 1778, 886; protected from Brit ̈ h,

## INDEX. 1053

March, 1776, 866-7; ship-building on, 924.
Quincy Point, 61, *note*.
Quincy, town, site of, "Massachusetts Fields" embraced within, 14, *note;* within the territory granted to Robert Gorges, 131, *note;* Morton's Passonagessit, 166; site of William Hutchinson's house, 536, *note;* its records of William Coddington, 546; Edmund Quincy's mansion at, 679, 680, 701; Josiah Quincy's dwelling on Hancock lot, 703; new spirit of the age in, 644-5; road to Boston, 673; character in early years of century, 741; survival of old-time taverns, 793-4; prior to 1830, daily papers not received at, 804; little accustomed to reading, 805; 857; religious development in, 944. *See* Braintree.
1792, North Precinct of Braintree, incorporated, 590, 642, 747, 903; named for John Quincy, 701, 904, 905; strong party for name of Hancock, 904; small-pox hospitals, 906;
1793, action to preserve national neutrality, 906;
1812, town-records, void of notice of war of 1812, 910; its militia not in service, *ib.;* alarm on reported arrival of enemy at Scituate, 911-12; joint action with Hingham and Weymouth for defence, 912; its contribution to expenses of war, *ib.;*
1826, celebration of July 4, 1826, 920; day of John Adams' death, *ib.;* J. Q. Adams' reflections on visit to, 921; Granite Railway built, 591;
1860-5, war of Rebellion, 961-4; Charles Francis Adams its contribution to national defence, 961;
1888, discussion of incorporation as a city, 996-7; principles of charter of 1888, 998-1000; terms of charter, 1000-3;
1889, January, becomes a city, 1003.
———, Burying-ground, its condition prior to 1809, 905-6; title to, conveyed to town, 906.
———, Church, 1792, 590; 1792-1800, Anthony Wibird, minister of, 642-3; 1800-43, Peter Whitney, minister, 643-4; change from orthodoxy to Unitarianism, 643; Mrs. Josiah Quincy's account of, 741; 1824, church becomes Congregational Society, 748; increase of membership, 1639-1739, *ib.;* renewal of covenant by members, 1739, *ib.:* Other religious societies : Congregational, 930; Episcopal, *ib.;* Universalist, *ib.;* Evangelical Congregational, *ib.;* Methodist Episcopal, *ib.;* Roman Catholic, 931-2; granite quarry given by John Adams to provide material for a new meeting-house, 1822, 919; Universalist meeting-house built, 1832, 930.

———, Finances, bad system, 916; rectified by Greenleaf, 917; town expenses, subsequent to 1792, 912-15; taxation, 1815-29, 912-13; its public debt, 950, 972; civil war taxation, 963; 1790-1885, 987.
———, Industries, ship-building, 924; granite quarries, 924-8, their value to the town, 927-8; development of tanneries, 928; shoemaking, 929-30; the town under industrial influences, 930; change in its business character, subsequent to 1830, 946 *et seq.;* occupations of inhabitants, 986.
———, Libraries, Christ Church, its library, 804; John Adams' library bequeathed to town, 804; 920; free public library established 1871, 940-1; Crane Memorial Hall, library building, 942.
———, Paupers, 1792, paupers warned to leave, 723; care of, put up at auction, 729; expense for, prior to 1820, 730; support of, 914, 916; 917, 918; almshouse built, 1815, 905.
———, Political characteristics of, 945 *et seq.;* contests in, *ib.;* a Federalist town, 909; vote of, 915; party politics in, 915-17; influence of the shoemaker in, 947; support given to Know-Nothing party, 958-9; effect of labor-unions, 1887, 988.
———, Population, 689-98; 1810-30; 915; 1865, 965, character of community, *ib.;* 1865-85, 984-5; 1875, 954; 1885, 985, *note;* its foreign-born inhabitants, 1875, 985; of granite village, 928.
———, Post-office, established, 1795, 803.
———, Schools, 776-7; 1812-24, 913; 1827-75, 933-40; Academy founded by John Adams, 941.
———, Social life, 699-721; character of inhabitants, 915; settlers prior to 1800, of pure strain of English blood, 922; English names in records, 923; alien infusion, 946 *et seq.*
———, Temperance reform, 950; 1838, ardent spirits provided for town laborers, 792; people opposed to temperance, 1840, 975.
———, Town Hall, burnt and rebuilt temporarily, 905; site of new one, *ib.;* the permanent building, 918; scene in, pictured, 969.
———, Town-meeting, refuses to authorize vaccination, 1809, 906; its protest against privateering, 1793, *ib.;* regulates tolling of bell, 907; buys bass-viol for meeting-house, 1804, 906-7; management of church affairs, 907; psalmody, *ib.;* salary of minister, 908; church music discussed, *ib.;* administration of government under, 916-18; development of, 918; 966 *et seq.;* causes derangement of public business, 971 *et seq.;* reform caused by J. Q. Adams, 2d, 1870, 973, changes

in municipal system of, 982-3 ; its modern needs, *ib.;* growth of business, 986 ; articles for consideration at, 1887, 989 ; revolt caused by labor-unions, 990 *et seq.;* story of the last, 1887, 990-6 ; 1888, 1006-7 ; adoption of city charter, 1007-8.

Quonahassit, *i. e.* Cohasset, Indian quarrel with Smith at, 5.

Rabelais, 390.
Railway at Quincy, for carrying granite, 926.
Raleigh, Sir Walter, 45 ; compared with Gorges, 105 ; who was connected with family of, 106 ; informed of the Essex plot, 1601, 113 ; 317.
Rainsford Island, Boston Bay, 911.
Rahl, Johann Gottlieb, Hessian commander, 874.
Randolph, Edward, 624.
Ranters, religious sect, persecuted at Boston, 542.
Rasdell, ——, in charge at Passonagessit, 168 ; turns over the colony to Fitcher, *ib.;* supposed to have come with Wollaston's servants, 1626, 174 ; follows him to Virginia, 1626, *ib.*
Ratcliff, Philip, 250 ; his offence at Salem, 1631, 259 ; 261 ; mitigation of punishment, *ib.;* a servant of Gov. Craddock, *ib.;* 266 ; his case described by Morton, 259 ; his encounter with Thomas Dexter, 260 ; his sentence compared with Prynne's, 262 ; witness for Gorges in attack on charter, 1632, 263 *et seq.;* 268 ; 1634, witness before Privy Council, against Mass. Bay Company, 278 ; his statement as to religious affairs at Boston, 279 ; 283, 347.
Rawson, Edward, Secretary of Mass. Bay, 306.
Rawson, Jonathan, of Braintree, 835.
Rawson, William, his offspring, 609 ; permitted a family pew in meeting-house, 1698, 753 ; 823.
Reading in colonial New England, 804-6.
Rebellion in Mass., Shays', 1786-7, 893, 895, 896, 897.
Rebellion in United States, 1860-5, 957.
Reconciliation meeting, 1636, Dudley and Winthrop, 377-80.
Redemptioners, bound servants, in colonial times, 722.
Regicides, execution, at Charing Cross, 376, *note.*
Revell, Thomas, of Braintree, 724, 819.
Revenue bills introduced in Parliament, 1767, 846-7.
Revivals in religion, New England, 1735-41, 749.
Revolution, war of, 641 ; 642 ; Braintree's immunity from trouble in time of, 827 ; 1766 election its first struggle of, 843 ; the new phase after evacuation of Boston, 868-9 ; difficulties after 1776, in Massachusetts, 869 *et seq.;*

incapacity and improper methods in conduct of, 874 ; finances, 883 *et seq.*
Rheumatism, in colonial times, 800.
Rhode Island, Winslow's first excursion to, 1621, 10 ; Morton visits, 1644, 346 ; William Coddington the father of, 365 ; Wheelwright refuses asylum in, 481, 539 ; dread of banishment to, salutary for Boston, 534 ; Mrs. Hutchinson's misfortunes in, 535, *note;* William and Mary Dyer remove to, 549 ; Life guard, escort of Governor Bellomont, 1699, 718 ; military expedition to, 1777, 874 ; 884, 886.
Rice, ——, master of Braintree grammar school, dismissed, 1775, 855 ; enters army, 856.
Richards, John, agent of Mass. Bay, London, 1692, 654.
Richardson, Henry Hobson, architect, 942.
Richelieu, Cardinal, Wentworth of his type, 273 ; Gorges refuses to deliver the Neptune to, 317 ; 318.
Richmond Island, Maine, 343 ; Morton visits, 1627, 351 ; Bagnall's trading station, 352 ; murdered at, 260, 352, 353, 354 ; relics found at, 354.
Rigby, Sir Alexander, buys from Cleeve, Plough patent to Maine, 314 ; his claim sustained by Parliament, 315 ; Morton, agent of, 344 ; 345.
Roads, Boston to Braintree and Quincy, 1641-1803, 673 ; between Boston and Plymouth, 1637, 581, 594, 666-79 ; Dorchester to Weymouth, 1648, 594 ; use of, prior to 1830, 676-7.
Roberts, Thomas, of Piscataqua settlement, 556.
Robinson, Rev. John, 46 ; on the killing of Wituwamat and Pecksuot, 99 ; his advice to conciliate the Indians, 102 ; 142.
Robinson, William, Quaker, hanged on Boston Common, 1659, 408 and *note;* 409-10, *note;* 550.
Rochelle, France, 317.
Rodgers, John, Commodore U. S. N., 1812, 911.
Roman Catholics, no tolerance of, in Mass. charter, 1691, 644 ; 931 ; first Mass said at Quincy, *ib.;* development of Church at Quincy, 932 ; burying-ground of, *ib.*
Rome, 452-3 ; 967 ; 989.
Rose, British frigate seized in Boston harbor, 1689, 818.
Rosier, James, 24, *note.*
Rossiter, Edward, Assistant of Winthrop's colony, death of, 1630, 237.
Rouen, siege of, 1591, 106 ; Gorges at, 313.
Rowe's Wharf, Boston, 784.
Rowley, Mass., 677.
Roxbury, settlement 1630, 238 ; 324, 525, 533, 535, 536, 726, 836 ; on route to Cambridge, from Boston, 454 ; Mrs.

INDEX.                                                                    1055

Hutchinson's sojourn at, 1637, 509;
  513, 601, 1719, noted for its schools,
  766.
Roxbury Neck, 671.
Royal Commission for governing New
  England, 1634, 277 et seq.
Royal governor question, 1635, in Mass.
  Bay, 811-12.
Royal proclamations, 195, 202, 222.
Ruggles, John, of Braintree, 772; 821.
Rum, use of colonial times, 786 et seq.
Rupert, Prince, at Long Ashton, 313;
  347.
Russell family, Sir Ferdinando Gorges
  connected with, 106.

Sabbath, limits of, defined by General
  Court, 893.
Sachem's Knoll, Chickatabot's residence,
  15.
Saco, Maine, seat of William Gorges'
  government, 308.
Sacheverell, Rev. Henry, 368.
Sagamore, John, son of Nanepashemet,
  consents to the settlement of the
  brothers Sprague at Mishawum, 217.
St. Botolph's Church, Boston, England,
  393.
St. Croix River, northern boundary of
  territory allotted at Greenwich meet-
  ing, 1623, 139; 209.
St. George's Church, New York, place
  of burial of Rev. Edward Winslow,
  633.
St. Giles' Church, Edinburgh, Laud's
  liturgy not permitted to be read in,
  300, 302.
St. James, Court of, John Adams, U. S.
  Minister at, 888; Charles Francis
  Adams, U. S. minister at, 961.
St. John, New Brunswick, La Tour's
  fort at, 358.
St. Louis, Mo., bridge across the Missouri River at, 668.
St. Petersburg, J. Q. Adams, U. S. minister at, 909.
Saleby, Lincolnshire, Wheelwright's
  birthplace, 368; 369.
Salem, Asa and Uzzia, cases cited by
  Winthrop in his justification, 512.
Salem, Mass., 201; the ship George
  brings settlers for Endicott's colony,
  1629, 217; Morton gains favor with
  Gorges because of his opposition to
  the new colony, 223; the famine and
  sickness at, winter of 1629-30, 228;
  the Mary and John brings new settlers, 1630, 228-30; John Winthrop arrives, 1630, 233; first residence of Isaac
  and Lady Arbella Johnson, 234; people of, in severe straits, ib.; famine
  and sickness at, 1630, 240; 241; offence committed by Ratcliff, 259; his
  affair with Endicott, 261; northern
  limit of territory allotted to Lord
  Gorges, partition of 1635, 283; Endicott mutilates royal banner at, 287;

Rev. George Burdet at, 1634, 310;
  Edward Gibbons' conversion and subsequent disorderly behavior at, 355,
  356; northern boundary of European
  settlement in Mass. Bay, 1630, 363;
  first emigrants to, called Separatists,
  568; 666; Mr. and Mrs. John Adams
  drive to, 1766, 677; 854.
Salisbury, James Cecil, third Earl, of the
  Plymouth Company, under charter of
  1620, 122; his influence at court in
  behalf of charter, 124; member of
  Privy Council, sustains the charter,
  125.
Saltonstall, Leverett, defeated for Congress, 1860, by C. F. Adams, 961,
  note.
Saltonstall, Sir Richard, Assistant of
  Mass. Bay, 1630, 155, 241, 256, note;
  in defence of charter, 1632, 265; 275,
  278, note; 282; of the English gentry,
  364; his farm lands, 365.
Samoset, Indian, 9; visits Plymouth
  with Squanto, 1620-1, 28.
Sancho Panza, 149.
Sanders, Martin, tavern-keeper of Braintree, 787.
Sandwich, Mass., 31; formerly Manomet, 69.
San Francisco Bay, California, visited
  by Drake, 122; City, 927.
Saunders, John, in command at Wessagusset, 1622, 62; attempts to buy and
  extort food from Indians, 66; informs
  Plymouth of his intention, 66-7;
  strengthens the stockades of Wessagusset, 66; warned by Bradford, 67;
  his perilous voyage in Swan, 68; 69,
  76, 91, 96; Thomas Weston informed
  by him of troubles at Wessagusset,
  146.
Saunders, John, Vestryman, Christ
  Church, Braintree, 622; his gallery
  seats in meeting-house destroyed,
  1720, 736-7.
Sassacus, Pequot chief, his scalp brought
  to Boston, 466.
Savage, James, statements concerning
  Mary Grove, 256, note; as to Ratcliff's
  sentence, 262.
Savage, ——, at Daniel Quincy's wed-
  ding, 706.
Savage, Thomas, attempts defence of
  Mrs. Hutchinson, 520; reproved and
  silenced by church, 520-1.
Savil, Benjamin, Lieut. Deacon, 821.
Savil, Dr. Elisha, 824; John Adams'
  comments on party at his house, 1758,
  841-2.
Savil, Mrs., John Adams reads Ovid's
  Art of Love to, 805.
Savil, Ned, privateer, in Plymouth jail,
  1781, 879.
Savil, Samuel, his gallery seats in meet-
  ing-house, 1720, 736-7.
Savill, William, 819-20.
Savin Hill, Mass., 15.

# 1056  INDEX.

Savonarola, 385.
Saxon customs in New England, 655; theory of derivation of town-meeting from folk-mote, 814, 815.
Say and Seale, Lord, project to emigrate to New England, 299; of Parliamentary commission for plantations, 315; a proprietor of Connecticut, 374; Sir Harry Vane his agent, *ib.*
Scarborough, Maine, 331.
Schneider, Johann, *see* Agricola, John.
Scholarship in Mass. town-schools, 1879, 937.
Schools, provision for, at Braintree, 723, 724; reorganized, 1790, 900-1; influence of, in New England, 765; Mass. Bay law of 1647, 766; at Quincy, 913; system at Quincy, 1827-75, 933-40.
School-books of colonial New England, 778-80.
School discipline, 938.
School-houses, 780.
School instruction, 781.
School lands at Braintree or Quincy, 546, and *note.*
School Street, Boston, site of Winthrop's house, 1630, 239; John Stephenson a resident in, 1659, 324.
Scituate, Mass., 338, 582, 911; Gridley Bryant's family, dwellers at, 926.
Scotchmen, emigrants to Mass., 1651, 922.
Scotland, disregarded in England, 1635, 294; interference of Laud in Church of, 297; influence on affairs of New England, 298 *et seq.*; the League and Covenant, signed, 1638, 304; rebellion over Laud's liturgy, 306; General Assembly of 1638, at Glasgow, *ib.*; its seventeenth century intellectual condition, 566.
Scott, Sir Walter, Old Mortality cited, 438; Woodstock cited, 745, *note.*
Scottow, Joshua, account of Edward Gibbons' conversion, 355.
Scrooby, England, a home of the Separatists, 142; John Smith's birthplace, 369.
Second Colony, afterwards Plymouth Company, incorporated 1606, 118.
Sedgmuir, England, battle of, 705.
Sensible, French frigate, brings John Adams home from France, 1779, 887.
Sentry Hill, Boston, 269; after April, 1635, called Beacon Hill, 288; Blackstone's residence on, 322.
Separatists, 142; Plymouth people so-called, 222; also first emigrants to Salem, 568.
Sergeants, of Boston, refuse escort to Winthrop, 1637, 461, 462; prosecuted by General Court, 509-10.
Sermons, circulation of, in manuscript, 1637, 456.
Servants, articled, brought by Captain Wollaston to New England, 1625, 162; carried by him to Virginia, 168; 722-3.

Servetus, 385.
Sewall, Judge Samuel, journey from Boston to Cambridge, 1711, 453; visit at Quincy mansion, Braintree, 605, 679, 680; contempt of Book of Common Prayer, 626-7; mention of Ebenezer Miller at Braintree, 1727, 629; characterization of Col. Edmund Quincy, 654; his funeral, 1698, 701; Mrs. Edmund Quincy's funeral, 1700, 678-9; journey from Plymouth, 1712, 679; winter weather 1716, 682; marriage of Daniel Quincy, 1682, 706; death of Mrs. Brattle, *ib.*; gives Mrs. John Quincy a psalm-book, 707; psalm-tuner, South Church, Boston, 739; his blunder in tuning, *ib.*; prayer for peace in Braintree Middle Precinct church, 740; 741; on dog fights in church, 744.
Shakespeare, 119, 390, 537; his works in houses of colonial gentry, 805.
Shannon, British man-of-war, engagement with U. S. Chesapeake, 911.
Shawmut, afterwards Boston, 167; included in territory granted to Endicott, 211; 239, 252; Blackstone's residence at, 322.
Shays, Daniel, his rebellion in Massachusetts, 1786, 893, 895, 896, 897, 899, 995.
Sheep Island, Boston Bay, Braintree men drive British foraging party from, 1775, 857.
Sheffield, Lord, 210.
Shepard, Anna, grand-daughter of Rev. Thomas Shepard, marries 1st, 1682, Daniel Quincy, 707; 2d, 1701, Moses Fiske, 615, 678, 706, 707; John Quincy her son, *ib.*; death of, 1708, *ib.*
Shepard, Thomas, minister of Cambridge, said by Mrs. Hutchinson not to preach Covenant of Grace, 427; silenced by Laud from preaching in England, 447; 456; at Synod of 1637, 470; 484; at trial of Anne Hutchinson, 487; dissatisfied with her confession, 525; in her further persecution, 526; 529, 530; his New England's Lamentations, cited, 564, *note;* his wife, daughter of William Tyng, 707; his grand-daughter, wife of Daniel Quincy, 706, 707; and of Rev. Moses Fiske, *ib.*; at wedding of Daniel Quincy, 706.
Shepard, Mrs. Thomas, daughter of William Tyng, inherits Mount Wollaston farm, 1661, 707; she bequeaths same to grandson, John Quincy, *ib.*; death of, 1709, *ib.*
Shephard, ——, fined for drinking, 356.
Sherman, Goodwife, her quarrel with Captain Keayne, 456.
Ship-building on Quincy Bay, 924.
Ship-money tax, writs of 1635, 290, 295, 296; English judges in favor of, 299, 302, 306.

Shirley, Governor William, negatives election of Paul Dudley a delegate to General Court, 708.
Shoemakers in Quincy politics, 947.
Shoemaking industry at Quincy, 929-30.
Shoals, Isle of, touched by ship Sparrow, 1622, 52; Morton removed from Plymouth to, 1828, 207.
Shrewsbury, Mass., John Adams' account of evening at, 1774, 783-4.
Shrimp, Captain, Morton's name for Standish, 205.
Sidney, Sir Philip, 317.
Simon, Bishop of Ely, Commentaries of, in Christ Church library, Quincy, 804.
Skelton, Rev. Samuel, 225.
Sketwarroes, Indian said to have been kidnapped, 24, note.
Slany, John, Squanto in his service at London, 25.
Slaves owned at Braintree, 923.
Slave-trade, Braintree discontinues, 1775, 855.
Slavery question in Quincy politics, 955, 956.
Sleswick, origin of town-meeting government traced to, 980.
Sluys, Gorges at siege of, 106.
Small-pox epidemic among Indians, 1633-4, 3, 4; periodical epidemics of, colonial times, 801; hospitals, Quincy, 1792, 906.
Smelt Brook, Roxbury, 238.
Smith, Elizabeth, wife of Rev. William, daughter of John Quincy, mother of Abigail, Mrs. John Adams, gives a grandson her father's name, 711; her death, 1775, 863.
Smith, Sir Hugh, his widow, wife of Sir F. Gorges, 315.
Smith, Captain John, describes Massachusetts, 1614, 4-5; Indian attack on French traders, 1614, 8; 19, 23, 45; compared with Gorges, 105; commands expedition sent to New England, 1615, 119; his enthusiasm for New England, 134; cited, 134-5; about Greenwich meeting, 1623, 139; his map of New England, ib.; 152, 157, 163; Passonagessit on his map, 167; mouth of Charles River inaccurately represented, 231-2; Scrooby, England, his birthplace, 369.
Smith, Rev. Ralph, not permitted to remain at Salem, 230; takes temporary residence at Nantasket, 231.
Smith, Toulmin, cited, 1005.
Smith, William, minister of Weymouth, his wife, daughter of John Quincy, 711; father of Mrs. John Adams, ib.; and of Mrs. R. Cranch, 904; his church burned, 1752, 743; sermon on Stamp Act, 841.
Snake in Cambridge meeting-house, 600.
Social rank rule, in Harvard catalogue, 733; in meeting-house seats, 738.

Society for Propagation of the Gospel, London, library sent to Christ Church, Braintree, 1701, 622, 804; aid to church, 622.
Southampton, England, the Mayflower joins the Speedwell at, 47; dispute between Pilgrims and Weston at, 1620, ib., 50; 125.
Southampton, Henry Wriothesley, Earl, associated with Gorges in expedition to Martha's Vineyard, 1614, 119; of the Plymouth Company, 122.
South Boston, 233, 910.
South Church, Boston, Judge Sewall its psalm-tuner, 739.
Southcot, Richard, emigrant in the Mary and John, 232.
Souther, ——, of Braintree, 914.
Souther, Francis L., of Quincy, killed at Big Bethel, Va., 1861, 962, 963.
South Precinct, Braintree, schools in, 1790, 901.
South Virginia Company, 124.
Spain, English expedition against Ferrol, 1597, 106; vessels of, capture Gorges' expedition, 1606, 118; 270; war with, 275; 476; trade between New England and, 698; war with England, 1718, 703; treasure ship of, captured by Yankee merchantman, ib.
Sparrow, ship, sent by Weston and Beauchamp to coast of Maine, 1622, 51, 58, 59, 130; arrival at Plymouth, 42-3, 52; letters to the Pilgrims, brought by, 52-3.
Spear, Nathaniel, of Braintree, 720.
Spear, Samuel, in Braintree records, 725; his insane sister, ib.; 726, 818, 820.
Special providences, Puritan belief in, 503.
Spectacle Island, Boston Bay, 867.
Spectator, Addison's, in houses of colonial gentry, 805.
Speedwell, sails from Delft Haven, August 1, 1620, and joins Mayflower, 47.
Spenser, Edmund, 390.
Spirit-drinking in colonial New England, 785 et seq.; its effects, 791.
Spiritual Milk for American Babes, by John Cotton, a school-book, 778-9.
Sports and games in New England, 179-81.
Sports, Book of, by King James, 336.
Sprague, the three brothers, Ralph, Richard and William, come to New England in ship George, 1629, 217; settle at Mishawum, ib.; they name the place Charlestown, 218; addition to their party under Thomas Graves, ib.
Springfield, Mass., property of Saltonstall at, 365.
Spring Gate, Boston, 238.
Spring Lane, Boston, 238.
Squanto, or Tisquantum, Indian of Pokanoket tribe, kidnapped, 23-4, 25; taken to England by Dermer, 1615, 25;

1058                             INDEX.

returns with him to New England, *ib.*;
saves Dermer's life, 26; his name
given to Squantum, 21, 22; teaches
Plymouth people to plant corn, 21;
other services to them, *ib.*; tells of
the beaver, 35; a guide to Standish,
1621, 15; urges plundering of squaws,
18; interpreter in embassy to Massasoit, 30–1; also to redeem boy stolen
by Indians, 31; important to Plymouth, 33–4; challenged by Canonicus,
35, jealous of Hobamack, 36–7; his
conspiracy, 37; his death demanded
by Massasoit, 1622, 41; compliance
evaded, 42–3; pilots Swan around
Cape Cod, 43, 62; obtains food for
Wessagusset, 63; his death, 29, 44, 62,
64, 105; Bradford's tribute to, 29.
Squantum, Mass., 14, *note*, 15, 19; origin of name, 20, 21, 22; 34, 167; settlement at, 183; first occupied by David Thompson, 191; residence of his
widow, 321; 583, 699, 868; colonial
militia stationed at, 1775, 860;· 861;
proposed fortifications, 1776, 867.
Squaw Rock, another name for Squantum, 21, *note*.
Squaw Sachem, widow of Nanepashemet, 16; Standish's search for, 1621,
17–18.
Squeb, Captain Thomas, assistant to
Francis West on New England coast,
1622, 136; in command of Mary and
John, arrives at Hull, 1630, 228; lands
passengers at Nantasket, 231; his familiarity with coast, 232; his employment by the Council for New England, *ib.*; his meeting with Winthrop
at Nantasket, 1630, 234.
Squidrayset, Indian sagamore of Casco
Bay, at Richmond Island, 352; his
party kill Bagnall, 353.
Stage coaches, Boston and Providence
line, established 1767, 677; between
Boston and Braintree, *ib.*
Stamford, Conn., Underhill removes to
from New Hampshire, 558, *note*.
Stamp Act, 1765, 642; 1765, Braintree's
protest, 838–9; John Adams' zeal in
opposing it, *ib.*; 840; influence of
Episcopalian Church in favor of, *ib.*;
Braintree's instructions to representatives on, 849; attitude of clergy towards, 841–2; affects Braintree election, 1766, 842–4; repeal, 1766, rejoicing at Boston, none at Braintree,
845; effect of repeal, 846.
Standish, Miles, explores Boston Bay,
1621, 13–22, 583; leads expedition to
surprise Corbitant, 34; 37; on expedition to prevent attack of Indians,
1622, 38; 58; asked by Indians to settle near them, 60; commands the
Swan in expedition round Cape Cod,
1622, 62; falls ill on the way, 63; replaced in command by Bradford, *ib.*;
expedition in search of food, 1623, 65;

expedition for food to Manomet, winter of 1622–3, 69; encounter with
Wituwamat, *ib.*; repulses him, 70;
his system with Indians, 70–1; obtains corn from Canacum, 71; apprehensions from the Indians, *ib.*; in
defence against the Indians, 1623, 75;
retaliation for insult at Manomet, 76;
his plan to stop Indian conspiracy, 89;
goes to Wessagusset, April, 1623, 90;
kills Pecksuot and Wituwamat, 92–3,
196, 200; completes his expedition,
93–4; fails to find Aberdecest, 94;
returns to Plymouth, 95; conveys
offer of refuge to Wessagusset people,
96; provisions the ship Swan for the
Wessagusset people, *ib.*; takes Wituwamat's head to Plymouth, 97; his
system with Indians discussed, 101;
102; feared by Indians, 103; the
value of his action at Wessagusset,
103–4; his last fight with Indians at,
104; 136, 167, 183; gives original
name, Trevore, to Thompson Island,
191; arrests Morton, 1628, 203–4;
loses and recaptures him, 205–6; en-
raged by moderate counsels, 207; 209,
217, 224, 245, 285; impatience with
Morton, 345; 351; serves in war with
Narragansetts, 1645, 359; 699.
Star Chamber Court, 202; Morton's
case before, 221; William Prynne
punished by, 262; 1634, 270; 278.
Stark, General John, 764.
Stearns, George, one of three who
first split granite with iron wedges,
925.
"Steenie," familiar name of Buckingham, 124.
Stephenson, George, inventor of loco-
motive engine, 926.
Stephenson, John, his widow, wife of
William Blackstone, 324; her death,
325.
Stevenson, Marmaduke, Quaker, hanged
on Boston Common, 1659, 408, and
*note*; 409–10, *note*; 550.
Stiles, Ezra, account of church proceed-
ings against Mrs. Hutchinson, pre-
served by, 518, *note*.
Stirling, Earl, allotted territory in New
England, partition of 1635, 283; meet-
ing of Council for New England at his
house, 1635, 292.
Stoke Pogis churchyard, 710.
Stone, Rev. Samuel, 466.
Stone's tavern, Boston, 1758, 788.
Stone Temple, Quincy, 930.
Stone-wall, a drink of colonial farm-
hands, 790.
Stoniefield day, July 23, 1637, Laud's
liturgy rejected in St. Giles' Church,
Edinburgh, 300.
Stony Point, capture of, 874.
Stony Sabbath, *see* Stoniefield day.
Storrs, Richard Salter, minister of Brain-
tree church, 944.

## INDEX. 1059

Story, Joseph, cited as to effect of separation of church and state, 590, note.
Stoughton, Israel, in command of the Mass. troops, Pequot war, 466; permits Wilson to return to Boston, ib.; returns from Pequot war, 470; appointed Wheelwright's keeper while in Massachusetts, 481; 494, 577; granted right to bridge the Neponset, 668, 670; his mill of 1634, 668; his widow relieved from obligation to maintain bridge, 1652, 670–1.
Stoughton, William, Deputy Gov., his death, 1701, 719.
Strafford, Earl of, see Wentworth, Thomas.
Strong, Caleb, Federalist governor of Mass., 909–10.
Strongbow in Ireland, 652.
Stuart dynasty of England, overthrown, 817.
Stubs, Philip, May-day in England, 1585, 182.
Study hill, William Blackstone's home in Rhode Island, 325.
Sudbury, Mass., 136.
Suffolk County, Mass., noted for free schools, 1719, 766; intemperance in, 1750, 788.
Suffolk regiment, commanded by Edward Gibbons, 358; Edmund Quincy [4th], colonel of, 702; Josiah Quincy [1st], colonel of, 703; John Quincy major of, 707; John Gooch takes colonelcy from John Quincy, 1742, 708, 715; John Adams [1st] declines captaincy in, 708, 715; John Marshall's services in, 717, 718; its character, 765; called out, rebellion of 1786, 897.
Sulpicius, 452.
Sumner, W. H., cited as to Maverick, 329, note.
Sunday in colonial times, 803; books read, ib.; John Adams' observance of, 806; tedium of, ib.; Sunday law, Mass., 893.
Superior, Lake, 122.
Superstition in New England, 388–9.
Surrey, Earl of, his land in New England, partition of 1635, 283.
Swallow, ship, 86.
Swan, vessel fitted out by Weston for trade with New England, 1622, 54; brings the main part of his 1622 company, 58; 59; returns to Plymouth, August, 1622, 60; expedition for food round Cape Cod, 62; returns to Boston Bay, 64; continues search, ib.; abandoned by Bradford, 65; Indian plot to seize her, 85; 90; provisioned for transportation of Weston's people, 96; 146, 147; seized by R. Gorges, 150–1; Gorges sails in, spring of 1624, 152; restored to Weston, 154.
Swine, Saxon law forbidding, in churches, 745, note.

Symmes, Sarah, wife of Moses Fiske, 609.
Symmes, Zachariah, minister of Charlestown, doubts Mrs. Hutchinson's orthodoxy, 397; 476; attends her trial, 486–7; his evidence at trial, 492; his daughter wife of Moses Fiske, 609.
Synod of 1637 at Cambridge, 467, 468–74; questions considered by, 472; its course discussed, 562–3; sessions held in Cambridge meeting-house, 485.

Taft, Rev. ——, preaches in Braintree church, June 25, 1775, 860.
Tanneries, Quincy, 929.
Tarratine tribe of Indians not affected by pestilence of 1616–17, 4; Obbatinewat's fear of 1621, 16; 17, 24, note.
Tasso, 390.
Tattler, in houses of colonial gentry, 805; 809.
Taunt, William, in Braintree records, 727.
Taunton River, 10; 255.
Tavern influence, New England, 783 et seq.; 809.
Taxation, system of, at Braintree, during Revolution, 882; 1780, 892; 1785, 899; in Mass., 1786, a cause of Shays' Rebellion, 895–6.
Tax-collecting, difficulties of, Braintree, 823–4.
Tax collectors of Braintree, their difficulties, 882.
Taylor, Major ——, muster master, 1709, 720.
Taylor, ——, amount received as selectman, 1829, 914.
Taylor, Zachary, President, 955, 956.
Tea, not in common use, colonial times, 785; destroyed, Boston Harbor, 1773, 642; 850.
Teacher of New England churches, functions of, 596.
Teachers, Quincy schools, support of, 933–5.
Temperance movement in New England, 786; John Adams' efforts in cause of, 789–90; at Quincy, 975 et seq.
Ten Hills, Medford, Gov. Winthrop's farm at, 258, 364.
Tennent, Gilbert, 620.
Terry, General Alfred H., in capture of Fort Fisher, 1865, 705.
Terry family, Connecticut, descended from Joanna Hoar, 705.
Texas, annexation of, 955.
Thacher, Col. ——, of Barnstable, 713.
Thacher, Oxenbridge, comments on Col. Thacher of Barnstable, 713.
Thayer, Ebenezer, his tavern, Braintree Middle Precinct, 743; 834, 835; delegate to General Court, 1766, 845; delegate to Boston convention, 1768, 849; 1774, delegate to county convention, 850; not elected to General Court, July 10, 1775, 860; 871.
Thayer, Ephraim, 660.

Thayer, Isaac, 830.
Thayer, Jonathan, overseer of poor, Braintree, 1786; 728.
Thayer, Capt. Peter, with company, joins colonial army, 1757, 836; 837.
Thayer, Richard, 1692, his claim under Indian land-title to Braintree township, 654-5; in charge of frontier post on Bridgewater road, 829; his character and exploits, ib.; Braintree disallows his bill, ib.
Thayer, Sarah, her offspring, 609; commemorated in verse, ib.
Theer, Isaac, disciplined by Braintree church, 757-8.
Theological controversies, in history and literature, 366.
Theopolis Americana, a favorite book in early New England, 391.
Theocracy in Mass. Bay, 513; extinguished by charter of 1691, 819.
Thompson, David, Agent for the Council of New England, 1622, 58; considers plan of emigration to America, ib.; learns from Trevore of Boston Bay, 130, note; protects Thomas Weston at Piscataqua, 146; his complaint against him, ib.; visited at Piscataqua by R. Gorges, 1624, 152; first occupant of Squantum and Farm School Island, 191; comes a traveller in 1621, ib.; receives patent of land in New England, ib.; settles, 1623, ib.; removes from Piscataqua to his island in Boston Bay, 192; title of his island confirmed to his son, 193; 198, 329; his widow a resident at Squantum or Thompson's Island, 321; 342; 582-3.
Thompson, John, General Court confirms his title to Island, 342.
Thompson's Island, Boston Bay, Standish anchors near, 1621, 13; names it Trevore, 14; 15, 20; settlement at, 183; within the territory granted to Endicott, 211; the residence of David Thompson's widow, 321; granted to John Thompson by General Court, 1648, 342; sold for debt, ib.; becomes property of Lynde family, 1666, ib.; 867.
Ticonderoga, forces from Mass. at, 1758, 836.
Tisquantum, see Squanto.
Tithingmen, overseers of boys in meeting-houses, 746.
Tiverton, Joseph Marsh minister of, 617.
Tobacco, early New England settlers propose to make it a staple, 219; dislike of it, of James I., ib.; used as currency in Virginia, ib.
Tocqueville, Alexis de, his "Democracy in America," 813; his account of town-meeting, 814, 966, 969.
Tokamahamon, Indian guide and interpreter, 31; brings a challenge to Squanto from Canonicus, 35.

Toleration in religion, secured in Mass. by charter of 1691, 819.
Tompson, Benjamin, Braintree schoolmaster, 1678-1704, 769; his support, ib.; fire-wood for, 769-70; graduate of Harvard, 769; a physician, ib.; 771, 772; his character, 771; town-clerk, 772; his scholarship, ib.; his progeny, ib.; buried at Roxbury, ib.; a poet, ib.; 773; 936.
Tompson, Deacon Samuel, father of "the prodigie of pride," 755; 757.
Tompson, Samuel, disciplined by Braintree church, 1697, 755-6.
Tompson, William, first minister of Braintree church, 1639, 586; ordained, 595; length of pastorate, 596; his character, ib.; goes a missionary to Virginia, 1642, 597; shipwrecked, 598; driven from Virginia, 599; mental infirmity, 601; resignation of pastorate and death, 1696, ib.; 643, 647; his son schoolmaster of Braintree, 771; 773; goes chaplain to Indian war, 1645, 828; 908; Mather's verses on, 598, 602; his lack of thrift, ib.; buried at Quincy, ib.; 954.
Tory party at Braintree, Episcopalians, comprised in, 632, 840, 850; and the gentry, ib.; 852; persecution of, 853-4.
Town meeting government, inefficient in social problems, 731; system in New England, 810-26; usual study of its origin, 813, 814-15; improved conditions under charter of 1691, 819; during Revolution, 875, 876; 930; its condition at Quincy, 965 et seq.; breaks down, 967 et seq.; duration of, 981; a scene at one pictured, 970.
Town records of Massachusetts, 813.
Town River, Quincy, 594.
Townshend, Charles, introduces a revenue bill in Parliament, 1767, 846.
Trade, restrictions imposed on, with New England, 132; 133, note; Plymouth and Wessagusset inconvenient for, 160; stations for, established elsewhere, ib.; between New England and foreign countries, 697.
Traders on New England coast kidnap Indians, 1614-9, 5, 6, 7; attacked by Indians, 8; number in Boston Bay, 1628, 197.
Training-field system in New England, its influence, 764.
Transcendentalists, Mrs. Hutchinson, Vane and Wheelwright forerunners of, 435.
Travel in New England, 1641-1786, 673-9.
Treaty of peace, United States and Great Britain, 1783, 893.
Trevore, William, accompanies Standish round Boston Bay, 1621, his name given to Thompson's Island, 14, 191; 58; 120; comes, 1622, to New England in the Fortune, 130; informs Weston and Thompson of Boston Bay, 130,

INDEX.                               1061

*note;* gives information to Robert Gorges, 136; 137, *note.*
Trimountain, first English name of Boston, 1630, 236; 288.
Trinity Church, Newport, 621.
Trumbull, J. Hammond, cited as to church difficulties at Weymouth, 341, *note.*
Tucker, Commodore Samuel, U. S. N., of frigate Boston, 886, 887, 951.
Tully, *see* Cicero.
Tun of Germany, theory of derivation of town-meeting from, 814; 815.
Tupper, Lieut. Colonel, in protection of Quincy Bay, March, 1776, 867.
Turner, ——, Captain of Colonial militia stationed at Germantown, Mass., 1775, 860.
Tyler, John, President of United States, 952.
Tyng, William, Boston merchant, buys farm at Mount Wollaston, from Coddington, 1639, 707; death of, 1661, *ib.;* he bequeaths farm to his daughter, Mrs. Shepard, *ib.*

Underhill, John, Captain of train band, comes over with Winthrop, 551; captures Gardiner, 256; of Mrs. Hutchinson's faction, 552; signer of Boston remonstrance, 510; prosecuted and disfranchised, *ib.;* his religious buffoonery, 511; an "opinionist," *ib.;* his character and career, 551; a soldier under Prince Maurice, *ib.;* answers General Court, *ib.;* banished, 553; asks land in New Hampshire, 551; follows Wheelwright thither, *ib.*, 554; charged with immorality, *ib.*, 553, 554, 555; his reply, 553; Winthrop's account of his conduct, 553-6; authorities of Mass. Bay try to destroy his credit in New Hampshire, 554-5; chosen Governor of Piscataqua, 555; writes threatening letter to Cotton, *ib.;* visits Boston and confesses to church, *ib.;* deposed from governorship, *ib.;* again humiliates himself to Boston church, 557; received into communion again, 558; resides at Stamford, Conn., *ib.*, *note;* removes to Long Island, N. Y., *ib.*, *note;* death at Oyster Bay, *ib.;* 568.
Unitarianism in New England, 643; at Quincy, 944.
United States Arsenal, Watertown, 233.
United States, Articles of Confederation, 1778, approved and amended at Braintree, 890; treaty of peace with Great Britain, 1783, 893; war with Great Britain, 1812-14, 909-12.
Universalist Religious Society, established at Quincy, 1831, 930.
Untruthfulness an attribute of servility, 795.
Ursuline Convent, Charlestown, destroyed, 932.

Uzzia, Asa and Salem, precedents cited in his justification by Winthrop, 512.

Vaccination, Quincy refuses, 1809, 906.
Van Buren, Martin, nominated for presidency by Free-Soilers, 1848, 955.
Vane, Sir Henry, 1638, at meeting of Lords Commissioners, 304; his position at Court, 373.
Vane, Sir Henry [younger], an etherealized Puritan, 372; his court influence, 374; sent to New England by Charles I., *ib.;* October, 1635, aged 23, lands at Boston, 373; Hugh Peters, his companion, 374; probably, also, Henry Flynt, 603; admitted to church, 376; 1636, concerned in reconciliation of Winthrop and Dudley, 377-9; chosen governor, 380; seen in a vision by Mrs. Hutchinson, 399; one of her adherents, 400; supports her in quarrel with Wilson, 411; his advanced religious tenets, 413; supports project to make Wheelwright assistant minister, 414; controversy with Winthrop, 418-20; loss of popularity, 419; resolves to return to England, 420; conduct at meeting of General Court on retiring from office, *ib.;* vacillation about governorship, 422; presides at discussion with Cotton, 423; rebuked by Peters, *ib.;* their subsequent friendly relations, 425, *note;* not in sympathy with Wilson, 426; attacks him at meeting of Jan. 1637, 428; his relations with Mrs. Hutchinson, 1637, 430; name Antinomian misapplied to, 435; the political phase of Antinomian struggle between Winthrop and, 436; at meeting of General Court, March, 1637, 442-3; leader of the Wheelwright party, 445; protests against the judgment in Wheelwright's case, 445-6; record of his protest refused, 446; 447; opposes removal of General Court to Cambridge, 449-50; candidate for governorship, May, 1837, 451; opposed by Winthrop, *ib.;* attempts to prevent election, 452; defeated, 455; his halberd-bearers refuse to attend Winthrop, 461; General Court prosecutes them, 509-10; elected delegate by Boston, 455; election annulled, *ib.;* reëlected, 456; attacks alien law, 459, *note;* refuses to sit at church with magistrates, 461; as governor escorted by halberdiers to church, 462; discourtesies to Winthrop, *ib.;* declines an invitation from him and goes to dine with Maverick, 331, 462; returns to England, August, 1637, 464, 466; loss of his support serious to Wheelwright, 466; effect of his departure on Cotton's position, 469; 1643, of Parliamentary Commission for Plantations, 315; his character 372; dulness of his writings, 373;

## 1062　INDEX.

Milton's sonnet to him, *ib.*; Cromwell's ejaculation concerning him, *ib.*; described by Clarendon, *ib.*; Winthrop's first opinion of him, 374; holds to tenet of predestination, 457; compared with Winthrop, 465; of less importance than Winthrop to colony, 465–6; 474, 485, 567, 569, 571, 574, 577, 593, 594.
Vassall, Leonard, his house at Quincy built, 1731, 681; bought by John Adams, 1787, *ib.*; 833.
Vassall family, of Braintree Episcopal Church, 632; 698; slaves owned by, 923.
Veasey, William, his argument in favor of Stamp Act, 842.
Veasey family, favorers of Stamp Act, 841.
Veazie, Benjamin, 628.
Veazie, Eleazer, disciplined by Braintree church, 1741, 762.
Veazie, William, one of earliest members of Braintree Episcopal Church, 1689, 621, 622; a Jacobite, fined for not observing Thanksgiving, 1696, 625; put in pillory, 626; refuses to pay tax for support of town minister, 1713, *ib.*; gives land for Christ Church, 628.
Vengeur, sinking of, cited, 83.
Venice Preserved, 806.
Verres, Caius, 350.
Versailles, treaty of peace, United States and Great Britain, 1783, signed at, 893.
Vestry of England, theory of derivation of town-meeting from, 814, 815, 816.
Vines, Richard, not affected by Indian pestilence, 3.
Vinton, Captain John, of Braintree, 851, and *note;* stationed at Squantum, 1775, 860.
Vinton, Thomas, contention with Braintree over fish in Monatiquot River, 1736, 831–4.
Virginia, Dermer takes refuge in and dies, 1620, 28; Weston's ship Charity goes to, 1622, 59; 61; Indian massacre of 1622, 74; Robert Gorges' ship bound to, 1623, 144–5; 151; some of his colonists go to, 154; Weston goes to, *ib.*; 163; Rasdell goes to, 174; Lyford removes to, and dies, 190; tobacco used as currency in, 219; Morton would have been unmolested in, 225; 286; Samuel Maverick's visits to, 330, 331; 339; William Tompson and John Knowles go as missionaries to, 1642, 597; their work there, 599; driven away from, *ib.*; grants to London Companies, 651; John Adams' receipt for making a New England in, 732, 764, 783.
Virginia Company of London, incorporated by royal patent, 1606, 117–8; opposes the 1620 charter granted to Plymouth Company, 124; defeated, 125; assails Plymouth Company in House of Commons, 1621, 126–7.

Walford, Thomas, establishes himself at Mishawum, now Charlestown, 161; 193, 217, 220, 233, 252; his career in New England, 336–7; difficulties as an Episcopalian, 336; fined and banished, 1631, 337; pays fine by killing a wolf, and removes, *ib.*; 340, 342.
Wampatuck, Braintree land title, 1665, 654, 655, 829.
War, colonial period, 827.
War, right of Congress to declare, objected to, at Braintree, 890.
War with Great Britain, 1812–14, 803, 909–12.
Ward, ——, at synod of 1637, 470.
Ward, Silas, overseer of poor, Braintree, 1787, 728.
Warwick, Earl, of the Plymouth Company, 122; at meetings of Council for New England, 131; his share of New England, drawn at Greenwich, 1623, 139; concerned in forwarding Endicott's schemes, 210; an agent in obtaining Mass. Bay charter, 274; 275; disassociated from Gorges, 283; 286, proprietor of Connecticut Valley, 299; supersedes Laud as head of Commission for Plantations, 315.
Washington, George, his military expedition on the Ohio, 641; 710, 765; informed of British fleet in Boston Bay, 866–7; remark on one year enlistments, 873; recruits from Braintree for his army, 876; 878, 879.
Washington, D. C., J. Q. Adams' death at, 920.
Washington Street, Boston, site of Winthrop's house, 1630, 239; site of E. Gibbons' house, 358.
Washington temperance movement, 975.
Waters, Henry P., Winthrop's map of 1634, discovered at London by, 61, *note.*
Watertown, Mass., U. S. Arsenal at, 233; 238; Saltonstall's property near, 365; 454; George Phillips pastor of church of, 486.
Watts, Isaac, his hymns authorized in Braintree church, 741.
Webb, Benjamin, buys first Braintree school-house, 774.
Webb, Jonathan, 619.
Weld, Joseph, given custody of Mrs. Hutchinson, 508, 509; liberates her to be excommunicated, 516; 525.
Weld, Rev. Thomas, his description of Mrs. Hutchinson, 381; her career at Boston, 399; as to Jane Hawkins, 400, *note;* public contempt of Mrs. Hutchinson for Boston preachers, 401; 423; said by her not to preach clearly the Covenant of Grace, 427; at examination of Mrs. Hutchinson, Dec. 1636, 426–8; introduces Laud's

INDEX. 1063

practices in General Court, 446; silenced in England, 1631, by Laud, 447; 456; at synod of 1637, 470; 476; on Wheelwright's amenability to the law, 477, *note;* attends trial of Mrs. Hutchinson, 486; his remarks concerning her, 491; his evidence, 492; cause of his bitterness towards her, 493; altercation with her, 496; called on to take oath, 507; made her guardian at Roxbury, 509; tries to convince her of errors, 513; his conduct at trial, 514; his satisfaction in her misfortunes, 535, *note;* purpose of his Short Story, 563; citation from same, 563–4.
Wells, Maine, Wheelwright removes to, 1641, 539.
Wenape, Indian kidnapped by Hunt, 24, *note.*
Wendell family, descendants of "Dorothy Q.," 605.
Wentworth, Thomas, Earl of Strafford, 247; not connected with the policy of New England affairs, 273; his character as a statesman, *ib.;* 275; proposed a member for royal commission for New England, 1634, 277; in correspondence with Laud concerning Ireland, 1637, 297; letter to him concerning tax for army, 299; advocates abstaining from war, *ib.;* 313; his scheme of "Thorough," 318–9; 570.
Wesley, John, separates men and women in meeting-houses, 733; free pews, *ib.*
Wessagusset, Weston's company settle at, 61; site identified, *ib.*, *note;* scarcity of food at, winter of 1622, 62; severity of winter, 1622–3, 63; its miseries, 84–5; colonists accused by Indians of robbery, 64; their condition grows worse, 65; charged with illusage by Indians, 66; Indian conspiracy to destroy, 1623, 73: revealed by Massasoit, *ib.;* demoralization at, 76; scarcity of food, 77–8; mortality at, 77; treatment of Indians, 78; the settlers punish those who steal from Indians, 1623, *ib.;* a thief hanged, 79; story of the hanging in literature, 79–83; relations with the Indians, 85; Standish goes in defence of settlers, 90; kills Pecksuot and Wituwamat, 92–3, 196, 200; abandoned, April, 1623, 96; stragglers remain, 104; no evidence that Weston's patent covered site of settlement, 130, *note;* occupied, 1623, by R. Gorges' colonists, 105, 144; its disorders, cause of complaint in Council for New England against T. Weston, 145; news of troubles at, reach him in Maine, 146; duration of Morell's stay at, 156; the scene of his literary work, 157; fate of Gorges' settlement at, 159; not a good trading station, *ib.;* or a good seaport, 160; the settlers attempt to establish trading stations, *ib.;* 163; Wollaston's company find there some of R. Gorges' people, 1624, 165; Oldham and Lyford exiled to, 190; population of, 1627, 193; Morton captured at, 203–4; 206; within territory granted to Endicott, 211; the residence of Jeffreys, 1630, 252; 285; story of original settlers at, 321 *et seq.;* condition of colony, 1634, 337–42; described, 1633, 339; its name changed to Weymouth, 1635, 339–40; wildness of region round about, 338, 364, 582; means of communication with Plymouth and Boston, 1637, 581; ferry communication with Mount Wollaston, 1635, 672. *See* Weymouth.
West, Christopher, one of Robert Gorges' Council in New England, 141.
West, Captain Francis, commissioned Admiral for coast of New England, to protect the fisheries, 1622, 135; 141; little known to history, 136; fails to control the fishermen, 153; Squeb employed by him, 232.
West Indies, Gibbons suspected of piracy in, 357; trade between New England and, 697; rum supplied to New England, 786.
Westminster, London, 109, 110.
Westminster Confession of 1643, 394, *note.*
Westminster Hall, London, scene of Essex trial, 112; 114; 316.
West Quincy, iron works, 696; labor agitation of 1887, 988, 990.
Weston, Andrew, employed by his brother Thomas, 1622, 55; his character, 57; in charge of ship Charity, 59; returns to England, 62; 79, 96, 163.
Weston, Thomas, his character, 45; Treasurer of Merchant Adventurers of London, 46; his association with the Pilgrims in Holland, *ib.;* his influence on their destiny, 47; charters the Mayflower in company with Cushman, *ib.;* his mercenary treatment of Pilgrims, 47–8, 55; abandons them, 48; expectations of returns from Plymouth, 48; reproves Bradford, 49; Bradford's reply, *ib.;* demands fulfilment of agreement with Pilgrims, 50; dissatisfaction with their first shipment, *ib.;* abandonment of colonists, 51; separates from the company of Merchant Adventurers, *ib.;* 54; sends out the Sparrow to coast of Maine, 1622, 51; his trading scheme, 1622, 54 *et seq.;* his patent, 130, *note;* sources of his information of Mass. Bay, *ib.;* influenced by John Smith, *ib.;* his expedition to Boston Bay, 1622, 34; in Sparrow sails from England, 130; arrival of pioneers of, May, 1622, 42, 43; arrival of party in charge of his brother Andrew, June, 1622, *ib.;* piloted by Squanto round Cape Cod, *ib.:* his crew, vagabonds, 55; intercepts clandestine let-

1064    INDEX.

ter to Bradford, 56; his company in New England, 1622, 59; their treatment by Plymouth colonists, 60; settle at Wessagusset, 61; site of settlement, *ib.*, *note;* Indians complain of ill usage and theft, 61, 79; Wessagusset abandoned, 96-7; compared with R. Gorges, 105; to evade arrest in England comes in disguise to coast of Maine, 1623, 145-6; sought for in Maine by R. Gorges, 1623, 145; his offence discussed, *ib.;* his adventures in attempt to visit Wessagusset, 1623, 146; sheltered at Piscataqua, *ib.;* appears at Plymouth, 147; obtains skins under false pretences, *ib.;* finds the Swan, and goes on trading expedition, *ib.;* discovered by R. Gorges at Plymouth, 148; threatened with arrest and transportation to England, 148-9; Bradford intervenes, 148-9; discharged, 149; arrested and the Swan seized by R. Gorges, 151; removed to Wessagusset, *ib.;* taken to Piscataqua, 152; 153; released and his vessel restored to him, 154; reappears at Plymouth, *ib.;* goes to Virginia, *ib.;* connected with the mutiny of the Little James, *ib.;* returns to England, *ib.;* dies at Bristol, 1645, *ib.;* the effect of his enterprise in New England, 155-6; 163, 192; his methods with Indians revived by Morton, 197.

Weymouth, Captain George, 23-4, *notes;* 31; excites the interest of Gorges in the New World, 117; Indians kidnapped by him, *ib.*

Weymouth, Mass., site of, 61, *note;* within R. Gorges' territory, 131, *note;* 338; receives name, 1635, by order of General Court, 340; men furnished for Pequot war, 1636, *ib.;* the number of inhabitants, 1636, *ib.;* service in Indian war, 1645, 828; road to Dorchester, 1648, 594; iron works, 696; meeting-house a powder magazine, 743; burns, 1752, powder explodes, *ib.;* its attitude towards indemnifying sufferers from Boston riots, 1765, 845; instructions to delegates to Boston convention, 1768, 849; alarm from British foraging party, 1775, 857; Mrs. John Adams removes to, 1775, 863; provisions for defence, war of 1812, 912. *See* Wessagusset.

———, church, established, 1635, 586; turmoils, 1638, 340-1; Joseph Hull, minister of, 368; 607; William Smith, minister, 711, 717; his Stamp Act sermon, 841.

Weymouth Bay defined on Smith's map, 5.

Weymouth Fore-river, Hunt's Hill on, site of Wessagusset, 61, *note;* the Swan moored at, 1623, 65; British man-of-war, with foraging party in, 1775, 857.

Weymouth River, 61, *note*, 90.

Wheelwright, John, birth and education, 367-9; relations with Cromwell, 369; marriage and ministrations in England, *ib.;* death of first wife, 370; second marriage, *ib.;* with sister of William Hutchinson, 381; removal to New England, 1636, 370; 381; cited as to Jane Hawkins, 400; project to make him teacher at Boston, 1636, 370-1, 411-12; unsuccessful, 415; at ministerial conference of 1636, 413; allotted lands at Mount Wollaston, 1637, 366, and *note;* made minister of Mount Wollaston Chapel-of-ease, 415-17; 584; probable site of his chapel, 593; his setttlement fails to give peace to Boston, 418; not in sympathy with minister Wilson, 426; at examination of Mrs. Hutchinson, Dec. 1636, 426-8; name Antinomian misapplied to, 435; his caution respecting this term, 435, *note;* not fully in sympathy with Mrs. Hutchinson, 436; effect of her opinion on his reputation, *ib.;* considered her representative, 437; contrasted with Cotton, 436; his fast-day sermon at Boston, 437; its character, 438; extracts from, 439-40; as a divine, 441, *note;* summoned before General Court, March, 1637, 443; first examination secret, 444; refuses to answer questions, *ib.;* following examinations public, *ib.;* account of examination, 445-7; justifies his sermon, 445; judged guilty of contempt and sedition, *ib.;* sentence postponed, 446; Vane appeals the case to people, 452; not sustained, 455; 456; shows disposition to yield, 457; his case in General Court, 1637, 457-67; refused an appeal to the King, 458; 459; loses his supporter Vane, 464; 466; desire to reconcile him with Wilson, 468; Wilson's concessions, 469; at synod of 1637, 471; his theological views considered, 472-4; not sustained, 474; deprived of Cotton's support, *ib.;* his friends fail of election to new Court of 1637, 475; does not submit to decision of Synod, *ib.;* magistrates determine to exile him, 476; within the grasp of law, 477; case before General Court, Nov. 1637, 479; his adherents among the deputies expelled, *ib.;* refuses to acknowledge error, 480; charged with cause of dissension, *ib.;* banished, 481; refuses asylum in Rhode Island, 539; removes to Piscataqua, 481-2; followed by his family, April, 1738, 482; his residence at Exeter, 482, 539, 581; 483, 489, 492, 503; deluded by Mrs. Hutchinson, 505; 508, 511, 514; 1641, removes to Wells, Maine, 539; 1642, his letter of reconciliation to Winthrop, 540; refuses to visit Boston, *ib.;* 1644, sentence of banishment remitted, *ib.;*